THE PRINCIPLES
OF
EDUCATIONAL MANAGEMENT

Other titles in the University of Leicester MBA Series

Research Methods in Educational Management by Daphne Johnson

Leadership and Strategic Management (Core module 1) by John West-Burnham and Derek Glover

Managing the Curriculum (Core module 2) by Mark Lofthouse, John West-Burnham and Derek Glover

Human Resource Management in Education (Core module 3) by John O'Neill, David Middlewood and Derek Glover

Managing Finance and External Relations (Core module 4) by Marianne Coleman, Tony Bush and Derek Glover

The principles
of
educational management

edited by

Tony Bush and John West-Burnham

LONGMAN

Educational Management Development Unit
University of Leicester

PRINCIPLES OF EDUCATIONAL MANAGEMENT

Published by Longman Information and Reference, Longman Group Ltd, 6th floor, Westgate House, The High, Harlow, Essex CM20 1YR, England and Associated Companies throughout the world.

A catalogue record for this book is available from The British Library

10 9 8 7 6 5 4

ISBN 0-582-23904-4

Printed in Great Britain by Bell and Bain Ltd, Glasgow

Contents

Contributors

Tony Bush is Professor of Educational Management and Director of the Educational Management Development Unit at the University of Leicester. He was formerly a teacher in secondary schools and colleges and an assistant education officer with the London Borough of Harrow. He was senior lecturer in educational management at the Open University where he was responsible for the production of post-graduate educational management courses. His principal publications include *Theories of Educational Management* and *Managing Autonomous Schools: The Grant Maintained Experience* (with Marianne Coleman and Derek Glover), both published by Paul Chapman.

John West-Burnham is Director of the Distance Learning Programme, Educational Management Development Unit, University of Leicester. He has previously worked as an LEA officer, lecturer in a college of higher education and he taught in schools, colleges and adult education for 15 years. He is the author of *Managing Quality in Schools* (Longman) and the co-director of the Centre for Total Quality in Education and the Community. John's research interests include total quality in education, mentoring and management learning and the management of colleges after incorporation.

Marianne Coleman is a lecturer in educational management in the Educational Management Development Unit at the University of Leicester. She has extensive experience in education, mainly teaching in secondary schools, and also working in the advisory service of a large LEA. She is the co-author of *Managing Autonomous Schools: The Grant Maintained Experience*.

Brent Davies is Principal Lecturer in Educational Management at Leeds Metropolitan University. He is the course leader, at Leeds, for an International MBA in Educational Management for Leaders of Self-Managing Schools. He is a visiting professor at the University of Southern California where, as co-director with Professor David Marsh, he runs an annual International Principals' Institute. Brent has lectured and published widely, with six books and over forty articles, on many aspects of self-managing schools in Australia, Canada, the UK and the United States.

Mark Lofthouse is a senior lecturer in education at the University of Leicester. He was formerly a teacher in primary schools, before becoming a lecturer in the field of initial teacher training. His current responsibilities include leadership of continuing professional development in Northamptonshire. He is author of a history of 'The Church Colleges', one of several publications in the field of religious and denominational education.

John O'Neill lectures in educational management with the Educational Management Development Unit. He spent ten years teaching students with SEN in mainstream and special education. John's research interests include middle management development and inter-school collaboration.

Colin Riches is a lecturer in educational management in the Centre for Education Policy and Management at the Open University. He has a wide experience of teaching, having taught in special schools, a secondary school, colleges of FE and education and a polytechnic, prior to joining the Open University. He has written extensively on human resource management issues and skills for educational management courses and has special interests in leadership, interviewing and support staff in education. Among other publications he has edited (jointly with C. Morgan), *Human Resource Management in Education.*

Preface

The purpose of this book is to provide a systematic and analytical introduction to the study of educational management. It offers an integrated and comprehensive review of the key theoretical perspectives in the management of schools and colleges. At a time of ever-increasing research and publication in the field of educational management, this book presents an overview of the main themes and issues which are relevant to the practical issues facing managers in the education system.

The book has been designed to serve as the foundation text for the MBA in Educational Management by distance learning of the Educational Management Development Unit of the University of Leicester. However, the editors believe that it is equally relevant to educationalists studying for qualifications on a wide range of courses and to the interested professional and lay person.

Each chapter represents a distillation of key theoretical perspectives and an introduction to the study of a specific aspect of educational management. The book as a whole helps to set an agenda for study, review and reflection appropriate to the challenges and demands on managers of educational organizations.

The editors wish to express their sincere thanks to Marianne Coleman, Brent Davies, Mark Lofthouse, John O'Neill and Colin Riches for their skill and scholarship in developing their contributions to the book. We wish to thank Christopher Bowring-Carr for preparing the index. We also wish to record our gratitude to Felicity Murray, Theresa Murray and Claire Klapproth for their work in producing the manuscript of this book, and to Carolyn Vincent who has managed the overall production of this text.

Tony Bush
Professor of Educational Management

John West-Burnham
Lecturer in Educational Management

Series Editors

Introduction: enduring principles in a climate of change

Tony Bush and John West-Burnham

The pace of educational change in the United Kingdom and internationally has been accelerating in the 1980s and 1990s. The faltering economies of most developed countries have heightened the demand for strong links between education and the perceived needs of industry and commerce. Schools and colleges are increasingly required to 'deliver' students prepared to contribute to the economic success of their country.

In the United Kingdom, the search for higher educational standards to enhance economic performance has led to substantial legislative change. The 1988 Education Reform Act (ERA), and subsequent legislation, have transformed the educational landscape which is now very different from the pre-ERA scene. The major changes are probably the following:

- The *National Curriculum* which specifies in considerable detail the content of the curriculum and the assessment arrangements for pupils at ages seven, eleven, fourteen and sixteen

- *Local management of schools* (LMS) which devolves funding and resource management to governing bodies and school staff and limits the powers of the local education authorities (LEAs)

- *Open enrolment* which removes artificial limits on the capacity of schools and enables parents to choose the school their children will attend, subject only to its physical capacity. School budgets are linked closely to pupil numbers, encouraging schools to compete for pupils in order to sustain or increase their income

- The provision for schools to 'opt out' of LEA control and become *grant-maintained*, receiving their revenue and capital budgets from a funding agency whose members are appointed by the Secretary of State for Education

- The *incorporation* of further education colleges as autonomous bodies, independent of LEAs

- The introduction of a nationally controlled *inspection* regime which will ensure that all schools are inspected once every four years according to criteria established by the Office for Standards in Education (OFSTED)

Many of these developments represent a trend towards institutional autonomy hypothecated on the assumption that decisions should be made by those who best understand the needs of the students and the local community. Governing bodies and senior staff have substantial powers for managing schools and colleges.

The move towards autonomy for schools and colleges has many international parallels. Caldwell and Spinks (1988, 1992) document this development which they describe as 'self-management':

> A self-managing school is a school in a system of education where there has been significant and consistent decentralisation to the school level of authority to make decisions related to the allocation of resources ... The school remains accountable to a central authority for the manner in which resources are allocated (Caldwell and Spinks 1992, p.4).

The authors argue that self-management is now so widespread that it merits classification as a 'megatrend', with government schools becoming largely self-managing. They also claim that the case for self-management is justified on the basis of findings from studies of school effectiveness. They quote Finn's (1984) view that transforming the findings of effective schools research into improved educational practice is facilitated by school-level autonomy.

Caldwell and Spinks (1992, p.14) expound the case for self-managing schools in these terms:

> It is simply more efficient and effective in the late twentieth century to restructure systems of education so that central bureaucracies are relatively small and schools are empowered to manage their own affairs within a centrally determined framework of direction and support. Two arguments have usually been offered, one is concerned with responsiveness, the other with priorities for resource allocation in times of economic restraint or budgetary crisis.

Autonomous schools and colleges may be regarded as *potentially* more efficent and effective but much depends on the nature and quality of internal management if the anticipated benefits of autonomy are to be realised.

The many extra responsibilities imposed on schools and colleges place a premium on high quality management. The management of finance and staff requires different skills from those needed to plan and deliver the curriculum. Headteachers and senior staff are primarily successful teachers who have been promoted to management positions largely on the basis of good performance in the classroom rather than successful experience as managers. Training is a vital component in the acquisition of managerial competence as is a clear understanding of how to ensure the successful implementation of change.

Caldwell and Spinks (1992) argue that self-management should be accompanied by internal devolution of power if it is to lead to successful outcomes for the school and its pupils. Improvement is dependent upon dispersed management within the school or college as well as autonomy for the institution. It also requires high quality leadership at all levels, which they describe as 'transformational':

> The need for outstanding and widely dispersed leadership is palpable ... This leadership must be more transformational than transactional, with the former implying a capacity to engage others in a commitment to change, while the latter is more concerned with maintaining the status quo by exchanging an assurance of a secure place of work for a commitment to get the job done (p.19).

Beare et al. (1992) argue that a large measure of school autonomy is a precondition for successful implementation of change. They endorse Purkey and Smith's (1985, p.358) view that school-site management *and* collaborative decision-making are essential components of the framework for successful change:

> The staff of each school is given a considerable amount of responsibility and authority in determining the exact means by which they address the problem of increasing academic performance. This includes giving staffs more authority over curricular decisions and allocation of building resources.

If this view is accepted, autonomy is a necessary but not a sufficient condition for school improvement. It has to be accompanied by devolution of power to teachers if higher standards are to result from the changes in government policy in England and Wales and elsewhere.

The rapid pace of educational change inevitably means that school and college managers have to absorb and interpret externally imposed change while facilitating internal innovation. These requirements pose considerable difficulties for those concerned with the training of educational managers. It would be understandable if principals and other leaders were to focus on short-term issues rather than adopt long-term strategies for school or college development. This 'fire-fighting' approach is an important element of management but should be accompanied by a vision of what the institution should be achieving in the years ahead.

The academic field of educational management is relatively new in the United Kingdom but by the early 1990s had progressed from the largely descriptive and prescriptive approach which characterized the subject in the 1960s and 1970s. There is now a body of analytical literature which establishes the essential canons or principles of educational management. This book brings together these major principles in a single volume. The editors' underlying assumption is that there are significant aspects of theory and principle which are relatively enduring and applicable in a variety of educational contexts in Britain and elsewhere.

The importance of theory is discussed in Chapter 2 but the essential arguments can be rehearsed here. Theory provides a basis for action. Without conceptual underpinning, decisions could become purely arbitrary. It is not sufficient simply to note the facts of a situation and to make a decision based on those facts. All such evidence requires interpretation. Theory provides the framework for understanding and interpreting events. The principles of educational management presented in this volume provide conceptual frameworks to help managers address the increasingly complex issues facing schools and colleges as they approach the millenium. Understanding and applying these principles are essential requirements for educational managers.

In Chapter 1, *Management in Educational Organizations*, John West-Burnham examines the concept of management in the context of the increasing autonomy of schools and colleges. He demonstrates that management concepts, techniques and processes can be applied to education without detriment to educational values. Rather, he contends that the task of education will be compromised without effective management.

Tony Bush explores the relationship between *Theory and Practice in Educational Management* in Chapter 2. He argues that understanding of theory can illuminate practice and bridge the 'theory/practice divide'. He presents five theories which represent different ways of 'seeing' the events and situations that occur in schools and colleges. He advocates the development of 'conceptual pluralism' to enable practitioners to select the most appropriate theory to help in the resolution of managerial problems.

Chapter 3 features a discussion of *Leadership in Educational Management*. Marianne Coleman suggests that leadership theories are useful analytical tools for the examination of behaviour and effectiveness in all organizations. She stresses the need for leaders to have a vision for the school or college and to be able to communicate this vision to others. She advocates the development of 'transformational leadership' in order to enthuse others with a commitment to the goals of the school or college.

In Chapter 4, John West-Burnham emphasizes the centrality of *Strategy, Policy and Planning* to the management of schools and colleges. He argues that strategic management is fundamental to the process of linking vision and values to the deployment of resources. Long-term planning is crucial in helping to ensure that the school or college does not simply react to externally imposed change but has a clear sense of direction based on its own values.

John O'Neill examines *Organizational Structure and Culture* in Chapter 5, presenting them as complementary perspectives on organizational activity. Structure focuses on the pattern of roles, relationships and lines of authority while culture represents organizational values and beliefs. He argues that a clearly defined and strongly articulated organizational culture can enable schools and colleges to develop an appropriate management response to new and unfamiliar areas of educational activity.

The next two chapters by Mark Lofthouse both relate to aspects of curriculum management. In Chapter 6, *Managing Learning*, he argues that there is a tension between the bureaucratic imperatives of educational organizations and the learning opportunities and outcomes offered to their students. He stresses that pupil learning is more important than teachers' teaching and suggests that management should focus on supporting the vitally important learning process.

In Chapter 7, *Managing the Curriculum*, Lofthouse explores different definitions of the curriculum and examines the pressures exerted by various interest groups in promoting their version of the curriculum. He assesses what senior managers and curriculum co-ordinators need to do in order to manage the curriculum successfully. He also points to the contradiction of a nationally imposed curriculum within the framework of a market-oriented educational system.

John West-Burnham explores the relationship between effective management and *Inspection, Evaluation and Quality Assurance* in Chapter 8. He argues that the demands for external accountability may well not meet the needs for understanding and improving management processes in schools and colleges. He advocates a model of prevention, based on quality assurance, as an alternative approach for self-governing institutions.

Marianne Coleman considers the position of *Women in Educational Management* in Chapter 9. She shows that women are inadequately represented in managerial positions in schools and colleges. She examines strategies to promote equal opportunities through recruitment, professional development and appraisal. She concludes that those gender qualities identified with the feminine side of human nature are amongst those required to manage an effective school or college.

In Chapter 10, John O'Neill addresses the important issue of *Managing Human Resources* in the context of institutional autonomy. He argues that self-managing schools and colleges require more flexible and responsive staffing structures to allow for future budgetary changes. In this unstable environment, he concludes that the challenge is to balance expectations of high performance with a concern for individual welfare and development.

Colin Riches examines the concept of *Motivation* in Chapter 11 and considers its relevance for management. He stresses that of all the resources at the disposal of the school or college, only people can grow. Motivation has a central role in that process of development. He assesses several of the main theories of motivation and examines the implications of these concepts for educational managers.

In Chapter 12, Riches explores the nature of *Communication* in schools and colleges. He defines communication and examines several models. He also considers barriers to effective communication and the different types of communication flow. He stresses that communication goes beyond the spoken word to include various non-verbal signals. He concludes by examining the managerial implications of communication theory.

Chapter 13, by Marianne Coleman and Tony Bush, addresses *Managing with Teams* in schools and colleges. The authors argue that teams are a suitable vehicle for the devolution of responsibility to smaller groups. They explore the nature of team-work and examine team membership, team building and leadership. They identify certain weaknesses in the operation of teams but conclude that team decisions are likely to be both appropriate and acceptable to those who have to implement them.

Managing Professional Development is the theme of Chapter 14 written by John O'Neill. He examines the relationship between personal and organizational improvement, the management of adult learning and models of professional development. He argues that professional development should take account of the needs of individual teachers, functioning groups and the school or college as a whole. He concludes that effective professional development depends on the provision of appropriate support networks.

Tony Bush addresses the issue of *Accountability in Education* in Chapter 15. He presents several models of accountability and argues that the shift to self-managing schools and colleges has changed the pattern of accountability in England and Wales. Accountability to public bodies and to the market have both increased in significance. Professional accountability has been de-emphasised as the British government has sought to reduce 'producer' influence in the management of public services.

The next two chapters by Brent Davies both address aspects of financial management in education. Chapter 16, *Managing Resources*, examines budgeting and the costing assumptions that form part of that process. He stresses that budgeting is part of the overall educational management process and not a separate activity. He considers the nature of costing in educational organizations and argues that cost-benefit analyses are essential components of educational decision-making.

In Chapter 17, Davies examines *Models of Decision-Making in Resource Allocation*. He considers the rational and political frameworks for resource decision-making. Rational models assume that organizations relate their expenditure to their objectives while in the political framework budgeting forms part of the battleground between competing factions. The author also examines models of effective decision-making in decentralised financial systems. He argues that financial decision-making should be devolved to faculty or departmental teams.

Chapter 18 by Marianne Coleman addresses *Marketing and External Relations*. She discusses marketing in the context of the relationships that schools and colleges have with their customers, including parents, LEAs and the wider community. She considers the marketing process, including audit, market research and the marketing plan. She examines the extent and nature of parental involvement in schools and addresses the management implications of external relations.

The editors believe that the issues presented and discussed in this volume are enduring principles that will withstand the shifting sands of educational policy-making. The twin tests of its efficacy remain at the heart of educational improvement. Does it enhance professional development and promote organizational effectiveness? If the book succeeds on both counts, the editors will be well satisfied.

References

Beare, H., Caldwell, B. and Millikan, R. (1992) 'A model for managing an excellent school' in Bennett, N., Crawford, M. and Riches, C. (Eds) *Managing Change in Education*, London: Paul Chapman.

Caldwell, B. and Spinks, J. (1988) *The Self-Managing School*, London: Falmer Press.

Caldwell, B. and Spinks, J. (1992) *Leading the Self-Managing School*, London: Falmer Press.

Finn, C.E. (1984) 'Towards Strategic Independence: Nine Commandments for Enhancing School Effectiveness', *Phi: Delta Kappan*, Feb, pp. 518–524.

Purkey, S.C. and Smith, M.S. (1985) 'School reform : the district policy implications of the effective schools literature'. *The Elementary School Journal*, **85**.

1 Management in educational organizations

John West-Burnham

Introduction

The purpose of this chapter is to explore the issues surrounding the concept of 'managing' educational institutions. The growth in the autonomy of schools and colleges has been paralleled by an increasing emphasis on the need to manage education. This in turn has given rise to a significant growth in the literature about school and college management. At its heart the debate is about whether management is an appropriate conceptual framework to apply to the processes associated with the learning of children and young people. At its most basic the sceptical view is expressed thus:

> (Management theory may be applied with) ... uncertain enthusiasm, with possibly unforeseen and illiberal consequences that are inimical to the values embodied in the broader educative task of the school ... There is so much that is important that cannot adequately be described in management terms (Taylor 1979, pp. 37, 49).

This chapter, and indeed this book, seeks to demonstrate that appropriate management concepts, techniques, skills and processes can be applied to education without detriment to educational 'values' or that which is educationally important. Indeed, it is the contention that without effective management the 'educative task' will be significantly compromised.

The fact that there is a continuing debate (e.g. Bottery, 1992) about the relevance and applicability of 'management' to education indicates the depth of a fundamental misapprehension about the nature of management. In *The Concept of Mind*, Ryle (1949) advances the notion of the category-mistake as a means of analysing confusions in the definition and elucidation of key concepts. Ryle illustrates a category-mistake by describing how a visitor to Oxford is shown colleges, libraries, science departments and then asks to be shown the university. The visitor had not realised, nor was it initially explained, that 'university' is a generic term covering all the elements seen. The mistaken assumption was that 'university' was in the same category as the other, constituent institutions.

When a category (e.g. a university) is made up of a number of elements (e.g. colleges) it is common practice to use the elements to help define, describe and clarify the proposition. However, it is misleading to take one of those terms in isolation and then argue that it characterizes the proposition or justifies a claim to distinctive processes and independent existences. An example of this is found in Ball and Goodson (1985, p.10):

> The concept of management is drawn from the methods of organization, administration and control employed in industry and it contains a set of assumptions which are derived from the work of F.W. Taylor.

In characterizing management as being derived from Taylor, Ball and Goodson describe it as being 'authoritarian', 'dehumanizing', and concerned with control, measurement and efficiency. They go on to propose participation as an alternative to management fundamentally confusing an element of the proposition (participation) with the proposition itself (management). Thus the status of 'participation' is significantly modified from that of constituent to that of generic alternative.

This error is compounded by two false premises. Firstly that management is derived from the work of F.W. Taylor, and secondly that there is a distinctive, homogeneous entity called industry. Both premises are problematic in that Taylor is only one (early and significant) contributor to management theory:

> ... whose theory of scientific management published in 1911, carries less credibility than Bohr's theory of the atom or even the philogiston theory of combustion. Taylorism (is) a historical relic (Everard, 1992, p.21).

It is worth including a brief summary of Taylor's work as it is the basis of many of the objections to the use of management concepts in schools and colleges. The key elements of his approach are:

1. The introduction of scientific methods into the design of working practices, i.e. measuring and analysing a process to find the 'best way'

2. Selecting and training workers to carry out work according to the best way

3. Careful definition of roles and responsibilities

Supporters of Taylor point to greater efficiency, rational organization and improved earnings. Opponents argue that his approach is mechanistic, dehumanizing, based on power and control through hierarchy.

The second premise is also problematic. Just as Taylorism is not synonymous with management theory so there is no generic classification of industry. Few farmers would make good bankers, few chemical engineers would run a successful retail enterprise. If profit is the sole unifying factor for industry then by negative corollary, the characteristics of non-profit organization would argue that education and the military could or should be run on the same principles as both are for the 'public good', cannot be judged by short-term results, use public funds, are subject to political control and are staffed by people with a vocation to serve. This is patently nonsense unless underlying values are explored and management is then seen as a means to an end and not as an end it itself. Thus management and education are in different categories and to argue that they are mutually exclusive, inconsistent or unreconcilable is to perpetuate a fundamental category-mistake.

Management is not *the* purpose of any organizations — it is a 'how?' not a 'what?' Symptomatic of the underlying problem is the tendency in education to use 'management' as a noun rather than a verb — to see it as a descriptor of the few rather than the activity of the many. The nature of this 'activity' will be contingent upon the context, desired outcomes, resources and relevant values. This chapter therefore explores three main issues: the problem of defining *educational* management, objections to the use of 'industrial' models of management and the factors involved in describing a model of management in education.

Defining educational management

There are three components to the process of producing a definition of education management; nomenclature, pedigree and content. The fact that each of these is problematic does not in any way diminish the academic or intellectual pedigree of education management as an academic subject or body of knowledge. Almost every subject studied in the context of higher education goes through periods of reinvention and realignment. Literary criticism and the chemistry of carbon are two recent examples. What is specifically difficult about education management is its relatively limited history (from 1970 in Britain) and its confused parentage. A potentially powerful synthesis of disciplines applied to a specific context can also be regarded as parasitism, expediency and pragmatism. The definition of educational management is made more complex by semantic ambiguity on the part of its practitioners — policy, management and administration are used almost interchangeably by some, and with very rigid and specific meanings by others. These uncertainties are further compounded by a genuine debate as to the actual components of the subject.

❏ The nomenclature of educational management

The issue of nomenclature could be resolved by reference to national differences. What is management to the British reader is administration to the American or Australian reader; the issue is one of comparative custom and practice. However, this is to oversimplify the issue and ignore significant implications for determining the special nature of management in educational institutions in Britain. Glatter (1979) proposes a distinction between educational policy and management in that the former is concerned with 'relationships of power, influence and control' between the protagonists in the educational system and the latter is concerned with the 'internal operation' of educational institutions. Glatter argues for the interchangability of the terms 'management' and 'administration'. However, there has been an increasing trend towards using administration as a specific designation of a type of organizational activity to be contrasted with management and leadership, i.e. a lower order, responsive function. Torrington and Weightman (1989) argue that administration is 'work that can be done by an intelligent 16-year-old' i.e. routine functions requiring limited individual discretion.

Historically leadership was defined as a subset of management, e.g. for Fayol (1916) 'commanding' was a component rather than a separate category of organizational behaviour. However, the work of Peters and Waterman (1982), Bennis and Nanus (1985), Sergiovanni (1984), Caldwell and Spinks (1988), as well as empirical studies such as that by HMI (1976) reinforced the notion of leadership as a distinctive component of organizational effectiveness which needed to be differentiated from management and administration. Hodson (1987) proposes a model which differentiates leadership and management in terms of mission and implementation. West-Burnham (1992), following Torrington and Weightman (1989), proposes a three-way dichotomy between leadership, concerned with values, vision and mission, management, concerned with execution, planning, organizing, deploying, and administration concerned with operational details. The important issue is the consistency of usage and awareness of the implications for the application of analytical models to practice. Semantic confusion can be easily overcome through explicit definition; conceptual confusion is more problematic in that the relationship between leadership, management and administration implies significant value judgements about the nature of schools and colleges as organizations. Bush explores these issues in chapter 2 and Coleman explores the issue of leadership in more detail in chapter 3.

❑ The pedigree of educational management

This section explores the relationship between changes in the structure and organization of the education system and the emergence and significance of theoretical models to explain organizational behaviour. The chronology is derived from that proposed by Williams in his introduction to Cooper and Shute (1988). Although based on analysis of the situation in England and Wales it is suggested that there are significant international comparisons. The sequence of theoretical perspectives is derived from Hughes (1985).

The danger of an attempt at classifying a complex evolutionary process is that artificial boundaries are created to facilitate understanding. The reality of course is that almost all the themes and perspectives identified are still current to a greater or lesser degree and some are essentially re-inventions of previous models; in essence the caelocanth is still with us! What is difficult to demonstrate is the causal relationship between the practice of educational management and the theoretical perspectives. This raises the significant question of the purpose of the study of educational management, i.e. the role of theory. Willower (1993, p.158) argues that,

> Administrators who seek to make reasonable value judgements need to be able to make informed estimates of what will happen when particular courses of action are pursued ... Here, social science concepts and theories can be especially helpful.

The pedigree of educational management might thus be seen as a continuing tension between the context (political, economic and social) in which schools and colleges have to operate, the management strategies and behaviours which are adopted in response to that context and the commentary upon the arguments used to justify those strategies and behaviours. The role of educational management theory may be regarded as:

- clarifying implicit values
- predicting outcomes
- facilitating comparative analysis

Thus the development of theoretical perspectives on educational management may be viewed as a gradual shift from a scientific, positivist view through a

Date	Features of the educational system	Management themes	Theoretical perspectives
1950s	Steady state	Professional control, ……, dependency models	Scientific administration, Normative, Empirical, Role theory
1960s	Comprehensive re-organization Growth Curriculum innovation	Democracy, participation Bureaucracy	Organizations as social systems Organizational climate
1970s	Falling rolls Accountability	Management by objectives Systems Competition	Subjective … Multi-disciplinary studies Contingency theories Economics of education
1980s		Change Effectiveness School improvement Excellence	Integration
1990s	Economic stringency Central control Institutional autonomy	Quality, leadership, Entrepreneurship	Grounded theory

Figure. 1.1 The pedigree of educational management

concern with values and subjective perspectives towards an integration of perspectives and the use of grounded theory in as interactive process which seeks to enhance understanding and effective practice. This process can be represented as in Figure 1.2:

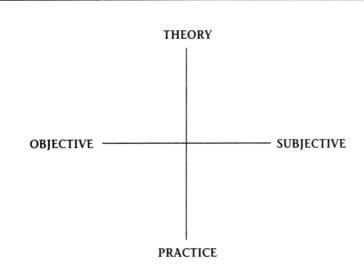

Figure 1.2 The iterative process in educational management

The nexus of the variables in Figure 1.2 might be defined as the paradigm which is felt to be most appropriate for a given situation at a given time. The decision as to the appropriateness or otherwise will be determined by the extent to which consistency with the prevailing values is demonstrated.

Hughes (1985) provides an elegant analysis of the changing theoretical perspectives and of the relationship between them. This discussion has been extended by Bottery (1992) and Evans and Lakomski (1991). All argue for a dynamic and integrative process in which theories 'compete', are applied, tested and reviewed and then modified. This process resolves in adoption, integration, assimilation or rejection and that is a critical component of the development of educational management as a discipline.

This approach is exemplified in a series of publications in the 1980s. Bush (1986) provides a clear model of integration and assimilation in order to develop a range of models to facilitate the process of clarification, prediction and analysis. The resulting framework offers a means of both investigating practice and informing and revising theory (see chapter 2).

Another example of the interactive process is the development of the self-managing school concept by Caldwell and Spinks (1988). Beare et al. (1989, pp.135–137) argue that the evolution of their model of effective management followed an explicit process i.e.

1. Identification of a need for development activities related to effective resource management

2. Investigation of perceived good practice

3. Development of a model synthesizing that practice

4. Dissemination of the model

5. Feedback, review and comparative analysis

6. Revision and extensions of the model

What is particularly relevant in the context of this discussion is the way in which the whole project was a collaboration between theorist and practitioner. The development of educational management can be seen as moving into what Willower (1993, p.158) characterizes as:

> (first) an adequate conception of inquiry, the second is more explicit attention to values and valuations, and the third is a view of practice that emphasises what the Greeks called praxis, that is, thoughtful practice.

The concept of grounded theory is helpful in characterizing this reflexive process which establishes a critical dialogue between theory and practice, is tested against methodological considerations and explores the inherent values. This process may help to bridge the demands of practitioners for practical strategies and the need to test and verify.

One of the key factors in determining the approach to issues such as the nature of leadership will be the view taken of the intellectual and academic pedigree of educational management. It can be viewed as a polyglot of a range of academic disciplines, e.g. political theory and science, sociology, organizational psychology, economics, philosophy as well as industrial and commercial practice. To this synthesis must be added views as to the nature and purpose of education and the tension between descriptive /analytical and prescriptive/ normative models.

Political theory and science are major contributors to the canon of educational management notably in the area of policy making; the study of the relationships and dynamics in the generation and continuation of policy at national and local level, and the impact on institutions and the relationship with stakeholders such as trade unions, parents' groups etc. Another significant contribution has been in the study of micro-politics, the exploration of influence, bargaining and coalitions at institutional level (see chapter 2).

Sociology has been an element in the evolution of educational management most notably in the area of organization theory. The study of bureaucracy has long been central to the understanding of how schools and colleges actually function. Equally significant influences are the human-relations approaches and the systems-based analysis of organizational life. These perspectives have informed discussions of organizational design and structure and the impact of social stratification on perspectives such as the nature of professional status. Sociology has also been crucial in the development of methodologies for research in educational management (see Johnson, 1994).

Organizational psychology has provided many of the 'practical' theories of management in general and educational management. Work on teams, motivation and social relationships has done much to inform actual practice. Equally, much of the empirical research that has been done in schools and colleges has focused on perceptions and behaviour. Many of the issues surrounding teacher appraisal, classroom management and the relationship between meetings and decision-making have links to organizational psychology.

The application of economic theory to the management of educational institutions is relatively underdeveloped. Significant work has been done at the macro-economics level on issues such as supply and demand and costing. However, much of the work at school and college level has focused on budgetary issues and accounting procedures. There is still a great deal of work to be done in understanding market-place economics in the context of educational institutions.

Only in recent years has philosophy emerged as a significant contributor to the evaluation of educational management. This has taken two main forms; first, providing a conceptual context for the debate between the rational/positivist, and subjective/phenomenological debate as to the nature of the discourse about organizations. This debate is at the heart of philosophical explanation and may be characterized as the tension between objective, empirical and logical interpretations of the world and individual responses as the basis for understanding. Secondly, philosophy is informing the increasing awareness of the problematics surrounding discussions about the values and ethical imperatives which underpin management behaviour in schools and colleges.

Industrial and commercial practice is a major source of theory and practice in educational management and is equally the most problematic and contentious. Although the debate about the nature of educational management is derived from established academic disciplines, much of the discussion of *school* practice is directly derivative of industrial and commercial sources. Although interpreted, refined and applied the conceptual framework and actual practice maintains a high correlation with the originals, e.g.

Target setting (Drucker, 1992)
Motivation (Herzberg, 1968)
Total quality (Deming, 1986)
Teams (Belbin, 1981)
Leadership (Adair, 1973)
Management learning (Kolb, 1983)
Interpersonal relationships (Beare, 1989, Harris, 1978)

Equally there are areas in educational management where there is a unique contribution from educational writers, notably Fullan (1991) on change and the whole area of the technology of learning, i.e. curriculum management (see chapters 6 and 7). Local management of schools in England and Wales owes much of its principles and operational detail to the commercial organization Coopers and Lybrand. There are many other areas where it is almost impossible to establish the precise genealogy of principles and practice, e.g. time management, marketing, staff development, planning etc.

The issues raised by this complex relationship are discussed in the next section of this chapter.

Objections to industrial models of management in education

A synthesis of the main concerns about the use of industrial management practices and concepts in education and anxieties about the nature of educational processes (Maw et al., 1984; Handy and Aitken,1986; Squire, 1987 and Bottery, 1992) produces the following list of caveats:

1. Management theory is primarily concerned with profit; education is not

2. Management is mechanistic, education should be organic; systems are hostile to the essential creativity of education

3. Management is about clear goals; educational aims are diffuse, varied and conflicting

4. Management denies professional status

5. Management theory is pragmatic and expedient

6. Management theory is pseudo-scientific

7. Management theory cannot be reconciled with the special status of children

Each of these concerns deserves a detailed examination and response; however a general point can be made at the outset. Critics of management in education rarely cite specific texts or examples of management practice. Management theory is usually found to be derived from Fayol or Taylor and 'practice' is usually anecdotal and not discriminated. The writers in Maw et al. (1984, p.13) make frequent references to 'managers in industry' or 'industrial practice'. There is a real danger of gross over-simplification or unwarranted assumptions of homogeneity, e.g.

> The role of morality in the commercial world is similar to that of a safety net: by and large its function is only active, or indeed recognized, when things go wrong ... Quite the reverse is true of education, where morality imbues not only the ends which are pursued but also the means ...

This may be true of some commercial concerns in some situations at some times but it is no more valid than claims by industrialists that schools produce young people who are unfit for employment. It is significant that Maw and her colleagues refer to only one industrially based text and provide no specific examples of industrial practice. Many of the objections to management in education are based on a false premise, a caricature of industrial practice. Bottery (1992, p.33) uses the building of the great pyramids as a metaphor for bureaucracy pointing out that without control, roles, planning, etc. they would not have been built but questions the 'inhuman treatment' of the builders. Current research argues that in fact the pyramids were built by independent, skilled craftsmen who were a 'labour aristocracy'. Great care is needed to avoid debating the nature of educational management using stereotypical and false premises.

On this basis the objections listed above will be examined in detail:

❑ Management theory is primarily involved with profit; education is not

If management theory is primarily and fundamentally about profit then there is a clear problem in transferring it to educational institutions. However, the 'profit motive' does not feature significantly in most contemporary management texts. Although it may appear purely semantic the emphasis is on the achievement of goals — which include making a profit. However, making a profit may be interpreted as a function of customer satisfaction. Drucker (1992) provides two powerful rejoinders to the notion of profit as the primary motivation of business:

> They are, however, surely wrong in defining 'performance' as nothing but immediate, short-term gains for shareholders. This subordinates all other constituencies ... to the immediate gratification of people whose only interest in the business is short-term pay-offs. No society will tolerate this for very long (p.18).

> ... in a market economy there is no 'profit' but only 'profit and loss'; no 'reward', but only 'risk and reward'; and that freedom is not just the absence of restraint but self-discipline and responsibility (p.123).

❑ Management is mechanistic; education should be organic; systems are hostile to the essential creativity of education

The work of Taylor and the supremacy of Management by Objectives (MBO) in the 1950s and 1960s created a view of management as being essentially authoritarian, concerned with the creation of systems to which individuals are subordinated and where the primary function of managers is to ensure compliance. MBO is the management approach which organizes work tasks into specific, measurable and negotiated short-term outcomes which dominate the individuals approach to the job. For Morgan (1985, p.37):

> Mechanistic organization discourages initiative, encouraging people to obey orders and keep their place rather than to take an interest in, challenge and question what they are doing.

It is the latter characteristics which are deemed appropriate for the education sector:

> The school is seen as an organism, a body, living, growing, flourishing, decaying ... We are firmly in the land of culture, where values not structure, belonging not organization, are paramount (Shipman 1990, p.143).

The truth is probably that schools, like almost all other organizations are both mechanistic and organic. These terms are used as metaphors to explain and understand the social reality of the organization. The issue centres on the extent to which the metaphor is extrapolated into a model which then becomes prescriptive — when an 'is' becomes an 'ought'. Shipman's classification of the school as organic has precise parallels in industrial management theory:

> In the past we have generally followed the principles of management proposed by Taylor. Under this regime, the manager's role is to plan, organise, direct and solve problems. The worker's role is to carry out tasks as directed by managers.

> TQM requires us to recognise the contributions which every employee can make ... individuals must be provided with skills, tools and authority ... managers ... must create an open atmosphere (Monro-Faure 1992, p.9).

❑ Management is about clear goals; educational aims are diffuse, varied, conflicting

Most industrial managers would be surprised to learn that they work in the context of clear, unambiguous and non-contentious goals. The manager of a chemical plant will have to balance demands for output against quality, safety against expediency, profitability against environmental concerns, conflicting motivation and expectations of the work force as well as personal issues related to responsibility, authority and career development. The situation is as complex as that of any educationalist. However, the chemical engineer can see a tangible product, which, it is argued the educationalist does not.

This is to significantly over-simplify the process; a bag of fertiliser is but one aspect of the possible outcomes, most of which are intangible or potentially contradictory. Customer satisfaction, perceived value for money, health and safety regulations will all produce different perceptions of the product. To argue that the outcomes of educational processes are so diffuse and intangible that they cannot be managed is to ignore the reality of what actually happens in schools and colleges. Educational processes are made up of a wide range of specific, concrete and time-constrained activities: lesson plans, schemes of work, examination syllabuses, timetables, job descriptions, etc. Of course there are intangibles but these are of a different order of significance to the activities which actually constitute the aspects of educational life which have to be managed; by definition, the intangibles the long-term outcomes cannot be managed in the same way. To paraphrase Wittgenstein (1922): 'where of we cannot manage, there of we must keep silent'. St Augustine said that we pray for miracles but work for results — the work and results are the proper subject of management. The hope, aspiration and values are vital but they must be translated into action:

> Strategy converts a non-profit institution's mission and objectives into performance ... The whole point of strategy is not to look at recipients as people who receive bounty, to whom the non-profit does good. They are customers who have to be satisfied (Drucker 1990, p.75).

The purpose of a school or college might be to produce an 'educated' young person, however 'educated' might be defined; for example a love of literature can be encouraged by a systematic exposure to examples of literature and the development of skills to help understanding. These processes can be managed, and are on a daily basis, i.e. it is possible to translate the educational process into specific activities and outcomes which can be managed.

❑ Management denies professional status

One of the most significant perceived tensions between management and education is what is often characterized as the 'bureaucratic – professional interface'. In essence this comes down to an explanation of the relative weight to be given to the claims of the individual to exercise personal judgement in an autonomous manner and the claims of the organization to insist on conformity to common values, purpose and activity. Thus being a professional and being managed are inimical.

However, the debate is essentially circular and sterile and the way forward is not to focus on relative social status but rather upon the way in which tasks are carried out, i.e. professionalism.

The issue then develops into the question 'what sort of management is consistent with supporting and enhancing professionalism?' The tension changes from the notion of a clash of cultures to one of appropriateness and effectiveness and as such is not restricted to the education service. Anxieties about the nature and values of management are found across the public and private sectors. The issue is not to debate the relevance of management theory *per se* but rather to identify the appropriate means of understanding and informing practice (see chapter 2).

❏ Management theory is pragmatic and expedient

The criticism that management theory is pragmatic and expedient is largely derived from a negative reading of contingency theory, e.g. Fielding (1984, p.15) refers to:

> ... an approach which proclaims that 'there is no single right or wrong style of leadership' and advocates an 'accurate diagnosis' and the selection of 'an appropriate style.'

> ... the key words here are 'accurate' and 'appropriate'. One cannot help but feel that the accuracy has more to do with expediency than principle and that appropriateness is self-confirming.

By this interpretation contingency theory is, at worst, cynical and manipulative and an attempt at legitimation of random management behaviour. However, this critique assumes that schools are internally homogeneous and consistent and operate in a stable environment. Neither of these suppositions can be regarded as accurate in the current educational climate. Hoyle (1986, p.19) argues that 'the basic tenet of contingency theory is that there is no eternally 'right' way of structuring and managing organizations'.

In essence one writer's pragmatic, manipulative approach is another's organic response to structural relativism, high levels of differentiation and a complex environment, making varying and sometimes contradictory demands. The rejection of contingent or situational approaches is based upon the problematic assumptions that educational institutions operate in a 'steady-state' and that there is 'one best way' to respond to the variables impinging on organizations. Burns and Stalker (1961, p.125) argued that 'the beginning of administrative wisdom is that there is no optimum type of management system'.

❏ Management theory is pseudo-scientific

There is little doubt that much management theory is pseudo-scientific, claiming a spurious legitimacy from claims of foundations in observation, scientific-method or mathematical models. The works of Taylor, management-by-objectives, deterministic theories of motivation, statistical measurement are most frequently cited. The debate centres on the concept of efficiency which

> ... tends to be wedded to a simplistic and limited vision of both rationality and science which assumes that one can plan down to the last detail the way in which things will happen (Bottery 1992, p.29).

Greenfield is equally critical of the implications of the scientific approach:

> The paradox of control-orientated science is that its consequences are exactly the opposite of those claimed, means supplant ends and become their own ends ... a management science focused upon control in the organizations brings with it an unfortunate consequence in education: 'The separation of administrative and educational concerns' (Greenfield and Ribbins 1993, p.220).

The objections to the 'scientific' approach centre on doubts about the applicability of efficiency, the problematic of predicting educational outcomes, concern over the concept of control and the danger of the system assuming greater significance than the intended outcome.

These concerns are shared by most management writers outside education. To some extent Bottery and Greenfield are challenging an historical model. Whilst the debate is live and real in terms of the epistemology of management theory it is less so in management practice. It could be argued that it is the most significant current manifestation of the search for

> ... predictabilities, for law-like interpretations of complex social phenomena, perhaps even for a mechanism or quasi-mechanistic system of interactions which can be managed, directed, planned. (Hodgkinson in Greenfield and Ribbins ibid. p.xi).

The emphasis is on prevention through definitions, control and conformity — yet all that it guarantees is conformity; there is no reference to content. It is not difficult to find management writers whose rejection of such an approach is as direct as Greenfields:

Shortcomings of rational management
- to be rational is often to be negative
- the exclusively rational approach leads to heartless philosophy
- the numerative component has in-built conservative bias

- today's version of rationality devalues experimentation
- anti-experimentation leads to over-complexity

(Peters and Waterman 1982, p.57)

Peters and Waterman were describing the characteristics of successful business — reversing their critique produces the following key components of excellence management:

- a positive approach
- a caring philosophy
- a radical bias
- a respect for experimentation
- a bias towards simplicity

The objections to scientific management are as strong in the industrial sector as they are in the educational sector. In both areas the emphasis on values is shared:

> Values lie beyond rationality. Rationality to *be* rationality must stand upon a value base. Values are asserted, chosen, imposed or believed. They lie beyond qualification, beyond measurement (Greenfield and Ribbins 1993, p.182).

> Managerial reality is not an absolute; rather, it is socially and culturally determined (Pascale and Athos 1982, p.22).

Both educational management and industrial management are moving away from certainty, control and measurement to relativism, ambiguity and, crucially, debate — management theory is becoming the basis for learning rather than that which has to be learnt.

In this context positivist, rational and scientific approaches have a limited contribution to make. But it would be wrong to deny their validity as a component of understanding. A work of art is responded to in terms of values, creativity and skill but the artist will have calculated the pigments to be used exactly and will understand the mathematics of proportion and perspective. The issue is to avoid a paint-by-numbers approach to art and to management.

❑ Management theory cannot be reconciled with the special status of children

Those who argue that management is inimical to the special status of children are probably right if they are referring to management as practised in many organizations and expounded by many theories. But by the same token it is equally inappropriate for adults. The previous sections of this chapter have sought to demonstrate that management is a multi-faceted concept and that the definitions of management as being concerned with power, control, measurement, etc. are rejected as much in some elements of business as in some parts of education.

There is a real issue in that too few educational management text-books place the learning, social and moral development of young people at the heart of every process. Management techniques are too often assumed to be self-legitimating and do not use children's development as the bench mark of appropriateness. Shipman (1990, p.1) expresses this most powerfully:

> Schools exist to promote learning. That is the end of management ... learning is individual and children are a varied lot. We know little about how they learn or the best way to help them ... yet these difficulties are not excuses for writing about school management as if it had no end beyond the establishment of efficient routines.

Two issues emerge from this critique, first the extent to which school and college management should serve as an educative model of social processes. This leads to the second issue; how far children, students and all adults should be involved in the management of *their* schools and colleges. This is not to advocate a spurious notion of democracy or reinforce the problematic virtues claimed for collegiality (see chapter 2) but rather to propose an integrated model of measurement and learning which applies as much to children as to adults and reinforces the exemplifications of values through school behaviour.

The important thing about the model in Figure 1.3 is that it was developed by the students themselves. It is a relatively simple task to extend the model into management relationships and so propose an holistic view of managing and learning.

Handy and Aitken (1986) point out the problems in coming to terms with 'children' in managing schools and colleges. In some (primary schools) they appear to be treated as workers, in others (secondary schools) as products and in others (colleges) as clients. This division is not the result of the applications of Philistine management techniques to secondary schools, but rather the emphasis on knowledge delivery rather than individual learning, the compartmentalization of activities and the emphasis on control and accountability.

26

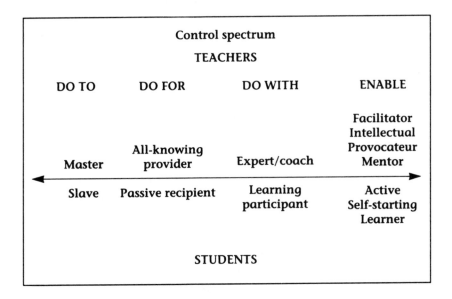

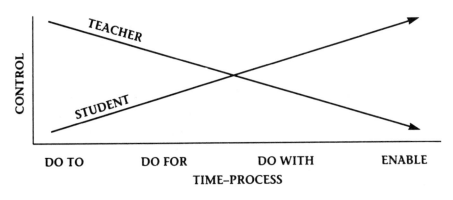

Figure 1.3. The learning model at Mt. Edgecombe High School

Few *effectively* managed industrial organizations would create a system that reflects so little concern for the individual or lack of trust. To re-phrase the title of this section: inappropriate management theory cannot be reconciled with the special status of children or anyone else. Inappropriate management theory and behaviour is not the monopoly of industrialists.

Management works through people. *It should encourage leadership at all levels* [my emphasis], (Shipman 1990, p.155).

Describing a model of management in education

The purpose of this final section is to offer a series of propositions which are derived from the preceding discussion. It is hoped that these will help to inform the reading of the other chapters in this book and other texts on educational management.

Management is a verb, not a noun One of the most significant barriers to the effective assimilation of management concepts and behaviour into educational organizations is the perpetuation of the notion that management refers to a senior group of staff. It therefore becomes associated with notions of status and power and because of the nature of the promotion process is often perceived as being male dominated. Indeed predominantly male behaviour is almost inevitable. The important shift is to move away from the notion of management as descriptor to management as an activity which is engaged in by all members of an educational organization, i.e. senior staff, teaching staff, non-teaching staff and children or students. Managing is doing things, making things happen, it is about the processes that all people engage in in the course of their life in organizations. Management is generic to all organizations.

Following what has been argued in the paragraph above it follows that the process of managing is found in every situation where individuals gather together for a common purpose and to achieve agreed outcomes. Whilst there may well be very significant differences in the way that the concept of management is interpreted in different organizations, these will be a natural response to variations in size, technology, staffing, and outcomes. Profound differences in values and purposes do not diminish the basic requirement to manage.

Management is a contingent concept The argument is that there is no 'one best way' to manage. Management is not an absolute which can be universally applied irrespective of the particular context in which it has to operate. It has meaning only when it is interpreted in a specific situation and the concept of management becomes meaningful when contextualized.

Understanding management is a process requiring adoption, integration and assimilation The canon of management exists only in the abstract as a result of the presentation of effective practice or the application of theoretical models. The process of managing effectively is the result of taking theory and described practice and applying them to the specific situation so that they are made relevant to the specific context. The process is therefore one of adoption, i.e. taking over practice; integration in the sense of incorporation of appropriate models and procedures from other organizations and assimilation in the sense of adjusting alternative practice to meet specific contextual needs.

Becoming a manager is learning to engage in the debate about purpose and values Management is purposive, i.e. it is concerned with achieving outcomes. The existence of outcomes implies a set of values about both the nature of the outcomes and the means by which they are to be attained. Becoming an effective manager is therefore developing the capacity to understand the nature of the outcomes and to relate them to appropriate value systems. Management is not and cannot be neutral in terms of values or outcomes.

Management learning is an heuristic process People learn to become effective managers only by managing. The interaction between theory and practice is crucial in allowing one to inform and extend the other. However, effective management is also a matter of organizational relationships in which mistakes are perceived as opportunities for enhancement and development. The organization which regards mistakes as failure is unlikely to be one that develops and grows.

Management is expressed in behaviour If management is about action then the ultimate criterion for effectiveness is the extent to which outcomes are achieved and intentions are translated into observable change. In complex organizations the vast majority of management outcomes will be expressed in terms of relationships and it is the impact of those relationships that must be perceived as the most important single arbiter of effectiveness. The effective manager is able to come to terms with a range of complex situations and issues. The management of the tension between theory and practice, values and expediency and the ultimate complexity of social relationships are fundamental to the management process. This presumes skills of analysis, prioritisation and communication.

Managing involves changing John Henry Newman argued 'to be perfect is to have changed often'. Effective management requires a process of sustained responsiveness to personal and environmental demands. The tensions and stress that are often found in educational institutions in the 1990s are frequently the result of imposed change and failure to accept the need to become capable of changing rather than trying to manage change.

Bibliography

Adair, J. (1973) *Action-centred Leadership*, Aldershot: Gower.

Ball, S.J. and Goodson, I.F. (1985) *Teachers Lives and Careers*, London: Falmer Press.

Beare, H., Caldwell, B.J. and Millikin, R.H. (1989) *Creating an Excellent School*, London: Routledge.

Belbin, R.M. (1981) *Management Teams: Why They Succeed or Fail*, London: Butterworth–Heinemann.

Bennis, W. and Nanus, B. (1985) *Leaders*, London: Harper & Row.

Bottery M. (1992) *The Ethics of Educational Management*, London: Cassell.

Burns, T. and Stalker, G.M. (1961) *The Management of Innovation*, London: Tavistock.

Bush, T. (1986) *Theories of Educational Management*, PCP.

Caldwell, B.J. and Spinks, J.M. (1988) *The Self-Managing School*, Lewes: Falmer Press.

Cooper, B.S. and Shute, R.W. (1988) *Training for School Managment*, Institute of Education, University of London.

Deming, W.E. (1986) *Out of the Crisis*, Cambridge University Press.

Drucker, P. (1990) *Managing the Non-Profit Organization*, Oxford: Butterworth–Heinemann.

Drucker, P. (1992) *Managing for the Future*, Oxford: Butterworth–Heinemann.

Evans, C. and Lakomski, G. (1991) *Knowing Educational Administration*, London: Pergamon.

Everard, B. (1992) 'Review of Bottery M. (1992), 'The ethics of educational management'. *Educational Change and Development*, **13**,1.

Fayol, H. (1916) *General and Industrial Administration*, London: Pitman.

Fielding, M. (1984) 'Asking different questions and persuing different views', in Maw, J. et al. (ibid).

Fullan, M. (1991) *New Meanings of Educational Change*, Teaching College Press.

Glatter, R. (1979) 'Educational policy and management: one field or two?'. *Educational Analysis*, **1**, 2.

Greenfield, T. and Ribbins, P. (1993) *Greenfield on Educational Administration*, London: Routledge.

HMI (1976) *Ten Good Schools*, HMSO.

Handy, C.B. and Aitken, R. (1986) *Understanding Schools as Organizations*, Harmondsworth: Penguin.

Harris, T.A. (1978) *I'm OK — You're OK*, Avon Books.

Herzberg, F. (1968) *Work and the Nature of Man*, Stephens Press.

Hodson, P. (1987) 'Managers can be taught but leaders have to learn'. *ICT*, Nov/Dec.

Hoyle, E. and McMohon, A. (1986) *The Management of Schools*, London: Kogan Page.

Hughes, M. (1985) 'Theory and practice in educational management' in Hughes, Ribbins and Thomas (1985), ibid.

Hughes, M., Ribbins, P. and Thomas, H. (1985) *Managing Education*, London: Holt.

Johnson, D. (1994) *Research Methods in Educational Management*, Harlow: Longman.

Kolb, D.A. (1983) *Experimental Learning*, Englewood Cliffs, NJ: Prentice Hall.

Maw, J. et al. (1984) *Education Plc?* London Institute of Education, London: Heinemann.

Monro-Faure, L. and M. (1992) *Implementing Total Quality Management*, London: Pitman.

Morgan, G. (1985) *Images of Organizations*, Beverly Hills: Sage.

Pascale, R.T. and Athos, A.G. (1982) *The Art of Japanese Management*, Harmondsworth: Penguin.

Peters, T. and Waterman, R. (1982) *In Search of Excellence*, London: Harper and Row.

Ryle, G. (1949) *The Concept of Mind*, Harmondsworth: Penguin.

Sergiovanni, T.J. (1984) 'Leadership and excellence in schooling'. *Educational Leadership*, February.

Shipman, M. (1990) *In Search of Learning*, Oxford: Blackwell.

Squire, W.H. (1987) *Education Management in the UK*, Aldershot: Gower.

Taylor, W. (1979) 'The head as manager' in Peters, R.S. (Ed) *The Role of the Head*, London: Routledge & Kegan Paul.

Torrington, D. and Weightman, J. (1989) *The Reality of School Management*, Oxford: Blackwell.

Torrington, D., Weightman, J. and Johns, K. (1989) *Effective Management*, Prentice Hall.

West-Burnham, J. (1992) *Managing Quality in Schools*, Harlow: Longman.

Willower, D.J. (1993) 'Explaining and improving educational administration'. In *Educational Management and Administration*, **21**,3.

Wittgenstein, L. (1922) *Tractatus Logico — Philosophicuz*, London: Routledge and Kegan Paul.

2 Theory and practice in educational management

Tony Bush

Introduction

The purpose of this chapter is to explore the relevance of theory to management in education. We shall examine the relationship between theory and practice and address the nature of theory in educational management. Five major theories of educational management will be presented and discussed. Finally, we shall consider certain over-arching theories.

The theory/practice divide

Management is usually regarded as a practical activity. The tasks of defining aims, making decisions and evaluating effectiveness all involve action. Simply repeating these actions might be thought to lead to managerial excellence — 'practice makes perfect'. As Hughes (1985, p.31) points out:

> It has been customary for practitioners to state the dichotomy in robust terms: airy-fairy theory versus down-to-earth practice.

Dearden (1984, p.4) suggests that 'teachers commonly regard theory with ... suspicion because its bearings are unclear on the detailed decision as to what to do next Monday morning.'

If practitioners shun theory then they must rely on experience as a guide to action. In deciding on the most appropriate response to a problem they draw on a range of options suggested by previous encounters with the issue. If pressed to explain decisions, teachers are likely to say that they are just 'common-sense'. However, such 'common-sense' decisions are often based on implicit theories — unacknowledged but nonetheless influential:

Commonsense knowledge ... inevitably carries with it unspoken assumptions and unrecognized limitations. Theorizing is taking place without it being acknowledged as such (Hughes 1985, p.31).

Theory provides a rationale for decision making. It helps managers by giving them a basis for action. Without a frame of reference decisions could become purely arbitrary. It is not sufficient simply to note the facts of a situation and to make a decision based on those facts. All such evidence requires interpretation. Theory provides the framework for understanding and interpreting events.

The relevance of theory

The arguments in support of the systematic acquisition of theory have been stated by this and other authors (Bush 1986, Bush 1989, Hughes 1985, Hughes and Bush 1991). These factors can be summarized as follows:

1. Reliance on facts as the sole guide to action is unsatisfactory because all evidence requires *interpretation*. Practitioners cannot make decisions simply on an event-by-event basis if decision-making is to be consistent and not simply arbitrary and disconnected. Frames of reference are needed to provide the insights for decision-making.

2. Dependence on experience alone in interpreting facts is narrow because it discards the accumulated experience and ideas of others. Practitioners can be more effective if they deploy a range of experience and understanding in resolving problems. 'It is only fools who learn by experience. Wise men do not have to learn of the existence of every brick wall by banging their nose into it' (Jennings 1977, p.vii).

3. Disastrous errors of judgement can occur while experience is being gained. Mistakes are costly in both material and human terms. Money is scarce but the needs of pupils and students are even more important. 'In education we just cannot throw away the flawed product as waste and start again' (Hughes 1984, p.5).

4. Experience in one situation is not necessarily applicable in another. Organizational variables may mean that practice in one setting has little relevance in the new context. To interpret behaviour and events in the fresh situation a broader awareness of possible approaches is necessary

(Hughes and Bush 1991 p.223).

Landers and Myers (1977, p.365) stress the relevance of theory to practice:

> There is nothing more practical than a good theory ... It can ... help the practitioner to unify and focus his [sic] views on an organization, on his role and relationships within the organization, and on the elusive phenomena of leadership and achievement.

Theories are most relevant when they provide fresh insight on events and problems. They can identify new ways of understanding practice and lead to a significant reduction in the theory/practice divide. They cannot then be dismissed as irrelevant to the needs of teachers.

The nature of theory in educational management

There is no single all-embracing theory of educational management. This is because it comprises a series of perspectives rather than an all-embracing 'scientific' truth:

> [Theories] 'describe' or operate in a social or political world that is itself changing ... The perspectives rest more upon a professional consensus of what is possible and relevant and valued than upon a scientific consensus as to what is true ... The perspective is a 'way of seeing' a problem rather than a rigid set of rules and procedures (House 1981, p.20).

The existence of several different perspectives creates what Bolman and Deal (1984) describe as 'conceptual pluralism'. Each theory has something to offer in explaining behaviour and events in educational institutions. It also means that educational management theories tend to be normative or prescriptive in that they reflect the theorists' views or preconceptions of how schools are, or should be, managed. These perspectives are sometimes advocated so zealously that they tend to obscure rather than illuminate reality:

> Students of educational management who turn to organizational theory for guidance in their attempt to understand and manage educational institutions will not find a single, universally-applicable theory but a multiplicity of theoretical approaches each jealously guarded by its particular epistemic community (Ribbins 1985, p.223).

The many different perspectives may be presented as five distinct theories of educational management (Bush 1986). These are the bureaucratic, collegial, political, subjective and ambiguity perspectives. We turn now to examine these five theories.

Bureaucratic theories

Bureaucratic theories are associated strongly with the work of Weber (1947) who argued that bureaucracy is the most efficient form of management. Livingstone (1974, p.9) suggests that bureaucracy is an almost inevitable consequence of increasing size and complexity:

> Bureaucracy describes only the simple truth that as organizations grow and become more complex, more formal systems of regulation replace the informal understanding that is often sufficient for effective co-ordination in the smaller, simpler units.

The main features of bureaucratic theories are as follows:

- a **hierarchical authority structure** with formal chains of command between the different positions in the hierarchy
- a **goal orientation** Organizations pursue those goals determined by their official leaders
- a **division of labour** with staff specializing in particular tasks on the basis of expertise
- decisions and behaviour are governed by **rules and regulations** rather than personal initiative
- decisions are made through a **rational process** involving definition of the problem, assessment of possible solutions and choice of the most appropriate solution to fit the organization's goals
- the **authority of leaders** is a product of their official positions within the organization
- leaders are **accountable** to the organization's sponsoring, or governing body

Schools and colleges have many bureaucratic features, including a hierarchical structure with the headteacher or principal at the apex. Teachers specialize on the basis of expertise in secondary schools and colleges and, increasingly, in primary schools also. There are many rules for pupils and staff, whose working lives are largely dictated by the 'tyranny of the timetable'. Heads and senior staff are accountable to the governing body and external stakeholders for the activities of the school or college. Partly for these reasons, bureaucratic theories pervade much of the literature on educational management but they have several weaknesses when applied to educational organizations:

- Bureaucratic theories characterize organizations as *goal-seeking* entities but in practice it may be difficult to ascertain the goals of educational establishments. Many schools have formal written statements of their objectives but these may have little operational relevance. Official goals are often vague and general and do not indicate how they are to be achieved. The increasing importance of development planning in England and Wales has begun to reduce the gulf between aims and practice but the gap still exists in many schools and colleges;

- Bureaucratic theories portray decision-making as a *rational* process. Managerial action is said to follow a careful evaluation of alternatives and a considered choice of the most appropriate option. In practice, however, much of human behaviour is irrational and this inevitably influences the nature of decision-making in education:

  > People in organizations, including educational organizations, find themselves hard pressed either to find actual instances of those rational practices or to find rationalized practices whose outcomes have been as beneficent as predicted, or to feel that those rational occasions explain much of what goes on within the organization (Weick 1976, p.1)

- Bureaucratic theories focus on the organization as an entity and ignore or underestimate the contribution of *individuals* within organizations. They assume that people occupy preordained positions in the structure and that their behaviour reflects their organizational positions rather than their individual qualities and experience. This stance has been criticised by Greenfield as we shall see in the section on subjective theories

- Bureaucratic theories assume that power resides at the apex of the pyramid. Heads and principals have authority by virtue of their position as the appointed leaders of the institution. This focus on official authority leads to a view of educational management which is essentially *top-down*. Such hierarchical approaches are most relevant for organizations which depend on tight discipline for their effectiveness. Soldiers, for example, are expected to carry out their orders without any questioning or elaboration. In education the perceived legitimacy of hierarchical authority is more ambiguous. Schools and colleges have large numbers of professional staff and tend to exhibit signs of tension between the twin demands of professionalism and the hierarchy. Professionals claim an authority of expertise which may come into conflict with the positional authority of the principal

- Bureaucratic approaches are most appropriate in *stable* conditions but are much less valid in periods of rapid change. In changing, dynamic, unstable organizations there may be little time or opportunity to engage in a rational process of choice. Bureaucratic perspectives require a measure of predictability to be useful as portraits of organizational behaviour. Yet, as March and Olsen (1976) point out, 'individuals find themselves in a more complex, less stable and less understood world than that described by standard theories of organizational choice'

The changes introduced in England and Wales by the 1988 Education Reform Act and subsequent legislation have modified the previous structure of education. Schools and colleges are increasingly self-managing institutions with an enhanced role for governing bodies. In many schools and colleges, this has led to new arrangements with professional and lay teams operating alongside, and to some extent supplanting, the hierarchical structure. Elsewhere, however, the reforms have served to re-inforce the bureaucratic authority of the formal leaders, and professionals and lay governors are given little opportunity to influence decision-making (Bush et al. 1993, Thompson 1992).

Collegial theories

The collegial approach is increasingly advocated as the most appropriate way to manage schools and colleges. Wallace (1988) refers to collegiality as 'the official model of good practice' while Campbell (1985) suggests that this 'contemporary image of good practice has been promoted by the Inspectorate since 1978'.

Collegial approaches developed within the colleges of Oxford and Cambridge universities. According to Becher and Kogan (1980, p.67), 'collegium designates a structure or structures in which members have equal authority to participate in decisions which are binding on each of them'.

The main features of collegial theories are as follows:

- They assume an **authority of expertise** in contrast to the positional authority associated with the bureaucratic models. Professional authority occurs when decisions are made on an individual basis rather than being standardized

- They stress a **common set of values** shared by members of the organization. These are thought to emanate from the socialization which occurs during training and the early years of professional practice. These common values are expected to lead to shared organizational objectives

- They assume that decisions are reached by a process of discussion leading to **consensus**. The belief that there are common values and shared objectives leads on to a view that it is both desirable and possible to resolve issues by agreement. The decision-making process may be elongated by the search for compromise but this is regarded as an acceptable price to pay to maintain the aura of shared values and beliefs.

Collegial theories may be regarded as highly normative and idealistic. They are attractive approaches because they encourage the participation of teachers in decision-making, leading to a sense of ownership and an enhanced prospect of successful innovation.

However, collegial theories also have several weaknesses when applied to schools and colleges. The main limitations are the following:

- The collegial literature often confuses *descriptive* and *normative* approaches. 'Are the writers saying that the university *is* a collegium or that it ought to be a collegium?'. (Baldridge et al. 1978, p.33). The same criticism could be applied to collegial theories in schools and colleges

- The assumption of decision-making by consensus is flawed because schools and colleges have *sectional interests* which may lead to conflict rather than agreement. 'The collegial model ... fails to deal adequately with the problem of conflict ... (it) neglects the prolonged battles that precede consensus and the fact that the consensus actually represents the prevalence of one group over another' (Baldridge et al. 1978, pp.33–34)

- Collegial approaches may be difficult to sustain in view of the *accountability* of the principal to external stake-holders. The requirements of accountability limit the extent to which heads are prepared or are able to share their power with their professional colleagues.

Hargreaves (1993) takes a sceptical view of collegial approaches. He cautions against the imposition of collegiality by government agencies and outlines five characteristics of what he describes as 'contrived collegiality':

- administratively regulated rather than spontaneous
- compulsory rather than discretionary
- oriented towards implementation rather than policy formulation
- fixed in time and place rather than informal and opportunist
- predictable outcomes rather than open discussion

The implementation of a nationally-determined curriculum in England and Wales lends support to the notion of contrived collegiality. If discussion takes place in 'directed time', and is geared largely to implementation of policies determined by institutional leaders or the government, this is a limited form of collegiality which barely justifies use of the term.

In many schools and colleges, however, more open approaches, which might be regarded as collegial, are increasingly prevalent. When staff meet to determine policies, or to engage in development planning, they are collaborating in the decision-making process. Its effectiveness depends primarily on the attitudes of heads who have to cede power in order to liberate the creative talents of their colleagues.

Political theories

Political theories characterize decision-making as a bargaining process. They assume that members of organizations engage in political activity in pursuit of their interests. In sharp contrast to the idealism of collegial theorists, political approaches adopt the view that conflict is an endemic feature of organizations. Political activity is not confined to *party* politics and is likely to occur elsewhere, including schools and colleges.

The main features of political theories are as follows:

- they focus on **group activity** rather than the school or college as an entity. Interaction between groups is at the heart of political approaches whereas bureaucratic and collegial theories stress the institutional level. In education much of the political analysis centres on the influence of academic departments in schools and colleges and their sectional approach to decision-making

- Political theories are concerned with **interests** and **interest groups**. Individuals are thought to have a variety of interests which they pursue within the organization. Individual interests may lead to collaboration and the formation of interest groups, which may be temporary or enduring

- Political theories stress the prevalence of **conflict** in organizations. Individuals and groups pursue their different objectives, leading to conflict between them. Baldridge argues that conflict is welcome as well as inevitable, and is 'a significant factor in promoting healthy organizational change' (Baldridge et al. 1978, p.35)

- Political theories assume that the **goals** of organizations are ambiguous and contested. Individuals, interest groups and coalitions pursue their own objectives and disputed goals may become a significant source of conflict between factions

- Decisions emerge after a complex process of **bargaining and negotiation**. Interests are promoted in committees, and at unofficial encounters, and differences may be resolved only after a long and multi-stage process

- The concept of **power** is central to political theories. The decision-making process is likely to be determined ultimately according to the relative power of the participating individuals and groups.

Baldridge (1971 pp.23–24) identified five stages of the policy process in articulating his political model:

1. **Social structure** This is a configuration of social groups with different life styles and political interests. These differences often lead to conflict, for what is in the interest of one group may damage another

2. **Interest articulation** Groups with conflicting values and goals must translate them into effective influence. They try to exert pressure, make promises or threats and seek to translate their desires into political capital

3. **The legislative stage** Legislative bodies such as committees respond to pressures, transforming the conflict into politically feasible policy. In the process, many claims are played off against one another, negotiations are undertaken, compromises are forged, and rewards are divided

4. **The formulation of policy** The legislators determine policy which is the official climax to the conflict and represents an authoritative, binding decision to commit the organization to one set of goals and values

5. **The execution of policy** The conflict comes to a climax and the resulting policy is turned over to the bureaucrats for routine execution. However, this may not be the end of the matter because the losers engage in a new round of interest articulation and the execution of policy may cause a feedback cycle leading to a new round of political conflict

Political theories are persuasive descriptors of events and situations in schools and colleges. They serve to capture the reality of life in organizations, as Bolman and Deal (1984, p.144) suggest:

[For many people] the political frame presents the only realistic portrayal of organizations ... The political frame says that power and politics are central to organizations and cannot be swept under the rug.

Although political approaches are both valid and plausible, they have several limitations when applied to schools and colleges:

- Political theories are immersed so strongly in the language of power and conflict that they neglect other standard aspects of organizations. The outcomes of bargaining and negotiation are endorsed, or may falter, within the formal authority structure of the school or college. 'Many decisions are made not in the heat of political controversy but because standard operating procedures dominate in most organizations'. (Baldridge et al. 1978, pp.42–43).

- Political theories stress the influence of interest groups on decision-making and give little attention to the institutional level. This aspect of political theories may be inappropriate for primary schools which do not have a departmental structure or other apparatus which could be a focal point for political activity

- In political theories there is too much emphasis on conflict and a neglect of the possibility of professional collaboration leading to agreed outcomes. Teachers may well be engaged in genuine debate about the best outcomes for the school rather than evaluating every issue in terms of personal and group advantage

- Political theories may be regarded as unattractive by many educationists. The cynicism and amorality of the approach raises questions of values. Does it 'ratify and sanctify some of the least humane and most unsavoury aspects of human systems?' (Bolman and Deal 1984, p.146).

Despite these weaknesses, political theories have much to offer to an understanding of schools and colleges. Interest groups may have a potent influence on policy formulation. Collegial teams may become the setting for group conflict rather than a vehicle for consensual decision-making. The emphasis on conflict is a useful counter to the optimistic harmony bias of collegial theories and may represent a more realistic portrayal of decision-making in many secondary schools and colleges although it is less applicable to the primary sector. One secondary head refers to the 'traditional political power of heads of departments' and criticizes their sectional approach to school policy-making:

> The status and self-esteem of heads of department seems to be increased the narrower the view and decreased if they develop a broader vision ... the good team leader is felt by the team as one who demands adamantly, ostentatiously, and consistently for more teachers, more space, more money, more equipment, more rooms, more pupils, smaller groups, and, above all, more of the pupils' time (Marland 1982, pp.122–123).

Subjective theories

Subjective theories focus on individuals within organizations rather than the whole institution or its sub-units. Each individual is thought to have a selective and subjective perception of the organization. Events and situations may have different meanings for each of the participants. Organizations are portrayed as the manifestations of the values and beliefs of individuals rather than the concrete realities presented in bureaucratic models.

Subjective theories became prominent as a result of the work of the Canadian writer Thomas Greenfield (1973, p.571) who was very critical of conventional (largely bureaucratic) theory:

> Most theories of organization grossly simplify the nature of the reality with which they deal. The drive to see the organization as a single kind of entity with a life of its own apart from the perceptions and beliefs of those

involved in it blinds us to its complexity and the variety of organizations people create around themselves.

The main features of subjective theories are as follows:

- They tend to focus on the beliefs and perceptions of **individual** members of organizations rather than the institutional level or interest groups. In schools and colleges, individual teachers, support staff and pupils have different values and aspirations according to their own background and motivations. 'The school is not the same reality for all its teachers. Each teacher brings a perspective to the school ... which is to some extent unique' (Ribbins et al. 1981, p.170)

- They are concerned with the **meanings** placed on events by the individual members of organizations. The focus is on individual interpretation of behaviour rather than the situations and actions themselves. In schools there may be differences of interpretation between the head and other staff, for example:

    When a head talks about his school on public occasions teachers often remark that they do not recognise the place ... the head and the teachers see the world differently with each perspective having its own legitimacy (Hoyle 1981, p.45)

- They treat **structure** as essentially a product of human interaction rather than something which is pre-determined or fixed. 'A structure cannot be imposed on an organization, it can only derive from what people do' (Gray 1982)

- They emphasize the significance of **individual purposes** and deny the existence of organizational goals. The portrayal of organizations as powerful goal-seeking entities is treated with disdain. 'What is an organization that it can have such a thing as a goal?' (Greenfield 1973).

Best et al. (1983) conducted an empirical study of pastoral care at 'Rivendell' comprehensive school and concluded that subjective meanings were an important analytical tool. In asking teachers for their perceptions of school pastoral care policy, they identified five broad perspectives arising from teacher responses:

- child-centred
- pupil-centred
- discipline-centred

- administrator-centred
- subject-centred

The 'Rivendell' research serves to illustrate the point that schools and colleges are not monolithic organizations with a single set of objectives pursued enthusiastically by all members of the institution. Rather, the portrayal shows that the school's official policy of a child-centred pastoral policy is only one of a wide range of interpretations held by staff and provides powerful evidence to support the validity of subjective theories.

Subjective perspectives can be regarded as 'anti-theories' in that they emerged as a reaction to the perceived weaknesses of bureaucratic theories. The focus on individual interpretation of events is a valuable contribution to theory development but subjective theories are strongly normative and do have some significant weaknesses:

- In emphasising the interpretations of individuals, subjective theories neglect the institutions within which individuals behave, interact and derive meanings. They assume the existence of an organization but do not explain it

- The focus on individual meanings underestimates the significance of the common professional background of teachers which often results in shared meanings and purposes

- They fail to explain the many similarities between schools

- They provide no guidelines for managerial action beyond the need to acknowledge the legitimacy of individual meanings. Greenfield himself acknowledges that 'this conception does not make them easy to control or change' (Greenfield 1980)

One way of understanding the relationship between bureaucratic and subjective theories may be in terms of scale. Theodossin (1983, p.83) argues that the bureaucratic approach is most useful to provide a broad overview of organizations while the subjective theory illuminates relationships between individuals.

Ambiguity theories

Ambiguity theories stress uncertainty and complexity in organizations. The emphasis is on the instability and unpredictability of institutional life. Cohen and March (1974), in their classic study of *organized anarchies*, claim that ambiguity is a prevalent feature of educational institutions which tend to exhibit the following characteristics:

- **Problematic goals** The organization appears to operate on a variety of inconsistent and ill-defined preferences. It can be described better as a loose collection of changing ideas than as a consistent structure

- **Unclear technology** The organization does not understand its own processes. It operates on the basis of a simple set of trial-and error procedures, the residue of learning from the accidents of past experiences, imitation and the inventions born of necessity

- **Fluid participation** The participants in the organization vary amongst themselves in the amount of time and effort they devote to the organization; individual participants vary from one time to another

The authors suggest that the decision process can be likened to a *'garbage can'* into which various problems and solutions are dumped by participants. Decisions are the products of the interaction of four independent streams — problems, solutions, participants and choice opportunities. The outcomes of such decision processes are claimed to be unpredictable (Cohen and March, 1974).

The relevance of the ambiguity theory has been tested empirically at 'Oakfields', a newly amalgamated comprehensive school in the East Midlands. (Bell, 1989). He found that the school was characterized by ambiguous goals, unclear technology and fluid membership, as suggested by Cohen and March (1974). He concludes that:

> The traditional notion of the school as an hierarchical decision-making structure with a horizontal division into departments and a vertical division into authority levels needs to be abandoned. Such a conceptualization is unsuitable for the analysis of an organization attempting to cope with an unstable and unpredictable environment (Bell 1989, p.146).

The turbulence of educational policy in England and Wales during the late 1980s and the 1990s lends credence to ambiguity theories. The rapid pace of curriculum change, and the vagaries of school and college funding, lead to multiple uncertainty which can be explained adequately only within the ambiguity framework. However, ambiguity theories do have three significant weaknesses:

- It is difficult to reconcile ambiguity theories with the customary structures and processes of schools and colleges. Participants may move in and out of decision-making situations but the policy framework remains intact and has a continuing influence on the outcome of discussions. Specific goals may be unclear but teaching staff usually understand and accept the broad aims of education

- They exaggerate the degree of unpredictability in education. Schools and colleges have a number of predictable features which serve to clarify the responsibilities of their members. As Baldridge et al. (1978) point out, 'the term organized anarchy may seem overly colourful, suggesting more confusion, disarray and conflict than is really present'

- The applicability of ambiguity theories depends crucially on the degree of turbulence. Unstable situations, such as that at 'Oakfields', can be characterized as ambiguous but many schools and colleges are more stable and the ambiguity theory is not appropriate for such institutions

The major contribution of the ambiguity theory is that it uncouples problems and choices rather than assuming a rational decision-process. The notion of unpredictability is an important concept that carries credibility in periods of turbulence such as those facing British schools and colleges in the 1990s.

Over-arching theories

Bolman and Deal's notion of 'conceptual pluralism' discussed earlier provides a framework for the analysis of educational management theory. The five theories discussed in this chapter each provides important insights into school and college management but they are all uni-dimensional. Individually, they are partial and selective but taken together they represent a powerful means of analysing and understanding events and situations in education:

> Understanding organizations is nearly impossible when the manager is unconsciously wed to a single, narrow perspective ... Managers ... can increase their effectiveness and their freedom through the use of multiple vantage points. To be locked into a single path is likely to produce error and self-imprisonment (Bolman and Deal, 1984, p.4).

Several writers have developed syntheses of two or more theories in an attempt to provide a more complete explanation of events and behaviour than any single approach. Ellstrom (1983 p.236) makes the case for such a synthesis:

> Each model emphasizes certain variables, while others are de-emphasized or ignored. Consequently, each model can be expected to give only partial understanding of the organizational reality ... it might be possible to obtain a more comprehensive understanding of organizations by integrating the models into an over-arching framework ... the models are viewed as compatible, rather than as mutually exclusive alternatives.

Enderud (1980) and Davies and Morgan (1983) have developed integrative models incorporating ambiguity, political, collegial and bureaucratic theories. These authors claim that policy formation proceeds through four distinct phases. An initial period of ambiguity is followed by a phase of bargaining and negotiation. A possible solution emerges which is subsequently tested in collegial settings. The agreed outcome is then passed to the bureaucracy for implementation. The Davies and Morgan version of the model is illustrated in Figure 2.1.

Enderud (p.241) stresses that the significance of each phase varies according to the different perceptions of participants as well as the nature of the issue:

> With its four phases, the model ... reflects a mix of different realities in ... decision-making — an anarchistic, a political, a collegial and a bureaucratic reality — which may all be part of any one joint decision process. This composite picture will be one of the reasons why different participants often can interpret the same decision as largely anarchic, political, collegial or bureaucratic, according to the phase which is most visible to them, because of their own participation or for other reasons.

Although Enderud acknowledges that the individual interpretations of participants may influence the visibility of the models, the subjective theory is not featured explicitly in his synthesis or in that of Davies and Morgan.

The Enderud model is plausible but it is certainly possible to consider alternative links between the theories. For example, an apparently collegial process may lead to conflict and become political or ambiguous. The optimum sequencing of the theories cannot be predicted with confidence.

While the Enderud model does not have universal applicability, it is reasonable to conclude that the notion of a multiplicity of theories is likely to enable practitioners to achieve a fuller and deeper understanding of events

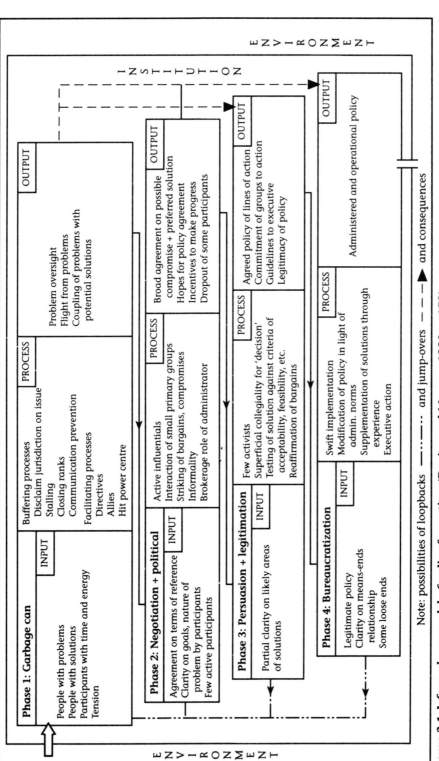

Phase 1: Garbage can

INPUT
People with problems
People with solutions
Participants with time and energy
Tension

PROCESS
Buffering processes
Disclaim jurisdiction on issue
Stalling
Closing ranks
Communication prevention
Facilitating processes
Directives
Allies
Hit power centre

OUTPUT
Problem oversight
Flight from problems
Coupling of problems with potential solutions

Phase 2: Negotiation + political

INPUT
Agreement on terms of reference
Clarity on goals, nature of problem by participants
Few active participants

PROCESS
Active influentials
Interaction of small primary groups
Striking of bargains, compromises
Informality
Brokerage role of administrator

OUTPUT
Broad agreement on possible compromise + preferred solution
Hopes for policy agreement
Incentives to make progress
Dropout of some participants

Phase 3: Persuasion + legitimation

INPUT
Partial clarity on likely areas of solutions

PROCESS
Few activists
Superficial collegiality for 'decision'
Testing of solution against criteria of acceptability, feasibility, etc.
Reaffirmation of bargains

OUTPUT
Agreed policy of lines of action
Commitment of groups to action
Guidelines to executive
Legitimacy of policy

Phase 4: Bureaucratization

INPUT
Legitimate policy
Clarity on means-ends relationship
Some loose ends

PROCESS
Swift implementation
Modification of policy in light of admin. norms
Supplementation of solutions through experience
Executive action

OUTPUT
Administered and operational policy

INSTITUTION

ENVIRONMENT

ENVIRONMENT

Note: possibilities of loopbacks ┈┈┈┈ and jump-overs ─ ─ ─ ▶ and consequences

Figure 2.1 A four-phase model of policy formation (Davies and Morgan 1983, p.172)

and situations than any single theory. Reflective practice grounded in theory will contribute to a reduction in the theory/practice divide. Creative tension between theory and practice may serve to improve practice and lead to further theory development.

Summary

This chapter has sought to show how theory can illuminate practice and reduce the perception of a 'theory/practice divide'. Educational management theory comprises a series of alternative perspectives rather than a single widely accepted theory. Five main theories have been identified and applied to schools and colleges. Over-arching theories serve to integrate some of the perspectives and lend credence to the notion of 'conceptual pluralism'.

Further reading

Bush, T. (1986) *Theories of Educational Management*, London: Paul Chapman.

This book provides an extended treatment of the ideas and theories discussed in this chapter and applies them to practice in schools and colleges.

Bush, T. (1989) *Managing Education : Theory and Practice*, Milton Keynes: Open University Press.

This edited volume contains extracts from the writing of several leading theorists of educational management, imcluding the main exponents of the five theories discussed in this chapter. It also includes chapters on the application of these theories to British schools and colleges.

References

Baldridge, J.V. (1971) *Power and Conflict in the University*, New York: John Wiley.

Baldridge, J.V., Curtis, D.V., Ecker, G. and Riley, G.L. (1978) *Policy Making and Effective Leadership*, San Francisco, CA: Jossey Bass.

Becher, T. and Kogan, M. (1980) *Process and Structure in Higher Education*, Aldershot: Gower.

Bell, L. (1989) 'Ambiguity models and secondary schools: a case study' in Bush, T. (Ed) *Managing Education: Theory and Practice*, Milton Keynes: Open University Press.

Best, R., Ribbins, P., Jarvis, C. and Oddy, D. (1983) *Education and Care*, London: Heinemann.

Bolman, L.G. and Deal, T.E. (1984) *Modern Approaches to Understanding and Managing Organizations*, San Francisco, CA: Jossey-Bass.

Bush, T. (1986) *Theories of Educational Management*, London: Harper and Row (reprint 1988 published by Paul Chapman).

Bush, T. (1989) 'The nature of theory in educational management' in Bush, T. (Ed) *Managing Education: Theory and Practice*, Milton Keynes: Open University Press.

Bush, T., Coleman, M. and Glover, D. (1993) *Managing Autonomous Schools : The Grant Maintained Experience*, London: Paul Chapman.

Campbell, R.J. (1985) *Developing the Primary School Curriculum*, London: Holt, Rinehart & Winston.

Cohen, M.D. and March, J.G. (1974) *Leadership and Ambiguity: The American College President*, New York: McGraw-Hill (reprint 1986 by the Harvard Business School Press, Boston).

Davies, J.L. and Morgan, A.W. (1983) 'Management of higher education in a period of contraction and uncertainty' in Boyd-Barrett, O., Bush, T., Goodey, J., McNay, I. and Preedy, M. (Eds) *Approaches to Post-School Management*, London: Harper and Row.

Dearden, R.F. (1984) *Theory and Practice in Education*, London: Routledge and Kegan Paul.

Ellstrom, P.E. (1983) 'Four faces of educational organizations', *Higher Education*, **12**, pp.231–41.

Enderud, H. (1980) 'Administrative leadership in organized anarchies', *International Journal of Institutional Management in Higher Education*, **4**, 3, pp.235–53.

Gray, H.L. (1982) 'A perspective on organization theory' in Gray, H.L (Ed) *The Management of Educational Institutions*, Lewes: Falmer Press.

Greenfield, T.B. (1973) 'Organizations as social inventions: rethinking assumptions about change'. *Journal of Applied Behavioural Science*, **9**, 5, pp. 551–74.

Greenfield, T.B. (1980) 'The man who comes back through the door in the wall: discovering truth, discovering self, discovering organizations'. *Educational Administration Quarterly*, 16, 2, pp. 26–59.

Hargreaves, A. (1993) 'Contrived collegiality : the micropolitics of teacher collaboration' in Bennett, N., Crawford, M., Riches, C. (Eds.) *Managing Change in Education : Individual and Organizational Perspectives*, London: Paul Chapman.

House, E.R. (1981) 'Three perspectives on innovation' in Lehming, R. and Kane, M.(Eds.) *Improving Schools : Using What We Know*, Beverly Hills: Sage.

Hoyle, E. (1981) 'The process of management' in *E323 Management and the School*, Block 3, Part 1, Milton Keynes: Open University.

Hughes, M.G. (1984) 'Educational administration: pure or applied'. *CCEA Studies in Educational Administration*, 35, pp. 1–11.

Hughes, M. (1985) 'Theory and practice in educational management' in Hughes, M., Ribbins, P. and Thomas, H. (Eds) *Managing Education : The System and the Institution*, London: Holt, Rinehart and Winston.

Hughes, M. and Bush, T. (1991) 'Theory and research as catalysts for change' in Walker, W., Farquhar, R., and Hughes, M. (Eds) *Advancing Education: School Leadership in Action*, Lewes: Falmer Press.

Jennings, A. (1977) 'Introduction' in Jennings, A. (Ed) *Management and Headship in the Secondary School*, London: Ward Lock Educational.

Landers, T.J. and Myers, J.G. (1977) *Essentials of School Management*, Philadelphia: W.B. Saunders.

Livingstone, H. (1974) *The University : An Organizational Analysis*, Glasgow: Blackie.

March, J.G. and Olsen, J.P. (1976) 'Organizational choice under ambiguity' in March, J.G. and Olsen, J.P. (Eds) *Ambiguity and Choice in Organizations*, Bergen: Universitetsforlaget.

Marland, M. (1982) 'The politics of improvement in schools'. *Educational Management and Administration*, 10, 2, pp.119–134.

Ribbins, P. (1985) 'Organization theory and the study of educational institutions' in Hughes, M., Ribbins, P. and Thomas, H. (Eds) *Managing Education : The System and the Institution*, London: Holt, Rinehart and Winston.

Ribbins, P., Jarvis, C., Best, R. and Oddy, D. (1981) 'Meanings and contexts : the problem of interpretation in the study of a school', *Research in Educational Management and Administration*, Birmingham: British Educational Management and Administration Society.

Theodossin, E. (1983) 'Theoretical perspectives on the management of planned educational change'. *British Educational Research Journal*, **9**, 1, pp. 81–90.

Thompson, M. (1992) 'The experience of going grant-maintained: the perceptions of AMMA teacher representatives'. *Journal of Teacher Development*, **1**, 3, pp.133–140.

Wallace, M. (1988) 'Towards a collegiate approach to curriculum management in primary and middle schools'. *School Organization,* **8**, 1, pp.25–34.

Weber, M. (1947) in Parsons, T. (Ed) *The Theory of Social and Economic Organization*, Ill. Glencoe: Free Press and NY: Collier–McMillan.

Weick, K.E. (1976) 'Educational organizations as loosely coupled systems'. *Administrative Science Quarterly*, **21**, 1, pp. 1–19.

3 Leadership in educational management

Marianne Coleman

Theories of leadership have application to all types of organizations, and the styles and models of leadership first described are drawn from organization theory. Where possible, references are to leadership in education, and attention is drawn to issues which are specific to leadership in schools and colleges.

The chapter continues with an overview of the strong links between leadership and the effective school and the relationship of leadership to school improvement. Consideration is given both to the variety of external pressures on leaders in education and to the fact that they are increasingly faced with leading more autonomous institutions. Finally the chapter touches on the importance of development and training for the leaders of today's schools and colleges.

Organizations and leadership

Organizations are linked with the existence of leadership:

> The concept of organization, ... with its implications for the differentiation of responsibility roles, does permit the study of leadership as an aspect of the relationships between members who are co-ordinating their efforts for the achievement of common goals (Stogdill 1969, p.41).

The implications are that leadership exists where:

1. An organization has common goals

2. There are different roles, within the organization, one role being that of leader

3. There are systems and structures to allow the co-ordination of efforts to achieve the common goals

Leadership is not necessarily confined to one person in an organization, nor is there one style of leadership.

Styles of leadership

Styles of leadership may be labelled as autocratic or authoritarian on the one hand and democratic or participative on the other.

The Tannenbaum–Schmidt continuum (see Figure 3.1) indicates that there may be a range of styles between autocratic and democratic that are open to the choice of the individual leader.

Boss-centred leadership ----------------------- Subordinate-centred leadership

Figure 3.1 The Tannenbaum-Schmidt continuum of leadership behaviour

The leader can choose along this continuum, ranging from making a decision and announcing it, to permitting 'subordinates to function within limits defined by superior' (Tannenbaum and Schmidt, 1973, p.164).

Perhaps the best known discussion of styles of leadership centres on the division of leaders into two groups, those who tend to be more 'task' or 'results' orientated and those who tend to be more 'people' or 'relationship' orientated.

Results   --- Relationships
orientated   orientated

Figure 3.2 Two leadership styles

The implication that a leader tends to be either results or relationships orientated at all times and in all situations is modified by a more sophisticated analysis of styles of leadership by Blake and Mouton (1964):

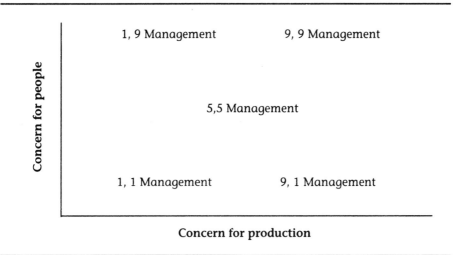

Figure 3. 3 The managerial grid

This two-dimensional grid allows the positioning of management styles along nine point axes labelled 'concern for people' and 'concern for production'. It is theoretically possible to identify 81 management styles, but the analysis generally places leaders into one of five main styles:

9,1 (results rated high, relationships rated low)
This type of leadership is identified as 'achievement orientated' and as personifying 'the entrepreneurial spirit' (p.18)

1,9 (results rated low, relationships rated high)
Leaders encourage their workers, 'the group, not the individual, is the key unit of the organization,' (p.80)

1,1 (results rated low, relationships rated low)
This approach indicates a passive approach which may apply 'to those that have accepted defeat' (p.85)

5,5 (results rated moderate, relationships rated moderate)
This middle range approach means that 'satisfactory... solutions are found through equilibrium or compromise processes. ' (p.110)

9,9 (results rated high, relationships rated high)
For this leader the basic aim is to 'promote the conditions that integrate creativity, high productivity, and high morale through concerted team action.' (p.142)

The analysis was not intended to identify personality types:

> The point to be emphasized here is that managerial styles are not fixed. They are not unchanging. They are determined by a range of factors. Many are subject to modification through formal instruction or self training. (p.13)

Leadership style can be analysed in terms of gender considerations, and further attention will be given to this in chapter 9.

The analysis of styles of leadership has been the basis for the development of many of the theories of leadership in organizations.

Leadership in organizational theory

The theories relating to leaders in organizations can be categorized into those which emphasize the qualities of an individual leader or even propose an ideal leader, and those which emphasize the importance of the situational variables interacting with the leader. The latter are known as contingency theories.

❑ Theories concerning the qualities of the individual

(a) 'The great man' theory

The view, particularly in the political world, that leaders are born and not made, carries the implications that the process of selection of leaders is crucial, and that training and development in leadership is to no account.

(b) Personality traits

Some theorists have worked on the assumption that certain personality traits determine success in leadership. Stogdill found that some traits were common to successful leaders, but there has been difficulty in identifying them consistently. There are also difficulties in agreeing definitions of traits as abstract as dependability and, in measuring to what degree a leader may have such a trait.

Stogdill (1969, p.127) recognised that, despite the observation of particular traits in leaders, situational factors would play their part:

> The findings suggest that leadership is not a matter of passive status, or of the mere possession of some combination of traits. It appears rather to be a

working relationship among members of a group, in which the leader acquires status through active participation and demonstration of his (*sic*) capacity for carrying cooperative tasks through to completion. Significant aspects of this capacity ... appear to be intelligence, alertness to the needs and motives of others, and insight into situations, further reinforced by such habits as responsibility, initiative, persistence and self confidence.

(c) The high, high leader

Leadership style can be analyzed on a two-dimensional grid as indicated above in Figure 3.3. Whilst this model allows for different combinations emerging in leadership style, the emphasis is still on the qualities of the individual. The language used to describe the 9,9 leader, rated high on both results and relationships, implies that this is an 'ideal' leader. Just some of the qualities possessed are the ability to 'help staff members to find solutions to poor performance', to 'face up to conflict calmly', and to 'take decisions as and when needed'.

(d) System 4 leaders

Working on the basis that a good leader will improve efficiency, Likert (1967) identified an 'ideal' leader from four basic styles of management, identified as Systems 1 to 4 and placed this ideal (System 4) at the democratic/participative end of the continuum. Under such a leader there is group participation in all decisions and individuals feel responsible for the goals of the organization. He concluded that:

> Research findings support the perceptions of managers that management systems ... toward System 4, are more productive and have lower costs and more favourable attitudes than do those systems falling more toward System 1 [autocratic] (p.46).

The theories of leadership that are based on the qualities of one person omit any emphasis on situational factors, particularly the dynamic relationship between the leader and those who are led.

❏ Contingency theories

By their nature these theories are complex, since they recognize the interaction of leaders and their environments. They allow for the fact that appropriate and successful leadership style and behaviour will vary in different situations.

(a) The model developed by Hersey and Blanchard identifies both directive and supportive behaviour in a leader, which can be modified according to the level of development, experience and commitment of the subordinate.

1. For the most experienced and committed staff the style would be basically that of *delegation*, low on direction and support. The expectation is that such staff would need little direction because of their experience, and little support because of their commitment

2. A young but keen subordinate would receive high *direction* because of lack of experience and low levels of support because of high motivation. (A combination that is certainly inconsistent with educational practice, and the concept of mentoring)

3. A more experienced worker with low commitment would be expected to benefit from the *coaching* style of high levels of both direction and support

4. The experienced middle manager with varying levels of motivation and commitment would be expected to need high levels of *support* but little direction

A simple version of the application of these principles can be found in *The One Minute Manager* (Blanchard K. and Johnson, S.,1982)

Intuitively this theory seems generally credible, but it relies on leaders being knowledgeable about the development of their employees and sophisticated in switching behaviour when appropriate.

(b) The model developed by Fiedler (1967) combines an analysis of the leader's style with an analysis of the situation in which he or she is working. The style of the leader is analysed in terms of the familiar results/relationship orientation. The situation is analysed in terms of three variables and to what extent they favour the leader (see Figure 3.4).

Favourable situation for leader	**Unfavourable situation for leader**
good relationship with subordinate	poor relationship with subordinate
task clearly stated	task not clearly stated
high level of formal authority	low level of formal authority

Figure 3.4

The major innovation in Fiedler's work is that he takes into account the situation, including the relationship with subordinates as well the the style of the leader (p.261):

> Leadership performance depends then as much on the organization as it depends upon the leader's own attributes. Except perhaps for the unusual case, it is simply not meaningful to speak of an effective leader or of an ineffective leader; we can only speak of a leader who tends to be effective in one situation and ineffective in another.

Fiedler's research has shown that when the situation is particularly favourable or unfavourable to the leader a task-orientated leader is more effective. When the situation is neither particularly favourable nor unfavourable a people orientated leader is more effective.

The training implications of this theory are important in that leaders may be trained to modify their work situation to suit their personality and leadership style, rather than the more obvious training option of modifying leadership behaviour.

Some consideration of training for leadership is given at the end of the chapter. We now turn to an examination of the particular nature of leadership in schools and colleges.

Leadership in schools and colleges

Leadership in schools and colleges is not confined to the headteacher and may be assumed by or dispersed to others including deputy heads, team leaders, curriculum leaders and class teachers.

There is much concerning leadership that is generic. However, it is possible to identify ways in which educational leadership differs from leadership in other areas. These can be summarized as:

- professionalism
- the dual role model
- mission/vision
- educational values

❑ Professionalism
The existence of a leader implies the existence of followers and that they recognize the right of the leader to exercise authority.

Weberian analysis of authority distinguishes between:

> legal/rational authority, for example that which derives from the statutes of central government, and gives the school leader/s the authority to ensure, for example, that the National Curriculum is delivered in the school

> charismatic/affective authority which is dependent on the personal qualities of the leader and is therefore not truly 'rational'

> traditional authority, which inclines followers to defer to those who they see as having 'the right' to lead

The classification of these three types of authority is useful in analysing the legitimation of leadership, but there is another basis for authority in schools and colleges. Whilst the authority of a headteacher or principal may derive partly from legal, charismatic and traditional authority, it is also underwritten by the recognition of his/her professionalism.

> in general leaders in the educational system are finding that their bases of authority are changing. The popular view of the leader as one who possess legal rights, with powers by virtue of his (*sic*) position to impose sanctions and rewards, is being upstaged by his need to display *superior competence* (our emphasis) and possess those leadership qualities as an individual which encourage his views to be adopted (Harling 1984, p.12) (Harling 1989, p.25).

Teachers as professionals

Professional expertise is not restricted to leaders in schools and colleges. Leaders of an educational institution will be faced with particular difficulties in managing a set of professionals.

1. Professionals expect a degree of autonomy of operation in view of the extent of their training.

   > One of the defining characteristics of the professional is his [*sic*] avowal of a code of practice which commits him to the independent exercise of his own trained judgement (Noble and Pym, 1989, p.29).

   However, it may be that autonomy is a 'privilege granted by the head on certain terms and conditions' (Ball 1987, p.121). Without the approval of the head, a teacher could find sanctions, e.g. difficulties over resources, used against them. In addition:

   > the maintenance of strong boundaries between teachers and between departments provides a basis for 'divide and rule' (Ball, 1987, p.123).

2. They may be less willing to accept 'traditional' authority.

    Professionals are well aware that technical expertise does not necessarily increase with position in the formal hierarchy (Hughes, 1988, p.7).

3. There may be a tendency for professionals to relate to colleagues in other institutions, to be 'cosmopolitan' in their outlook. In that they may relate to the profession as a whole they may not have complete loyalty to their own institution.

❏ The dual role model of leadership

A headteacher or college principal is the leader of the institution, with the appropriate management responsibilities, but also maintains a role as a professional in education.

This gives rise to ambiguities as well as opportunities (Hughes, 1988, p.11).

Hughes postulates a dual role model which applies:

when the chief executive of a professionally staffed organization may also be considered to be its leading professional (p.11).

However, despite the division of tasks of the leading professional-chief executive, e.g. the guidance given to staff undertaken as leading professional, and the allocation of resources as chief executive, research has established that in practice it is artificial to divide the two roles.

In general the research confirmed a substantial inter-penetration of the two sub-roles. In seems that the professional-as-administrator does not act in some matters as a leading professional and in others as a chief executive. Professional knowledge, skills and attitudes are likely to have a profound effect on the whole range of tasks undertaken by the head of a professional organization. (Hughes, 1988, p.15)

When 500 secondary heads were asked to categorize their style, the largest group (43.5 per cent) opted for the professional role, whilst 16.5 per cent considered themselves as 'Senior Teacher', and only 27.5 per cent of the 400 responded as 'leading professional and chief executive' (Jones, 1987, p.232). It would be interesting to see if these perceptions have changed following the trend towards autonomous schools in the UK and elsewhere.

❏ The importance of mission/vision

The importance of a vision is recognized by business as well as education. However, it can be argued that the objectives of education are different in kind:

> The *objectives* of educational institutions are much more difficult to define than the purposes of commercial organizations. There are no clear-cut educational equivalents to such major private sector objectives as profit maximization, output maximization or product diversification. Schools and colleges are expected to develop the personal capacity of individuals, to inculcate the accepted values and beliefs, to look after children and young people for set periods of each day and to prepare pupils and students for the next stage of education, for employment or, increasingly, for unemployment (Bush, 1986, p.5).

There has been general recognition amongst those writing about educational leadership in the 1980s and 1990s that it is essential that the leader of a school or college has a vision or mission for the institution and that the leader can transmit their own commitment into one that can be shared by others. Hoyle (1986, p.102–103) drawing attention to the political nature of leadership, comments:

> there is still something else missing ... It would seem that the 'something' is the leader's capacity to grasp the configuration of forces at work in the environment, to construct an achievable mission — the art of the possible — to convey this mission to others often through the skilful use of language and symbol, and to attain a commitment to the mission.

The objectives of education are difficult to define, and in comparison with other spheres of life, it is difficult to measure outcomes and test success. According to Hodgkinson (1991, p.62–3) this provides the very environment in which a leader has real opportunities to develop a vision:

> the opportunity to discover, clarify and defend the ends of education, to motivate towards those ends, the opportunity to discover means and invent process, ... and the opportunity to create and establish morally grounded evaluation and legitimate it for all the participants in the great cooperative educational project.

Hodgkinson considers that the highest form of leadership contains:

> some element of charismatic commitment or enthusiasm, ... and [leadership] will then embrace the added functions of vision and mystique (p.159).

Beare et al. (1993, p.155) have produced a set of ten generalizations about leadership gleaned from studies of leadership of the last decade. Three of these generalizations relate to leadership and vision:

— Outstanding leaders have a vision for their organizations

— Vision must be communicated in a way which secures commitment among members of the organization

— Communication of vision requires communication of meaning.

In making the distinction between management and leadership, West-Burnham (1992a, p.102) divides the operational concerns of management from the vital 'components of leadership in a quality environment', listing the latter as:

— vision

— creativity

— sensitivity

— empowering

— managing change

Resulting demands on leaders

The expectation that leaders will have a vision for their institution and will communicate it, seems to rely on the charismatic basis of authority for leadership. Although this implies a concentration on the strength of an individual personality, the demands should be seen in the context of the more collegial styles of management and the emphasis placed on 'ownership', for example in the work of Hargreaves (Hargreaves and Hopkins, 1991) on school development.

> All contribute to the culture of the school, so all should contribute to the management arrangements the purpose of which is to empower.

The implication is that leadership should be dispersed throughout the school and that teams with a designated leader take on the policies identified as priorities within the school or college, as in the models developed by Caldwell and Spinks (1988, 1992).

It could be that, without this dispersal of leadership, demands which are too great or are potentially conflicting are being made on the school or college leader.

The idea that heads are the owners of the schools' vision has implications for the meaning of collaboration. Where heads hold the vision and encourage teacher collaboration the head, tacitly or otherwise, may only be developing teacher interaction as a vehicle for the implementation of his or her wishes (Southworth 1993, p.82).

Leaders of schools are nevertheless expected to perform on all levels. An NFER study of 16 new heads, including interviews with around 300 teachers showed:

that many staff had very high expectations of the new head but these proved to be unrealistic and most heads were not able to live up to them (Weindling and Earley 1987, p.75).

❑ Educational values — the moral dimension

Leaders are perceived to be invested with authority and to have the ability and opportunity to direct or support others in the achievement of the aims of the organization. More recently:

attempts to explain the concept of leadership penetrate more deeply than 'the organization' and the activities associated with goal setting and goal accomplishment. Attention now is also given to meanings and values (Beare, Caldwell and Millikan1993, p.143).

Whilst a clear vision for the future of any school or college is important, some would argue that educational leadership carries a moral dimension. Education has a unique role in society, 'No other institution or complex organization attends to the general aims of life in quite the same way.' (Hodgkinson 1991 p.143) The leaders of educational institutions, it is argued, therefore carry a moral responsibility with regard to the values that inform the culture and mission of the school.

A research project on primary school staff relations found that:

... each of the five schools involved in the project had its own culture embodying strongly held beliefs about the social and moral purposes of education. These beliefs originated with the headteachers. (Southworth, 1993, p.74).

The educational reforms of recent years in England and Wales, open enrolment, the publication of league tables and the reduction in the role of the local education authorities, have led to a more consumer-orientated education system, where schools are in competition with one another. Such a change means that school and college leaders must mediate between different sets of values.

> Heads must have more confidence in their own ideas and cultivate those ideas. They must recognize that well-thought-out philosophy and values are still a potent force in society; indeed, they are probably the most important force in our increasingly atomized, individualistic and dislocated society. For this reason they require more explicit professional attention (West 1993, p.45).

Whilst schools and colleges have 'a formally instituted pattern of authority and an official body of rules and procedures' (Harling 1984, p.7) the alternative view is of schools and colleges as communities, where value systems are more important than formal structures:

> Communities are defined by their centres. ... Centres govern the school values and provide norms that guide behaviour and give meaning to school community life (Sergiovanni 1992, p.41).

Leadership and links with school effectiveness and school improvement

Whilst school effectiveness is generally concerned with outcomes such as examination results, staying-on rates or pupil attitude, the work on school improvement is generally concerned with the introduction of change into schools. Both bodies of investigation have considered the variable of leadership.

> these traditions of educational research have shared input and process variables. ... Concern with leadership, for example, directed the school effectiveness inquirers to the issue of whether the behaviours or expectations of the principal were distinguishable in effective and less effective schools. The school improvement researchers examined the impact of the school leader on the ability of the unit to invent, adopt, or adapt practices that would make the school more responsive to contemporary knowledge in education (Clark et al. 1989, p.160).

❑ School effectiveness

Leadership is consistently recognised as being a vital factor in school effectiveness. The 'purposeful leadership of the staff by the headteacher'

(Mortimore et al. 1988, p.118) heads a list of factors necessary for effective junior schooling. In relation to *Ten Good Schools* it was stated that: 'Without exception the most important single factor in the success of those schools is the quality of leadership at the head' (HMI 1977).

The defining of an effective school as 'one which responds to individual pupil and staff needs and to the changing face of the community in which it is placed' (Murgatroyd and Gray 1984, p.39) highlights the importance of the nature of the leadership of such a school. Indeed the emphasis given here is very much on the inter-personal skills of the leader, in this context:

> Leadership is not about skills, rules or procedures but about the person and the quality of their relationships with others (Murgatroyd and Gray 1984, p.47).

In presenting *A Model for Managing an Excellent School*, Beare et al. (1992) state that: 'Such a model should be consistent with what is known about outstanding leadership', and go on to mention the importance of values, commitment, collaborative decision-making and the sharing of leadership roles (p.149).

❑ School improvement

The literature relating to school improvement also stresses 'the less tangible, more subtle aspects of management' (Glatter 1988, p.128). At the same time there is recognition that leaders in education are expected to both act as a change agent and maintain the day-to-day running of a stable institution.

The International School Improvement Programme (ISIP) working in fourteen countries, emphasized the importance of the school leader in school improvement:

> our observations point to some common factors: in particular, the difficulty and complexity of the task and that ... a great deal depends on less tangible, even elusive qualities such as judgement, sensitivity, courage, imagination, perseverance, personal stability, practical sense and professionality (Glatter 1987, p,197).

Despite the difficulty of observing, measuring or inculcating these qualities, the conclusions drawn from the ISIP work include the recommendation of four major tasks for leadership in school improvement:

1. Taking a long-term view

2. Ensuring a 'corporate educational strategy' agreed to by all involved

3. Working towards integration, they have 'to glue the results of successful improvement work on to the normal work of the school' (Glatter 1987, p.116)

4. The management of external relations, relating the school or college to its wider environment

❏ Transactional and transformational leadership

The development of a wider concept of leadership is implicit in the types of leadership associated with effective schools and school improvement. A useful distinction is that made between transactional and transformational leadership.

Transactional leadership describes the 'contract' made between leader and follower:

> ... from the followers, an agreement to work toward the achievement of organizational goals; from the leader, an agreement to ensure good working conditions or, in some other way, satisfy the needs of followers (Caldwell and Spinks 1992, p.49).

The introduction of change, as in school improvement, cannot be guaranteed by such leadership. Rather what is termed transformational leadership ensuring the commitment of followers is required:

> leaders and followers are united in pursuit of higher-level goals common to both. Both want to become the best. Both want to shape the school in a new direction (Sergiovanni 1990, p.24).

Sergiovanni has developed a model of the stages of leadership as linked with school improvement. The implication is that the leadership must develop through these 'evolutionary' stages if improvement is to be achieved.

1. Leadership by bartering, transactional leadership

2. Leadership by building, providing support to increase potential, motivating leader and thus encouraging 'higher levels of commitment and performance' (p.24)

3. Leadership by bonding, commitment to mutually agreed aims 'elevates school goals and purposes to the level of a shared covenant that bonds together leader and follower in a moral commitment' (p.24)

4. Leadership by banking, the institutionalisation of the values of improvement.

External pressures on educational leaders

Leaders have to mediate on behalf of schools or colleges. The broadest possible external pressures are recognized in the 'strategic leadership' outlined by Caldwell and Spinks (1992), in particular their suggestion that leaders should be aware of world-wide 'educational mega-trends'.

> Schools in the 1990s will require a high-level capacity for strategic planning; that is, to see 'the larger picture' and, on a continuing basis, set and re-set priorities in a simple school development plan which will provide the framework for the annual operational plan (p.10).

Examples of these world-wide educational 'mega-trends' include the move towards centralization, for example the establishment of a national curriculum in England and Wales, a concern about quality in education and a recognition that to be economically competitive there is a need:

> ... for a highly responsive system of education that equips citizens with required knowledge, skills and attitudes. (p.9)

A further educational 'mega-trend' is identified as the move towards the more autonomous school; this, in apparent contradiction with the trend towards centralization. The growth of the GM sector, and of LMS is evidence of a movement towards self management in England and Wales and school leaders are faced with the external pressure of a statutory requirement to consider GMS annually (DFE 1993).

Other reforms, particularly those included in the Education Reform Act (1988), have explicitly or implicitly increased the pressures on leaders in the world of education. Government education policy has emphasized the role of parents, and made schools and colleges susceptible to the demands of the market.

> by specifying that the allocation of delegated budgets should be primarily pupil-led, the Education Reform Act 1988 ensured that parental choice

directly influences individual schools—the more pupils a school attracts, the larger its budget (DFE 1992 para. 1.17).

External pressures require a response from the school or college. The possible modes of response from headteachers have been categorised as:

1. The reactive head, who simply responds to change by taking on the values of the day

2. The 'closet' head, who, whilst not agreeing wholeheartedly with the dominant values of the day, appears to do so

3. 'Oasis' headship, the school is united in attitudes and views but may be out of step with the wider environment

4. The proactive head who shares with parents. 'Instead of suppressing the potential for value conflict, heads and governors must learn to bring it into the open for general examination and sometimes allow their communities to resolve these differences themselves through a process of mutual education' (West, 1993, p.62).

Leadership in the autonomous school and college

The removal of further education from the local education authority and the development of LMS and GMS for schools in England and Wales is mirrored by moves to greater autonomy in other countries, particularly in the English speaking world. The increased level of autonomy both imposes extra responsibilities upon the management of institutions and creates opportunities for new modes of leadership. This area has been explored by Caldwell and Spinks (1992, p.47) who state that:

> It is clear that special kinds of leaders and leadership are required for school self-management, both at the system level and at the school level. For example, there is no place for an autocratic leader who is unwilling to empower others.

The requirements of leaders of the self-managing school are seen to be:

1. Cultural leadership, working with others to establish a recognised ethos and value system, and 'sustain a culture of excellence.'

2. Strategic leadership, including the ability to look at wider issues, already discussed in terms of awareness of 'mega-trends.'

3. Educational leadership, 'in the final analysis, the case for self-management must be based on benefits for students in terms of gains in learning outcomes' (p.57).

4. Responsive leadership, the accountability of the school to parent and pupil and to the wider community.

Whilst these demands of a leader may seem excessive, the underlying philosophy of the kind of 'transformational leadership' (Sergiovanni, 1990) envisaged is that the responsibilities are shared across the school or college. Such leadership may carry implications for management structures, in particular the existence of team-based management. This is consistent with the idea that: 'Both in theory and in practice teams are seen as fundamental to the management of quality in organization' (West-Burnham, 1992b, p.52).

The management of primary schools is often of a collegial type, but Yeomans (1987) concludes not just that primary schools may enjoy participative management cultures, but that 'leadership and membership' are both 'activities performed by the same individuals' within the group formed by a primary school staff (Yeomans 1987, p.139).

Training and development for educational leaders

The importance of the quality of leadership in relation to improvement and effectiveness in schools is widely recognized, and has been highlighted in official publications:

> Strong leadership of teachers and pupils usually means articulating a clear academic mission for the school, setting standards and creating a recognisable ethos. These are not ends in themselves. But they are necessary conditions for good management (DFE 1992 para. 1.35).

> Much of the research on school effectiveness reported over the last decade has pointed unambiguously to the quality of leadership and management as the pre-eminent factor underlying differences in educational outcomes between otherwise similar schools (DFE, School Teachers' Review Body, 1993, para. 148).

The need for training and support for management in education was recognised by the establishment of the School Management Task Force (SMTF). Their recommendations, including the school-based approach to management development, drew attention to the responsibility of the head and governors for management development, whilst recognizing the need for external support, particularly from LEAs.

The policy implications of ISIP were spelled out in terms of suggested types of development for school leaders. The key requirements for effective development were considered to be:

— an adequate period of time for learning

— scope for reflective learning

— a focus on concrete situations

— application of learning in collaboration with colleagues (Glatter 1987, p.198)

It was also suggested that development should continue and form part of a career-long training process. The recommendations, particularly the last two with their references to learning within the work place, echo the recommendations of the SMTF.

In a survey of headteachers (Jones 1987) 400 heads responding to a question on training needs identified leadership as the first choice for training for heads. The establishment of a school ethos is considered to be of prime importance for school effectiveness and 'philosophy' ranked second only to leadership in the rating of heads' training needs.

Weindling and Earley (1987) in their research on new heads found that:

> The introduction of change to improve the school was a major concern for the vast majority of new heads. Recent research has provided a clearer understanding of the process of innovation and heads need access to this information in order to use the appropriate strategies during each phase (p.189).

Southworth (1993) reflecting on headship in the light of two projects on leadership in primary schools, concluded that:

> Although both projects showed that primary heads can be visionaries, at the same time, they also showed that the heads tended to create the conditions for teachers to be dependent upon them. As such their leadership may be 'effective' in the instrumental sense but it is ethically questionable since it overrides teachers' professionality.

His recommendation is then that:

> As leaders in school cope with all the educational and organizational changes which recent legislation has created, they may also need to contemplate changing the way they lead (p.85).

Much of the more recent theoretical work on leadership in education has focused on the need for the leader to have a vision for the institution and to be transformational and empowering, dispersing the leadership function throughout the institution.

The emphasis on the supportive and empowering role of a leader in the effective school has been translated into a training programme by Murgatroyd and Gray (1984).

> Finally, training for leadership cannot be normative, prescriptive, skill-based or problem-centred. Instead it needs to focus upon the personal and interpersonal qualities of the person. It needs to develop and sustain openness, empathy and warmth and to encourage exchange, acceptance and exploration. Though the aims may be pursued by means of studying specific problems or issues or by exploring key concepts and research, such training needs to be person-centred (pp.47–8).

Summary

Theories and styles of leadership are useful analytical tools for the examination of behaviour and effectiveness of all organizations. Educational institutions may differ from other organizations in significant ways, largely because of the predominance of professionals, and the nature of the 'products' of the educational system. It is argued that there is a moral dimension to leadership in education.

The necessity for a leader in education to have a vision for the school or college and to be able to communicate this vision to others is linked with effective schools and school improvement. It is also argued that the autonomous school requires such a visionary leader.

The development of the notions of transformational leadership and of empowerment of others points towards a different kind of leader, but one of whom much is demanded. Caldwell and Spinks (1992, p.203) counter the possible criticism that they are describing a 'super-person' as leader:

This will only be the case if one conceives of leadership residing with one or a few people. Consistent with the value of empowerment, ... we cannot stress too highly the need for widely dispersed leadership in the school. This also implies a capacity and commitment on the part of the principal to establish and utilise structures and processes for empowerment.

Further reading

Reading on the theories of leadership can be found in:

Beare, H. Caldwell, B. and Millikan, R. (1993) 'Leadership' in Preedy M. (Ed) *Managing the Effective School*, London: Paul Chapman.

Caldwell, B.J. and Spinks, J.M. (1992) *Leading the Self-Managing School*, London: Falmer Press.

Useful collections of writings on leadership issues include:

Harling, P. (Ed) (1984) *New Directions in Educational Leadership*, London: Falmer Press.

Riches, C. and Morgan, C. (Eds) Section II on Leadership and motivation in *Human Resource Management in Education*, Milton Keynes: Open University Press.

References to values in headship can be found in:

Jones, A. (1987) *Leadership for Tomorrow's Schools*, Oxford: Blackwell.

Southworth, G. (1993) 'School leadership and school development: reflections from research'. *School Organization*, **13**, 1., relates particularly to leadership in primary schools.

References to classic theories of leadership in organizational theory can be found in:

Gibb, C.A. (1969) *Leadership: Selected Readings*, Harmondsworth: Penguin.

References

Ball, S.J. (1987) *The Micro-Politics of the School: Towards a Theory of School Organization*, London: Routledge.

Beare, H., Caldwell, B.J. and Millikan, R.H. (1993) 'A model for managing an excellent school' in Bennett, N., Crawford, M. and Riches, C. (Eds) *Managing Change in Education: Individual and Organizational Perspectives*, London: Paul Chapman.

Beare, H. Caldwell, B. and Millikan, R. (1993) 'Leadership' in Preedy M. (Ed) *Managing the Effective School*, London: Paul Chapman.

Blake, R.R. and Mouton, J.S. (1964) *The Managerial Grid*, Houston, Texas: Gulf Publishing Co.

Blanchard, K. and Johnson, S. (1983) *The One Minute Manager*, London: Fontana.

Bush, T. (1986) *Theories of Educational Management*, London: Paul Chapman.

Caldwell, B.J. and Spinks, J.M. (1988) *The Self-Manging School*, London: Falmer Press.

Caldwell, B.J. and Spinks, J.M. (1992) *Leading the Self-Managing School*, London: Falmer Press.

Clark, D., Lotto, L., and Asuto, T. (1989) 'Effective school and school improvement: A comparitive analysis of two lines of inquiry' in Burdin J.L., (Ed) *School Leadership: A Contemporary Reader*, Newbury Park: Sage

DES (1977) *Ten Good Schools*, Her Majesty's Inspectors, London: HMSO.

DFE, (1992) *Choice and Diversity: A New Framework for Schools*, (Cmnd 2021), London: HMSO.

DFE, (1993) School Teachers' Review Body, Second Report 1993, (Cm 2151), London: HMSO.

DFE, (1993) Education Act, London: HMSO.

Fiedler, F.E. (1967) *A Theory of Leadership Effectiveness*, New York: McGraw-Hill.

Glatter, R. (1987) 'Tasks and capabilities' in Stego, N.E., Gielen, K. Glatter, R. and Hord, S. (Eds) *The Role of School Leaders in School Improvement*, Leuven: Acco.

Glatter, R. (1988) 'The management of school improvement' in Glatter, R., Preedy, M., Riches, C. and Masterton, M., *Understanding School Management*, Milton Keynes: Open University Press.

Gray, H. (1989) 'Gender considerations in school management: masculine and feminine leadership styles' in Riches, C. and Morgan C. (Eds) *Human Resource Management in Education*, Milton Keynes: Open University Press.

Handy, C. and Aitken, R. (1986) *Understanding Schools as Organizations*, Harmondsworth: Penguin.

Hargreaves, D. and Hopkins, D., (1991) *The Empowered School: The Management and Practice of Development Planning*, London: Cassell.

Harling, P. (1984) 'The organizational framework for educational leadership' in Harling P. (Ed) *New Directions in Educational Leadership*, London: Falmer Press.

Harling, P. (1989) 'The organizational framework for educational leadership' in Bush, T. (Ed) *Managing Education: Theory and Practice*, Milton Keynes: Open University Press.

Hersey, P. and Blanchard, K.H. (1977) *Management of Organizational Resources Utilizing Human Resources*, NJ, Englewood Cliffs: Prentice-Hall.

Hodgkinson, C. (1991) *Educational Leadership: The Moral Art*, Albany: State University of New York Press.

Hoyle, E. (1986) *The Politics of School Management*, London: Hodder and Stoughton.

Hughes, M. (1988) 'Leadership in professionally staffed organizations' in Glatter, R., Preedy, M., Riches, C. and Masterton, M. *Understanding School Management*, Milton Keynes: Open University Press.

Jones, A. (1987) *Leadership for Tomorrow's Schools*, Oxford: Blackwell.

Likert, R. (1967) *The Human Organization: Its Management and Value*, New York: McGraw-Hill.

Mortimore, P., Sammons, P., Stoll, L., Lewis, D. and Ecob, R. (1988) *School Matters : The Junior Years*, Wells: Open Books.

Murgatroyd, S. and Gray, H.L. (1984) 'Leadership and the effective school' in Harling, P. (Ed) *New Directions in Educational Leadership*, London: Falmer Press.

Noble, T. and Pym, B. (1989) 'Collegial authority and the receding cus of power' in Bush, T. (Ed) *Managing Education: Theory and Practice*, Milton Keynes: Open University Press.

Sergiovanni, T.J. (1990), 'Adding value to leadership gets extraordinary results'. *Educational Leadership*, May pp 23–27.

Sergiovanni, T.J. (1992) 'Why we should seek substitutes for Leadership'. *Educational Leadership*, February, pp 41–45.

Southworth, G. (1993) 'School leadership and school development: reflections from research'. *School Organization*, **13**, 1.

Stogdill (1969) 'Personal factors associated with leadership: a survey of the literature' in Gibb, C.A. (Ed), *Leadership*, Harmondsworth: Penguin.

Tannenbaum, R. and Schmidt, W.H., (1973) 'How to choose a leadership pattern' in the *Harvard Business Review*, May–June, pp 162–180.

Weindling, R. and Earley, P. *Secondary Headship: The First Years*, Windsor: NFER-Nelson.

West, S. (1993) *Educational Values for School Leadership*, London: Kogan Page.

West-Burnham, J., (1992a) *Managing Quality in Schools: A TQM Approach*, Harlow: Longman.

West-Burnham, J. (1992b) 'Total quality management in education' in Bennett, N., Crawford, M., and Riches, C. (Eds) *Managing Change in Education: Individual and Organizational Perspectives*, London: Paul Chapman.

Yeomans, R. (1987) 'Leading the team, belonging to the group?' in Southworth, G. (Ed) *Readings in Primary School Management*, London: Falmer Press.

4 Strategy, policy and planning

John West-Burnham

Introduction

Strategy, policy and planning are inextricably related management activities in that each requires the others in order to translate aspiration into action. Historically all three have had limited significance at institutional level in education in that they have been perceived as the prerogative of national and local government. The move towards institutional autonomy has led to increased significance being attached to the development of clear principles for managing and the anticipation of a medium- to long-term view of desired outcomes.

One of the characteristics of successful commercial organizations is the ability to work in an extended time frame. This has been perceived as less significant for non-profit organizations. However, the absence of profit does not remove the significance of value-driven management. An emphasis on proactive rather than reactive management and the potential benefits of more effective resource management, staff deployment and the possibility of evaluation follow the use of systematic planning. Strategy is central to effective management in that it:

> ... converts a non-profit institution's mission and objectives into performance. Despite its importance, many non-profits tend to slight strategy. It seems so obvious to most of them that they are satisfying a need, so clear that everybody who has that need must want the service ... (Drucker 1990, p.75).

> ... good intentions don't move mountains; bulldozers do. In non-profit management, the mission and the plan ... are the good intentions. Strategies are the bulldozers (ibid. p.45).

The purpose of this chapter is to examine the principles behind strategic planning and policy making in educational institutions. The issues discussed are:

1. Defining strategy, policy and planning

2. The strategic planning process

3. Organizational structures and roles

4. Managing the process

Defining strategy, policy and planning

Caldwell and Spinks (1988) provide a detailed definition of what they call 'corporate planning' which contains many of the essential components of strategic planning:

> ... a continuous process in administration which links goal-setting, policy-making, short-term and long-term planning, budgeting and evaluation in a manner which spans all levels of the organization, secures appropriate involvement of people according to their responsibility for implementing plans as well as of people with an interest or stake in the outcomes of those plans, and provides a framework for the annual planning, budgeting and evaluation cycle (quoted in Beare et al. 1989 p.142).

This analysis coincides almost exactly with the Peters and Waterman (1982) view that the purpose of management is to 'keep the herd heading roughly west' i.e. moving in unison towards a common goal. A number of key components emerge from the Caldwell and Spinks definition; planning:

— is an integrative process

— involves all staff and stakeholders

— changes in response to evaluation

— informs other management processes

— is a continuous process

— works from a long–term perspective

This view places strategic planning at the heart of management processes in that it moves management away from a response based on expediency into the value–driven approach which is founded on consent and consensus. It is also an integrative model in that it informs all management processes and outcomes. Thus decisions relating to resources and staffing are derived from a set of premises founded on common principles.

It is possible to take these elements and propose a model to indicate the relationship between strategic planning and other institutional processes (see Figure 4.1).

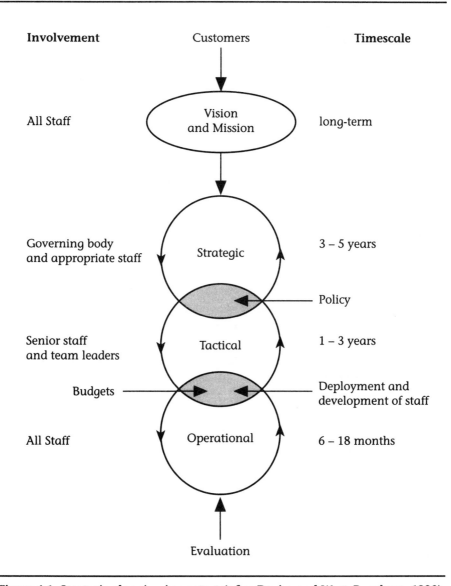

Figure 4.1. Strategic planning in context (after Davies and West–Burnham, 1990)

The terms strategic, tactical and operational may be problematic because of their military connotations. However, they are helpful because they emphasize both the time–scale and the level of significance in organizational and individual terms. The key features of this model are:

1. Everything is driven by the values and mission of the organization and these have been developed and are owned by all staff

2. Strategic planning has a three- to five-year time-frame, i.e. beyond the contingent and reactive, and is primarily the responsibility of senior staff and community representatives

3. Once agreed, strategy has to be translated into policy which serves as the basis of decision–making notably for annual budgets and the deployment and development of staff

4. Medium-term planning is primarily concerned with translating policies into action, most significantly through annual development plans, objective budgeting and planning for the deployment and development of staff

5. This in turn facilitates the negotiation of short-term targets so that each individual is working to optimum effect

6. Because the vision has been translated into individual activities, evaluation is based upon the aggregation of specific outcomes allowing the matching of intention and actual achievement

For an educational institution strategic planning is essentially a matter of bridge building or mapping the route between the perceived present situation and the desired future situation. The effectiveness of the process is largely contingent upon the clarity of the situational analysis and the skill in translating the vision into tangible outcomes. One way of viewing strategic planning is to think of the answer to the question asked by the parents of a child about to start secondary education — 'What will this school be like in five years time?' A detailed answer will exemplify both the vision and the strategic planning.

A school or college's strategic plan will deal with the key areas of management activity and will refer to specific examples of desired change, e.g:

Key area	*Change sought*
1. Student learning	50 per cent of the curriculum covered by self–managed learning
2. Staff management	Appraisal scheme fully operational
3. Resource management	Non-student-generated income increased by 20 per cent
4. Student attendance	Unjustified absences reduced by 75 per cent

The model outlined in Figure 4.1 and described above is problematic. In the first place it requires operating with long horizons when the tradition is to function with very short horizons. Limited time-frames in planning are exemplified in incremental budgeting, replication in the delivery of the curriculum and 'cloning' in staffing. This type of response may be explained by:

(a) the emphasis in schools and colleges on the short–term task, i.e. teaching

(b) the existence of a dependency culture where strategic decisions were taken outside the institution

(c) limited awareness of and skills in planning

(d) a limited awareness of the potential for strategic planning at institutional level

It is argued that because institutional planning is often at the mercy of national political policy changes, the response can only be reactive. However, increasing institutional autonomy increases the scope for planning, bearing in mind that plans are intentions which may have to be modified in response to changing circumstances. It is doubtful if any organization in any context at any time has delivered to an unmodified plan.

> The basis of flexibility is a process of more or less continual creation, monitoring and adjustment of the rolling plans ... In this way it is possible to become fully informed and to respond to the many spasmodic, often unpredictable, internal short–term crises and longer-term issues that arise, along with changing information about external innovations (Wallace 1992, p.163).

The second reservation about this model is that it assumes that all those involved in its execution accept the rationality of the process and outcomes. The reality is that the planning process is unlikely to be characterised by logical incrementalism — it is much more likely to be a political process dealing in ambiguities in order to obtain necessary support. (See Bush's discussion of the political and ambiguity models in Chapter 2.) However, it is contended that it is important to move away from a definition of the planning process which is purely descriptive of historic management behaviour towards a normative model that challenges expediency and reification of the status–quo. However, the model postulated in Figure 4.1 coincides with the characteristics of effective organizations, i.e.

— value-driven planning

— visionary leadership

— clear delegation

— objective budgeting

— integral evaluation

Although the model proposed is normative it is not abstract but an extrapolation of successful practice. For such a model to work a number of antecedents and related processes have to be in place.

The combined effects of institutional autonomy, public accountability, formula-based funding, parental and student choice mean that failure to plan is no longer an option. The world will not be in the future as it has been in the past. Murgatroyd and Morgan (1993, pp.128–130) identify a range of responses to the notion of planning which will become increasingly untenable:

1. Short-range focus for planning — one year or less

2. Difficult to measure goals

3. Measurable goals which are not measured

4. Opaque and ignorable goals

5. Long–range goals that do not relate to the reality of daily life

6. Plans without teeth

7. Planning as a political process rather than a learning agenda

8. Excellent planning poorly communicated

On the basis of what has been discussed in this section it is possible to offer the following definitions:

Strategic planning A process operating in an extended time-frame (three to five years) which translates vision and values into significant, measurable and practical outcomes. Although the primary responsibility of senior management, the process requires two-way communication at all stages and has to be focused on the core purpose and practical activities of the school or college.

Policy The statement of how the strategic plan will actually function for the main areas of the school or colleges activity, e.g. curriculum, staffing, resource management. A policy statement describes the content of a strategic plan and is closely related to the critical success factors and critical processes described below.

Development planning A short-term process (12–18 months) which identifies how the strategic plan is to be implemented in a way consistent with the policy. The development plan mediates between the long-term aims and short-term priorities which are supported by the deployment of human, financial and physical resources.

The whole process of planning can be reduced to answering the question 'who will do what by when and how?'. The reason 'why?' returns to the issue of vision, values and mission.

The strategic planning process

Marsh (1993), in a detailed account of a strategic planning process that has actually been successfully applied in education and industry, identifies (p.13) eight steps in the strategic planning process. These are outlined below.

1. Customers The first and crucial step in the strategic planning process is to identify the customers of the organization. Customers are those who receive an 'output from a process' or are 'those people served by the process' (ibid. p.15). This process is essentially setting the school or college in context by identifying primary and secondary customers, partners and controllers. Thus Marsh identifies (p.18) the context of an English Comprehensive School:

First line Customers:	Students
	Parents
Second line Customers:	Employers
	Further and Higher
	Education
	Community
Partners:	Feeder Schools
	LEA
Controllers:	DFE
	Curriculum bodies.

The importance of customer identification is reinforced by Drucker 1990 (p.75):

... strategies begin with research and research and more research. They require organized attempts to find out who the customer is, what is of value to the customer, how the customer buys. You don't start out with your product but with the end, which is a satisfied customer.

2. Customer needs Having identified an organization's customers it then becomes necessary to identify, accurately, wants and needs. This may involve market research, involvement in a strategic review, etc. This stage of the planning process involves careful *listening* to customers and their *integration* into the appropriate processes.

3. Performance indicators Once customer needs have been established then it is necessary to translate them into performance indicators, which are measures of the extent to which the need has been met. As far as possible they are quantifiable, or at least they are objective, and they translate external, i.e. customer needs, into measurable outcomes. Examples could include examination grades, attendance rates, etc.

4. Purpose statement This is made up of three elements:

Vision	—	where we are going
Mission	—	how we are going to get there
Values	—	what is important to us

Schools and colleges are increasingly familiar with managing in the context of a mission statement which serves as focus for all significant activities, i.e.

— producing a sense of direction and purpose
— setting criteria for policy making
— generating consistency of action

5. Critical success factors These are internal to the organization and provide a means of establishing the extent to which vision, mission and values, as well as customers' wants and needs, are being met.

The definition of a critical success factor is an outcome, or a group of outcomes, the absence of which will jeopardise achievement of the purpose and customer satisfaction. These are pre-requisites, not desirables, for success (Marsh 1993 p.37).

6. Critical processes
Marsh argues that the application of the Pareto principle is fundamental to meeting mission, needs, performance indicators and success factors. In essence the Pareto principle, or 80/20 rule, identifies the 20 per cent (or critical

few) that are actually significant. 'It assists in identifying those areas that if improved will deliver the greatest return' (ibid. p.43). By focusing on the key 20 per cent it is possible to achieve disproportionate improvement. Thus for a school or college the critical processes might include:

— managing classroom behaviour
— personal relationships

Changing these will have a significance over and above their relative weighting, i.e. they will have a disproportionate impact because they are fundamental to the effective functioning of the institution.

7. Planning process improvement Once the critical processes have been identified the next stage is to improve them by getting all those involved in the process to identify the required end results by specifying indicators of success. Improvements might include reductions in process time, increases in reported satisfaction, fewer errors, etc. Examples of this in a school or college might include:

— a reduction in truancy resulting from improved methods of monitoring attendance
— changes in the management of meetings so that more is achieved in less time
— increased attendance at parents' consultation evenings following changes in reporting procedures
— improved examination results following the adoption of consistent learning strategies

8. Aligning objectives to strategy

A strategy is worthless unless there is the means to convert it into focused action ... This kind of focus enables more effective prioritisation and better resource decisions. Strategy is not a top-down process (ibid. p.55).

The process that Marsh outlines challenges some of the concerns about strategic planning outlined above. It minimises the problems of varying perceptions and the vested interests of stakeholders by having the whole process driven by customers in the context of explicit vision, mission and values. The relationship is shown in Figure 4.2.

However attractive this model may appear in terms of coherence and relative simplicity it is not unproblematic. Any rational approach to planning will inevitably be compromised by a number of factors.

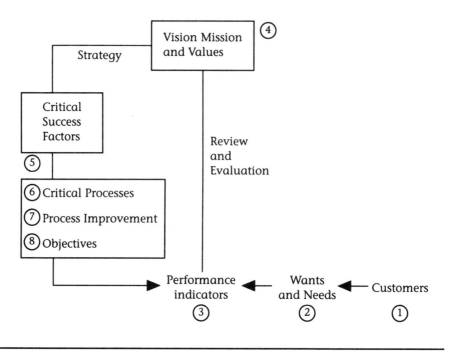

Figure 4.2 The strategic planning process (after Marsh, 1993)

1. The extent to which vision and values are shared — cultural homo-geneity is an aspiration rather than the norm in most educational institutions

2. The problems in identifying a vision which is capable of changing to meet the perceptions and legitimate demands of all stakeholders over a significant time-scale

3. The purposive nature of Marsh's model could be seen as inhibiting the capacity of individuals and the organization to be directly responsive—perceived as crucial when dealing with the learning of children and young people

4. The concern that the dominance of one vision can over-simplify reality and thereby inhibit creativity, i.e. the organization becomes mechanistic

The issue is one of establishing the extent to which educational organizations which adopt a strategic planning approach are perceived to be more effective than those which do not work in an extended time-frame (and lack an explicit consensual framework.) There is limited empirical evidence. However Rutherford (Leithwood, et al. 1986) in analyzing the work of effective principles identifies the following characteristics:

1. Having clear vision and goals

2. Translating that vision into practice

3. Creating a supportive environment focused on learning

4. Monitoring activity in school

5. Responding to monitoring by supportive or corrective activity

These principles have a high correlation with the model proposed by Marsh.

Organizational structures and roles

The approaches outlined in Parts 1 and 2 of this Chapter represent a challenge to established ways of working for many schools and colleges. The movement to working in a longer time horizon and the focus on differentiated long-, medium- and short-term planning have implications for the way in which the process is managed. If there is to be a shift away from short termism and pragmatic policy making to a long-term, value-driven model with consistent application then the appropriateness of existing structures and roles has to be considered.

In essence the implications of the model proposed in Figure 4.1 have to be applied to the organizational structure of the school. A simplistic response would be to seek to replicate the hierarchy of strategy, tactics and operational activities in terms of senior managers, middle managers and teachers. However, this would ignore a number of highly significant factors:

1. In most schools and colleges individuals will work at all three levels; there will not be the sharp differentiation of function related to status found in many public-sector organizations

2. The process is a dynamic one and each 'level' depends upon interaction, either directly or indirectly, with the other levels. Thus the

quality of strategic thinking will be directly proportionate to the extent
of the involvement of all those involved in implementation

3. A hierarchy of functions does not necessarily require a hierarchy in
    terms of status; this is particularly true in professionally staffed
    organizations but is increasingly found in total quality businesses
    where all staff have a shared sense of involvement and commitment

Handy (1989, p.71), somewhat optimistically, reviews the culture shift that is
taking place thus:

Organizations used to be perceived as gigantic pieces of engineering, with
largely interchangeable human parts. We talked of their structures and
systems, of inputs and outputs, of control devices and of managing them as
if the whole was one large factory. Today the language is not that of
engineering but of politics, with talk of cultures and networks, of teams and
coalitions, of influence or power rather than control, of leadership rather
than management.

The extent to which this is taking place in secondary schools and colleges is
debatable; the response to change by educational institutions often seems to
involve:

1. A greater emphasis on hierarchy with an emphasis on status

2. Bureaucratisation of working procedures

3. Introduction of 'need to know' management of information

4. Formalisation of working relationships

In primary schools the increase of administration has led to changing
priorities for senior staff. These responses are not unique to education; they
are found in almost any organization that perceives itself to be under threat
and where the available options are not understood:

... a single-dimensioned organizational structure is no longer sufficient for
an educational enterprise, and the key operators, including the school
principal, will need to be adept at changing administrative tactics and
structures according to the task in hand (Beare et al. 1989, p.88).

Beare, Caldwell and Millikan go on to point out that for planning and
developmental tasks the most appropriate mode is the project or task force

approach. This view is reinforced by Davies and West-Burnham (1990, p.257) who argue that:

> The composition of these temporary groups should represent available expertise both in terms of technical knowledge and of the skills necessary to produce effective and relevant outcomes. They should not just be microcosms of the main body nor should issues of status compromise the ability of the group to solve problems and generate policies ... it is essential that (these groups) are trained to work effectively in order to achieve the task.

According to Peters (1987, pp.215–217) the characteristics of successful team development include:

1. Multi-functional involvement, i.e. customers, suppliers, plus representatives of all elements with an interest or potential contribution

2. Simultaneous full-time involvement, i.e. the task should be the dominant feature of the team members' working life; diffusion of purpose can only compromise the integrity of the outcome

3. Co-location, i.e. team workers should 'live' together

4. Communication, i.e. regular, open and complete movement of information

5. The 'shared-resource' trap, i.e. the project has access to its own dedicated resources

6. Outside involvement, i.e. those whom the project is going to impinge on become 'partners for development'

There are obvious problematics in applying these maxims to schools and colleges, e.g. students cannot be told to stay away so that strategic planning can take place. However, the issues of involvement, commitment, resourcing and integration identified by Peters, all point to a very different organizational structure. The issues are discussed in detail by O'Neill (Chapter 5), but in the context of strategic planning for schools and colleges some specific issues emerge:

1. If the team/task approach is right, then it should be implicit to the organizational structure and not 'bolted-on'. It may be necessary to

explore in more detail the justification for the essentially hierarchical bureaucratic structure of most schools and colleges. If the response to critical questioning is 'It doesn't actually work like that', then there is an even stronger case for questioning the validity of a structure that only exists as a diagram in a handbook. West-Burnham (1992) argues for an organizational structure that is based around teams with functions rather than status and administrative convenience.

2. The fluidity of teams being assembled for a specific purpose, completing it and then being re-formed coincides with Weick's (1976, p.3) view of educational organizations as 'loose assemblies' and 'soft' structures:

> It is conceivable that preoccupation with rationalised, tidy, efficient, co-ordinated structures has blinded many ... to some of the attractive and unexpected properties of less rationalized and less tightly related clusters of events.

3. Roles will need to be reviewed to reflect the reality of a job and to indicate the relative significance of the components of the job. Thus if vision and strategy are perceived as significant as the basis for the effective management of the school or college, then this should be reflected in the role description of the individuals concerned and given operational significance in terms of workload, support, etc.

Torrington and Weightman (1989), Hall, Mackay and Morgan (1986) and Jones (1987) all identify 'problems' in senior staff in schools finding time for, or being comfortable with, the issues of strategic planning and policy formulation. Earley and Fletcher-Campbell (1989, p.43) found a similar situation for middle managers:

> Their work, like that of their senior management counterparts, tended to be characterized by fragmentation ... little time was found for planning, evaluating, reflecting or observing colleagues; crisis management appeared to be much more the norm.

Handy and Aitken (1986) proposed three specific solutions to these issues:

1. Distinguish between leadership and administration, delegating the latter to appropriately qualified staff

2. Separate policy and execution with different mechanisms for each

3. Turn teachers into managers and pupils and students into individuals capable of managing their own learning

The impact of these changes will be to create time and the opportunity to use that time to reflect on values, their translation into outcomes and the deployment of resources to meet those outcomes. In order to achieve this situation a number of very practical steps are necessary:

— reformulation of job descriptions to include responsibility for mission and strategy

— empowerment of junior and support staff to release leadership time

— training for leaders in conceptualisation, quality planning techniques, creative thinking and problem solving

— reformulation of structural 'teams' into task teams, e.g. abolish the senior management team and replace it with a strategy team

— involve all staff and stakeholders to avoid making the future the property of a few

— have the values and mission on the agenda of every decision-making meeting as the benchmark for effectiveness

These broad principles represent a significant culture shift for many schools and colleges, in essence a move away from a controlling and closed culture to one that is trusting and open. Within the Total Quality movement the natural extension of this strategic approach, based on a fundamentally different set of operating premises, is the process of setting outrageous goals, what in Japanese management is referred to as 'Hoshin'.

Murgatroyd and Morgan (1993, p.138) provide powerful examples of the way in which the application of Hoshin to a school can radically transform perceptions, expectations and performance. They provide examples of outrageous goals from a Canadian school:

1. Reduce paper use by 80 per cent
2. Reduce discipline problems to zero
3. Involve every family in a parenting course
4. Increase the student population from 170 FTE to 225 FTE

The school used three crucial techniques to ensure that outrageous goals become attainable. First, the use of 'champions' to drive the process and communicate, and secondly the translation of the goal into specific action planning with clear targets. (Goal 2 above has 20 targets). Thirdly, everyone in the school knowing the goal and focusing on it. The Hoshin approach will rarely produce anything dramatically new — what is different is the total commitment and consistent effort applied.

> The purpose of Hoshin planning is to focus the energies of the organization through the creation of challenging goals to which individuals and teams feel that they can be committed. Through the setting of challenging goals, the school can achieve beyond its comfort zone—it can become more like the school of its vision statement and can propagate its strategy (Murgatroyd and Morgan 1993, p.140).

Managing the process

One of the crucial determinants of the success of Hoshin planning is the emphasis that is placed on the process as well as the outcomes. The planning process is seen as an opportunity for development, communication, team-building, integration and enhancing personal relationships. Even if the Hoshin approach is felt to be too radical these principles can be applied to any other systematic planning technique.

The classic, rational, formulation for decision making is well understood:

1. Definition of objective
2. Collection of data
3. Generation of alternative solutions
4. Evaluation and selection of optimum solution
5. Implementation
6. Monitoring and feedback

Few decisions will follow the neat logic of this process. As Bush indicates in Chapter 2, the formal, rational approach has to be set against subjective, ambiguity and political models. However, a more effective approach to strategic planning (i.e. long-term decision making) is possible if it is derived from:

1. An explicit and shared vision
2. Consensus about the future of the organization
3. The use of mature teams
4. The use of appropriate process techniques
5. Clear commitment to the outcomes

The formal stages in the strategic planning cycle are shown in Figure 4.3.

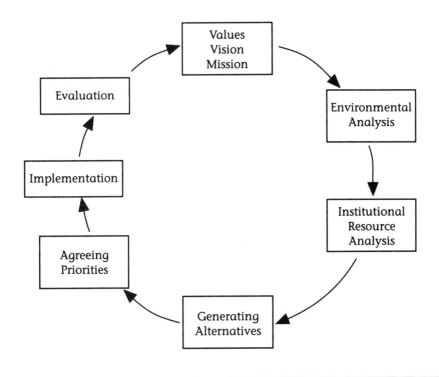

Figure 4.3 The strategic planning cycle

The significant elements of this cycle are:

— it is value driven, the organization's mission is the starting point for the central management process

— the mission is interpreted through environmental and institutional needs in order to identify the statutory or other imperatives which need to be given priority

— the generation and selection of alternatives is the major opportunity for consultation and involvement

— implementation is the point at which strategy (what we are going to do) and policy (how we are going to do it) are translated into specific commitments, action plans and individual targets

— because of the specificity of action plans and targets the evaluation process is very much one of measurement (a) against intentions and (b) of consistency with the mission

The relationship of a strategic, long–term plan to short term, i.e. annual planning cycles, is shown in Figure 4.4. Strategic planning is thus an interactive process being modified in response to changing situation and constantly informed by the annual planning and budgetary cycles. Thus a three or five year plan is constant only in terms of vision and values, the outcomes are subject to regular renegotiation and development.

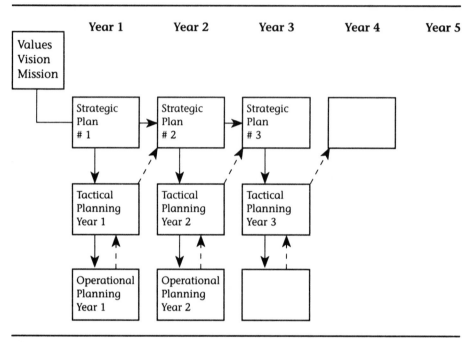

Figure 4.4 The strategic planning process

The strategic planning process is thus heuristic and an essential component of organizational development. Because it is always translated into team and individual actions the process also provides an agenda for individual development programmes and succession planning. As Hargreaves and Hopkins (1991) argue:

> Where a school lacks the appropriate culture, development planning is a means of achieving it. The recognition of this fact is a real and important condition of development planning. This is the key insight ... development planning is not just about implementing innovation and change, but about changing its culture — or in more concrete terms, its management arrangements — to improve its capacity to manage (other) changes (in Preedy 1992, p.239).

Finally, if the budget is perceived as a form of tactical planning which is geared to long– and medium– term outcomes, then objective rather than historic budgeting is possible and resource management is curriculum- or learning-driven.

Summary

This chapter has shown the centrality of strategic planning to the management of schools and colleges in that it is fundamental to the process of linking vision and values to the deployment of resources. Although difficult in any organization, long-term planning is crucial in helping to ensure that the school or college moves from reaction to anticipation. A model of strategic planning has been outlined which is problematic in that it assumes a high degree of rationality. However, the planning process is as much about the development of the capacity to plan as it is about defining outcomes.

The proposed model helps to integrate a number of variables in the management of any organization:

- vision, values and core purpose
- external demands, expectations and influences
- focus on clients
- prioritising the deployment of resources
- managing complexity and uncertainty

The absence of both a strategic plan and its related processes can only compromise the capacity of a school or college to translate the aspiration of its aims or mission into management action.

The means by which this process takes place is closely intertwined with notions of leadership (Chapter 3), teams (Chapter 13) and decision making about resources (Chapter 16).

Further reading

Beare, H. Caldwell, B. Millikan, R. (1989) *Creating an Excellent School*, London: Routledge.

Drucker, P.F. (1990), *Managing the Non-Profit Organization*, London: Butterworth-Heinemann.

Marsh, J., *The Strategic Toolkit*, IFS International

West-Burnham, J. (1992), *Managing Quality in Schools*, Harlow: Longman.

Bibliography

Beare, H. Caldwell, B. Millikan, R. (1989) *Creating an Excellent School*, London: Routledge.

Caldwell, B.J. and Spinks, J.M. (1988) *The Self-Managing School*, Lewes: Falmer Press.

Drucker, P.F. (1990) *Managing the Non-Profit Organization*, London: Butterworth-Heinemann.

Davies, B. and West-Burnham, J. (1990) 'School governors—an effective management force or another bureaucratic layer of school management?' *School Organization*, **10**, 2 & 3.

Earley, P. and Fletcher-Campbell, F. (1989) *The Time to Manage? Department and Faculty Heads at Work*, Windsor: NFER–Nelson.

Hall, V. Mackay, H. and Morgan, C. (1986) *Headteachers at Work*, Open University Press

Handy, C. (1989) *The Age of Unreason*, Business Books Ltd.

Handy, C. and Aitken, R. (1986) *Understanding Schools as Organizations*, Harmondsworth: Penguin.

Hargreaves, D. and Hopkins, D. (1991) 'School effectiveness, school improvement and development planning,' in Preedy, M. (1992).

Jones, A .(1987) *Leadership for Tomorrows Schools*, Oxford: Blackwell.

Leithwood, K.A., Rutherford, W. and Van der Vegt, A. (1986) *Preparing Schoolteachers for Educational Improvement*.

Marsh, J. (1993) *The Strategic Toolkit*, IFS International.

Murgatroyd, S. and Morgan, C. (1993) *Total Quality Management and the School*, Milton Keynes: Open University Press.

Peters, T. (1987) *Thriving on Chaos*, London: MacMillan.

Peters, T. and Waterman, R.H. (1982) *In Search of Excellence*, London: Harper and Row.

Preedy, M. (1992) *Managing the Effective School*, PCP.

Torrington, D. and Weightman, J. (1989) *The Reality of School Management*, Oxford: Blackwell.

Wallace, M. (1992) 'A key to the management of multiple innovations', in Bennett et al. (1992).

Weick, K.E. (1976) 'Educational organizations as loosley coupled systems'. *Administrative Science Quarterly*, **21**.

West-Burnham, J. (1992) *Managing Quality in Schools*, Harlow: Longman.

5 Organizational structure and culture

John O'Neill

This chapter explores the management of schools and colleges from two distinct yet complementary perspectives. Analysis of organizational structures focuses on visible and tangible features of educational organizations. Cultural analysis examines those seemingly intangible and invisible characteristics of organizations which, nevertheless, contribute directly to managerial and organizational effectiveness within any institution.

Theoretical analysis of structure and culture varies according to interpretations of three essential terms: organization, structure and culture. The relationship between the three is a major theme of the chapter. Principles of, and models for, structure and culture are presented and examined. The chapter concludes with a discussion of the implications of recent developments in education for the management of organizational structure and culture.

Organization, culture and structure

> Organizations are essentially collectivities of people, who define policies, generate structures, manipulate resources and engage in activities to achieve their desired ends in keeping with their own individual and collective values and needs (Beare et al. 1989, pp.172–173).

A distinction between culture and structure is helpful because it highlights the potential tensions between structures and policies, which constitute the official goals and formal relationships in the organization, and the values and informal networks of relationships which represent the practice and aspirations of the people who make up the organization.

> Every organization has a formally instituted pattern of authority and an official body of rules and procedures which are intended to aid the achievement of those goals. However, co-existing alongside this formal aspect of the organization are networks of informal relationships and unofficial norms which arise from the interaction of individuals and groups within the formal structure (Harling 1989, p.21).

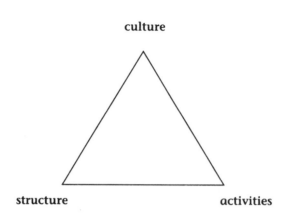

culture

structure   activities

Figure 5.1 Dimensions of educational organizations

Figure 5.1 illustrates the interdependent relationship of the three dimensions which determine the character of individual educational organizations. Each *organization* has broadly similar educational aims and objectives. The particular educational *activities* or curricula which are undertaken will depend on an interpretation of those aims and objectives within the individual institution. The activities comprise the official curricula which schools and colleges are required to deliver together with other broader areas of activity which collectively make up the organization's intended whole curriculum. How the whole curriculum is interpreted will reflect the common values, beliefs and priorities of those within the school or college community. Those shared values constitute the *culture* of the organization. The chosen activities will reflect an accommodation between the values and beliefs, or culture, of those people who comprise the institution, and the goals of those in the wider community who sponsor the organization. The collective commitment of those working in the organization to carry out those activities will, in turn, be reflected in a customised management *structure* to support agreed policies and accompanying procedures.

Educational organizations exist within an external environment which *licenses*, in the case of local or national government, or *patronizes*, in the case of parents and students, the educational services offered by each institution. It is in the organization's interests, therefore, to ensure an appropriate match between the school or college's expressions of value or belief, and those of the wider community (Meyer and Rowan 1988). Equally, changes in community values or expectations impinge directly on organizational practice, and, as suggested in Figure 5.1, on other dimensions of the organization.

The complexities of educational organizations demand appropriate management structures to promote effective and efficient development and delivery of the whole curriculum. According to the cultural perspective (e.g. Morgan 1986) these structures and processes are themselves cultural artifacts, designed, in part, to support and maintain the desired organizational culture. The relationship between structure, culture and activities is one of interdependence because changes in any of the three dimensions will affect the established balance between all. The effective management of educational organizations involves the establishment and maintenance of an appropriate balance among those various structural and cultural elements (Everard and Morris, 1990).

Organizational culture

The importance of understanding organizational culture lies in the notion that the officially agreed and sanctioned areas of organizational activity produce only a partial picture of how and why an organization functions as it does. Educational managers, therefore, need an analytical framework in order to identify the undocumented, unofficial and intangible elements which influence the way the organization functions. An awareness and understanding of the influence of shared values and attitudes are essential in order to fully appreciate the possibilities for effecting educational change and improvement (Holly 1987; Deal 1988; Westoby 1988). Indeed, for some writers, culture is perceived as a primary determinant of the level of organizational effectiveness (Reynolds and Reid 1988; Campbell and Southworth 1992).

The invisible, intangible and informal nature of culture presents a considerable difficulty for managers seeking to change or influence the existing culture because, typically, it is described using terminology and frameworks which are themselves opaque and imbued with mystique.

> Organizational culture is the characteristic spirit and belief of an organization, demonstrated, for example, in the norms and values that are generally held about how people should treat each other, the nature of the working relationships that should be developed and attitudes to change. These norms are deep, taken-for-granted assumptions that are not always expressed, and are often known without being understood (Torrington and Weightman, 1989, p.18).

Nevertheless, it is possible to chart those deeply held values and beliefs by analyzing the various ways in which they are enacted in terms of overt

103

organizational activity and behaviour. *Implicit* aspects of culture are those which reflect underlying beliefs and values whereas *explicit* aspects are those which are documented and enacted through procedural, ceremonial and symbolic activities which help maintain and reinforce the culture of the organization (Handy and Aitken, 1986; Hoyle, 1986).

Cultural analysis serves four management purposes:

1. It offers an indicator of the match between internal organizational and external environmental values

2. It leads to a more complete understanding, through observation, of how things are done in a particular institution (Deal, 1988)

3. It facilitates assessment of which areas of individual and organizational activity are in conflict with the desired organizational culture

4. It suggests areas of activity which may be open to influence in order to promote desired organizational values (Beare et al. 1989; Morgan, 1986).

Figure 5.2 illustrates the chain of factors which contributes to the development and maintenance of organizational culture. The diagram demonstrates the link between external environment and internal organizational culture. It acknowledges that the well-being of schools and colleges depends increasingly on their ability to relate successfully to their external environments. As such they are open rather than closed systems. It is therefore fundamentally important that the organization is able to offer visible and tangible manifestations of cultural 'match' to that environment.

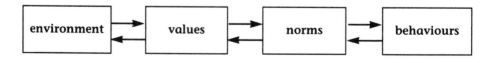

Figure 5.2 The development of organizational culture

School or college culture, in Figure 5.2, is represented in terms of values, norms and behaviours. Values and norms inform the behaviour of organizational members. Equally, changes in behaviour help modify established norms and values. Hence, tangible manifestations of culture are of primary importance within the organization. They help to promote and reinforce that translation of cultural values into appropriate norms and behaviours.

In educational organizations it is not difficult to identify a range of staff, student and community oriented activities which are used as part of this 'collective programming' (Sergiovanni 1984). The significance of the socialization, or conditioning, process is that it encourages and helps people within the school or college to adopt the official, preferred norms of the organization, 'since organizational culture exists only if internalised by individuals' (Westoby 1988, p.xv).

Cultural demonstrations are important then in two respects.

- They publicise the existence of complementary values and beliefs to sponsoring groups in the external environment
- They provide internal opportunities for establishing and reinforcing those values and beliefs (Deal 1988) amongst organizational members

❏ Expressions of culture

Deal (ibid pp. 203–207) identifies several elements of culture which are enacted in a variety of forms and activities.

- shared values and beliefs expressed in written form
- heroes and heroines who typify desirable organizational behaviours and personal qualities
- rituals which allow members to come together and reinforce core values
- ceremonies which celebrate those values
- stories which communicate and disseminate philosophy and successful practice
- an informal network of cultural players which serves to maintain the culture in the face of pressures for change

In the context of Deal's taxonomy it is axiomatic that schools and colleges not only have a clear awareness of what their core values are, but that those values are regularly and collectively expressed, maintained and reinforced. Within educational organizations it is possible to identify various areas of educational activity which act as expressive vehicles for the elements of culture listed above.

Beare et al. (1989), for example, suggest that culture is expressed in three modes:

1. *Conceptually or verbally* through, *inter alia*, definition of the curriculum, use of language, and the identification of organizational aims and objectives

2. *Behaviourally* through, *inter alia*, rituals, ceremonies, pedagogy, rules, support mechanisms, and patterns of social interaction

3. In a *visual or materiél* mode through, *inter alia*, facilities and equipment, memorabilia, and mottoes, crests and uniforms.

Culture is thus manifested via a complex multi-sensory amalgam of symbols, routines and physical resources. It presents significant management opportunities inasmuch as 'symbols are not only the means whereby established meanings are communicated but are central to the process of constructing meaning.' (Hoyle 1986, p152). Hence it becomes possible for managers to influence the development of organizational culture by attending to the way it is demonstrated and symbolised in all areas of organizational activity.

By focusing on cultural rather than purely structural aspects of organizational activity, managers are:

- addressing values, attitudes and beliefs at a 'deep' level (Cheng, 1993)
- acknowledging that attempts at managerial control which conflict with the existing values and norms are unlikely to be successful (Holly, 1987; Sergiovanni, 1989)
- accepting that effective educational management is as much about the adroit manipulation of 'connotative symbols' (Hoyle, 1986) as it is about the development of structures and procedures

Nias et al. (1989) indicated that, in addition to those factors identified above:

1. Maintenance of the culture was a significant leadership role. Leadership was exercised primarily by the headteacher but also by other members, both teaching and non-teaching, of the school community

2. Maintenance of the culture was threatened by changes in both group membership and practice. A strong culture could thus contribute to the socialization of new members and to the integration of demands for changes in activities

3. Maintenance of the culture depended, critically, on the recognition of both the individuality and the interdependence of group members. Such recognition led to the development of interpersonal openness in an atmosphere of security and mutual affection

It is possible, then, to identify four interdependent elements of organizational activities which contribute to the prevailing culture.

Purpose
This refers both to the official educational purposes of the organization and the interpretation of those purposes by the people who work in the organization and its immediate educational community.

Symbolism
This refers to the 'connotative' aspects of organizational activity, i.e. the implicit messages which particular pedagogies, management structures and styles, and ceremonies and rituals convey.

Networks
This refers to patterns of professional and social interaction, i.e. the way people in the organization communicate, meet and work together in all areas of organizational activity.

Integration
This refers to the extent to which disparate areas of activity and different groups of people are brought together and given opportunities to share in a unifying and unified organizational culture (Fullan and Hargreaves, 1992).

Culture and structure

The cultural 'mix' within any school or college will depend on, in addition to the people involved, the balance between the demands of the current activity portfolio of the organization, the way the organization is structured, and its size (Handy and Aitken 1986, pp.91–92). The prevalence of 'sub-cultures' (Goodson, 1988), or 'counter-cultures' (Beare et al. 1989) increases with the size, complexity and diversity of the organization, thereby placing additional management constraints on those attempting to establish a dominant culture. In this sense, the relationship between organizational structure and culture is of crucial importance. A large and complex organizational structure increases the possibility of several cultures developing simultaneously within the one organization. A minimal organizational structure, such as that found in most primary schools, enhances the possibility of a 'solid culture' (ibid.) guiding all areas of organizational activity.

Handy's (Handy and Aitken, 1986) typology of organizational cultures provides a useful bridge between the related concepts of culture and structure.

Handy identifies four cultures in educational organizations:

- club
- role
- task
- person

For Handy, none of the four cultural models is of itself inherently good or bad, but rather each is viewed as appropriate for different types of organizational activity and with different groups of people. Indeed, it is possible, argues Handy, that elements of each culture will be represented in all schools and colleges.

The strength of the Handy typology is that from each model it is possible to extrapolate, given the distinct emphasis of each culture, the likely characteristics of the resultant organizational structure. The major shortcoming, as Handy readily acknowledges, is that awareness of culture and prevailing norms, offers no ready indicator of the most effective way to structure the school or college in order to harmonise the potentially competing demands of the four cultures.

The **club** culture is likened to a spider's web in which informal networks of influence and like-minded people support the vision of the central leader of the organization. Communication channels are short and informal, and power is centralized. The strength of the club culture lies in its ability to respond immediately to new demands. The major weakness is its dependence on the leader. The club culture will reflect both the virtues and shortcomings of its leader. Handy suggests that club cultures are most effective in smaller (i.e. less than 20 people) organizations.

The **role** culture is articulated in terms of the impersonal sets of roles or job boxes which relate to each other in an ordered, logical fashion. The focus in role cultures is on the work of the organization. Communication channels are formalized and are used to support chosen procedures and systems. Role cultures are most appropriate in stable and predictable environments. They struggle to cope with change and unpredictability.

The **task** culture, described as a flexible net, concentrates on the organization of human and other resources to meet the demands of specific problems, projects or new areas of activity. Thus the task culture is perceived as a response to the inflexibility of a pure role culture. As such it tends to be non-hierarchical. Communication takes place in meetings which are used to plan co-ordinated responses to unfamiliar tasks. Task cultures are seen as expensive in terms of time and energy.

The **person** culture is oriented towards organizational support for the talent and initiative of particular individual 'stars', or, alternatively, 'clusters' of individuals. The organization serves to provide a minimal support structure within which talented individuals operate with a great deal of autonomy.

Management structures

> Structure is simply a description of what people do and how they relate; organization structure is a grossly simplified description of jobs and relationships (Gray 1988, p.147).

> I use structure in the sociological sense to include organizational arrangements, roles, finance and governance, and formal policies that explicitly build in working conditions that, so to speak, support and press for improvement (Fullan 1992, p.124).

In the context of this chapter structure embodies both a formal description of roles, authority, relationships, and positions within the organization (Stewart, 1970; Paisey, 1981), and also the pragmatic notion that structural design should promote and facilitate organizational effectiveness. Structure, in that sense, does not exist *per se* but, instead, is created to distribute and co-ordinate the work of people in the pursuit of organizational goals and objectives (Mullins, 1981). Here, the examination of organizational structure focuses on both the internal considerations which affect the design of management structures and also on the way in which organizations may be structured to enable them to respond to external demands.

Effective management structures, it is suggested, are not permanent but subject to change and development in order to incorporate new demands made upon the organization. In turn this may create internal tensions and management difficulties because the 'formal structure may be poorly adapted to the actual ongoing activity' (Meyer and Rowan 1988, p.110).

Aspects of structure

Mullins (1981, p.73) identifies the following *objectives* for structure:

1. The economic and efficient performance of the organization and the level of resource utilisation

2. Monitoring the activities of the organization

3. Accountability for areas of work undertaken by groups and individual members of the organization

4. Co-ordination of different parts of the organization and different areas of work

5. Flexibility in order to respond to future demands and developments, and to adapt to changing environmental influences

6. The social satisfaction of members working within the organization

These objectives are of direct and immediate relevance to educational organizations in that they focus on individual and organizational needs, on relationships with the environment, on the effective and efficient use of resources, and on visible accountability for actions.

In addition, Paisey (1981, p.86) lists a set of *variables* which allow analysis and comparison of organizational structures in educational organizations.

1. The degree of specialization of function; that is, the division of work

2. The degree of standardization of procedures; that is, the existence of rules

3. The formalization of documentation; that is, the commitment of rules and other types of information to writing

4. The degree of centralization of authority; that is, the location of decision-making

5. The configuration of positions; that is, the 'shape' which the structure assumes

6. The flexibility of structure; that is, the capacity of structure to meet new conditions and accept new tasks.

Together these two sets of criteria constitute a powerful tool for the analysis of educational organizations in terms of effective structure. The *objectives* of structure may be deemed common to all types of educational organizations; the balance and emphasis amongst the *variables* will alter according to the size and type of institution and the range of activities undertaken by the school or college. The actual structure will be determined in large part by the culture within the organization, ultimately being an accommodation between the demands of

- the organization's activities
- the existing roles of people in management positions
- the degree of motivation of people within the organization

Bolman and Deal (1984) provide a comprehensive synthesis of structural approaches to the management of organizations which aids identification of those factors influencing the balance of variables within organizational structures. They suggest that the basic dilemma in organizational design is the tension between differentiation and integration.

❏ Differentiation
- the allocation of tasks and responsibilities amongst individuals and groups
- the definition of specific roles and responsibilities

❏ Integration
- the linking together of roles to promote interdependence

Roles and interdependencies are co-ordinated vertically by authority and rules and laterally through meetings, task forces, teams and co-ordinators (ibid. p.42).

This need for both lateral and vertical relationships is endorsed by Packwood (in Packwood and Turner 1988, p.74) who argues that the hierarchy, in its most elaborate form 'is far more than a system of manager-subordinate relationships, including a wide and complex structure of lateral relationships'.

He makes a distinction between lateral co-ordinating and vertical managerial relationships. The former is seen as an essential element of a broader definition of hierarchy; one which allows for the active participation, rather than control, of professionals in the decision-making process.

Bolman and Deal suggest that organizational structure is determined by the *technology* of the organization and its *environment*. Technology is defined as the central activities of the organization, environment as everything outside the boundaries of the organization (pp. 43–44). The major pieces of educational legislation during the 1980s and 1990s may be seen to have exerted considerable influence on both the technology and the environments of autonomous educational establishments. Schools and colleges are now seen to depend directly on their external environments for their well-being whilst increased centralized control over curricula has dictated many changes in their technology.

Galbraith (1973) implies that the influence of technology and environment on organizational structure depends largely upon the level of *uncertainty* faced by organizations. In a stable environment, where activities and responses are predictable, it is possible to develop rules, procedures and decision-making mechanisms to cope with the demands made upon the school or college. In a turbulent environment, however, the reverse is true. Activities become unpredictable and it is, therefore, impossible to plan responses in advance because the necessary information is not to hand. In order to be able to continue to make effective decisions, organizations need to adapt their structures by, for example,

- creating more efficient information management systems; or
- distributing decision-making powers more widely within the organization

Adaptive structures

The need for flexibility in organizational structure, incorporating elements of both vertical and lateral co-ordination, is articulated by Peters and Waterman (1982) in terms of 'loose' and 'tight' qualities. The loose/tight distinction is of particular relevance to educational organizations as their external relationships exert greater influence over the type and organization of internal activities (e.g. Handy and Aitken 1986, Beare et al. 1989) because it implies a need to devolve increased authority and responsibility to those teams which interact directly and most closely with the organization's customers or clients (e.g. Jenkins 1991, West-Burnham 1992).

As yet, there is conflicting evidence concerning changes in management practice within educational organizations (Torrington and Weightman, 1989). It is possible to identify, for example in primary schools, a substantive move towards 'team or collegial' management (Bolam et al. 1993, p.125), prompted by the demands of educational reform. Empirical data from the secondary sector (Earley and Fletcher-Campbell 1992, Bolam et al. op. cit.), however, would suggest that, in larger and more complex organizations, the development of flexibility in organizational structure is problematic. In these studies effective management is characterised by clearly defined areas of authority and autonomy at subject department or faculty level. Conversely, difficulties within the organizational structure arise, to a large degree, from both a lack of clarity concerning the role and authority of middle managers and an absence of inter-departmental collaboration. Nevertheless, in both the secondary and further education sectors there is a growing body of evidence which indicates a perceptible trend towards less bureaucratic, hierarchical structures (Gillborn, 1989; Further Education Staff College, 1990; Roberts and Ritchie, 1990).

Handy (1990) postulates three radical organizational structures, designed to meet the demands of ever-changing environments and activities. The structures offer significant signposts for educational organizations because they highlight the need:

1. For flexible staffing structures to cope with demographic changes and economic constraints

2. For flexible authority structures with decision-making powers devolved to functioning units

3. For functional structures which allow greater access to information and which encourage the constant generation of ideas

The various structural perspectives outlined above exemplify a chronological move from readily defined organizational goals to unclear goals and uncertain responses. Traditional bureaucratic, hierarchical structures find ready application within organizations, or parts of organizations, which operate in stable environments with clear objectives (Turner, in Packwood and Turner 1988). Conversely, it is ineffective to predetermine organizational structures to meet the demands of turbulent environments and uncertain tasks; hence the growth of interest in more flexible organizational structures which are determined by the demands of the task and the shared values of organizational members. Roles, authority and positions in more flexible structures are defined according to the nature of the tasks and the capabilities of the individuals or groups who undertake them; in effect a contingency theory of management.

> The appropriate structure, management style, etc., are contingent on what the organization (or part of it) is there to do (Everard and Morris 1990, p.163).

Structure, culture and organizational flexibility

The international 'restructuring' of education movement (e.g. Caldwell and Spinks, 1992) represents a sharply focused set of threats and opportunities for individual institutions. Educational organizations now experience similar pressures to respond to the needs of their 'clients' as those in other sectors where demographic and economic pressures have seen the development of flatter, more responsive organizations. The major changes brought about by the Education Reform Act (ERA) and subsequent pieces of legislation mean that educational organizations exhibit, at both system and individual institution level, the characteristics of 'wild' organizations (Carlson, 1975). Individual schools and colleges operate in a market environment and, as such, have to be responsive to the demands of the market in order to survive. Educational organizations, however, differ significantly and paradoxically (Campbell-Evans, 1993) from other types of organization. Central control over curriculum delivery has been substantially increased whilst at the same time autonomous schools and colleges are held responsible and accountable for their ability to effectively manage a host of delegated financial and related responsibilities.

In such an environment streamlined bureaucratic structures are needed to cope, instrumentally, with the administrative requirements of more formal accountability. Equally, radical, flexible structures are demanded to simultaneously assimilate multiple changes (Wallace, 1991) in organizational tasks and community relationships. The link between a changing environment and organizational structure has been recognised in the non-education sector for many years. Burns and Stalker (1961) for example, distinguished between 'mechanistic' structures, appropriate for stable conditions, and more flexible, 'organic', forms of structure needed to respond to changing environmental conditions. That basic distinction has characterized much of the theoretical debate concerning effective organizational structure in subsequent decades (e.g. Galbraith 1973; Mintzberg 1979; Bolman and Deal 1984; Handy and Aitken 1986; Beare et al. 1989).

Figure 5.3 illustrates the principal differences between the two types of structure, here labelled 'traditional' and 'radical'. In a traditional organizational structure new activities are accommodated within existing procedures for the distribution and control of work. In a radical organizational structure new activities trigger a flexible organizational response according to the demands of the task itself. Thus structures become ad-hoc rather than permanent. In such an environment hierarchical lines of authority and established procedural norms are inappropriate responses when 'adaptive, short-run decisions are made at the front-line' (Turner in Packwood and Turner 1988, p.81).

Traditional	Radical
Solid	Fluid
Closed	Open
Form	Function
Role	Task

Figure 5.3 Characteristics of organizational structure

In the radical organizational structures suggested by figure 5.3 the cohesion hitherto provided through clarity of structure and authority no longer exists. Responses to new areas of activity, in the absence of appropriate rules and procedures, are perforce guided by the shared core values and beliefs of the organization:

> When visible structures and formal means of control are soft or loose, habits
> and attitudes assume greater importance (Westoby 1988, p.xv).

The, comparatively recent, increased focus on organizational culture (e.g. Peters and Waterman 1982, Bolman and Deal 1984, Morgan 1986, Beare et al. 1989, Nias et al. 1989, Torrington and Weightman, 1989) has, in part, directly paralleled the move, discussed above, in educational organizations away from rigid, hierarchical management structures. The shift may be interpreted as a desire on the part of managers and organizational members to understand more clearly those features of organizational activity which help provide meaning and commonality of purpose in an environment of uncomfortable change. As a result, a more complete understanding of organizational culture appears to have become something of a touchstone to those educationists wishing to promote continued educational improvement in an increasingly turbulent environment.

The effective schools movement (e.g. Mortimore et al. 1988) typifies attempts to identify the apparently elusive aspects of curricular organization and management which contribute to increased effectiveness in educational organizations. Significantly, however, Sergiovanni (1989, p.32) suggests that 'schools are not managerially tight and culturally loose, but rather are culturally tight and managerially loose'. This implies that effective management depends as much on an ability to influence culture as it does on the effective design of organizational structure.

Normative models of task-driven organizational management have been characterised by a call for more distributed forms of leadership (e.g. Caldwell and Spinks, 1992) with managerial authority devolved to autonomous teams (e.g. Jenkins 1991, West-Burnham, 1992). These trends have been accompanied by attempts to identify appropriate values, norms and organizational behaviours which enable members of the organization to work in a flexible, creative way. The appearance of labels such as 'problem-solving culture' (Schmuck, 1980), 'culture of consent' (Handy, 1990), 'culture of collaboration' (Nias et al., 1989) and 'culture of expectation' (West-Burnham, 1992) are intended to embody a desirable and attainable collective approach to the pursuit of organizational goals.

The increased use of such cultural descriptors in the literature of educational management is significant because it reflects a need for educational organizations to be able to articulate deeply held and shared values in more tangible ways and thereby respond more effectively to new, uncertain and potentially threatening demands on their capabilities. Organizations, therefore, articulate values in order to provide form and meaning for the activities of organizational members in the absence of visible and certain organizational structures and relationships. In this sense the analysis and influence of organizational culture become essential management tools in the pursuit of increased organizational growth and effectiveness.

Numinous organizations

Effective educational organizations, it is argued, are well led (Mortimore et al. 1988, Caldwell and Spinks, 1992) and have strongly articulated and expressed cultures (Campbell and Southworth, 1992) which are used to inform responses to new demands. In terms of Handy's typology, discussed earlier, these schools and colleges appear to have developed a judicious balance between role and task and between club and person cultures. They are structured flexibly in the present educational environment to enable them to respond appropriately to a constantly changing set of demands from their various stakeholders. They reflect, also, Peters and Waterman's simultaneous 'loose-tight' properties. Routine administrative procedures are rigorously monitored, yet, where necessary, individuals are delegated authority to act independently. In these instances tight administrative control is replaced by tight cultural control.

Effective educational organizations manifest an ability to successfully adapt and respond to external demands. This visible success reinforces shared values internally and the organization's reputation externally. As such they may be described as *numinous* organizations, which, irrespective of cultural nomenclature, exhibit three core characteristics.

1. They attract attention and loyalty because of a clearly articulated set of shared core beliefs and values which guides all areas of activity

2. They attract a certain degree of awe and respect because of their ability to respond positively and creatively to new demands and challenges

3. They value and achieve successful relationships with all their stakeholders

Numinous organizations provide several essential indicators for managers in aspiring but less successful educational organizations.

*   Traditional bureaucratic structures are appropriate and necessary continuing responses to routine administrative demands
*   Radical management structures are needed to respond to constantly changing demands on the resources and expertise of the organization
*   As 'open' systems, educational organizations are required to interact successfully with their environments in order to survive
*   Core values and beliefs are essential organizational guides to the interpretation and integration of new areas of organizational activity
*   Shared values and beliefs need to be developed, maintained and reinforced via a range of multisensory approaches in all organizational activities

The development, maintenance and articulation of a strong organizational culture is a leadership (e.g. Campbell and Southworth, 1992) activity which serves as an essential guiding and unifying influence in radical organizational structures. Numinous organizations are characterised by a synergy of culture, structure and activities. As such they exhibit loose-tight properties in both cultural and structural dimensions of organizational activity. The relationship is illustrated in Figure 5.4.

117

Activities	Culture	Structure
unpredictable	explicitly articulated	radical
routine	implicitly articulated	traditional

Figure 5.4 The relationship between culture and structure in numinous organisations

Summary

This chapter has analysed organisational culture and structure within a management context. Each offers alternative but complementary perspectives on organizational activity. Organizational structure focuses on the pattern of roles, relationships and lines of authority within the organization. Organizational culture focuses on values and beliefs which are collectively held and demonstrated through a variety of organizational activities. Traditional management structures are seen as an inadequate vehicle for responding to discontinuous change. The importance of culture as a management perspective in educational organizations may be attributed to the emergence of 'wild' or 'open' autonomous educational organizations which depend for survival on their ability to respond to external demands.

In this respect a systems perspective, which places schools and colleges in their external environment, is of some use in analysing potential strategies for coping with new and increasing external demands on the internal operation of educational organizations. Centralized accountability for curriculum delivery reinforces the need to maintain bureaucratic structures for enlarged but routine site-level administrative functions. Increased boundary relationships and a need to respond effectively to community aspirations have demanded the development of flexible responses to cope with new and unpredictable areas of educational activity. A clearly defined and strongly articulated organizational culture is perceived to provide a significant code of conduct within which schools and colleges can structure an appropriate management response to new and unfamiliar areas of educational activity.

Further reading

Beare, H., Caldwell, B. and Millikan, R. (1989) *Creating an Excellent School: Some New Management Techniques*, London: Routledge.

Bolman, L. and Deal, T. (1984) *Modern Approaches to Understanding Organizations*, San Francisco: Jossey Bass.

Morgan, G. (1986) *Images of Organization*, London: Sage Publications.

Westoby, A. (Ed) (1988), *Culture and Power in Educational Organizations*, Milton Keynes: Open University Press.

References

Beare, H., Caldwell, B. and Millikan, R. (1989) *Creating an Excellent School: Some New Management Techniques*, London: Routledge.

Bolam, R., McMahon, A., Pocklington, K. and Weindling, D. (1993) *Effective Management in Schools: A Report for the Department for Education via the School Management Task Force Professional Working Party*, London: HMSO.

Bolman, L. and Deal, T. (1984) *Modern Approaches to Understanding Organizations*, San Francisco: Jossey Bass.

Burns, T. and Stalker, G. (1961) *The Management of Innovation*, London: Tavistock Publications.

Caldwell, B. and Spinks, J. (1992) *Leading the Self-managing School*, Lewes: Falmer Press.

Campbell, P. and Southworth, G. (1992) 'Rethinking collegiality: teachers' views' in Bennett, N., Crawford, M. and Riches, C. (Eds) *Managing Change in Education*, London: Paul Chapman Publishing.

Campbell-Evans, G. (1993) 'A values perspective on school–based management' in Dimmock, E. (Ed) *School-based Management and School Effectiveness*, London: Routledge.

Carlson, R. (1975) 'Environmental constraints and organizational consequences: the public school and its clients' in Baldridge, J. and Deal, T. (Eds) *Managing Change in Educational Organizations*, Berkeley: McCutchan.

Cheng, Y.C. (1993) 'Profiles of organizational culture and effective schools'. *School Effectiveness and School Improvement*, **4**, 2, pp.85–110.

Deal, T. (1988) 'The symbolism of effective schools' in Westoby, A. (Ed) *Culture and Power in Educational organizations*, Milton Keynes: Open University Press.

Earley, P. and Fletcher-Campbell, F. (1992) 'How are decisions made in departments and schools?' in Bennett, N. Crawford, M. and Riches, C. (Eds), *Managing Change in Education*, London: Paul Chapman Publishing.

Everard, K.B. and Morris, G. (1990) *Effective School Management*, second edition, London: Paul Chapman Publishing.

Fullan, M. (1992) 'Causes/Processes of implementation and continuation' in Bennett, N., Crawford, M., and Riches, C. (Eds) *Managing Change in Education*, London: Paul Chapman Publishing.

Fullan, M. and Hargreaves, A. (1992) *What's Worth Fighting for in Your School*, Milton Keynes: Open University Press.

Further Education Staff College (1990) *Managing Colleges into the Next Century*, Coombe Lodge Report, 22(5), Bristol: Further Education Staff College.

Galbraith, J. (1973) *Designing Complex Organizations*, Reading, Mass: Addison Wesley.

Gillborn, D. (1989) 'Talking heads: reflections on secondary headship at a time of rapid educational change', *School Organization*, 9, 1, pp. 65-83.

Goodson, I. (1988) 'Beyond the subject monolith: subject traditions and subcultures' in Westoby, A. (Ed) *Culture and Power in Educational Organizations*, Milton Keynes: Open University Press.

Gray, H. (1988) 'A perspective on organization theory' in Westoby, A. (Ed) *Culture and Power in Educational Organizations*, Milton Keynes: Open University Press.

Handy, C. (1990) *The Age of Unreason*, London: Arrow Books.

Handy, C. and Aitken, R. (1986) *Understanding Schools as Organizations*, London: Penguin.

Harling, P. (1989) 'The organizational framework for educational leadership' in Bush, T. (Ed), *Managing Education: Theory and Practice*, Milton Keynes: Open University Press.

Holly, P. (1987) 'Soaring like turkeys — the impossible dream?', *School Organization*, 6, 3, pp.346–364.

Hoyle, E. (1986) *The Politics of School Management*, London: Hodder and Stoughton.

Jenkins, H. (1991) *Getting it Right: A Handbook For Successful School Leadership*, Oxford: Blackwell.

Meyer, J. and Rowan, B. (1988) 'The structure of educational organizations' in Westoby, A. (Ed) *Culture and Power in Educational Organizations*, Milton Keynes: Open University Press.

Mintzberg, H. (1979) *The Structuring of Organizations*, Englewood Cliffs, NJ: Prentice Hall.

Morgan, G. (1986) *Images of Organization*, London: Sage Publications.

Mortimore, P., Sammons, P., Stoll, L., Lewis, D. and Ecob, R. (1988) *School Matters*, London: Open Books.

Mullins, L. (1981) *Management and Organizational Behaviour*, London: Pitman.

Nias, J., Southworth, G. and Yeomans, R. (1989) *Staff Relationships in the Primary School*, London: Cassell.

Packwood, T. and Turner, C. (1988) 'Hierarchy, anarchy and accountability: contrasting perspectives' in Westoby, A. (Ed) *Culture and Power in Educational Organizations*, Milton Keynes: Open University Press.

Paisey, A. (1981) *Organization and Management in Schools,* London: Longman.

Peters, T. and Waterman, R. (1982) *In Search of Excellence: Lessons from America's Best-run Companies*, New York: Harper Collins.

Reynolds, D. and Reid, K. (1988) 'The second stage: towards a reconceptualisation of theory and methodology in school effectiveness research' in Westoby, A. (Ed) *Culture and Power in Educational Organizations*, Milton Keynes: Open University Press.

Roberts, B. and Ritchie, H. (1990) 'Management structures in secondary schools', *Educational Management and Administration*, **18**, 3, pp.17–21.

Sergiovanni, T. (1984) 'Leadership and excellence in schooling', *Educational Leadership*, **41**, 5, pp.4–13.

Sergiovanni, T. (1989) 'Value-driven schools: the amoeba theory' in Walberg, H. and Lane, S. *Organising for Learning: Towards the 21st Century*, Virginia: National Association of Secondary School Principals.

Stewart, R. (1970) *The Reality of Organizations: A Guide for Managers*, London: Macmillan.

Torrington, D. and Weightman, J. (1989) *The Reality of School Management*, Oxford: Blackwell.

Wallace, M. (1991) 'Flexible planning: a key to the management of multiple innovations', *Educational Management and Administration*, 19, 3, pp.180–192.

West-Burnham, J. (1992) *Managing Quality in Schools*, Harlow: Longman.

Westoby, A. (1988) 'Introduction' in Westoby, A. (Ed) *Culture and Power in Educational Organizations*, Milton Keynes: Open University Press.

6 Managing learning

Mark Lofthouse

Introduction

'Do not let your son's schooling interfere with his education'. This saying from Mark Twain, uttered at a time before gender stereotyping made the bias visible, nevertheless gets to the heart of issues raised in this chapter. If Twain's quip is seen as being inclusive of all students, it asks sharp questions of what education does to, and for, young people. These questions are examined in this introductory section, where it is argued that an uneasy tension exists between the bureaucratic imperatives of schools as organizations and the learning opportunities and outcomes offered by them to students.

Having first identified some organizational constraints and opportunities, the central parts of this chapter consider the proposition that all schools exist primarily to provide all their pupils with quality learning experiences. The implications of this claim are examined and applied in order to illustrate the impact that prioritizing learning is likely to have upon the roles and responsibilities of senior and middle managers. In the light of these considerations the chapter concludes by re-examining the significance of Jerome Bruner's work on theories of instruction and learning.

Facing up to the bureaucratic imperative

'Always remember,' declared Blyth, 'that children's learning is more important than teachers' teaching' (1988, p.1). If this sounds like just another academic truism, let us pause long enough to consider its meaning. Think back to your own schooling; do you recall yourself and your learning needs as being central to the operation of institutions you attended? The memories of an older generation tend to focus not on the learning they experienced but rather on the conditions in which instruction was conducted. Blackie (1963, pp.51–53) captures a not too distant past when he asked, 'What do we as teachers give children? High windows through which they cannot look, forbidding staircases, bare, unlovely yards, smelly lavatories and dark classrooms.' If you were fortunate enough not to encounter the Victorian legacy and this description fails to evoke a shudder of recognition, I nevertheless want to suggest that a dispassionate review of your school days may confirm a suspicion that teachers were more important than children. 'Teachers knew things; they occupied roles which invested them with both power and authority. In such a one–sided relationship, the role of pupil was primarily one of obedience and diligence in remembering knowledge transmitted by the teacher' (Calvert, 1975).

It would be reassuring to suggest that all of this is now past history. However, without becoming side–tracked into on–going arguments concerning how far schools are still used as mechanisms of social control (Habermas 1972), I wish to argue that there is a bureaucratic imperative built into schools which, if unacknowledged, will invariably operate so as to draw them back into past practice. Facing confusing and diverse demands, it is fatally easy for senior staff in schools to allow their institutions to serve the needs of the providers, *teachers*, rather than confront the frequently unexpressed needs of their clients, *pupils*. This outcome, far from being the result of a conspiracy theory, may merely reflect intensifying pressures currently being exerted upon teachers to be *accountable* for both *what* they teach and *how* they teach. These pressures of accountability have once again revived the debate concerning the roles played by teachers. A critical gaze is now being cast by politicians and parents on how teachers relate to their pupils, in terms of both teaching styles and learning outcomes. Figure 6.1 summarizes the position.

		Teacher	
Do to	**Do for**	**Do with**	**Enable**
Master	Provider	Expert/coach	Facilitator Mentor
Slave	Recipient	Participant	Active learner
		Students	

Figure 6.1 The role of the teacher
Source: Mt. Edgecombe High School, Sitka, Alaska, (West–Burnham 1992)

There is a long research history (Bennett 1976, Galton 1980, Alexander 1985) pointing to the fact that teachers frequently change teaching styles and their relationships with pupils and students. Fitness for purpose combined with the application of professional judgement, are two powerful reasons why teachers should be free to make judgements concerning teaching methods. However, in the context of this chapter, it is significant that a teacher acting as enabler, facilitator and mentor creates the conditions for *active learning*. Now it could be argued that active learning is the final ingredient on the far right of the table because it is the logical end of a long, slow developmental process. While true in one sense, such a proposition is debatable. Active learning and participation in 'doing' are the very foundations of good practice for teaching young children. In short, active learning is an option for teachers and pupils from pre–school to postgraduate ages and stages.

These points would hardly merit amplification but for a sharp increase in the number of pressure groups currently urging a return to Victorian values and 'back to basics' approaches. While the 'back-to-basics' phrase and the associated political agenda lack clarity, when applied to learning such groups strongly support the role of the teacher as director and provider of selected information. The consequent role for the learner (as illustrated in columns one and two of Figure 6.1) is as a willing or unwilling recipient. Thus the means of learning are essentially passive. While formal teaching has a long history of what might be termed 'limited success', it also has an equally long history of being perceived as strong on control and weak on learning outcomes. The present championing of formal teaching seems something of an aberration when set against the promotion of autonomous and empowered schools (Hargreaves and Hopkins, 1991). As Caldwell and Spinks (1992, p.7) note:

> The dominant principle of organization has shifted, from management in order to control to leadership in order to bring about the best in people and respond quickly to change.

In the light of this judgement, excessive reliance upon formal methods as a means of promoting quality learning outcomes risks taking a very blunt instrument to a complex and delicate issue.

Schools and colleges as learning institutions

Given the complexity of what schools are expected to achieve within contemporary society (Musgrave, 1972) it is easy to lose sight of their key mission. I wish therefore to argue that *all schools exist to provide pupils with quality learning experiences.* From this there are three key words/terms which need further clarification: *pupils; quality; learning experiences.*

❑ Pupils

For 'pupils' read 'students' and, while many in the education service may feel uneasy with the terminology borrowed from industry, pupils may also be identified as *clients* or *customers.* In confronting this use of terminology we face a real stumbling block. Many teachers have a deep suspicion of industrial models. Such hostility to models and managerialism usually culminates in a teacher asserting, 'I am a teacher not a manager.' However, whether they like it or not, it has been established that all teachers are in fact managers. What becomes critical is the degree to which teachers are willing to *define* and *own* areas of their management domain. A personal example might serve to illustrate this issue. When I was a primary teacher, my first promotion was to a post of 'special responsibility'. While nothing was written down concerning my teaching or classroom, acceptance of the post of special responsibility attracted a long list of 'systems maintenance' functions, one of which was stock control. While my colleagues found it amusing, I found it tedious, that my new found managerial eminence rested on my ability to estimate, order and count sheets of sugar paper and boxes of felt tip pens. This is an illustration of the 'bureaucratic imperative'. Left to its own devices, this imperative will ensure that senior and middle managers may seek to justify their existence in terms of administrative competencies or 'trivial pursuits'.

It is precisely because teachers need to avoid the 'trivial pursuits' version of management, that they need to embrace the client-centred approach, which is delineated in 'customer first' policies, embedded in *total quality management* (TQM). TQM defines a customer as anyone to whom a product or service is provided. West–Burnham (1992), proceeds to draw the conclusion that in order to understand your customers or clients, you need information about their values, attitudes, educational level, expectations, preferences, social situation and commitment. TQM is dealt with extensively elsewhere in this book but, I want to stress the advantages it brings to managing two vital aspects of schools.

It has often been observed that traditional school management has been run on the 'polo principle' (the mint with the hole in the centre). The hole has been the lack of any conceptual glue to hold together the varying and competing agendas and management functions of any school. If consistently applied, the principles of TQM provide the values and processes to enable schools to work coherently and harmoniously together. In terms of values, it places pupils at the centre of the enterprise. Seeking to understand their values, attitudes, educational levels, expectations, preferences, social situations and commitment is the most effective method of determining how best to provide the right context for quality learning experiences.

❑ Quality

For too long quality has been in the eye of the beholder. Shared commitment to TQM enables all members of an institution to clarify what quality means in terms of teaching processes and observable learning outcomes. Teachers will find West–Burnham's (1992, p.26) eight point synthesis valuable in establishing a framework which is applicable to their situation: (see Figure 6.2).

---

1. Quality is defined by the customer, not the supplier
2. Quality consists of meeting stated needs, requirements and standards
3. Quality is achieved through continuous improvement, by prevention, not detection
4. Quality is driven by senior management but it is an equal responsibility of all those involved in any process
5. Quality is measured by statistical methods—the 'cost of quality' is the cost of non–conformity. Communicate with facts
6. Quality has to pervade human relationships in the work place; teams are the most powerful agent for managing quality
7. Quality can be achieved only by a valued workforce; education, training and personal growth are essential to this
8. Quality has to be the criterion for reviewing every decision, every action and every process

---

Figure 6.2 Key features defining quality

Of all the points identified, the emphasis placed on continuous improvement through persistent attention to quality processes is vital in creating the right environment for a range of learning experiences to be selected and put in place.

❑ Learning experiences

While risking being pedantic, I wish firstly to draw attention to the plural nature of the word 'experience'. This is necessary 'ground clearing' in the sense that the Victorian 'experience' of learning was predominantly rote learning as a product of didactic instruction, (Gosden, 1969). Clearly the work of Piaget (1932) and Bruner (1966) has established the developmental nature of learning, while work by Duignan and Macpherson (1992) on educative leadership encourages teachers to consider the plurality of learning outcomes.

Perhaps all of this work is simply leading the way back to cherishing what the Hadow Report (1931) had to say about learning and the curriculum:

> The curriculum is to be thought of in terms of activity and experience rather than of knowledge to be acquired and facts to be stored.

Implications for senior and middle managers

If the Hadow recommendations for activity and experience in the curriculum are to be delivered it poses a challenge to senior managers because, in order to achieve *quality in learning*, there has to be *quality in management*. In stating this we are firmly back to recognizing the pursuit of quality as the conceptual glue holding together institutional mission. Defining 'vision for mission' is a fundamental task for the member of a senior management team who need to address the following key issues in terms of their roles:

- Offering visionary and empowering leadership
- Building self-managing teams
- Focusing on the pupil, student, customer
- Paying attention to fitness for purpose
- Trusting colleagues and recognising achievement
- Celebrating growth in excellence

Now it may be objected that all the above are somewhat grandiose in conceptions; strategy unhinged from tactical deployment. These objections can be met by tracing through particular issues. While returning in a later section to the responsibilities a SMT bears for creating appropriate management cultures, I focus first on pupil, student or *customer* experiences. If you are a senior manager of a school or college reading this now, do you know what your students did today? Have you a firm idea, not only of what they learned, but how they learned it? If you don't know, where and from whom could you find out? Might the process of finding out include asking students? I pose these questions because, having been involved in a series of OFSTED inspections, I have some reservations concerning what knowledge senior managers possess relating to student learning. Sitting in front of impressive year planners and voluminous budget statements, some heads give the impression of having acquired a grip of the budget while losing sight of the curriculum.

If this view is both partial and unfair, let me suggest two ways of checking on the learning realities operating within a teaching institution. First a little

MBAW — Management by Walking About — will tell you an awful lot about what is actually going on as compared with what you might think or wish to be going on. Secondly, conducting a *pupil pursuit* can be a sobering way of monitoring learning experiences. Pupil pursuit involves tracking one pupil, at random, across a whole day within your school. If further time can be found (and you are feeling especially brave) the exercise can be continued for a week or longer. In a primary school which honestly believed it had 'customer first' policies in place, outcomes from pupil pursuits resulted in a series of sharply focused questions from children.

- Why do we have to have playtimes?
- What are withdrawal groups for?
- Why are dinner ladies different from teachers?
- Why are teachers different from headteachers?

Such questions provide useful feedback on a child's view of school culture. Further analysis at the end of a tracking exercise regarding what the child actually did throughout the day provides an indicator of prevailing learning styles and outcomes. Such evaluation may demonstrate how rhetoric and reality may be at odds. At a primary school which prided itself on pursuing progressive approaches to curriculum learning, an analysis of one week's activities showed an overwhelming proportion of pupils learning passively. Two–thirds of all class time across the school was devoted to listening, copying and writing. While staff were initially shocked they quickly came to appreciate the variables at work in this situation. Left to their own devices teachers will often unconsciously drift towards the 'comfort zone' of safe methods and predictable learning products, such as writing, because these are validated by pupils and parents. Passivity and formality in learning may therefore be prompted in part by a mixture of teacher exhaustion and pupil–parent approval (Lofthouse 1989).

I once had a tutor who, when you had spent half an hour constructing an elegant hypothesis, would look up and say 'so what?'. Addressing the same salutary question to this discussion, the following points are critical:

- Senior managers need to *Know* the range and quality of learning experiences being offered to their students. Knowing in these circumstances is not the same as wishful thinking
- Knowing involves *monitoring*, monitoring means putting in place *curriculum* and *learning reviews*, consistently and persistently
- Unless senior managers focus on the customer, and empower self-managing teams to meet customer/student needs, there will be a

regression to the mean in terms of time devoted to *passive* rather than *active* learning activities and outcomes

• If senior managers fail to *develop* their staff the above *regression* will be more *certain*, more *severe* and more difficult to *reverse*

All of these perspectives bring us to the potentially unenviable position occupied by middle managers. The huge 'down loading' of responsibilities to institutions, which has been a feature of the late eighties, has been accompanied by a rise in expectations. Expectations of school performance rise as more is expected from less, namely higher quality at lower unit costs. Harassed senior managers faced by such demands have often participated in what I call the 'hot rivet game'. Catch a rivet (the latest initiative) throw it on — don't worry too much where it lands — you have shifted it. However, if the hot rivet goes to hand, it is invariable the middle manager who catches it.

Such an experience can be distressing, especially in a traditionally organized school where downward delegation may be regarded as a sop to collegiality. In these circumstances the middle manager is delegated responsibility without authority, a situation not unfamiliar to some curriculum co-ordinators in primary schools. All co-ordinators are faced with the daunting task of attempting to connect their curriculum and learning responsibilities into a wider pattern of school and curriculum development planning. Heads of department in secondary schools and course leaders in colleges confront the same issues. All frequently have too little *time* for their tasks, a problem which compounds difficulties of access to *resources* (Edwards, 1993). Such tokenism is unhelpful in enabling middle managers to come to terms with the complexities associated with implementing policies for learning. Lacking genuinely collaborative structures, any middle manager is likely to find him or herself between a 'rock and a hard place', namely senior managers and the foot soldiers. In such trying circumstances the temptation for middle managers is to *limit* their responsibilities, so as to concentrate on classroom activities.

Making middle managers successful

In the context of an extensive literature detailing the problems associated with being a middle manager (Nicholls 1983, Firth 1985, Everard and Morris 1985) what factors promoting successful intermediate management can be identified? One very important ingredient is *clarity* of purpose and vision offered by senior managers. If ways forward are made clear to all, the next step is to ensure that those who define the *ends* establish the *means*. In terms of managing middle managers, this invariably means that they need to be allocated *time* and adequate *resources* to pursue their tasks. Time and resources, properly delegated, are powerful factors promoting cycles of good practice where achievement fuels institutional improvement. In such virtuous cycles, the middle manager is trusted and supported, support being both a recognition of what is being achieved and a catalyst for developing the middle manager further.

New cultures for self-managing schools

New cultures are emerging in schools. In the chapter on 'Managing the Curriculum', a Lawtonian model of cultural analysis for curriculum selection is described. Lawton's (1990) models are more illuminating if they are integrated and compared with models of *management cultures*. Fullan and Hargreaves (1992) clearly encapsulate contemporary shifts in emphasis (see Figure 6.3).

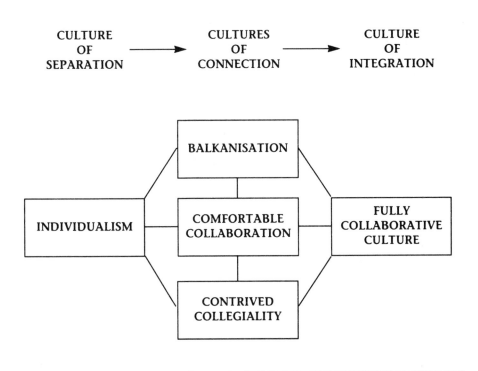

Figure 6.3 Management cultures (Day et al. 1993, p.9)

The cultures of separation, connection and integration in the diagram need further explanation. This is offered by Day, et al. (1993) from which this typology is drawn. For the purposes of this analysis a number of brief but salient points are sufficient. Hargreaves (1992, p.8) is sharply critical of the cult of teacher individualism, noting that under the guise of professional autonomy teachers continue:

> ... to teach largely within the isolated privacy of their own classrooms, insulated from observation and criticism ... are reluctant to share professional problems ... display the same anti–intellectual suspicions of talking seriously about education in general terms as opposed to gossiping about the particularities of school life

The sharpness of this comment may reflect something of Hargreaves' disappointment with school development planning having failed to achieve the promised gains in institutional improvement. While teachers may share both the blame and the sense of disappointment, a systems approach to school improvement relies on compatibility of systems. Sadly, if cogs don't connect they end up as fly wheels — driving nothing. Such an outcome is illustrated by *balkanisation* which is characterized by:

- Separate and competing groups whose first loyalty is to the group and its beliefs rather than those of the school, where these are different
- Squabbles over resources and territory
- Poor continuity and expectations of pupils (Fullan and Hargreaves, 1992)

❏ Comfortable collaboration and contrived collegiality

Management cultures may seduce teachers away from the excesses of individualism, yet still largely fail to capture the real potential of working in teams. For example, it is claimed in both cultures that planning is reactive rather than proactive and that the majority of teachers working within such systems have little contact with, or ownership of, theories and ideas generated outside the school or college. The central point is that the ideals of total quality management and educative leadership are best developed and expressed in *cultures of integration*, specifically fully collaborative cultures. Such cultures are characterized by:

- strong personal relationships (e.g. social interaction and cohesion)
- strong professional relationships (e.g. task–related working parties, curriculum leaders, paired teaching)
- commonly held social and moral intentions (e.g. beliefs about behaviour, pupil discipline)

- agreed curricular intentions (e.g. curriculum policy statements)
- failure and uncertainty are not protected or defended, but shared and discussed with a view to gaining help and support
- the individual and the group are simultaneously and inherently valued

The collective force of these six criteria is formidable — so formidable that senior managers in schools and colleges could be tempted to despair of ever achieving the ideal. Temptations towards despair should be tempered by situational analysis, a search for what might be achieved within 'the art of the possible'. Kanter develops a persuasive hypothesis that, 'excellence equals the capacity to change.' (Quoted in West–Burnham 1992, p.25). Applying this theory suggests that, once those pressures of change are initiated, teachers and schools join a moving continuum, where sharing in and evaluating change becomes a component of professionalism. In short, change becomes internalized, not as an event but as a process.

Once change becomes a process, the essential precondition has been achieved for managing learning in a dynamic sense. Assimilating change engages teachers in a process of *reflection*, a process which exposes and examines values, assumptions, personal and professional behaviours. Schon (1987) develops a model of reflection–on–action — a model I have described elsewhere (Lofthouse, 1993) as enabling teachers to consider action as thought and thought as action. The work of Schon, and modifications by Griffiths and Tann, (1991) are brought together in a five–level model of reflective practice, a matrix which enables teachers to move from consideration of the curriculum in action towards wider perspectives of the curriculum as concept (see Figure 6.4).

Reflection–in–action
1. Rapid reaction (instinctive, immediate)
2. Repair (habitual, pause for thought, on the spot)

Reflection–on–action
3. Review (time out to re–assess, over hours or days)
4. Research (systematic, sharply focused, over weeks or months)

Reflection–about–action
5. Re–theorise and re–formulate (abstract, vigorous, clearly formulated over months or years)

(Day et al. 1993, p.13).

Figure 6.4 A five-level model of reflective practice

These ways of seeing are important because they give teachers and senior managers a chance to confront the 'slings and arrows of outrageous fortune', described by Hoyle (1986) as, 'the contingent, the unexpected and the irrational' forces waiting to ambush the most rational of organizations. Hoyle's work on the *micropolitics* of organizations and management cultures has been a thorn in the flesh of systems and, particularly, management by objectives. The essence of Hoyle's argument is that behind images of organizational order and coherence, lurk irrational forces capable of creating disruption and disorder. If such forces develop unchecked, the result is likely to be institutional anarchy. Hoyle vividly describes this situation in terms of a window. The frame of the window constitutes the authority structure, the management model presented to the outside world. Within the frame are sections of glass, easily seen through and therefore easily disregarded. Hoyle argues that the glass constitutes the 'domain of micropolitics', partly invisible but in reality exerting a strong if uncertain influence upon the legitimate structure.

In attempting to pin down the nature of this influence, Hoyle (1982) defines micropolitics as, 'Strategies by which individuals and groups in organizational contexts seek to use their resources of authority and influence to further their interests'. Accepting this as a working definition, micropolitics is best perceived as a continuum, one end of which is virtually indistinguishable from conventional management but which at the other end, 'constitutes almost a separate organizational world of illegitimate, self-interested, manipulative interest sets' (Hoyle 1986, p.126).

This is clearly the area in which micropolitics is both most disruptive and most unacceptable on ethical grounds. The significant point is that on the map of management cultures, the destructive aspects of micropolitics thrive in those schools where individualism and balkanisation are dominant features. For example, in one large secondary school known to the author where the balkanisation of departments was both obvious and endemic, interminable rows concerning the proportion of subject time allocated on the time–table were understandable only in terms of recognizing that curriculum time equals staffing, resources and power. In bringing the struggle to a resolution, a great deal of organizational energy was dissipated. The result was seen in terms of 'winners' and 'losers' and only a select minority of staff knew what the game was. Bystanders experienced the discomfort of being dragged off the touch-line at critical points, and if, through lack of knowledge, they performed unsatisfactorily, were subsequently blamed for 'losing'.

Such games are clearly very expensive, in financial and human terms. However, in fully collaborative cultures they become redundant. A strong shared commitment to visible values, allied to openness of negotiated reflection on action, limits the need for teachers to participate in the 'cabals' and 'cliques' approach to curriculum planning identified by Hoyle (1986). While collaborative cultures on their own do not eradicate micro-politics, they do offer an environment where a resort to the darker dimensions of political activity becomes both unnecessary and a symbol of 'yesterday's culture'.

In terms of cultural shifts, schools and schooling are in danger of becoming antiquated, indeed being the principal representatives of 'yesterday's culture'. The theory of cultural lag — namely that most schools serve the needs of society as it was a decade ago, is being highlighted by the information explosion. In 1971 Ivan Illich wrote *Deschooling Society* and Everett Reimer declared, 'School is Dead' (1971). While parts of their thesis have been discounted, one central element continues to tick away like an unexploded bomb. Schools are very expensive places. The costs of schooling spiral upwards (Reimer 1971, pp.23–33). Therefore if you can obtain what is offered in schools more cheaply and more efficiently elsewhere, some very disturbing red lights are flashing with regard to the future of schooling.

This sense of impending danger is one of the reasons why this chapter has focused on the principles and frameworks of learning rather than devoting time to detailed discussions concerning the mechanisms of curriculum delivery. Not only are the latter dealt with extensively elsewhere (Easen 1985), but it is also the case that what is dealt with has a remarkably short shelf life. For example, Emerson and Goddard's (1984) book, describing the delivery of the National Curriculum in Britain, is now as much historical as contemporary in its analysis. Something more substantial than the shifting sands of practice is required and Bruner (1966, p.206) has supplied an important signpost:

> There is a dilemma in describing a course of study. One must begin by setting forth the intellectual substance of what is to be taught, else there can be no sense of what challenges and shapes the curiosity of the student. Yet the moment one succumbs to the temptation to 'get across' the subject, at that moment the ingredient of pedagogy is in jeopardy. For it is only in a trivial sense that one gives a course to 'get something across', merely to impart information. There are better means to that end than teaching. Unless the learner also masters himself, disciplines his taste, deepens his view of the world, the 'something' that is got across is hardly worth the effort of transmission.

Bruner is powerfully suggesting here that teaching is in jeopardy once it succumbs to the temptation of imparting knowledge. I would suggest that the future of education is seriously in jeopardy if teaching is more important than student learning.

135

Further reading

Those seeking models relating to learning need to consult:

Bruner, J. (1966) *Towards a Theory of Instructions*, Harward University Press.

If you are equally interested in learning and managing learning, a book which achieves a good balance is:

Bennett, N., Desforges, C., Cockburn, A., and Wilkinson, B. (1984), *The Quality of Pupil Learning Experiences*, NJ: Lawrence Erlbaum.

For those mainly interested in managing learning two books are recommended:

Nicholls, A. (1983) *Managing Educational Innovations*, London: George Allen and Unwin.

Day, C., Hall,C., Gammage, P. and Coles, M. (1993) *Leadership and Curriculum in the Primary School:The Roles of Senior and Middle Management*, London: Paul Chapman Publishing.

Two general texts which convey a more focused interest in secondary schools and associated management theories are:

Firth, D. (Ed) (1985) *School Management in Practice*, Harlow: Longman.

Everard, K.B. and Morris, G. (1985), *Effective School Management*, London: Harper Row.

Both of these texts should be compared with more recent work embodied in:

Duigan, P.A. and Macpherson, R.J.S. (1992), *Educative Leadership: A Practical Theory for New Administrators and Managers*, London: Falmer Press.

References

Alexander, R.J. (1985) *Primary Education in Leeds*, University of Leeds.

Ball, S.J. (1987) *The Micro–Politics of the School: Towards a Theory of School Organization*, London: Methuen.

Bennett, N. (1976) *Teaching Styles and Pupil Progress*, London: Open Books.

Blackie, J. (1963) *Good Enough for the Children*, London: Faber, pp.51–53.

Blyth, W.A.L. (1988) *Learning is More Important than Teaching*, Occasional Paper, University of Leicester.

Bruner, J. (1966) *Towards a Theory of Instruction*, Harvard University Press. p.206.

Caldwell, B., and Spinks, J. (1992) *Leading the Self-Managing School*, London: Falmer Press.

Calvert, B. (1975) *The Role of the Pupil*, London: Routledge and Kegan Paul. pp.1–7.

Day, C., Hall, C., Gammage, P. and Coles, M. (1993) *Leadership and Curriculum in the Primary School*, London: Paul Chapman Publishing.

Duignan, P.A. and Macpherson, R.J.S. (1992) *Educative Leadership: A Practical Theory for New Administrators and Managers*, London: Falmer Press. pp.1–85.

Easen, P. (1985) *Making School Centred INSET Work*, London: Croom Helm. See also, Southworth, G. and O'Shea, A. (1992) *Management of Learning in Schools*, Milton Keynes: Open University Press.

Edwards, A. (1993) 'Curriculum co-ordination: a lost opportunity for primary development?' *School Organisation*, **13**, 1,. pp.51–59.

Emerson, C. and Goddard, I. (1989) *All About the National Curriculum*, London: Heinemann.

Everard, K.B. and Morris, G. (1985) *Effective School Management*, London: Harper Row. pp.1–25.

Firth, D. (1985) *School Management in Practice*, Harlow: Longman.,

Fullan M. and Hargreaves, A. (1992) *What's Worth Fighting For in Your School?*, Milton Keynes: Open University Press.

Galton M. (1980) *Inside the Primary School*, London: Routledge.

Gosden, P.H.J.H. (1969) *How They Were Taught*, Oxford: Basil Blackwell. pp.33–76.

Griffiths, M. and Tanns, S. (1991) 'Ripples in the reflection' in Lomas, P. (Ed), *BERA Dialogues*, 5, pp.82–101.

Habermas, J. (1972) *Knowledge and Human Interests*, London: Heinemann. pp.56–89.

Hadow Report (1931) *The Primary School*, HMSO.

Hargreaves, D. (1992) *The New Professionalism: The Synthesis of Professional and Institutional Development*. Keynote Paper at Fourth International Symposium: Effective Teachers, Effective Schools, University of New England, NSW Australia, July 1992.

Hargreaves, D. and Hopkins D. (1991) *The Empowered School*, London: Cassell.

Hoyle, E. (1982) *Micropolitics of Educational Organisations*, British Educational Management and Administration Society, **10**, 2, pp.87–98.

Hoyle, E. (1986) *The Politics of School Management*, London: Hodder and Stoughton.

Illich, I. (1971) *Deschooling Society*, Harmondsworth: Penguin Books.

Lawton, D. (1990) *Education, Culture and the National Curriculum*. pp.86–87.

Lofthouse, M.T. (1989) *Crisis Management*, University of Leicester.

Lofthouse, M.T. (1993) *Teaching an Active Curriculum*, University of Leicester.

Musgrave, P.W. (1972) *The Sociology of Education*, London: Methuen .

Nicholls, A. (1983) *Managing Educational Innovations*, London: George Allen and Unwin.

Piaget, J. (1932) *The Moral Judgement of the Child*, London: Routledge and Kegan Paul. pp.411–12.

Reimer, E. (1971) *School is Dead*, Harmondsworth: Penguin.

Schon, D.A. (1987) *Educating the Reflective Practitioner*, San Francisco: Jossey–Bass.

West-Burnham, J. (1992) *Managing Quality in Schools*, Harlow: Longman.

7 Managing the curriculum

Mark Lofthouse

Introduction

'The school is the curriculum.' This simple but challenging definition, frequently used by HMI during school inspections, sums up the dilemmas facing anyone attempting the task of examining curriculum management. Do schools and colleges as institutions embody curriculum? If they do, which curriculum are we referring to? A National Curriculum? An academic curriculum? A vocational curriculum? The hidden curriculum?

This chapter addresses some of these questions. The opening section offers an historical perspective, where it is argued that fundamental issues concerning curriculum content and control are as contentious now as they were in early Greece. By reference to the work of Lawton and Kliebard the theme of curriculum ambiguity is developed. In this section it is suggested that curriculum content and methods of delivery can be interpreted only through an analysis of pressure groups striving to achieve curriculum control. In this confusing and contested context, the central part of the chapter examines what senior managers and curriculum co-ordinators need to do in order to manage the curriculum successfully. A major performance indicator of how successful they are in this formidable task is identified in the conclusion, namely how far real curriculum coherence and integration can be achieved.

The curriculum: a historical perspective

Who should teach what to whom has always been a contentious issue. Aristotle, (undated) writing in Book Eight of *The Politics*, lamented;

> At present there are differences of opinion as to the proper tasks to be set, for all peoples do not agree as to the things that the young ought to learn.

The passing centuries have done little to answer the dilemmas Aristotle posed. Pondering the proportions of time that should be properly allocated for students to follow 'pursuits that are practically useful' as compared with activities ' which are morally edifying', Aristotle initiated a debate that shows no sign of diminishing. Is the curriculum primarily a means of transmitting useful knowledge? Or does the curriculum have a moral dimension, where process is as important as content in shaping both the learner and the future citizen? In wishing the curriculum to serve more and more purposes, Aristotle was possibly the first, but certainly not the last, to promote what is currently identified as curriculum overload.

Overload is, in part, an outcome of the increasing sophistication and complexity of contemporary societies. In his book *The Struggle for the American Curriculum 1893–1958*, Herbert Kliebard (1987) examines the campaigns waged by four major pressure groups to achieve curriculum dominance in America during the opening half of the twentieth century. None of the interest groups, he argues, ever achieved total curriculum domination. In order to describe the ebb and flow of curriculum ideas Kliebard (p.208) asks us to think of a stream with several channels and varying currents:

> None ever completely dries up. When the weather and other conditions are right, a weak or insignificant current assumes more force and prominence, only to decline when conditions conducive to its new found strength no longer prevail.

The significance of Kliebard's analysis is his willingness to acknowledge, within the field of curriculum studies, ambiguities caused by overlapping and competing agendas. While Aristotle worried about the relationship of useful knowledge to moral principles, Kliebard examines the problematic nature of social efficiency, determinism and developmental models in contemporary curriculum planning. This willingness to engage with complex and multiple realities should encourage, rather than depress, teachers and managers everywhere. Instead of claiming simplicity where there is none to be found, Kliebard accurately defines the difficulties facing teachers when curriculum choices have to be made, choices which can no longer please everyone. The major task facing any curriculum manager is one of defining priorities. In undertaking this task Kliebard asserts that teachers will no longer hear a dominant voice, only a chorus of dominant voices. Pressure groups, parents, pupils and politicians all jostle for the right to shape the curriculum. In the midst of this debate the professional voice is now one among many.

A feature of the post-industrial society is the speed with which information can be distributed directly to institutions. The work of Schon (1971) and others on 'forward mapping' strategies suggests that centralized decision-making now results in the policies of the few being transmitted directly into the work place, school or college for implementation. For good or ill, teachers are no longer shielded or fettered by intervening layers of bureaucracy. The tasks of interpretation and delivery now fall to them. The net result, argues Kliebard (1977, p.262) is that on a yearly, termly and daily basis teachers are confronted with four critical questions:

1. Why should we teach this rather than that?
2. Who should have access to this knowledge?
3. What rules should govern the teaching of what has been selected?
4. How should parts of the curriculum be interrelated in order to create a coherent whole?

Although first posed in 1977, Kliebard's questions are excellent bench-marks for those seeking to understand the applied nature of curriculum theory. In the light of the curriculum context set out by Kliebard, it is now possible to examine more closely current issues facing curriculum managers.

The curriculum: making it work

Teachers are extremely busy people. Not unreasonably, they expect curriculum theories to be embedded in daily realities. Unfortunately, such is the business for all concerned, one person's view of reality is another person's vision of fantasy. In short, the view from the bridge is different from that in the engine room. Although this may appear a commonsense homily, it is nevertheless critically important for members of a senior management team (SMT) to be aware of the perils of curriculum overload and associated initiative fatigue. Such difficulties can be avoided by attention to forward planning and to the allocation and delegation of curriculum responsibilities. The 1988 Education Reform Act places upon the governing body and the headteacher primary responsibility for formulating a curriculum strategy. How these responsibilities are shared is identified in Figure 7.1.

In reflecting on the table it is important to note that the weight of mandatory legislation concerning curriculum allocation places upon the Head and SMT a 'first order' priority to ensure that a school is fulfilling its legal obligations. Increasing numbers of school inspections carried out under OFSTED regulations serve to point up just how many schools fail to conform to the law, notably in their provision for acts of collective worship.

The process of monitoring the curriculum for legality provides opportunities for a more pro-active stance to be achieved in relation to curriculum

Governing Body

Decides curriculum policy taking into account the National Curriculum, the LEA Curriculum Policy Statement and the view of the school and community

Approves arrangements for sex education and RE

Confirms the delivery of the curriculum and receives reports

Decides the number of staff required to deliver the curriculum

Headteacher

Proposes a detailed curriculum plan after consultation within the school which ensures delivery of the statutory elements

Organises the delivery of the curriculum; monitors and reports

Advises on number and skills of staff needed

Figure 7.1 Division of responsibilities for the curriculum (Hilditch 1993, p.162)

mapping. Given the pressures of time which have been intensified by National Curriculum orders, senior staff have a critical role to play in ensuring the efficient and effective deployment of curriculum time. In achieving this, curriculum strategy is translated into curriculum implementation. The transformation is not easy, not least because it is likely to bring into question all of the following factors:

Timing and organization of the school year and school day

Balance of time devoted to National Curriculum core subjects and cross curricular themes

Progression of the curriculum across Key Stage Assessments in relation to whole school assessment policies

Financial management and budgetary policies and practice, including deployment and payment of teaching and non-teaching support staff

Relationship of curriculum planning to school development plan, staff development plan, projected pupil profile and numbers

While this list can be extended, it is more important to define priorities. A senior management team needs to ensure that the curriculum is well planned, that changes are implemented and delivery is monitored. (Hilditch, 1993, p.162).

Curriculum co-ordinators play a key role in organizing, delivering and monitoring. In this context senior managers and curriculum co-ordinators have shared responsibilities for ensuring that staff have access to, and where appropriate, shared ownership of, curriculum process and content. As more and more schools become self-managing, curriculum planning increasingly becomes integrated into a pattern of *curriculum as process*. In these circumstances, all staff need to have a clear understanding of how, when and where curriculum policies and reviews are negotiated and planned (Caldwell and Spinks, 1992). While detailed planning models for achieving this process are available, (Hilditch 1993, p.163) it is unwise to be too prescriptive. Self-governing schools will develop their own systems. In the primary sector, where any form of planning competes for time with teaching, over-elaborate planning models are precisely the kind of devices which give theory a bad name.

Curriculum players and pressure groups

Theory and practice inform each other because 'theory without practice is sterile, practice without theory is blind'. However, if theory is to sustain its place in the partnership, practitioners need to be assured of its relevance. During the sixties and seventies it was customary for every book written on curriculum studies to commence with an exhaustive list of curriculum definitions. While the pursuit of definitions still has philosophic fascination, utilitarian benefits are more limited because cultural pluralism now suggests that one perfect, composite definition of the curriculum is unlikely ever to be found. In practical terms this means that any school manager or teacher has strong reasons to embrace multiple aims for the curriculum. In arriving at these, curriculum managers need to know more than a string of definitions. Particularly useful to the curriculum manager is a knowledge of the players and pressure groups active in the curriculum field. It is these groups, each with a curriculum emphasis and ideological preoccupation, who set the framework in which curriculum debates are resolved. The following groupings are derived from an analysis of the positions adopted by interested parties as defined by Kliebard (1977), Lawton (1975) and set out in a typology by Duignan and Macpherson (1992):

Neo-classical or humanists Represented by Hirst et al. (1974) and remembered for their 'forms of knowledge' approach to the curriculum. Often perceived as the guardians of cultural tradition, a tradition founded on reason and defended via objectivist–absolutist values. In placing emphasis on the conservation of an authoritative cultural tradition, the neo-classical definition of curriculum stresses the need for curriculum to embody worthwhile knowledge.

Vocational Emphasis placed on instrumental values where the needs of the individual are subordinated to the requirements of society. Employment and enterprise are perceived as vital to the growth of a free-enterprise society. With over-riding weight placed on individual survival through employment, vocational definitions of the curriculum stress the transmission of useful knowledge.

Liberal-meritocratic Believing in competitive equality of opportunity, members of this group can trace back affiliations to nineteenth century Liberalism. By embracing notions of a minimal state, liberal-meritocratic definitions of the curriculum accentuate the need for pupils to acquire personal autonomy within a framework of egalitarian freedoms.

Liberal-progressive In contrast to the above, this group embraces an interventionist as opposed to a minimalist state. Welcoming individual development, self-expression and cultural pluralism, this group looks to the state to encourage tolerance and understanding rather than competition and elitism. This group would promote a definition of the curriculum which places personal autonomy in the context of social and cultural harmony.

Socially critical Deriving from the work of Habermas (1972) and Kemmis et al. (1983), this group advocates that teachers, schools and the education system need to adopt a critical stance towards society. Believing that schools can and should change society, this group defines curriculum in terms of encouraging social change through educational action.

Religious Proponents of religious values test secular knowledge against the development within the individual of a system of beliefs and values. Frequently the latter derive from historic positions and seminal texts. Members of this group place secular knowledge in the context of transcendental values and wish the curriculum to explicitly convey spiritual values and beliefs.

Pragmatic Extensively reviewed and commended by Walker (1992) in his chapter 'A philosophy of leadership in curriculum development', from where this typology is drawn. Citing Dewey as intellectual originator, Walker commends a pragmatic stance to curriculum planning. He argues that a pragmatic stance to planning enables a proper focus to be placed upon coherent and mutually productive problem-solving and learning capacities of individuals and social groups.

The implications for school managers of all these curriculum players and pressure groups is to underline the changing and contested nature of the curriculum. For example, in Britain curriculum control currently shifts uneasily between cultural restoration policies as argued by humanists and the claims of vocationalists. From the clash of interested parties the only certainty to emerge is the unresolved nature of the curriculum.

All of the groups referred to exhibit a range of strengths and weaknesses. Given the evident difficulties associated with all the groupings explored, it is fatally easy to end up by default in the pragmatist camp. While Walker makes a persuasive case his claims upon Dewey as an originator and advocate of pragmatism are open to interpretation. As Kliebard (1977) is at pains to point out, Dewey was an enigmatic figure whose intellectual legacy is both exaggerated and flawed. However, it was Dewey who presciently predicted a pattern of 'oscillating between extremes' which is now only too evident in political approaches to curriculum planning. Without a firm grip on values it could be argued that pragmatism merely enables teachers to adjust to the 'violent enthusiasms' which Dewey both predicted and deplored.

In Britain in the 1990s, violent enthusiasms tend to be transmuted into legislative policy statements. No curriculum would last beyond a week if teachers and managers took seriously the ever increasing flood of prescriptive advice offered by politicians and pressure groups. Thus the role of 'gate keeper' has fallen upon senior staff, who have to take on the uncomfortable but necessary task of selection. In the field of curriculum studies senior managers have to weigh competing claims and, as Duignan and Macpherson (1992) argue, can do so only on the basis of extensive knowledge. An example is the issue of curriculum definitions. It is not difficult to perceive how uncomfortably neo-classical and vocational interpretations of the curriculum rub up against each other. If neo-classicists believe that the prime function of the curriculum is to initiate pupils into areas of worthwhile knowledge how does this fit with a vocationalist insistence that the curriculum is the vehicle for the transmission of useful knowledge? Any practitioner is left pondering, what is worthwhile and what is useful knowledge.

In answering difficult questions, teachers and managers might be wise to seek for *inclusive* as opposed to *exclusive* curriculum definitions. The problem with all the interest groups identified is that they each wish to say that the curriculum is more like this and less like that, whatever that is. Partiality is therefore the inevitable consequence. The temptations to be partial, or exclusive, are strong. Where a school decides that its curriculum is based on 'presented instructional content', they limit at a stroke their collective responsibilities to organized teaching. Does organized teaching, though, logically represent the curriculum of any school? Unfortunately, it is rather like a car owner saying that he or she will be responsible for the engine but has no interest in the bodywork. Inclusive definitions generally offer a more comprehensive portrait of the complex realities of contemporary schooling, but at the risk of making teachers responsible for areas such as 'the hidden curriculum'.

Cultural shifts and cultural mapping

Whether teachers accept responsibility or not for something as nebulous as the hidden curriculum, the contemporary thrust of worldwide legislation is creating a climate in which teachers and schools are being held accountable for curriculum delivery. Their collective task is made easier, or more difficult, by government legislation to 'nationalize curricula'. By invoking a national and therefore overriding interest, governments put in place some form or forms of national curricula. The key features of such curricula are:

- They embody and reflect perceived *national* needs and interests
- They are invariably conceived, administered and legislated for by *centralized* bodies and institutions
- Advances in information technology enable central policies to be transmitted directly to *autonomous* institutions
- Such 'forward mapping' strategies render intervening *bureaucrats* redundant

The interaction of the above factors provides curriculum leaders with a management context finely balanced between threat and promise. The threat is to accept the imposing monolith of a National Curriculum without ever owning it. Passive managers may arrive too quickly at a situation where curriculum orders, plus assessment regulations, equal curriculum. In one bound we are back to a situation where timetable equals curriculum. Such an outcome may arise when the power and persistence of cultural shifts are under-estimated. The monolithic structures of all forms of national curricula are more imposing than real. In Britain since the National Curriculum was first introduced one hundred and sixty–eight changes have been made during a two–year period, and it can be anticipated that the rate of such changes will increase (Finegold et al. 1993, pp.90–28). This prediction is based on the premise that any curriculum reflects competing claims within society and all societies are now subject to ever increasing rates of change. What was useful knowledge yesterday, may be redundant facts to-day.

While all of this may be threatening at a national level, the promise for self-governing schools is to achieve institutional curriculum coherence within a network of national frameworks. By reference to the latter (which by definition will reflect cultural shifts) teachers and managers can apply to their own school or college situational analysis derived from *cultural mapping*. Lawton (1975) argues that curriculum is a selection from the culture of society and this selection should be appropriate for all children. In order for curriculum to be accessible to all, Lawton examines the social and anthropological definition of culture as everything created by and within society. If this inclusive definition is adopted, Lawton argues that the way is cleared for a common curriculum to be built on the basis of cultural analysis. He suggests a five stage process of selection (see Figure 7.2).

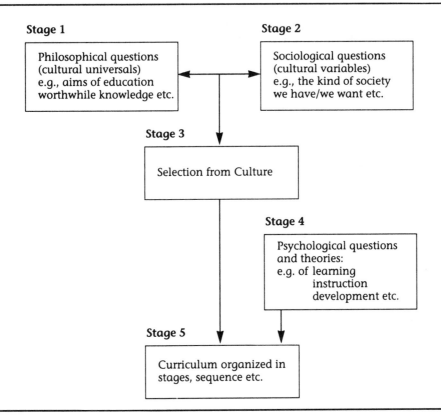

Figure 7.2 Curriculum planning: five stages of selection (Lawton, 1975)

❑ Curriculum planning: five stages of selection

By adopting this approach to curriculum planning Lawton has been a consistent advocate of a common, classless curriculum. Whether such a curriculum is either obtainable or desirable is still a matter of fierce controversy. In the context of this chapter, what is important about Lawton's approach is that it places in the hands of curriculum managers a useful analytical tool. Cultural analysis, applied at institutional level, offers one means of achieving and 'tooling up' ongoing processes of curriculum review. At a local level it compliments and, in a limited sense, replicates what has been identified as cultural shifts at national levels.

While Lawton's methods remain relevant and useful to teachers responsible for curriculum planning, his advocacy of a common curriculum has come under increasing attack. Criticism of his stance invariably derives from the slippery nature of the word culture. While Lawton is prepared to build a curriculum based on an inclusive anthropological definition of culture, neo-classicists hanker after Matthew Arnold's (1869 [1960]) definition of culture as 'the best that has been thought and said'. This high-culture definition attracts attack because of the perception of curriculum being equated with cultural imperialism. Keddie (1976) and Midwinter (1972) offer the counter argument of cultural relativism, namely that cultures are different but equal. On the basis of this argument you are culturally deprived only if you feel deprived. The problematic nature of this position is highlighted by Bantock (1968). If you offer children a curriculum based on popular culture which they know and understand, do you condemn them to a lifetime of knowing only what they know as compared to offering them insights into what they may wish to discard? It is these contradictory arguments which fuel the sense of crisis currently enveloping the curriculum debate.

When Lawton advocated a common curriculum to be delivered by a comprehensive system of schools he mirrored a time during the sixties and early seventies when egalitarian reforms were in the ascendant. With reference back to Kliebard's (1977) analogy, the egalitarian stream has now practically dried up. It has been replaced by market-driven objectives which have gained a world-wide impetus. While the following points are taken from educational reform plans currently being advocated in New Zealand, they are easily replicated in both Europe and America:

1. The creation of self-governing schools

2. The reduction of bureaucracy

3. The introduction of objective and visible formula funding

4. The exposure of services to competition

5. The raising of standards through competition between schools and among pupils

6. The development of a 'national curriculum' with clearly defined and monitored assessment processes and targets (Shenstone 1993, p.489).

Galton (1993) traces the development of the above agenda in terms of its impact upon the primary sector. However, two overall perspectives seem relevant in terms of the whole curriculum debate. First, the collapse of communist, collectivist systems has spurred forward market solutions, even when these solutions sometimes appear irrelevant to the sectors where they are applied. Secondly, the revolution in information technology systems enables governments to drive forward reforms. By communicating directly with institutions, and by publishing data and assessments regionally and nationally, competition within and between institutions becomes an ever-present reality. In this sense, the discipline of the market and the alleged stimulus of private enterprise solutions are currently being injected into schools on a world-wide basis.

At the heart of these reforms lie unresolved tensions. In pejorative terms it appears that those who create the market also wish to rig the market. The imposition within the United Kingdom of a prescribed National Curriculum is at odds with free-market solutions. As a parent in Britain, if you send your child to a state school, you may choose your school but you cannot select your curriculum. Wherever you go only the National Curriculum is on offer. It is reminiscent of Henry Ford's sales pitch: you can choose any car as long as it's black.

These philosophical inconsistencies are explained by Skidelsky (1993) in terms of the ideological complexity of modern conservatism. The tendencies towards market individualism and utilitarianism within conservative doctrines, argues Skidelsky, are now being tempered by 'a prescriptive moral appreciation of what constitutes right and wrong'. This latter prescriptive element means that in the field of education the market cannot be trusted to deliver the right solutions. Intervention in, and interference with, the market therefore becomes commonplace. Hence the very hasty imposition of a National Curriculum in the United Kingdom and the creation of ever tighter regulatory frameworks to monitor its delivery. While Skidelsky identified inconsistencies, a Marxist interpretation would point to a system designed to promote and establish social control while pretending to offer the illusion of choice.

149

For those who have to implement centrally prescribed systems, a number of issues becomes clearer by the day. Many programmes of study are in reality the vehicles for testable attainment targets. The collection of test data enables any central authority to monitor the progress of pupils and, by implication, test the efficiency of the school and the teachers working within it. Reactions to this regime depend on how far any individual considers it right and proper for publicly funded institutions and their staff to be held accountable in terms of measured outcomes. It is an ongoing debate but the Victorian experience within the area of state education is not an encouraging precedent. The imposition of Robert Lowe's Revised Code, which set up a system of 'payment by results', led to widespread cheating and collusion among teachers and their pupils. The ever increasing time and cost devoted to monitoring the application of the Code in schools, led to its abandonment.

Reference to an example culled from the history of education raises an issue also bearing on current reforms. Aldrich (1990) has deftly pointed out how the presently formulated National Curriculum in Britain almost exactly replicates recommendations issued by the Board of Education in 1907. While this provides the most startling example of historical revisionism, other notable examples are apparent in France, the United States and New Zealand.

The curriculum: back to the future?

It appears that as we approach the twenty first century, there is a widespread desire among politicians and the public to return to the apparent simplicity of earlier times. Three aspects in particular appear to exercise a continuing appeal. First, the simplicity and clarity of a curriculum based on subjects and the opportunity this affords of making curriculum equal timetable. Secondly, the clear cut moral purposes embodied within nineteenth century curricula. Thirdly, the tractable and docile qualities fostered in both pupils and teachers working within an elementary system. Whether these attributes still serve, or more importantly, can still be invoked within contemporary societies, is uncertain.

Towards a new vocationalism?

The viability and credibility of re-inventing 'old' for 'new' policies is nowhere more evident than in contemporary debates concerning vocational curricula. At the beginning of *Hard Times* (Dickens, [1854] 1961) Mr. Gradgrind demanded a curriculum founded on facts:

Teach these boys and girls nothing but facts. Facts alone are wanted in life. Plant nothing else and root out everything else.

This rooting-out process is a feature of pressure groups associated with vocationalism, so much so that the new Gradgrinds demand a curriculum founded on skills and competencies, a curriculum of 'proving by doing.' Such an approach has a powerful, if flawed, internal logic. Competency-based learning, as presently incorporated within systems of national vocational qualifications, offers a much needed alternative to the academicism prevalent within traditional 'A' level routes. The vocationalists' insistence upon active learning and skills-based approaches has served to open up the curriculum. It is no accident that modularity and individual action-planning first made progress within an FE sector offering distinctive, alternative learning approaches for those students unable or unwilling to pursue the 'fur–lined rut' of 'A' levels in the sixth form. In this instance, vocationalists can rightly claim to have shifted the curriculum emphasis from inputs towards outcomes, from an emphasis upon the pure acquisition of knowledge towards its application and demonstration.

It can be argued that many things are virtuous until carried to excess. The flawed internal logic of vocationalism derives from an excessive faith in believing that doing equals knowing. Smithies (1993a), in a sharply worded attack on the vocationalist agenda, argues that NVQs are designed to measure what people can already do rather than what they might do. Unsupported by something more demanding than competency- based assessments, Smithies argues that NVQs perpetuate a low skills, low expectations curriculum. Predicting that Britain is on the road towards a training disaster of epic proportions, Smithies claims that vocationalist obsessions with assessing competencies, 'relegate knowledge and understanding to the dustbins of academe' (Smithies, 1993b, p.6). The National Council for Vocational Qualifications, while protesting at the ferocity of Smithies' attack, offers little in terms of refuting the main points, namely that testing does not equal learning and doing does not equal knowing (NCVQ 1993, p.14). All of which leaves the two parties shouting at each other across a curriculum chasm. While both parties possess part of the truth, both ignore the necessity of achieving curriculum integration.

In terms of this curriculum debate, and especially issues relating to managing the curriculum, it is significant that a newly published book is entitled, *The Quest for Coherence*, (Weston et al. 1992). Achieving curriculum coherence seems to be the nub issue facing teachers in schools and colleges. Evidence from this chapter demonstrates how curriculum policies change in relationship to cultural movements, nationally and locally. Change is the key word because managing the curriculum has become another facet of managing change (Bennett et al. 1992, p.8). Evidence from this field provides two key points for curriculum leaders. First, practice makes perfect. While change can be threatening, participating in successful change empowers teachers to manage change. (Fullan, in Hoyle and McMahon 1986, pp.73-86). Secondly, as West-Burnham (1992, p.1) points out this latter phrase itself needs alteration:

> The important thing is not to manage change but to change the way we manage .

This is a powerful message at a time when unprecedented degrees of autonomy are being granted to schools. It argues that curriculum leaders are the authors of their own destinies.

Practitioners may protest that in the field of curriculum their autonomy is heavily circumscribed by national legislation. However, it has often been observed that, 'the law was made for the obedience of fools and the guidance of wise men and women'. A number of state as well as private schools are already demonstrating an ability to interpret rather than to obey centrally prescribed legislation. They are wise to do so because time is on their side. The logical end point of some 1990s reforms is a free market in which all schools are 'private schools', working within the freedoms and constraints of a market economy.

Good managers, in the private and public sectors, offer their institutions a sense of coherence and structure. In schools, structures have to deliver excellent quality learning experiences for pupils. How these are to be organized and achieved is the central topic of chapter 6. But within the curriculum domain it suggests that teachers have to be sharply aware of curriculum content and process and be able to apply tools of analysis to establish appropriate curriculum mapping. Teachers can do this only on the basis of extensive knowledge and a persistent willingness, individually and collectively, to pay attention to quality, especially the quality of pupil learning experiences.

In a sense nothing has changed since Aristotle considered the curriculum riddle, and yet everything has changed. One startling aspect of the reforms of the 1990s is that the rush to implement devolved powers to schools places upon teachers the responsibility to be their own Aristotle. In terms of being both practitioner and philosopher, the ideas embodied in educative leadership, and extensively referred to in this chapter, have much to offer teachers. But the stakes are high. As Macpherson points out, quality does not come cheap. It demands of teachers a willingness to engage in thought as action and action as thought. Viewed in this context, applied theory is not some kind of idle luxury to be dispensed with at the earliest opportunity. Owned and articulated theory is at the heart of quality schooling.

There is a well know slogan, 'If you think education is expensive, try ignorance'. Black (1993, p.137) has added a salutary rider:

> If you think the serious study of education is a waste of time, try educational policy based on prejudice.

Further reading

Collections of writings on the theme of managing the curriculum include:

Preedy, M. (Ed) (1989) *Approaches to Curriculum Management*, Milton Keynes: Open University Press.

Weston, P., Barratt, E. and Jamison, J. (1992) *The Quest for Coherence: Managing the Whole Curriculum 5–16*, National Foundation for Educational Research, Berkshire.

Curriculum issues linked to management dimensions are considered in:

Duignan, P.A. and Macpherson, R.J.S.(1992) *Educative Leadership, A Practical Theory for New Administrators and Managers*, London: Falmer Press.

Day, C., Hall, C., Gammage, P. and Coles, M. (1993) *Leadership and Curriculum in the Primary School, The Role of Senior and Middle Management*, London: Paul Chapman Publishing.

Day, C., Whitaker, P. and Johnston, D. (1990), Managing Primary Schools in the 1990s: A Professional Development Approach, London: Paul Chapman Publishing.

Particular approaches to curriculum planning are considered by:

Hilditch, B. (1993) *Managing the Curriculum* in Green, H. (Ed) *The School Management Handbook*, London: Kogan-Page.

West-Burnham, J. (1992), *Managing Quality in Schools*, Harlow: Longman.

A comparative review of curriculum development is offered by:

Holmes, B. and McLean, M. (1989) *The Curriculum: A Comparative Perspective*, London: Unwin Hyman.

Other recommended reading:

Eggleston, J. (1992) *The Challenge for Teachers*, London: Cassell.

Tomlinson, J. (1992) *The Control of Education*, London: Cassell.

Finegold, D., McFarland, L. and Richardson, W. (1993) *Something Borrowed, Something Blue? A Study of the Thatcher Government's Appropriation of American Education and Training Policy*, Oxford: Triangle Books.

References

Aldrich, R. (Ed) (1990) *History in the National Curriculum*, Institute of Education, London University.

Aristotle, *Politics* (Book 8) Loeb Classical Library.

Armytage, W.H.G. (1967) *The American Influence on English Education*, London: Routledge and Kegan Paul.

Arnold, M. (1869 [1960]) *Culture and Anarchy*, Cambridge University Press.

Bantock, G. H. (1968), *Culture, Industrialisation and Education*, London: Routledge and Kegan Paul.

Bennett, N., Crawford, M. and Riches, C.(1992), *Managing Change in Education*, Milton Keynes and London: The Open University and Paul Chapman Publishing.

Bennett, N., Desforges, C., Cockburn, A. and Wilkinson, B. (1984) *The Quality of Pupil Learning Experiences*, New Jersey: Lawrence Erlbaumn.

Black, P. (1993) in *Education*, 19 February.

Caldwell, B. and Spinks, J. (1992) Leading the Self Managing School, London: Falmer Press.

Dickens, C., (1854 [1961]) *Hard Times*, London: Everyman Edition, Dent and Son.

Duignan, P.A. and Macpherson, R.J.S. (1992) *A Practical Theory for New Administrators and Managers*, Lewes: Falmer Press.

Finegold, D., McFarland, L. and Richardson, W. (1993) *Something Borrowed, Something Blue? A Study of Thatcher Government's Appropriation of American Education and Training Policy*. Oxford: Triangle Books.

Galton, M. (1993) *Crisis in the Primary Classroom*, David Fulton.

Habermas, J. (1972) *Knowledge and Human Interests*, London: Heinemann.

Hirst, P.H. (1974) *Knowledge and the Curriculum*, London: Routledge and Kegan Paul.

Hirst, P.H. and Peters, R.S. (1970) *The Logic of Education*, London: Routledge and Kegan Paul.

Hoyle, E. and McMahon, A. (1986), *The Management of Schools*, London: Kogan Page.

Keddie, N. (1973) *Tinker, Taylor. The Myth of Cultural Deprivation*, Harmondsworth: Penguin.

Kemmis, S., Cole, P. and Suggett, D. (1983) 'Towards the socially critical school', Melbourne, Victorian Institute of Secondary Education, in Walker, J.C. *A Philosophy of Leadership in Curriculum Development*, ibid. Duignan and Macpherson.

Kliebard, H.M. (1977) *Curriculum Theory: Give me an Instance*, Curriculum Inquiry 6, 4, p.262.

Kliebard, H.M. (1987) *The Struggle for the American Curriculum, 1893–1958*, London: Routledge and Kegan Paul.

Lawton, D. (1975) *Class Culture and the Curriculum*, London: Routledge and Kegan Paul.

Lawton, D. (1980) *The Politics of the School Curriculum*, London: Routledge and Kegan Paul.

Lawton, D. (1983) *Curriculum Studies and Educational Planning*, London: Hodder and Stoughton.

Midwinter, E. (1972) *Priority Education*, Harmondsworth: Penguin.

Morgan, G. (1990) *Riding the Wares of Change*, Oxford: Jossey Bass.

Schon, D. (1971) *Beyond the Stable State*, New York.

Shenstone, M. (1993) 'The mirror of reform '. *Education*, 25 June.

Short, J., (1993) 'How will colleges manage?' *TES*, 10 December , p.23.

Skidelsky, Lord (1993) 'Test knowledge but not values'. *TES*, 30 July.

Smithies, A., (1993a) *All Our Futures: Britain's Education Revolution*, Gatsby Foundation and University of Manchester.

Smithies, A., (1993b) 'U.K. set for training disaster'. *TES*, 17 December, p.6.

Walker, J.C. (1992) 'A philosophy of leadership in curriculum development: a pragmatic and holistic approach' in Duignan, P.A. and Macpherson, R.J. (Eds) *Educative Leadership: A Practical Theory for New Administrators and Managers*, London: Falmer Press, pp.47–82.

West-Burnham, J. (1992) *Managing Quality in Schools*, Harlow: Longman.

Weston, P., Barrett, E. and Jamieson, J. (1992) *The Quest for Coherence: Managing the Whole Curriculum 5–16*, National Foundation for Educational Research.

8 Inspection, evaluation and quality assurance

John West-Burnham

Introduction

Most models of effective management can be reduced to a three-part process: plan, act, review.

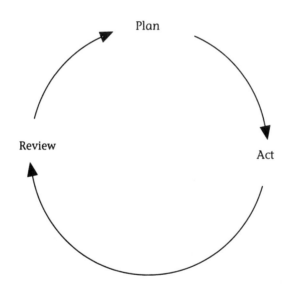

Figure 8.1 The management cycle

The other chapters in this book are largely concerned with the theoretical and practical components of planning and acting. This chapter identifies the components of the review element of effective management, discusses the implications of different approaches to review and outlines the relevant practical activities.

A significant initial difficulty is the problem of terminology. Many terms are used almost interchangeably in the context of organizational review. The following definitions are therefore proposed for use in this chapter:

Assessment a summative process providing measurements against objective criteria.

Assurance a process designed to remove the need for external, summative inspection by designing processes to guarantee conformity.

Audit an analysis of the current situation of the organization e.g. the prevailing strengths, weaknesses, opportunities and threats.

Evaluation an internal or external formative process designed to provide feedback on the total impact and value of a project or activity.

Inspection an external, summative process judging the extent to which an organization meets externally imposed criteria.

Monitoring the collection of data and evidence to inform other review activities.

Review a range of management procedures which collect data to establish the extent to which intentions have been achieved.

The appropriateness and effectiveness of each of these approaches will be discussed. What is not at issue is the significance attached to the review process in the management of schools and colleges:

> Basically, the implication of this ... for non-profit institutions is to keep an eye on the fundamental, long-term goal. Make sure you move towards it, and you'll gain credibility. And be sure you define performance and hold yourself accountable for it (Drucker 1992, p.106).

Drucker identifies a number of key components of the review process:

— the importance of explicit outcomes
— measuring progress
— the definition of performance relevant to the outcomes

Aspinwall et al. (1992, p.14) extend the definition of the purpose of formative feedback:

... evaluation needs to be seen as an integral part of the management process ... It must be a continuous subject of attention and must be soundly embedded in the structure and culture of the organization. If it is a stage in the process it can be put off; if it is integral to the process it cannot.

Garratt (1987, p.77) makes much the same point but, importantly and significantly, relates the process of review to learning:

Re-framing, by getting a better perspective through monitoring the external environment, rising above the immediate organizational problems, and identifying the wider issues allows ... learning.

He extends this view to argue for:

an integrative mechanism which acts as the central processor, the cerebral cortex of the organization which brings together the information flows, synthesizes them and allows adaptation to change of the whole (ibid. p.78).

Aspinwall et al. and Garratt provide further criteria as to the nature of review:

— It should be axiomatic to the management process
— It facilitates understanding, learning and so change

The sum of these definitions produces a view of the management process in which review is as significant an element as planning and acting. It is also a dynamic and integrated process where the impact of each factor is directly proportionate to the strength of the relationship with the other two. Equally significant is the extent to which the factors relate to actual practice. The whole process is summarized by Beare et al. (1989).

The judgements which are made are important factors in decisions on the formation of goals, the identifications of needs, the setting of policies and priorities, the preparation of plans and budgets and the ongoing implementation of school programmes.

However, this perception of review as an internal process linked to effective management for improvement through individual and organizational learning is problematic. The issues surrounding the process of review may be broadly classified as:

1. *Control:* who owns the review process?

2. *Perception:* how objective can the process be?

3. *Opportunity Costs:* does the process justify the cost?

These problems can be first elucidated in a non-education example. Workers on a production line are responsible for putting flanges on gizmos. As each unit is completed it is passed to quality control inspectors who decide whether the unit is acceptable, in need of re-working or scrap. The problem is that the workers don't know the criteria for acceptability, they only have a broad indication. They do not have the time or training or resources to produce perfect units. The system is geared to failure, waste is institutionalized, indeed the cost of failure may not be known. However conscientious the inspectors may be they are fallible and failures do slip through. The inevitable result is dissatisfied customers. A number of issues emerge from this example:

— the workforce is not trusted, with obvious implications for motivation and morale

— a significant number of units are therefore wasted

— customers do not receive what they ordered

— the inspectors represent a significant extra cost

In essence, the system presumes failure and systems are created which serve to diminish responsibility and autonomy, lessen the likelihood of satisfactory outcomes and increase overall costs.

The educational process does not produce simple physical products. There is a wide range of complex outcomes at every stage, some of them tangible, many of them intangible and subject to a range of interpretations. The issue is how to review the effectiveness of those things that can be measured e.g.:

• the appropriateness of teaching and learning strategies
• the effectiveness of meetings, pastoral procedures and communication systems
• the extent to which stated outcomes have been achieved
• the degree of conformity to agreed standards and procedures
• the efficient and effective use of resources

Historically, information on these issues has been gathered by two processes, external inspection and internal evaluation. There is an increasing awareness in education of a third strategy, quality assurance. This chapter will explore the components of, and the issues arising from, each of these approaches.

160

Inspection

The rationale for the external inspection of educational institutions can be found in the discussion of formal models of education management in Bush (1986, p.23).

> In formal models there is an emphasis on the accountability of the organization to its sponsoring body. Educational institutions, then, are held to be responsible to the local education authority. Within hierarchies heads and principals in particular are answerable to the director of education for the activities of their organizations.

The practical expression of this principle in Britain was a pattern of national and local inspection under the auspices of Her Majesty's Inspectorate and local education authorities respectively.

❑ National inspection

Marjoram (1989, p.49) identifies the classic role of HMI:

> The Inspectorate (1) assesses standards and trends and advises the Secretary of State on the performance of the system nationally; (2) identifies and makes known good practice and promising developments while drawing attention to weaknesses; (3) provides advice and assistance to those with responsibilities for institutions in the system. ... It is not HMIs task to right what is wrong; it is for others to act upon its assessments.

There is abundant evidence of the role of HMI in collecting, synthesizing and disseminating good practice and providing data to inform policy making at national level. However in the inspection of individual institutions the notion of accountablity is much clearer. Lambert, Ribbins and Thomas (1985) draw on a distinction between 'collaborative evaluation' (p.397) and various models of external inspection, the differerence being in the balance of inspection and advice, and the extent to which the process is designed to serve the needs of an external or internal audience.

This ambiguity of purpose was exacerbated by concerns about the methodology of HMI. Riches (1992) refers to his 1984 study concluding that:

> A major criticism is the unevenness of these reports: some seem sketchy and vague and are consequently misleading.

In 1991 (HMI) published reports on 2% of primary schools (a 50-year inspection cycle) and 10% of secondary schools (a 10-year inspection cycle (p.15).

A third issue that Riches identified was the lack of public or explicit criteria, and the failure of HMI to make consistent use of their internal criteria.

As a form of external accountablity the historic role of HMI appears to be highly problematic. There is no doubting the significance invested in their reports on individual institutions but their limited number and variable nature constrained any claim to a national system of inspection for accountability, not least because it was a model of external inspection resulting in advice with a commitment to action, resources or sanctions if that advice was not followed.

This model has been fundamentally modified by the new arrangements for school inspection introduced under the auspices of OFSTED in 1992.

❑ LEA inspection and advice

If the potential of HMI to manage accountability was problematical then inspection at local level would appear less so. LEAs were responsible for decisions relating to the opening, closure and character of maintained schools. They also had direct influence over budgeting matters and a statutory right to inspect. This latter power was enshrined in the Education Act 1944 (para. 77).

> Any Local Education Authority may cause an inspection to be made of any educational establishment ...

Parallel with this formal and strict view of inspection for accountability was the notion of the LEA in partnership with schools providing advice. This tension leads to what Lowe (1992) characterizes as a 'world of shadows and hints' and the 'Janus complex', i.e. the tension between external, formal inspection and a process of collaborative advice, support and development. However the notion of partnership was often constrained by the control that advisers had over resources. Advisers were often able to extend their sponsorship through involvement in staff appointments and the deployment of additional resources.

The ability of LEAs to operate in an advisory capacity has been systematically eroded since 1988 with increasing proportions of LEA budgets being devolved to schools and only funding for statutory functions being available to LEAs.

The combination of the limited capacity of the LEAs to inspect, a government belief that advice should be at the schools' behest and the constraints on HMI led to the establishment of OFSTED in 1992.

❑ The Office for Standards in Education

OFSTED represents a significant change in the notion of inspection linked to accountability. In a number of key respects the OFSTED arrangements meet the constraints identified above with respect to the HMI and LEA models for inspection. The key characteristics of the OFSTED model may be summarized as follows:

- All schools to be inspected on a four-year cycle
- Publication (in the Handbook for the Inspection of Schools) of:
  — a standardized inspection procedure
  — explicit criteria for the inspection
- Inspection of all aspects of the school
- Inspectors to be trained and impartial
- Involvement of governors and parents
- Publication of a standardized report to governors, the staff and a summary to parents
- Requirement for an action plan to respond to the report's findings

The nature of the inspection process is made quite clear in the 'Handbook':

> The report is an appraisal of the quality and standards of education in the school; some descriptive detail is obviously necessary, but the emphasis throughout should be on judgements and evaluation (p.17).

> The function of the report is to evaluate, not to prescribe or speculate; reports must be as objective as possible ... (p.17).

A significant element of the OFSTED process is that it has no role for the local education authority, reinforcing the polarisation of the responsibility for education between the institute and central government.

The changes in provision for schools in England and Wales are parallelled by changes in the arrangements for 16–19 education. The most significant development in the post-compulsory sector is the publication of *The Charter for Further Education*. This effectively sets agendas for college review procedures and external inspection. The Charter represents a response to a consumer-led market-place approach and establishes criteria to serve as the basis for external judgements. The Charter outlines students' rights and responsibilities with regard to:

- information
- application
- finance
- teaching and learning
- guidance and counselling
- student unions
- equal opportunities

Employers' and community entitlement are also set out as are the procedures for making complaints.

This Charter thus seeks to reconcile formal accountability through inspection with a consumer orientation. However, the capacity of a college to become genuinely responsive on the basis of customer feedback will inevitably be constrained by the use of a range of outcomes to determine funding which places the emphasis on course completion and success rather than recruitment. This is analogous to not paying for a motor-car until it has completed 100,000 miles of trouble-free motoring. However effective a course of study may be perceived to be on the basis of inspection and review, if it is not efficient in terms of completion then it will not be fully funded.

A major issue that is emerging is the range of potentially conflicting demands on colleges in terms of accountability:

> Nevertheless, there was still some concern that the definition of acceptable quality procedures might differ from one agency to another and that there was therefore a need to ensure that the procedures did not become an end in themselves ... (FEU, 1993, p.32).

The new arrangements for inspection have to be viewed in combination with the publication of league tables. These reinforce the notion of objective data being available to the community and to inform decision-taking and policy-making. However, a number of serious issues emerge:

1. Are the criteria valid and appropriate?
2. Are summative judgements based on 'objective' data possible in the educational context?
3. Will the standardized criteria and procedures allow valid comparisons to be drawn between schools?

4. Will the need to prepare for and respond to inspections create 'artificial agendas' for schools?

5. Is it possible to derive valid inferences from observations of classroom teaching?

6. Are the models of teaching, learning and managing implicit to the inspection process appropriate for autonomous schools and colleges?

7. Will the inspection process reinforce a dependency model and produce stereotypical schools?

8. If the criteria, analysis and judgements are external will there be 'ownership' of the need to change in schools and colleges?

9. Will responding to the process of inspection divert resources from school/college priorities?(partly derived from Ormston and Shaw, 1993)

The fact that these questions can be asked raises doubts about the notion of external inspection in the context of the effective management of autonomous schools and colleges.

Institutional evaluation

Most educational institutions engage in some kind of evaluative activity, often as a component of development planning or of a specific aspect of the school's or college's work, e.g. a maths scheme, communication with parents or a training day. Most such activities would meet one or more of the purposes of evaluation identified by Nixon (1992, p.21):

1. Creating a context of shared understanding within which schools can begin to realise the need for change

2. Improving the quality of classroom practice and of the wider organizational structures of schooling

3. Countering some of the simplistic expectations that are too often imposed upon educational institutions from the outside

Thus the purposes of evaluation might be summarized as changing perceptions, serving as the basis for action and informing on the basis of evidence. However, accountability to external bodies must also be added to this list as evaluation is often part of the contract between a funding body and the school or college. For example, in England and Wales the TVEI initiative required detailed evaluation as did work on records of achievement. Although in all three purposes evaluation is perceived as a component of a process, its usefulness is almost invariably constrained:

> It is rare ... for evaluation in schools to have the kind of direct and visible impact that it is so often expected to have. Educational evaluation may on occasions provide definitive answers; but, usually, only in response to questions which ... appear fairly simplistic (Nixon 1992, pp. 24–25).

Nixon argues that evaluation is about understanding, developing insights and encouraging reflection. As such it may be categorized as a central element in professional learning and an important element in the heuristic process of school improvement. However, there are a number of significant constraints on the management potential of this process.

Cuttance (1993) cites the findings of the Keeves Report *Education and Change in South Australia* in identifying weaknesses in school evaluation:

- weak linkage between the review and planning   processes
- the confidentiality of evaluation reports
- limited dissemination of the reports
- the evaluation process was time-consuming and expensive

A number of other weaknesses may be added to this list:

- the limited availability of expertise in designing, managing and acting on evaluations
- the absence of a culture of evaluation (i.e. the extent to which it is implicit to management processes, job descriptions, etc)
- the limited resourcing of evaluation in terms of training, time, clerical support, etc.

This is not to deny that effective evaluation takes place in educational institutions. Bolam et al. (1993, p.113) provide a practical example:

> ... each department was evaluated with a focus on a particular aspect that the SMT wished to explore. The evaluation had three broad components ... visits to classes ... pupil pursuits, and an interview ... of teachers and the head of department ... culminating in a written report ...

Although a significant process in its own right this model poses difficulties in a number of important respects:

— the agenda was determined by the SMT

— classroom observation, pursuit and interview are problematical methodologies

— the production of a report implies a summative judgement

However skilfully and sensitively managed, this approach raises two fundamental questions. Firstly, the extent to which the evaluation is owned by the department and secondly, that any successes, issues or problems identified are *post facto*. The information is historic and whilst it may benefit future generations it is of little comfort to those students whose current poor experience is simply the basis of improvement strategies. Aspinwall et al. (1992) summarize the problem in individual and organizational terms:

> It cannot be assumed that all members of an educational organization ... share a common view about purposes, priorities or practice; and if they do not, their responses are likely to be coloured by their perceptions of the likely impact of the evaluation on their interests (p.194).

> In general there is considerable evidence that, whatever the rhetoric, there are enormous pressures towards the marginalisation of evaluation activities ... The wider organization finds it difficult or impossible to respond ... (p.212).

Even if sophisticated strategies are developed to overcome individual rejection and organizational inertia, the fact remains that the subjects of a negative evaluation have moved on. In essence it is of little comfort to me to have it confirmed that my son was badly taught in some subjects, he will never repeat his time in school.

If evaluation, as a formal process in school or college management, describes, analyses and explains phenomena that have already occurred, and if implementation is problematic, then its place in the effective management of learning must be questioned. As with the outcomes of external inspection, institutional evaluation is a powerful tool in strategic planning but has very little to say about the actual experience of children and students now. Evaluation is a classic exemplification of a reactive culture at the micro level however significant it may be at the macro level. Inspection and evaluation are in the same relationship to the daily learning experiences of the current generation of young people as the post-mortem is to preventative medicine. This is not to diminish the significance of evaluation in terms of policy-making or strategic and development planning. However, short-term wastage or lost opportunities cannot be justified by reference to future generations.

167

In industrial and commercial management practice this tension is being increasingly recognized and is exemplified in the move from quality control to quality assurance.

Quality assurance

In essence quality control tells us that a product or service is wrong, quality assurance prevents it going wrong:

> Quality assurance is a management system designed to control activities at all stages ... to prevent quality problems and ensure only conforming products reach the customer. The key features of an effective quality assurance system are:
> (i) an effective quality management system
> (ii) periodic audit of the operation of the system
> (iii) periodic review of the system to ensure it meets changing requirements
> (Munro-Faure and Munro-Faure 1992, pp.6–7)

The fundamentals of quality assurance are meeting *specifications* through a *system* designed to ensure *prevention*. Assurance rejects the notion that mistakes are inevitable. The underlying principle is one of conformance to specification and management systems should be established which allow this.

The components of a management system to assure quality will include:

- clearly defined roles and responsibilities
- documentation to formalize procedures
- identification of customers' requirements
- a quality policy
- clear work instructions and process control
- procedures for corrective action
- management audit
- inspection and testing

Most schools and colleges will already have many of these factors in place, although not necessarily described in the terms used above, e.g.:

— the prospectus as a contract with parents and students and as a quality policy

— defined procedures for absence, break-time supervision

— process control through the timetable, lesson plans, reward and discipline systems

— inspection and testing through internal examinations, identification of special educational needs

— documentation to cover student records, etc. (BSI1993)

This approach is best known through the application of ISO 9000 (BS 5750 in Britain). This system provides explicit criteria to inform the design and management of a quality assurance system. It involves a process of external assessment which determines the extent to which the system conforms to the standard. However, it is for the institution to interpret and apply the standard and the assessment is of the consistency and integrity of the system — not the product or service. Although it has its origins in manufacturing, BS 5750 has been applied to service industries and an increasing number of schools and colleges in England and Wales have obtained or are seeking accreditation.

However significant concerns have been raised about the appropriateness of BS 5750 to a range of organizations. These concerns centre on its potential for bureaucracy, the fact that it does not involve all aspects of the organization and the fact that it makes no reference to the integrity or value of the product or service. However, an assurance process does recognize the need for an organization to accept responsibility for its own management processes.

It is in this last point that the crucial difference between inspection, evaluation and assurance arises. Assurance is an internal process concerned with ensuring the integrity of the relationship between intentions and outcomes. Thus the responsibility for quality rests directly with the organization itself and is expressed through its relationship with its customers. Quality assurance recognizes the autonomy of organizations and seeks to enhance their capacity to operate in a responsive way. It thus removes the notions of dependence, control and hierarchical accountability. These characteristics are reflected in the internal operations of a quality organization; individuals become responsible for the quality of their work within a context of agreed procedures, support, training and resources.

There are a number of examples of this approach operating in educational systems. Cusack (1992) describes the changes in the New Zealand education service which resulted in the replacement of the Inspectorate with the Education Review Agency. A number of significant features emerge in the working of the Agency:

1. 'The object of School Review is to check that schools are matching outcomes to what had been promised in their corporate development plans' (p. 7)
2. The review methodology is negotiated with the school
3. Schools record and collate their own data on school performance
4. A school's review is 'pre-occupied with appraisal of school self-evaluation systems' (ibid)
5. 'Actual classroom performances by teachers are seen as the responsibility of the school' (ibid)
6. 75–80 per cent of schools had implemented recommendations within *three months* (my emphasis).

The result of the new system is:

> Self-managing schools with ... direct local accountability and insistence on proof of performance (ibid).

This model would appear to go a long way towards meeting the concerns raised about inspection and evaluation and exploring the potential of a quality assurance approach.

Another, related, approach is found in the procedures for evaluation and accreditation of the European Council of International Schools. The purpose of the process is to:

> Further the pursuit of educational excellence by providing an instrument for periodic self–examination and an opportunity for outside appraisal (ECIS 1987, p.3).

The process involves five stages:

1. Preliminary visit, to clarify process and procedures and prepare for self-study

2. Self-study, in this stage the school examines its philosophy and objectives and carries out a detailed review using ECIS guidelines

3. External visit, by a team of administrators and teachers from other schools. The aim of the team
    > is not to impose extraneous models on the school but to view it in terms of its own philosophy and objectives and seek ways to be helpful to it in realising its potentialities. (ibid p.4).

4. Decision on Accreditation

5. Subsequent reporting

The significant features of this model are the emphasis on self-study and peer review. The model combines professional rigour with management relevance in the context of an autonomous institution.

The New Zealand and ECIS models would appear to offer a model of review for improvement that is far more consistent with autonomous schools and colleges operating in a market economy.

However, even these models can serve to diminish genuine responsiveness. For this reason a significant number of schools and colleges are exploring the possibilities of total quality as an answer to the problem of managing educational institutions in the final years of the twentieth century.

Total quality management

West-Burnham (1992), Murgatroyd and Morgan (1993) and Sallis (1993) have all provided detailed definitions, histories and rationals for the quality movement. A wide range of commercial organizations are working with schools and colleges to support the implementation of total quality (e.g. Royal Mail, ICI, ICL, Rover Group, British Gas, etc). There is significant anecdotal evidence of a large amount of activity in a number of areas of quality management.

Total quality can be seen as the logical extension in terms of organizational autonomy and maturity in that it focuses all aspects of management on its core purpose — the provision of appropriate services and products to customers.

West-Burnham (1992, p.26) identified the key features of total quality:

1. Quality is defined by the customer, not the supplier
2. Quality consists of meeting stated needs, requirements and standards
3. Quality is achieved through continuous improvement, by prevention, not detection
4. Quality is driven by senior management but is an equal responsibility of all those involved in any process

5. Quality is measured by statistical methods, the 'cost of quality' is the cost of non-conformance. Communicate with facts
6. Quality has to pervade human relationships in the work place, teams are the most powerful agent for managing quality
7. Quality can be achieved only by a valued work force; education, training and personal growth are essential to this
8. Quality has to be the criterion for reviewing every decision, every action and every process

In the context of this chapter the relationship between inspection and evaluation, assurance and total quality may be summarized as follows:

Inspection and evaluation identify what has gone wrong and allow remedial action to be instituted or confirm and reinforce that which is known to be working well and effectively.

Assurance establishes systems and processes to meet specifications so as to minimise the possibility of wastage or loss.

Total quality works to ensure that every aspect of the organization and every employee is focused all the time in meeting and then exceeding customer requirements.

In this respect it would appear that total quality has much to offer schools and colleges in that it is:

— value driven, i.e. has a clear moral imperative

— customer focused, i.e. existing for a driven by the needs of young people, parents and community

— based on prevention, i.e. concerned with optimising outcomes

In support of these principles, total quality offers a range of techniques; notably an emphasis on proactive leadership, autonomous teams, communication systems and, perhaps most importantly, quantitative methods which facilitate the meeting of customer requirements. There is only limited empirical evidence as to the appropriateness and effectiveness of total quality approaches in schools and colleges. Reference has already been made to schools and colleges seeking BS 5750 accreditation. A significant number of schools are exploring the applicability of 'Investors in People', a quality assurance system which relates to mission, planning, communication and training and development. At the time of writing there are no known documented examples of a school or college in Britain which has successfully implemented TQM and sustained it over a period of time.

The best known example of a total quality school is Mt. Edgecombe High School in Sitka, Alaska, USA. Larrae Rocheleau (1991, p.18) summarized the approach of the school thus:

> Quality is not more costly, it is cheaper. All the high school graduates that schools put out with extremely low academic and social skills are causing rework by the greater system. We need to do a better job the first-time. A parent remarked to me once 'My child only has one chance for a good education'.

Mt. Edgecombe is able to point to a number of significant quantifiable indicators which have improved since the introduction of total quality, e.g. attendance, disciplinary incidents, graduation rates, employment and completion of higher education. How far this approach is translatable and the results replicable is still highly problematic. It would be naïve to pretend that total quality is a panacea, it is a highly demanding system that challenges the existing culture of many educational systems:

— it challenges the control and dependency models implicit in inspection models

— it replaces notions of professional autonomy and collegiality with common purpose and team work

— it replaces 'knowledge as teacher control' with 'learning as student control'.

What total quality offers is a means of managing which ensures that accountability is direct, immediate and personal. As such it is essentially alien to a political context. The application of total quality to schools in Britain may well be constrained by the higher significance attached to political control and a system of accountability rather than a responsive culture.

Finally

> Quality cannot be imposed from outside — from outside the institution, outside the team, outside the individual. You cannot inspect in quality. You can't have externally-driven efficiency and accountability ...

Accountability can be distorting; it diverts teachers from concentrating on the known needs of children ... (Bowring-Carr and West-Burnham 1994, p.75).

Summary

This chapter has analysed the relationship between inspection, evaluation, assurance and total quality and argued that the first two may be inadequate tools for managing the learning process. Although inspection and evaluation have fundamentally important roles in public accountability, policy making and strategic planning, they are of limited value in the short-term management of learning. In this context, it is argued that some form of quality assurance is more appropriate and that total quality offers an holistic approach which has the potential to enhance outcomes and reduce costs. The tension may be one between quality and effective management and notions of political policy making and accountability.

References

Aspinwall, K., Simkins, T., Wilkinson, J. and McAuley, J. (1992) *Managing Evaluation in Education*, London: Routledge.

Beare, H., Caldwell, B. and Milliken, R. (1989) *Creating an Excellent School*, London: Routledge.

Bennett, N., Crawford, M., and Riches, C. (1992) *Managing Change in Education*, PCP.

Bolam, R., McMahon, A., Pocklington, K. and Weindling, D. (1993) *Effective Management in Schools*, HMSO.

Bowring-Carr, C. and West-Burnham, J. (1994) *Managing Quality in Schools: Workbook*, Harlow: Longman.

BSI (1993) *Management Systems of Schools*, BSI.

Bush, T. (1986) *Theories of Educational Management*, PCP.

Cusack, B. (1992) 'An end to school inspection', *Management in Education*, 6, 2.

Cuttance, P. (1993) 'School development and review in an Australian state education system', in Dimmock, C. (1993).

DFE (1993) *The Charter for Further Education*, DFE.

Dimmock, C. (1993) *School-Based Management and School Effectiveness*, London: Routledge.

Drucker, P. (1992) *Managing the Non-profit Organization*, London:Butterworth-Heinemann.

ECIS (1987) *Guide to School Evaluation and Accreditation*, ECIS.

Further Education Unit (1993) *Challenges for Colleges*, FEU.

Garratt, B. (1987) *The Learning Organization*, London: Fontana.

Hargreaves, D. and Hopkins, D. (1991) 'School effectiveness, school improvement and development planning', in Preedy, M. (1992).

Lambert, K., Ribbins, P. and Thomas, H. (1985) 'The practice of education' in Hughes, M., Ribbins, P. and Thomas, H. *Managing Education*, London: Cassell.

Lowe, P.A. (1992) *The LEA Adviser and Inspector*, Harlow: Longman.

Marjoram, T. (1989) *Assessing Schools*, London: Kogan Page.

Munro-Faure, L. and Munro-Faure, M. (1992) *Implementing Total Quality Management*, London: Pitman.

Murgatroyd, C. and Morgan, C. (1992) *Total Quality Management and the School*, Milton Keynes: Open University Press.

Nixon, J. (1992) *Evaluating the Whole Curriculum*, Milton Keynes: Open University Press.

OFSTED, *Handbook for the Inspection of Schools*, HMSO.

Ormston, M. and Shaw, M. (1993) *Inspection: a Preparation Guide for Schools*, Harlow: Longman.

Preedy, M. (1992) *Managing the Effective School*, PCP.

Riches, C. (1984) 'HMI reports go public', *Educational Administration and Management*, **12**, 2.

Riches, C. (1992) 'Inspecting the inspection of schools', *Management in Education*, **6**, 2.

Rochelau, L. (1991) 'Mt. Edgecumbe's venture in quality', *The School Administrator*, Nov 1991.

Sallis, E. (1992) *Total Quality Management in Education*, London: Kogan Page.

Wallace, M. (1992) 'A key to the management of multiple innovations' in Bennett et al. (1992).

West-Burnham, J. (1992) *Managing Quality in Schools*, Harlow: Longman.

9 Women in educational management

Marianne Coleman

Introduction

There is a recognition in education of both the importance of equal opportunities and the strengths that women bring to management. However, women are under-represented in the management of schools, colleges and LEAs.

This chapter begins with some statistical information on women in the workforce as a whole, and on the distribution of posts of responsibility between men and women in educational management. Four groups of theories analyzing inequality are examined, and links are made between the feminine management 'style' and effective schools. In addition the potential for change towards greater equality between individuals and within institutions and society is considered.

❏ The wider context — women in paid employment
It is expected that by the turn of the century women will make up 45 per cent of the total civilian labour force.

In 1990 there were 12 million economically active women in Great Britain in a civilian labour force of 28.1 million. These figures represented an average female economic activity rate of 52.8 per cent in 1990 compared with an average male activity rate of 74.2 per cent. The average rate masks differences between the socio-economic groups, and between those with and without dependent children. Of professional women 89 per cent with no dependent children are economically active, and a higher proportion of professional women worked full-time than any other socio-economic group whether or not they had children, and whatever the age of the child. (CSO, 1992)

Women have traditionally been employed in service industries, and are more likely to work part-time than are men. In 1990 women earned 76.6 per cent of men's gross weekly earnings and 68.2 per cent of men's gross hourly earnings (Davidson and Cooper 1992, p.6). Nearly 30 per cent of women work part-time and a large proportion of these: 'are in low-status, low-skilled occupations which rarely lead to promotion or more responsible positions' (Davidson and Cooper 1992, p.3).

Women are less likely to hold positions of responsibility in any area of paid employment. Davidson and Cooper (1992, p.11) quote that in 1988, women accounted for only 11 per cent of general managerial staff. Despite the large number of female teachers, particularly in the primary phase, there are disproportionately few women in positions of authority in educational management.

❑ Women in positions of responsibility in educational management

Of the total number of teachers in nursery and primary schools on 31 March 1991, over 80 per cent were women, but 51 per cent of the headteachers were men. Of women nursery and primary teachers, 51 per cent were on Main Scale with no allowance, whilst this was true for only 23 per cent of the male teachers.

Just under half the secondary school teachers were female, and of these, 38 per cent were Main Scale teachers with no allowance. As in the primary sector, 23 per cent of the male secondary teachers held no allowance.

In secondary schools, proportionately more women than men held incentive allowance A, and approximately the same numbers of men and women held incentive allowance B, but there was a greater discrepancy between the proportions of males and females holding the higher positions, for example 70 per cent of all D allowances were held by male teachers.

Table 9.1 Distribution of senior management posts by gender in secondary schools 31 March 1991

	Men	Women	Total
All teachers	103,103	96,911	200,014
Incentive allowance D	19,731	8,134	27,865
Incentive allowance E	6,697	2,156	8,853
Deputy Head	6,626	3,409	10,035
Headteacher	3,970	1,063	5,033

Table 9.1 is based on Table B12/91 (1993) provided by the Analytical Services branch of the DFE

In addition to holding fewer allowances at a senior level, it is also possible that women are working harder than men to qualify for these positions. Research carried out in the Management and Organisation in Secondary Schools (MOSS) Project showed not only that women held many fewer senior posts than men but that they tended to have 'two specific posts of responsibility at the same grade as men who only had one of the jobs.' (Weightman 1989, p.119).

In 1991, 16 of the 108 LEAs had female chief education officers; females accounted for four per cent of principals of colleges of further education, and three per cent of professors in universities (Darking, 1991).

Theories of inequality

Schmuck (1986) classifies the theories of inequality as 'individual socialization processes, organizational constraints to women's mobility, and gender-based career socialization' (p.176). Drawing on this classification, the theories are examined here under the following headings:

1. Overt and covert discrimination

2. Organizational constraints, with the implication that it is the culture that should change and not women

3. Theories of socialization of women, carrying the implication that women could and should be re-socialized

4. Male·cultural domination

❑ Overt and covert discrimination

Despite the fact that the Sex Discrimination Act 1975 makes direct or indirect discrimination illegal, women still rate discrimination and prejudice as the greatest deterrent to career progression. In their interviews of nearly 700 female managers and 185 male managers, Davidson and Cooper (1992) found that: 'sex was a disadvantage regarding job promotion/career prospects' (p.119). They also report that:

> the usual employer attitude — that women are 'poor training and promotional investments' who leave work on marrying and/or starting a family — is particularly detrimental to those who work continuously after

marriage and single women who do not marry, a profile which fits the majority of the women in management (p.120).

Women are numerically important in education but there still exists the attitude expressed by a male teacher, reported by Clwyd County Council in 1983, 'It grates to have a woman in any position of authority over me' (Al Khalifa 1992, p. 101).

It is unlikely that a woman candidate for a senior management position in a school or college today would be asked, as Margaret Maden was in 1969: 'did I really think I was strong enough to take on a job like this?' (Ozga 1993, p.38). However, more subtle forms of discrimination are still a factor in the career progression of women teachers. There may be a presumption that the male candidate is automatically more suited to a senior post. A female senior teacher who applied for a deputy headship reported that:

> They said I wasn't quite what they were looking for. ... I'm in my forties; with an MA in education and a diploma in educational management ... The job went to a smart young chap who had been an HoD for three years and had a BA. He was in exactly the same mould as the head! (Adler et al. 1993, p.25).

❑ Organizational constraints

At every level of an educational or other organization there appear to be barriers to the advancement of women. Some of these are:

- at the point of application for a promotion
- in planning a career path
- differential levels of opportunities within the post
- the differential expectations of others; and partially resulting from these expectations, the stereotypical roles that men and women tend to adopt in management

Such organizational barriers may operate not only against women, but positively in favour of men:

> At each step of administrative preparation, job seeking and selection, there are organizational processes which clearly indicate a preference for males (Schmuck, 1986, p.179).

Schmuck identifies:

- the 'grooming' of male teachers
- sex bias in the training offered by higher education

- males tending to mentor other males
- the lack of female role models in senior management
- more opportunities given for males to exhibit leadership
- male domination of selection committees, leading to discrimination

Whilst some of the more obvious aspects of discrimination are now identified and are being eliminated, the more subtle barriers remain.

Applications for promotion There is evidence to show that women are less persistent than men in applications for promotion, particularly when they are not supported actively in their application by a 'mentor':

> If the woman seeks a position on her own, ... and she doesn't get it, she'll try again only once or twice and then cease pursuing administration (Shakeshaft 1987, p. 67).

Women tend to be self-critical in weighing up their chances of successfully obtaining promotion:

> women can be scrupulous in self-evaluation and therefore more critical and selective about career moves than many men teachers (Al Khalifa 1992, p.96).

Men hold more positions of responsibility than women and tend to set the standards of what is expected from a manager; it is claimed that men are 'gatekeepers' to the profession:

> Through all the stages of preparation — from encouraging teachers to seek administrative positions to final selection of administrative candidates — the chances are that a man will be preferred to a woman. The exclusion of women is self-perpetuating, despite active efforts to change institutional practices (Schmuck 1986, p. 179).

Adjustment of aspirations If the barriers to women's advance are inherent in the institution, there is evidence to show that the lack of opportunities may result in women adjusting their aspirations accordingly (Kanter, 1977).

> Thus people who have very little opportunity to move up the hierarchy (women teachers), disengage in the form of depressed aspirations (Shakeshaft 1987, p. 91).

Lack of self-confidence It remains to be seen whether institutional practice is changing. Even where there is change there may be under-lying subtle pressures and influences hampering the career progress of women. Self-confidence is a necessary pre-requisite for successful job applications, and it has been suggested that women are more likely to be lacking in self-confidence than their male colleagues, tending, unlike males to apply only for jobs for which they are fully qualified (Shakeshaft 1993, p.51).

Research reported by Shakeshaft (1987, 1993) may be relevant to the issue of confidence. The research supports the perception that females are less criticized than males in the work situation. Whereas males obtain regular and critical feedback on their work, women are not criticized openly and therefore do not have the chance to improve or develop ways of dealing with negative comment. When they become aware of criticism they take it extremely seriously and 'tend to think it is an assessment of their very essence' (Shakeshaft 1993, p.55).

An increase in confidence is one of the major outcomes reported by those offering training in educational management to female teachers (Jayne, 1989, Atchison, 1993).

Potential role conflict Women may also be less inclined to advance into management given the potential stress of role conflict that such a move may bring. For where women carry the main burden of dependents:

> the balancing of different roles and responsibilities is a considerable organizational achievement, but is also experienced as a source of pressure. A move into management then comes to be seen as compounding this problem (Al Khalifa 1992, p.96).

Realistic assessment of commitment Promotion may not be sought by women, not through lack of aspiration, but because:

> Not wanting to take on two jobs ... rather reflects an accurate assessment of the number of hours in the day and the very real limits of the human body (Shakeshaft 1987, p.89).

There is evidence that women take an overview when contemplating a decision about an increase in work-load. Where a male teacher will apply for promotion as a simple career move, a female teacher does not separate the world of work from the rest of her life in the same way. Women tend to:

> seek to bridge the personal and professional aspects of their lives and to reduce the gap between public and private roles (Al Khalifa 1992, p.102).

Antipathy to 'male' concepts of management Alternatively the 'male' image of management, may be unappealing to women who would not wish to become part of a culture which they see as fostering:

> aggressive competitive behaviours, an emphasis on control rather than negotiation and collaboration, and the pursuit of competition rather than shared problem-solving (Al Khalifa 1992, p. 100).

Women may not identify with management as they see it practised:

> when women become managers they often have to take on definitions of management which exclude their experience and their understanding (Ozga 1993, p.3).

Al Khalifa (1992) has pointed out that when theories of management were first applied to schools, the application was seen as 'technical' and logical. Therefore those who practiced management were expected to have the 'male' qualities of 'analytical detachment, strong task direction, "hard-nosed" toughness' (Al Khalifa, p.98).

This identification of management with 'maleness' does not seem to allow for the very different ways in which existing women managers do carry out their work, nor for the increasing recognition of the benefits of 'feminine' style management considered below (see p.189 *et seq.*)

Evaluation of the worth of work It seems probable that many women in education choose deliberately to stay with classroom teaching rather than opt for a career that moves into school or college management. The same inclinations that make women in general: 'work for self-fulfilment, for social relationships and to feel that they are making a contribution' impel women teachers to: 'value classroom teaching and put it as a priority. For them teaching and not management is 'real work' (Thompson 1992, p.206).

Career path and planning The critical self-evaluation of women may be linked to the lack of career planning that has been typical of even successful women in education. Margaret Maden, Warwickshire CEO commented on her application for headship: 'Again, I was asked to apply for something — didn't do it on my own' (Ozga 1993, p.39).

Women managers in general tend either not to have a career plan, or to embark late upon one. Davidson and Cooper (1992) found that 50 per cent of the female managers they had interviewed had never had a career life plan at all. They also report that it is the belief of many female managers that: 'a large number of women just drift into senior positions without clearly planning their career strategy' (p.128).

A study of 24 educational managers in Scotland, carried out by Gerver and Hall, showed that the women 'thought that luck had influenced their careers rather than planning' (Darking, 1991).

Dual career families Women are strongly identified with the family:

> for years researchers studied the activities and attitudes only of women when they looked at 'family life', thus reinforcing the myth of separate worlds. The man was plugged in when he appeared, but he was not seen as carrying with him family membership when he went off to work. Employed women, however, were presumed to have, or want to have, a family (Kanter 1989, p. 289).

Where both partners are pursuing a career, it is still most common for women's career interests to be subordinate to those of the man if there are problems of geographical mobility. The Scottish study found that as a result of having to move homes:

> Many had 'tapestried' careers, where they had been forced to transfer skills from one professional area of work to another, rather than following more hierarchical career routes (Darking, 1991).

Difficulties of moving home or of trying to maintain two homes are commonplace, but even when faced with finding another position near to the partner there can be difficulties:

> If I gave my partner's location as my reason for wanting the job, I would be reinforcing that stereotype, and also devaluing my own commitment to the post and my capacity to do it, especially in competition with men who made reference only to 'professional' motives in support of their candidature (Whitehead 1993, p.77).

Career Breaks In educational management and in the world of work generally, career breaks are detrimental to women's career development. However, the average career break for employed women in the UK is 3.5 years (CSO). Statistics on career breaks would seem to indicate that:

Women are unfairly penalized by the majority of employers for taking a
career break, ... unlike the maternity breaks, breaks initiated by employers
(for example, study leave or transfer to other disciplines) are accepted as
being inevitable, essential or for the greater good (Davidson and Cooper,
1992, p.129).

In education, the career break still inhibits career development and the value
of women's experience outside the workplace is not generally recognized.

Differential levels of opportunity Schmuck (1986) contends that
educational institutions have 'a gender overlay', that high school principals
will interact more with male than female teachers and give more
encouragement to young male teachers with leadership potential. There is
also the claim that men are given extra responsibilities, like membership of
committees, and therefore more chances to exhibit those very qualities that
will recommend them for further responsibility. Research in British
comprehensives showed that:

Men tend to do the high profile, straightforward jobs that are part of the
natural progression up the hierarchy. The job of head of department or
faculty has a clear role that everyone understands and accepts. This enables
the postholder to be seen as being a manager and doing management work
(Weightman 1989, p.121).

These views of institutional preference for males are endorsed and reinforced
elsewhere:

the caution with which some women approach management posts and
promotion reflects an appreciation of the difficulties they may have to face
which men are not exposed to. In particular, women see that their future
work environment will be male dominated and both senior staff and those
they surpervise anticipate male leadership (Al Khalifa 1992, p.100–1).

Women managers outside education may be denied the back-up that a male
colleague would receive, in terms of informal advice and suggestions from
colleagues:

we assert that this type of informal training and development has often
excluded women, hence reducing their opportunities, visibility and skill
levels (Davidson and Cooper 1992, p. 98).

Differential expectations and resulting role stereotypes Some women
are successful in educational as in other areas of management. If this is the
case, the women in question may find that expectations of their behaviour

differ from those held about the equivalent male manager. In the broadest sense:

> many men still find it hard to cope with working with women as equals, having been burdened with their conditional stereotypes of women being mothers, wives or at the 'very most' secretaries (Davidson and Cooper 1992, p.106).

There may be a tendency for females in management positions, in this case in higher education, to be judged by 'male' values of leadership:

> I suggested, ... new non-sexist ways of working to try to allow for more democratic, cooperative methods. But this initiative was quickly misunderstood and interpreted to mean that I was a 'soft touch', incapable of providing a firm, directive framework of leadership (David 1988, p.211).

In cases where women are holding positions of power it is claimed that they do not receive the back-up of authority that would normally be accorded to a male leader within an institution:

> if a woman has achieved a position of power and responsibility she is supposed to be exceptional and must 'prove her worth', whereas the male is not expected to perform in such an exemplary manner (Schmuck 1986, p. 181).

A woman manager operating in the environment of a school or college is likely to find that her role is pre-defined consciously or unconsciously by her colleagues. In a recent study of six deputy heads it was found that:

> a number of the respondents had felt under pressure to conform to an accepted image of the old senior mistress role (Singleton 1993, p.166).

The same study noted that form tutors were selective about which deputy head to select on the basis of the nature of the problem:

> problems that appear to need a woman's touch, that is social or emotional problems, always end up outside my door (Singleton 1992, p. 166).

In mixed-sex groups men will tend to adopt the task-orientated roles and women the caring, people-orientated roles (Schmuck 1986, p. 181).

❑ Theories of socialization

The idea that women are less likely to be promoted because of the way in which they have been socialized:

essentially, blames the victim for her lack of achievement in school leadership. Its remedy is for women to be re–socialized so that they will fit into the male world (Shakeshaft 1989, p.82).

The presumption that a woman can succeed in management only by a re-socialization process and the adoption of male styles of management has been countered by the recognition that the more 'feminine' traits of participatory management and respect for relationships are to be valued. In a review of the British research on women in educational management, Hall points out that generally, management has been identified with masculine traits and women managers then measured against this stereotype. She contrasts the position of studies which 'have as their focus how women perform, not how they are different from men' (Hall 1993, p.38).

The socialization theory approach has also been criticised as simplistic because:

> It does not account for the complex interactions between personal motives and the structure of institutions. It does not account for the influences that institutions have upon the career motives and aspirations of workers (Schmuck 1986, p.177).

Theories of socialization do not allow for changes in motivation over time, and for the fact that what was true for one generation of men and women teachers will not be true for future generations. These socialization arguments 'merely describe a state of affairs at a given time period and offer little explanatory power' (Schmuck 1989, p.178).

❏ Male cultural domination

Shakeshaft (1987) states that: 'Men and women divide the labour on the basis of sex and male tasks are more valued than female ones' (p.94). This theory of male domination of society and culture, is applied to all areas of life including the world of education. Such theories of patriarchy and 'androcentrism' hold that a male-centred culture invests worth in male values and regards female values and experience as less significant.

With particular reference to the academic world, 'male' research methods and theories of management are criticized on this basis.

Male domination of research methods Whilst male domination may take the form of overt and covert discrimination referred to above, it is possible to identify more subtle forms of cultural domination in the androcentric bias of research methods.

187

As a teacher of women's studies, Spendiff (1992) has as a major objective to work 'democratically and supportively with her students'. When wishing to use a feminist approach to the evaluation of women's studies courses she commented:

> I suspect that such research would represent a triple non-conformity — of course content, teaching method and research methodology — and hence might be very difficult to implement in a conventional educational institution (Spendiff 1992, p. 126).

In some cases a 'feminist methodology' may overthrow what is considered to be androcentric traditional research methods and move towards a more intuitive approach, where 'the research process is grounded in the personal politics of the researchers' (Adler et al. 1993, p.62). One such research approach is described as: 'full of "the personal" and "the subjective". The research process was not very orderly or, at times, very coherent. I was however "inside" the culture and participating in the process' (Strachan, 1993, p.76). Whilst rich in descriptive material and intuitive insights, the outcomes of such research may lack the validity and applicability of more traditional methods.

Male domination of management theory Shakeshaft makes a case for the fact that:

> In developing theories of administration, researchers didn't look at the context in general and, therefore, were unable to document how the world was different for women. When female experience was different, it was ignored or diminished (Shakeshaft 1987, p.148).

Some of the most widely accepted theories and concepts used in educational management are criticized as being androcentric. For example, Shakeshaft criticizes Fiedler's theory of leadership effectiveness (see Chapter 3) on the grounds that his definition of leadership was 'based on the male-dominated corporate world of big business' (Shakeshaft 1987, p.154) and that whilst the theory is concerned with the interplay of situational variables and the relationship of the leader and led, no account is taken of the situational variable of gender. (Shakeshaft 1987, p.156)

Similarly Shakeshaft criticises Maslow's theory of motivation (see Chapter 11) which, by placing social needs well below self-realization in the hierarchy of needs appears to indicate that self-actualization through home and family is inferior to 'the full humanness of the male' (Shakeshaft 1987, p 157). Her analysis concludes that Maslow appears to devalue the female experience, since the theory implies that women may evolve beyond 'feminine' fulfillments to the public world of the male.

Male and female 'styles' of management

The identification of characteristics as being basically male or female can be modified by use of the term 'gender', which when applied to social roles is relatively value-free.

> 'Masculine' and 'feminine' represent coherent, consistent 'ideal types', which none of us are. Gender is not defined by physical sex so an individual may have a very clear identity as a man (male) while having a largely 'feminine' behaviour repertoire (Gray 1989, p.43).

Gray has identified two paradigms which can be used as a means of examining gender issues in schools.

The feminine or 'nurturing' paradigm:

caring,
creative,
intuitive,
aware of individual differences,
non-competitive,
tolerant,
subjective,
informal.

The masculine, defensive/aggressive paradigm:

highly regulated,
conformist,
normative,
competitive,
evaluative,
disciplined,
objective,
formal.
(Gray 1993 p.111)

However, rather than reinforcing any stereotypes, the types of qualities listed by Gray need not be mutually exclusive; each person can recognize that they have qualities from both lists:

> the better adjusted we are emotionally the easier it is for us to accept this 'fully androgynous' duality — we see it simply as a full description of a mature person, whether male or female being of little relevance (Gray 1989, p.39).

Despite the rational acceptance of some degree of gender 'androgyny' there is still a tendency for schools and places of work to expect that males and females will accord with the appropriate paradigm. Gray identifies the feminine paradigm with the accepted ethos of primary schools and sees the masculine as broadly being equated as an ideal type of secondary school. The implication of this is that there is potential tension and role conflict for women managers, particularly those in secondary schools and conversely for male managers in primary schools.

The tension between the traditionally 'male' role of secondary headteachers and their recognition of the need for the 'nurturing' qualities that are traditionally identified as female has been thrown into sharp relief by research on effective schools and school improvement.

❑ Effective schools and 'feminine' management

Studies show that effectiveness of schools is linked with qualities such as empathy, warmth, genuineness, concreteness (focusing on present issues) (Murgatroyd and Gray, 1984, p.41) The twelve key factors identified for effective junior schooling (Mortimore et al. 1988) emphasise involvement and good communication. School improvement:

> implies a very different way of thinking about change than the ubiquitous 'top-down' approach so popular with policy-makers (Hargreaves and Hopkins 1992, p. 234).

Good management is seen to be the 'empowering' of others through transformational leadership. The 'nurturing' qualities identified with women are being recognized as a strength in management. A head of department in teacher education saw the need to convince people that she could manage in the conventional 'male' way: 'good organisation and planning, clear aims, support for the department's policies ...' and also planned to bring to bear 'enabling, facilitative attributes which are generally seen as more "female"' (Whitehead 1993, p.79).

Much of the research reported by Shakeshaft (1987) therefore has implications for school effectiveness and improvement. Amongst the findings are that women have far more interactions with both subordinates and superiors, and are more likely to be informal in style than their male equivalents. Women tend to give more importance to differences between individual students and to emphasise academic achievement and the productivity of teachers.

Differences in styles of communication and decision-making also have relevance to effective school management. Studies undertaken in the United States and reported by Shakeshaft (1987, pp.179–186) show that women managers tend to be more democratic than males, their speech tends to be more polite, less aggressive and more tentative. For managers who seek to motivate and engage subordinates, female speech patterns may be more successful.

The study of female managers in 24 British comprehensive schools showed that women employed their communication skills to good effect in jobs that required 'cross-school liaison'.

> If there is a genuine difference in what men and women are good at, it seems the school is missing these cross-school influencing and diplomacy skills from their promotion lists (Weightman 1989, p.121).

There are similarities between the findings reported by Shakeshaft and others and the qualities that are being identified as crucial to effective schooling. These include:

— clear educational goals
— values that stress care and relationships
— a focus on educational issues
— co-operative decision-making
— monitoring of other's progress
— behaviour that promotes achievement and learning as well as high morale and commitment by staff (Shakeshaft 1987, p.200)

Routes to change

The theories stressing male cultural domination and the organizational constraints on achieving equality carry the implication that changes of the most basic kind are necessary:

behavioural changes in men and women, structural and legal changes in school and society, and attitudinal changes in everyone must be achieved. No one strategy will accomplish this revolution; many approaches must be used (Shakeshaft 1987, p.126).

Against this background, the possibilities of greater equality for women in educational management can be considered at the individual, institutional and societal levels.

❏ Specific strategies for change

For the individual
Generally these strategies are based on the assumption that the socialization of the female should be adjusted through training to enable her to cope better with the 'male' world. Such strategies are criticized as encouraging women to adopt 'masculine behaviours and values — to be competitive, aggressive; to look like men' (Ozga 1993, p.9) and it is feared that at worst, they may not build on the strengths that women can bring to management.

However reviews of training aimed specifically at women indicate that those receiving training gain in confidence and build support networks, leading to the conclusion that: 'management training, particularly if it contains a feminist input, can be one way of increasing the numbers of women in school leadership' (Jayne 1989, p.111).

A further question is raised as to whether women will benefit more from management training without men present. Al Khalifa (1992) makes a strong case for the effectiveness of women-only management training in terms of the increased confidence, empowerment and levels of support and opportunities for networking that such courses provide, but concludes that:

> Women's training is a form of positive action which assists women in their development but it is not an adequate solution to the problems and barriers impeding women's access to management (p.104).

For the organization
The existence of male 'gatekeepers' has been identified as a crucial organizational factor limiting the entrance of women to educational management. The inclusion of women on selection committees was found to raise the likelihood of a woman being hired from 20 per cent to 35 per cent (Schmuck 1986, p.179).

Appraisal as a formative instrument in schools and colleges may be used as an opportunity for the development of female management potential but as Thompson (1992, p.259) points out: 'gender stereotypes do need to be considered in appraisal training if appraisal is to be fair and equitable'.

Changes in management styles, linked with effective schooling and school improvement place a new emphasis on 'female' participative styles of management. Such changes may support the development of more female managers.

For society
Political will is required if change is to be under-pinned. Joanna Foster, Chair of the Equal Opportunities Commission states that:

> Neither employers and unions nor women themselves, despite their determination and public commitment, can do it by themselves. The leadership and, above all, action of Government will make the vital difference (Davidson and Cooper, 1992).

The development of equal opportunities in schools has been endorsed by Ofsted requirements (DFE, 1992) but on a wider front, the results of a survey of equal opportunities in *The Times Top 1,000 Index for 1987* was reported as painting 'a gloomy picture of the present or future development of equal opportunities' (Davidson and Cooper 1992, p.165).

For the general encouragement of equal opportunities there is the example of the 'affirmative action' that has been adopted as policy in the USA. This gives Government backing to positive recruitment strategies towards the employment of women.

As change is necessary on the micro and macro level to promote equal opportunities, the relevance of what women have to offer to educational management remains:

> The real measure of success will be seen both in an increase in the number of women in administration and in allowing those women to function as females, not as imitation men (Shakeshaft 1987, p.144).

Summary

Women are firmly established in the work-place, but despite the proportion and number of women who engage in paid work, there is inequality in both pay and opportunity. This inequality extends to the field of education and educational management despite the high proportion of women at work in schools and colleges.

Analysis of inequality encompasses theories of socialization and of organizational barriers with 'their subtle gender-based practices' (Schmuck 1986, p.180) Strategies for change include awareness of the need to promote equal opportunities through recruitment, professional development and appraisal. Change may be enhanced by the adoption of empowering and transformational management.

Despite the male cultural domination of traditional theories of management, there is growing recognition that those gender qualities identified with the feminine side of human nature are amongst those required in the management of the effective school. Therefore in attempts to redress the balance of inequality between male and female, it is important to recognise and value what women have to offer to educational management.

Further reading

Collections of writings on women in education include:

Ouston, J. (Ed) (1993) *Women in Education Management*, Harlow: Longman.

Ozga, J. (Ed) (1993) *Women in Educational Management*, Milton Keynes: Open University Press.

Theoretical issues are treated in:

Gray, H.L. (1989) 'Gender considerations in school management: masculine and feminine leadership styles' in Riches, C. and Morgan, C. (Eds) *Human Resource Management in Education*, Milton Keynes: Open University Press.

Hall, V. (1993) 'Women in educational management: a review of research in Britain' in Oustson, J. (Ed) *Women in Education Management*, Harlow: Longman.

Schmuck, P.A. (1986) 'School Management and Administration: an analysis by gender' in Hoyle, E. and McMahon, A. (Eds) *The Management of Schools, World Year-book of Education 1986*, London: Kogan Page.

Shakeshaft, C. (1987) *Women in Educational Administration*, Newbury Park: Sage.

Shakeshaft, C. (1993) 'Women in educational management in the United States' in Ouston, J. (Ed) *Women in Education Management*, Harlow: Longman.

A perspective on women in general management is given in:

Davidson, M.J. and Cooper, C.L. (1992) *Shattering the Glass Ceiling: The Woman Manager*, London: Paul Chapman Publishing.

Training women for educational management is covered in:

Gray, H.L. (1993) 'Gender issues in management training' in Ozga, J. (Ed) *Women in Educational Management*, Milton Keynes: Open University Press.

Jayne, E. (1989) 'Women as leaders of schools: the role of training' in *Educational Management and Administration*, **17**, pp.109–114.

Ouston, J. (Ed) (1993) *Women in Education Management*, Harlow: Longman.

Other recommended reading:

Al Khalifa, E. (1992) 'Management by halves: women teachers and school management' in Bennett, N., Crawford, M. and Riches, C. (Eds) *Managing Change in Education: Individual and Organizational Perspectives*, London: Paul Chapman Publishing.

Thompson M. (1992), 'Appraisal and equal opportunities' in Bennett, N., Crawford, M. and Riches, C. (Eds) *Managing Change in Education: Individual and Organizational Perspectives*, London: Paul Chapman Publishing.

Weightman, J. (1989) 'Women in management' in *Educational Management and Administration*, **17**, pp.119–122.

References

Adler, S., Laney, J. and Packer M. (1993) *Managing Women: Feminism and Power in Educational Management*, Milton Keynes: Open University Press.

Al Khalifa, E. (1992) 'Management by halves: women teachers and school management' in Bennett, N., Crawford, M. and Riches, C. (Eds) *Managing Change in Education: Individual and Organizational Perspectives*, London: Paul Chapman Publishing.

Atchison, H. (1993) 'Women and management training in the 1990s' in Ouston J. (Ed) *Women in Education Management*, Harlow: Longman.

Central Statistical Office (1992) *Social Trends 22*, London: HMSO.

Darking, L. (1991) 'The equalizers' in the *Times Educational Supplement*, 3 May.

David, M.E. (1988) 'Prima donna inter pares? Women in academic management' in Acker, S. (Ed) *Teachers, Gender and Careers*, London: Falmer Press.

Davidson, M.J. and Cooper, C.L. (1992) *Shattering the Glass Ceiling: The Woman Manager*, London: Paul Chapman Publishing.

DFE (1993) Provisional Data supplied by the Analytical Services Branch

DFE (1992) Ofsted Framework for the Inspection of Schools, London: DFE.

Gray, H.L. (1989) 'Gender considerations in school management: masculine and feminine leadership styles' in Riches, C. and Morgan, C. (Eds) *Human Resource Management in Education*, Milton Keynes: Open University Press.

Gray, H.L. (1993) 'Gender issues in management training' in Ozga, J. (Ed) *Women in Educational Management*, Buckingham: Open University Press.

Hall, V. (1993) 'Women in educational management: a review of research in Britain' in Ouston, J. (Ed) *Women in Education Management*, Harlow: Longman.

Hargreaves, D. and Hopkins, D. (1993) 'School effectiveness, school improvement and development planning' in Preedy, M. (Ed) *Managing the Effective School*, London: Paul Chapman Publishing.

Jayne, E. (1989) 'Women as leaders of schools: the role of training 'in *Educational Management and Administration*, **17**, pp.109–114.

Kanter, R.M. (1977) *Men and Women of the Corporation*, New York: Basic Books.

Kanter, R.M. (1989) *When Giants Learn to Dance: Mastering the Challenges of Strategy, Management, and Careers in the 1990s*, London: Unwin Hyman.

Mortimore, P., Sammons, P. Stoll, L., Lewis, D. and Ecob, R. (1993) 'Key factors for effective junior schooling' in Preedy, M. (Ed) *Managing the Effective School*, London: Paul Chapman Publishing.

Murgatroyd, S. and Gray, H.L. (1984) 'Leadership and the effective school' in Harling, P. (Ed) *New Directions in Educational Leadership*, London: Falmer Press.

Ozga, J. (Ed) (1993) *Women in Educational Management*, Milton Keynes: Open University Press.

Schmuck, R.A. (1986) 'School management and administration: an analysis by gender' in Hoyle, E. and McMahon, A. (Eds) *The Management of Schools, World Year-book of Education 1986*, London: Kogan Page.

Shakeshaft, C. (1987) *Women in Educational Administration*, Newbury Park: Sage.

Shakeshaft, C. (1993) 'Women in educational management in the United States' in Ouston, J. (Ed) *Women in Education Management*, Harlow: Longman.

Singleton, C. (1993) 'Women deputy headteachers in educational management' in Preedy M. (Ed) *Managing the Effective School*, London: Paul Chapman Publishing.

Spendiff, A. (1992), 'Learning brings us together: the meaning of feminist adult education' in Biott, C. and Nias, J. (Eds) *Working and Learning Together for Change*, Milton Keynes: Open University Press.

Strachan, J. (1993) 'Including the personal and the professional: researching women in educational leadership' in *Gender and Education*, 5, 1, pp.71–80.

Thompson M. (1992), 'Appraisal and equal opportunities' in Bennett, N., Crawford, M. and Riches, C. (Eds) *Managing Change in Education: Individual and Organizational Perspectives*, London: Paul Chapman Publishing.

Weightman, J. (1989) 'Women in management' in *Educational Management and Administration*, 17, pp.119–122.

Whitehead, J. (1993) 'The head of department in teacher education' in Ozga, J. (Ed) *Women in Educational Management*, Milton Keynes: Open University Press.

10 Managing human resources

John O'Neill

Introduction

Human resource management (HRM) is of critical importance in educational management given that educational organizations are 'service' organizations. They do not manufacture any tangible product but, rather, they provide a service to their community, to parents, and to students. Quality of service depends directly on the capability, commitment and motivation of the people who provide it as schools and colleges are 'resourced' predominantly by professional teachers together with significant numbers of non-teaching staff (NTS) employed in a variety of support roles. The human resources available to educational organizations thereby constitute both their most valuable asset and their greatest management challenge.

Effective formal education, it is suggested, results largely from the quality of relationships between teachers and students, which itself relies on the level of expertise which teachers can employ in the development and maintenance of that basic relationship. Thus the management of human resources, seen as an increasingly important management function in all types of organization, acquires an additional imperative in schools and colleges. Given that quality learning depends on the recruitment, retention and development of professional teachers, effective HRM in education assumes that the school or college has a set of well-planned and fully integrated strategies, processes and procedures which are intended to promote an optimum level of performance from the people who ultimately determine the quality of education offered by each institution.

> Every pupil should be entitled in each lesson to be taught by a teacher with the knowledge, training, competence and commitment to teach that lesson well (NCE 1993, p.193).

A number of the topics which traditionally appear under the umbrella term of human resources merit separate chapters in this volume. The purpose in this chapter, however, is twofold:

199

- first, to examine HRM in the context of the move towards autonomous schools and colleges; and
- secondly, to relate that context to the particular issues which need to be addressed at site level if individual institutions are to be able to manage their most valuable resource effectively.

This chapter, then, deals with human resource management at both strategic and policy levels.[1] It is argued that the significant challenge for school and college managers in the area of HRM is to ensure that the relationships which characterize the management of staff, and for that matter students, reflect, in both policy and practice, the underlying values of the institution (Drucker, 1988).

The scope of HRM

The HRM approach seeks to start from a consideration of what the strategies of an organization might be and then asks how the human resources can help formulate and accomplish those strategies, and what human development and motivation is required to meet those ends. (Riches and Morgan 1989, pp. 2–3)

Riches and Morgan's definition of HRM is helpful in two respects.

1. The focus is the strategic objectives of the organization. Thus, in educational organizations, HRM is seen to be driven by, and explicitly linked to, whole-school or college educational objectives. Such a view sits comfortably alongside the notions of public accountability and responsiveness expressed in educational legislation throughout the 1980s and 1990s

2. The role of human, rather than material or physical, resources is given due eminence in the pursuit of organizational objectives. Human resources, however, differ from other types of resource in the manner of their deployment and development. People's performance depends not so much on their innate ability as on the extent to which the organization can enable them to perform at an optimum level.

No organization can depend on genius; the supply is always scarce and unreliable. It is the test of an organization to make ordinary people perform better than they seem capable of, to bring out whatever strength there is in its members, and to use each person's strength to help all the other members perform (Drucker 1988, p.361).

Promoting an optimum level of performance is a management task. Associated issues include leadership style (chapter 3) motivation strategies (chapter 11), the creative use of teams (chapter 13), and approaches to professional development (chapter 14). Further, the school or college's policies on recruitment, selection, appraisal, development, remuneration and welfare will impact significantly on the commitment and performance of all categories of staff within the institution. Effective HRM, in short, incorporates both strategic and operational level activities; it is a dynamic management process rather than a set of administrative procedures.

This last point is of particular significance in the state education sector where, until recently, conditions of employment, remuneration and the welfare of staff have been negotiated and decided between national government, LEAs and professional teacher associations or trade unions. The implications of education-specific and more general employment-related legislation have yet to be fully appreciated in schools and colleges where the freedom to develop highly customised approaches to HRM remains constrained by national and local 'custom and practice'. The change from administration of policies decided elsewhere, to the management of school- or college-determined priorities (Coopers and Lybrand, 1988) creates significant challenges for senior staff and governors whose responsibilities in many areas of HRM, prior to the 1988 Education Reform Act (ERA), were limited. Nevertheless, the drive towards fully autonomous educational establishments suggests that HRM practice in the future will increasingly and more closely reflect the needs and priorities of the individual institution than it will those of the LEA:

> The loyalties of all concerned with the school — pupils, parents, governors and staff — are focused on the institution and not on its place in the local educational system. (Bush et al. 1993, p.209).

Personnel or human resource management?

A useful distinction between personnel and human resource management is provided by Guest (1987, p.507) in Figure 10.1. The HRM orientation appears particularly pertinent to the arguments elaborated throughout this volume as to the ways in which it is anticipated that the management of autonomous educational organizations will develop in a market environment. The HRM perspective articulated here is fully consistent with the notion of flexible, responsive schools and colleges.

	Personnel management	Human resource management
Time and planning perspective	Short-term reactive, (ad hoc) marginal	Long-term, pro-active, strategic, integrated
Psychological contract	Compliance	Commitment
Control systems	External controls	Self-control
Employee-relations perspective	Pluralist, collective, low-trust	Unitarist, individual, high-trust
Preferred structures/ systems	Bureaucratic, mechanistic, centralized, formal defined roles	Organic, devolved, flexible roles
Roles	Specialist/professional	Largely integrated into line management
Evaluation criteria	Cost-minimization	Maximum utilzation (human asset accounting)

Figure 10.1 Stereotypes of personnel management and human resource management (Guest 1987, p.507).

West-Burnham (1990, p.67) argues for a distinction between the largely bureaucratic elements of a narrowly defined personnel function in education, and the broader HRM focus which embodies elements of leadership and team-building.

> The danger in the education system is that there will be an emphasis on procedures and practices at the expense of personal growth and relationships.

For West-Burnham, the solution is to view HRM as a holistic management strategy which addresses individual and organizational needs and which permeates all levels of organizational activity (Figure 10.2). His model offers an exhaustive taxonomy of the activities which need to be undertaken at institutional level. In addition, however, there is an implicit emphasis on the basic 'management of learning' objectives of the organization. In West-Burnham's model, school and college managers would be supported, rather than directed, by a personnel function able to offer technical expertise and advice where appropriate. In this respect, the model proposed for the education sector replicates emerging and projected trends in other types of organization (Coulson-Thomas and Brown, 1989).

Principle	Processes	Skills/qualities
1 Leadership	Appointment procedures	Assertiveness
	Appraisal systems	Conflict management
	Career development	Counselling
	Consultative procedures	Decision-making
	Effective communication	Delegation
2 Team management	Employee services	Innovations
	Equal opportunities policies	Interpersonal skills
		Management of change
	Evaluation procedures	Negotiating
	Health and safety	Planning
3 Performance management	Industrial relations	Prioritising
	Job analysis	Problem solving
	Managing information	Stress management
	Organizational development	Target setting
		Time management
	Record keeping	Vision
4 Organisational design	Succession planning	
	Training design	
	Welfare systems	

Figure 10.2 The components of human resource management (West-Burnham 1990, p. 70)

We now turn to an analysis of how recent educational legislation has affected the opportunities and constraints on autonomous schools and colleges in relation to HRM.

Autonomous schools and colleges

The seminal changes incorporated in the ERA and subsequent education acts have led not only to fundamental changes in the internal organization and management of schools and colleges but also to a significant reframing of the relationship between LEA and individual institutions (Pryke 1992, Ranson 1992).

The transition of LEA services towards a 'demand-led' (West 1991, p.123), 'trading-agency' or 'business-unit' basis has implications for decisions about the management of HRM at school and college level. In the early years of LMS there is evidence that institutions are gaining in confidence in routine personnel administration yet they continue to expect the LEA to be able to provide 'expert and technical aspects of support', in the form of a 'consultancy' style, delivered in a 'slick, efficient way and on a high quality basis' (Pryke 1992, p.5). Further, evidence from the grant maintained (GM) sector suggests that governing bodies with fully delegated powers as employers are reluctant to move too far away from nationally or locally determined norms in the area of pay and conditions of service (Bush et al. 1993, p.149).

There is evidence, nevertheless, of educational organizations

1. Beginning to examine the 'lack of clear boundaries' (Mortimore et al. 1992, p.ix) between teaching and non-teaching roles within the institution. This has led to non-teaching staff (NTS) undertaking 'a broader (and increasing) range of tasks and responsibilities than hitherto, including some at the level of middle and senior management' (ibid.)

2. Seeking to exercise greater flexibility in the use of discretionary payments to teaching staff (Bush et al. 1993, p.150) within the overall resources available to the institution.

The picture which emerges is one of schools and colleges benefiting from increased levels of opportunity choice in relation to overall human resource deployment and the balance which it is possible to create between different types and grades of staff (Brunt, 1993). In addition, schools and colleges are faced with decisions about which aspects of HRM they wish to manage directly 'in-house' and which they prefer to buy from elsewhere.

Related central government initiatives, specifically in the area of HRM, have spawned a further set of school-based managerial requirements which relate to the training, support and development of professional teaching staff. These initiatives are examined briefly below.

New initiatives

The changing status of HRM, from administration to management (West-Burnham, 1990), reflects a combination of socio-economic trends. Riches and Morgan (1989, p.2) identify the following factors which have contributed to an increased focus on people in organizations in general:

- increased legislation with respect to fair employment and health and safety at work

- technological, economic and demographic pressures represented by the highly competitive global economy
- an increasing emphasis on economy and value for money as a resource allocation yardstick
- the increased use of performance indicators for evaluating what is being achieved in institutions

In the education sector these trends are reflected in a series of programmes, initiated by central government, which has the express purpose of improving the supply and performance of the teaching force at large:

- a broadening of entry routes into the teaching profession
- a strengthening of support arrangements for teachers at various career stages via:
    — induction guidelines
    — mentoring schemes
    — attempts to develop taxonomies of professional and managerial competencies
- the introduction of appraisal schemes
- funding for professional development activities
- the development of published performance indicators
- a preference for links between pay and performance
- an enhanced focus on the role played by NTS

The aim of central government would appear to be, then, to persuade schools and colleges to adopt a particular vision of sound management practice in general, and high quality HRM in particular, via:

- statutory responsibilities
- the dissemination of good practice
- the encouragement of regional networks of support and information

The dilemma for schools and colleges lies in attempting to establish an internal strategy for HRM which builds on the prevailing culture of the institution, yet is flexible enough to incorporate the many external demands for change and development. The challenge is not so much to adopt them wholesale but rather to adapt appropriate elements of these various initiatives so that they become integral features of the management of the organization rather than bolt-on extras. The next section, therefore, examines the management issues associated with a strategic level approach to HRM.

Strategic HRM

Moves, in the 1990s, towards school or college-based Initial Teacher Training (ITT) and continuing professional development (CPD) have allowed institutions to make choices about how much direct control they wish to exercise over the training and development of their human resources. This, combined with greater governing body discretion over staffing levels and associated pay policies, suggests that all educational organizations have the opportunity to become actively engaged across the full range of what are traditionally perceived as HRM or personnel functions.

As West-Burnham explains (see chapter 4), strategic management involves the institution in articulating a clear set of values and aims, and in making decisions about how that is reflected in the particular 'mix' of educational services the institution wishes to offer. The educational mix will vary from one institution to another (Murgatroyd and Morgan, 1993). HRM issues are an integral feature of that strategic process and will influence the school or college's development of policies in the following areas:

Social responsibility the philosophy of the organization towards the people it employs, covering areas such as equity, consideration of individual needs and fears, the quality of working life.

Employment the level of personnel the organization wishes to employ, the provision of equal opportunity and reasonable security.

Pay the level of pay and other benefits for employees and the extent to which pay systems are negotiated and disclosed.

Promotion the attitude of the organization to providing long-term career prospects and to promoting from within the organization.

Training the scope of training and staff development schemes and the extent to which the organization proposes to subsidise education and training.

Industrial relations policies on union recognition, closed shops, the role of teacher representatives and shop stewards and the approach to dealing with grievances, discipline and redundancy (adapted from Armstrong 1984, p.22).

The fragmentation of the role of the LEA, and increased discretion over the use of resources, are reflected in greater degrees of freedom at site level to make a considered institutional response to each of the areas above. HRM strategies, then, increasingly reflect the value placed upon human resources within that individual institution. In turn this creates a greater variety of approach to the management of staff from one establishment to another. The approach adopted will reflect the perceived importance of being able to attract and retain appropriate people within the institution.

The creation of an educational marketplace, via the ERA and subsequent legislation, now has direct relevance for the recruitment of staff just as much as students. With greater freedom to determine the range of benefits and working conditions on offer to individual staff, comes the realisation that, particularly when seeking to attract quality staff, institutions are in direct competition with each other. The institutions which are most successful are likely to be those which manage, within the resources they have available, to develop the most appealing balance of factors outlined by Armstrong, (1984).

The realities of that marketplace, however, suggest that strategic approaches to HRM in autonomous schools and colleges need to adopt a pragmatic approach to the very real prospect of a shortage of high quality professional staff in certain key areas. These shortages, at times chronic (Straker, 1991), impact significantly on the range and quality of educational services offered. The Audit Commission (1989, p.8) advocates consideration of four possible organizational responses to professional staff shortages in public sector services:

1. *Reviewing the sources of supply*, to see if contracting out is feasible and economic

2. *Reorganizing work* to achieve the best match of skills available to tasks needing to be performed

3. *Improving employment practices* to ensure that those scarce staff who are really indispensable are located, recruited, trained, retained and motivated

and if all these fail, or if shortages are critical

4. *Getting out of the business* by contracting-out functions that would be better performed in-house, or by cutting services (emphasis in original)

The requisite policy areas themselves are not new ones. What has changed since 1979 is the ability of individual institutions to influence what is offered to staff by way of an overall employment package which reflects the culture of the school or college, the employment market in which it operates, and the educational services it is attempting to staff.

Recruitment and retention policy

There are four substantive issues to be considered in attempting to obtain and retain high quality teaching staff.

1. The characteristics of the total pool of teachers available for employment and career progression (teacher *supply*)

2. The policy mix which persuades suitable candidates to apply for particular posts (teacher *recruitment*)

3. The 'mix' of teaching and non-teaching staff (teacher *deployment*)

4. The processes and procedures used to obtain optimum involvement and commitment from individuals (teacher *integration*)

❑ Teacher supply

NCE (1993, p.208) identifies three routes into the teaching profession:

*   young entrants
*   mature entrants
*   returners to the profession

The development of a variety of flexible entry schemes (NCE 1993, p.208), with which schools and colleges can become directly involved, has considerable implications for educational organizations operating either in isolation or as part of a consortium whose role it is to ensure adequate supply (Fidler et al. 1993; Griffiths and McLachlan, 1993). Entrants to the profession, to a greater extent than before, come from diverse backgrounds and experiences, bring differing aspirations and expectations to their employment, and, as such, create significant human resource management challenges and opportunities.

> Certain significant demographic trends and changes in the labour market environment confronting organizations, such as declining birth rates, an ageing population, an increasingly educated workforce and the increased participation of women, are making for a less homogeneous workforce which is placing a premium on the 'effective management of diversity' (Beaumont 1993, p.56).

Schools and colleges, in turn, will need to modify traditional approaches to HRM policy, to enable them to respond to the employment and development needs of staff who do not fit an increasingly anachronistic forty-year full-time career path pattern (Green 1992; NCE 1993).

❏ Teacher recruitment

Organizations are restructuring to reflect differing employment patterns and economic uncertainty. Handy (Handy, 1985; Handy and Aitken, 1986; Handy, 1990) chronicles the move, in all types of organization, away from large cores of full-time permanent contract staff which severely constrain the ability of managers to respond to different levels of activity within the organization and in the external environment. Handy argues that different types of activity within organizations, variable environmental influences and the disparate employment needs of individuals, combine to make a cogent case for closer linkage between staffing structures and the actual tasks undertaken by the organization itself.

In the education sector this suggests that schools and colleges:

(a) acknowledge that not all entrants to the profession will want permanent full-time contracts; flexible working and job-sharing opportunities may appeal to potential recruits

(b) accept that the precarious nature of educational funding requires institutions to adopt a more considered mix of different types of employment contract which promote rather than inhibit organizational flexibility

(c) differentiate between the levels of additional benefits which accompany each type of contract so that, for example, insecurity of tenure can be compensated for with higher pay levels or significant development opportunities not available in competitor institutions

It has been observed that differentiated approaches to the employment and payment of teachers is not without precedent (Thomas, 1985). Within an HRM framework, however, it is inevitable that any attempt to diverge from historical patterns of employment will create tensions and uncertainties at site level which have long been avoided at national and local government levels.

The failure to take account of, and adapt to, the realities of the labour market for teachers in no way diminishes the effect of the workings of that market. Hostility to market-oriented policies on the basis that they are diversionary, and divisive for the teaching profession, ignores their effect on learners. Under existing salary and supply policies some learners are not only diverted from effective learning by inadequately qualified teachers (e.g. maths) but obtain unequal (divisive) access to educational opportunities. And it is learners who are the most important resource in schools (Thomas 1985, p.95).

As NCE (1993, p.198–202) indicates, continuing problems with high teacher turnover in some inner city areas, shortages of subject specialists and mid-career torpor all point to the need for radical and flexible approaches to recruitment and retention initiatives.

The difficulties facing managers in autonomous schools and colleges, in attempting to match human resources to the level of activity within the organization, relate partly to the continuing constraints imposed on them by a comparatively inflexible collective bargaining machinery belonging to a pre-ERA age. It becomes clear that in order to respond effectively, individual institutions need to be able to exercise maximum discretion in the following three aspects of recruitment:

- the type and length of employment contract offered
- the linkage between pay and market forces
- the range of additional benefits which form part of a complete retention and development package

The various elements of that package will be drawn from the factors suggested by Armstrong above: i.e. professional development, promotion prospects, enhanced early retirement, and, in the specific context of educational organizations, such items as timetable remission, a high degree of autonomy, enhanced capitation and well-equipped teaching accommodation. The particular mix on offer will be dictated by the available resources and informed by the HRM philosophy of the individual institution, by market norms and, not least, by the level of determination of the school or college to closely match its ideal job and person specifications when recruiting staff.

❑ Teacher deployment

The 1988 ERA has transformed the issue of staffing within schools and colleges. This section examines the implications of the changes from an HRM perspective.

Within the provisions for LMS (LACSAB, 1990; DFE 1993; NCE, 1993) the governing body of a school or college enjoys a markedly greater degree of freedom in decisions concerning:

- the size and type of staffing structure
- the make up of individual job descriptions
- remuneration
- grade structures for posts
- appointment and dismissal of staff

Three broader aspects of LMS have direct implications for staffing decisions:

1. Funding on the basis of average rather than actual teacher costs places a significant premium on teaching experience. Prior to LMS, institutions could appoint the most experienced candidate at no extra cost to themselves

2. The move away from staffing quotas on the basis of pupil-teacher ratio (PTR) enables institutions to decide on their own mix of teachers, other professionals and 'para-professionals' (NCE 1993)

3. The devolution of funding, for services formerly provided at the centre by the LEA, allows institutions to decide whether to staff an activity or post in-house, or whether to buy it in as a service from a contractor

The shift can be described as a move from supply to demand led staffing. In this sense an appropriate model is Handy's shamrock organization which is made up of:

- the essential *core* of professional staff
- the *contractual fringe* which provides services to the organization for a fee
- the *flexible workforce* which is 'contracted labour' employed on a part-time or temporary contract basis (Handy, 1990).

It is not difficult to apply the model to autonomous educational organizations and envisage establishments staffed by a variety of permanent, temporary and supply contract teaching staff together with a range of individuals and agencies providing a myriad of professional, clerical and ancillary services on either a service agreement or fee-paying basis. The range of options available to schools and colleges in the staffing of educational activities has increased greatly. Equally, however, the need both to attract and retain high quality staff and, at the same time, to demonstrate effective student learning, creates difficult choices for institutions in terms of the level of qualifications and experience demanded for a post, type of contract, level of remuneration and the opportunities for advancement and development which are offered by the organization.

> Much of what teachers do in school does not require a teacher to do it (...)
> There should be far more people in schools who can support teachers by
> taking responsibility for some of these tasks, freeing teachers to implement
> their professional role. This would not only be a more effective use of
> resources but would also raise the morale of teachers. (NCE 1993, p.225)

There is, however some empirical evidence (Mortimore et al. 1992) of
organizations linking staffing more directly to the demands of a particular
activity. Mortimore et al. identified a significant post-1988 change in the
number and type of NTS in primary and secondary schools. This would
suggest that organizations are demonstrating both an awareness of the
relatively high cost of professional teacher time and of the variety of activities
that might usefully be carried out by other categories of staff, in the areas of:

- curriculum support
- support for the management and administration of schools
  (Mortimore et al. 1992, p.viii)

❏ Teacher integration

In this section we examine the management of staff from the perspective of
performance management; the effective integration of staff into the working
processes of the organization. This has two strands. In the first, the focus is on
the package of factors which may be used to attract, motivate and retain staff.
In the second, we analyse the strategies which are available in order to
support and evaluate the work of members of the organization.

The basic polemic in HRM is the achievement of a productive balance between
support and control, between empowerment and accountability, between
person- and performance-centred approaches, between process and outcomes.
The tension is between 'soft' management approaches which are regarded as
appropriate within collegial, professionally staffed organizations, and the
'hard', objective measures of attainment or competence typically used to
monitor and evaluate performance externally. An accommodation between
the two extremes is necessary in educational organizations which are required
to respond to the demands of external stakeholders, yet which depend for their
success on optimum levels of commitment from staff in order to maintain
high quality services.

The management of performance is a complex phenomenon which is
influenced at institutional level by management or leadership style (see
chapter 3), by motivation issues (see chapter 11), by external demands for
public accountability (see chapter 15), by monitoring and review processes
(see chapter 8) and, not least, by institutional culture (see chapter 5). In

addition, three factors have militated against the ready identification of measurable performance standards in education:

- the perceived difficulty of defining educational objectives
- the traditional classroom autonomy enjoyed by teachers in many institutions
- the historical antipathy in education towards 'managerial' approaches

The notion that performance management is inimical to the work of schools and colleges is strongly refuted by Trethowan (1987, p.1) who argues that effective performance is characterized by:

- clarification of goals or objectives
- feedback on performance

There is no effective management without appraisal. Once a person accepts that management is working with and through others to achieve organizational goals, then appraisal is part of that process. It is not an optional extra.

The analysis of performance has to be regarded as a *sine qua non* of the effective delivery of educational activities in schools and colleges. The issue then becomes one of who has ownership of the process, and to what degree. The way forward may well be encapsulated in the rationale provided by Drucker (1988, p.362):

1. The focus of the organization must be on *performance*. The first requirement of the spirit of performance is high performance standards, for the group as well as each individual. The organization must cultivate in itself the habit of achievement.
2. The focus of the organization must be on *opportunities* rather than on problems.
3. *The decisions that affect people* — their placement and their pay, promotion, demotion and severance — must express the values and beliefs of the organization. They are the true controls of an organization.
4. Finally, in its people decisions, management must demonstrate that it realises that *integrity* is one absolute requirement of managers, the one quality that they must bring with them and cannot be expected to acquire later on. And management must demonstrate that it requires the same integrity of itself. (emphases in original)

The usefulness of the Drucker criteria is that they emphasize both process and outcomes. The effective management of staff demands an equal focus on organizational decisions which gain the full commitment of individuals and on the management strategies which are needed to obtain optimum performance. Above all, suggests Drucker, the school's or college's approach to the management of performance must be consistent with the core values espoused by the institution, not just a bolt-on extra.

❑ Gaining full commitment

Managers in educational organizations are faced with a complex range of decisions in the attempt to devise a staffing structure which allows the organization flexibility to respond to changing circumstances, yet appeals to potential and existing employees in terms of security, remuneration and opportunities for development.

The starting point is an analysis of organizational staffing requirements (see Figure 10.3). In the figure a distinction is made between primary and secondary areas of activity (after Knight, 1983). *Primary* activities in educational organizations are those directly associated with the teaching and learning process. *Secondary* activities are those concerned with the administrative and managerial support mechanisms which contribute only indirectly to the quality of the learning experience.

	Type of contract		
	long-term	fixed-term	agency
Focus of activities primary			
secondary			

Figure 10.3 Analysing staffing requirements

The type of contract offered relates to the divisions of Handy's shamrock organization described above. Schools and colleges need to make decisions about which areas of organizational activity merit lengthy, semi-permanent contracts, which should be on a shorter-term basis and which should be contracted out to specialists. The dangers of staff exploitation via the routine use of short-term contracts are readily apparent (Mortimore et al. 1992; Beaumont 1993). Nevertheless, Drucker's dictum suggests that it is possible to retain flexibility in staffing providing that decisions are characterized by management integrity rather than short-term expediency. HMI (1992), for example, point to an increased use of inappropriate short-term contracts for newly qualified teachers. This may preserve organizational flexibility in terms of staffing costs but does little for the career or professional development of the individuals involved. Handy (1985; 1990) takes the argument a stage further by suggesting that it is essential to differentiate between levels of pay and other benefits offered to different categories of staff, so that lack of security is compensated for by higher wages or opportunities for rapid, high quality personal development.

There is a range of factors which might make up the package of benefits offered to staff on different types of contract (see Figure 10.4). Here they are categorized as either remuneration, welfare or development oriented. Significantly, there is a considerable degree of overlap between factors offered as benefits to staff and the strategies used to manage individual and collective performance.

Remuneration	Welfare	Development
starting salary	incapacity benefits	induction
salary progression	career-break entitlements	mentoring
performance-related pay	child-care provision	appraisal
	security of tenure	opportunities for career and professional development
	retirement provision	
	grievance and discipline mechanisms	
	counselling	
	working conditions	
	union recognition	
	redundancy	

Figure 10.4 Factors in the management of staff commitment

❑ Obtaining optimum performance

As suggested at the beginning of this chapter, optimum levels of staff performance are contingent upon effective management. The upsurge in interest in the management of human resources has been paralleled by an enhanced focus on the strategies or tools which are available to managers. The principal phases of performance management may be summarized as

- selection
- induction
- mentoring
- appraisal
- development

The history of education management practice is characterized by a lack of awareness of the importance of effective selection (Morgan et al. 1983; Evetts, 1991), induction (HMI, 1992) and professional development (Ofsted, 1993) as essential constituent parts of an overall approach to HRM. Effective practice, however, presupposes a considered school or college position in these areas so that, in each phase, the organization promotes clear expectations of performance and provides appropriate and adequate support mechanisms. The common theme or tension in each is the locus of control or ownership of the process. The willingness of individual professional staff to address either:

- performance failures; or
- development needs

in a meaningful way is entirely contingent upon the quality of relationship between the individual and his or her mentor, manager, appraiser or counsellor. A useful approach, which may promote reconciliation of both organizational and individual priorities, is suggested by the framework for management by objectives (MBO). This has three key elements:

1. Performance goals or targets initiated periodically by the employee.
2. Mutual agreement on a set of goals by the employee and his (*sic*) superior after discussion.
3. Periodic review by the employee and his superior of the match between goals and achievements.

(Schuster and Kindall, cited in Fidler 1988, p.4)

The three elements of the MBO approach provide a coherent structure for the management of performance, in all its phases, which might be adapted to suit the preferred management style within any institution. The value of the approach is that it emphasises the need for both 'managed' and 'manager' to play an active role in the process. In theory, therefore, the approach is readily applicable to the education sector because, used appropriately, it values both professional 'voice' and managerial responsibility.

As Guest's (1987) model (see Figure 10.1) suggests, a move from personnel to human resource management endorses the central importance of the line manager in terms of achieving an optimum level of performance from members of staff. The breadth of strategies adopted by managers is a reflection of the prevailing management culture of the institution. The important issue in performance management here, however, is the degree to which the phases of performance outlined on page 216, are fully integrated elements of management practice within the school or college.

The difficulties of applying such performance management approaches in education are articulated, with specific reference to appraisal, by Fidler (1988):

- the management of professionals
- the assessment of predominantly qualitative objectives
- limited range of rewards
- unclear linkage between teaching quality and learning
- individuals report to more than one superordinate
- lack of time
- fragmented infrastructure to support the process

Performance standards in this context are likely to be relative, as defined within the organization, rather than absolute measures. This places greater emphasis on the role of the organization, and team leaders or line managers, in the negotiation and agreement of acceptable performance standards. Thus the quality of relationships between staff, rather than the tools of performance management, is of primary importance. In an effective and trusting relationship, 'mentoring' accurately describes the predominant, supportive management style of the school or college whilst 'appraisal' embodies a collective commitment to the attainment of high standards of educational performance (e.g. Trethowan 1987).

Optimum levels of performance derive largely from a high degree of mutual trust between manager and managed. The danger is that the imposition of schemes for the management of performance on an alien school or college culture is likely to lead to 'safe mediocrity' (Drucker, 1988) rather than to higher standards of performance. The evidence, however, suggests that education managers may be unprepared for this relatively new additional role responsibility:

The more established heads of department had often learnt the skills of developing students and probationers from experience; 'newer' ones were sometimes uneasy about the role in that they had been given little guidance as to how best to go about it (Earley and Fletcher-Campbell, 1989, p.116).

The challenge for managers in educational organizations is to develop performance management frameworks which both empower professional staff and respond to external demands for quantifiable improvements in standards.

Summary

This chapter has examined the role of HRM in autonomous educational organizations. Schools and colleges are faced with opportunity choices which promote a high degree of self-determination in the training, development and performance management of professional and support staff. Environmental and economic variables constitute a formidable incentive for educational organizations to depart from traditional employment patterns and adopt more flexible and responsive staffing structures which do not act as a drain on the overall resources available for deployment. The uniqueness of human, as opposed to material or physical, resources suggests that effective HRM relies on the ability of managers to empower, motivate and retain high quality staff within the institution. The challenge is to balance expectations of high performance with a concern for individual welfare and development.

Note

1. The actual processes and procedures which are used to effect those policies, i.e., the details of recruitment, selection, induction, mentoring, appraisal, discipline, grievance, and redundancy all merit greater depth of analysis than can usefully be attempted here. This chapter is limited, perforce, to a broader discussion of the policy framework which is used to structure such procedures.

Further reading

Armstrong, M. (1991) *A Handbook of Personnel Management Practice*, fourth edn. London: Kogan Page.

Brunt, M. (1993) 'Personnel matters' in Morris, R. (Ed) *Education and the Law,* third edn. Harlow: Longman.

Fidler, B. and Cooper, R. (Eds.) (1988) *Staff Appraisal in Schools and Colleges,* Harlow: Longman.

Fidler, B., Fugl, B. and Esp, D. (Eds) (1993) *The Supply and Recruitment of School Teachers,* Harlow: Longman.

Mortimore, P., Mortimer, J., Thomas, H., Cairns, R. and Taggart, B. (1992) *The Innovative Uses of Non-teaching Staff in Primary and Secondary Schools Project, Final Report,* Institute of Education, University of London.

References

Armstrong, M. (1984) *A Handbook of Personnel Management Practice,* second edn. London: Kogan Page.

Audit Commission (1989) *People Management; Retaining and Recruiting Professionals,* management paper number 4, London: HMSO.

Beaumont, P. (1993) *Human Resource Management: Key Concepts and Skills,* London: Sage.

Brunt, M. (1993) 'Personnel matters' in Morris, R. (Ed) *Education and the Law,* third edn. Harlow: Longman.

Bush, T., Coleman, M., and Glover, D. (1993) *Managing Autonomous Schools. The Grant-maintained Experience,* London: Paul Chapman Publishing.

Coopers and Lybrand Associates (1988) *Local Management of Schools,* London: HMSO.

Coulson-Thomas, C. and Brown, R. (1989) *The Responsive Organization: People Management: The Challenge of the 1990s,* Corby: British Institute of Management.

DFE (Department for Education) (1993) *Schoolteachers' Pay and Conditions,* London: DFE.

Drucker, P. (1988) *Management,* London: Pan Books.

Earley, P. and Fletcher-Campbell, F. (1989) *Time to Manage? Department and Faculty Heads at Work,* Windsor: NFER–Nelson.

Evetts, J. (1991) 'The experience of secondary headship selection; continuity and change'. *Educational Studies,* 17, 3, pp.285–294.

Fidler, B. (1988) 'Problems of adaptation to education' in Fidler, B. and Cooper, R. (Eds) *Staff Appraisal in Schools and Colleges*, Harlow: Longman.

Fidler, B., Fugl, B. and Esp, D. (1993) 'Introduction' in Fidler, B., Fugl, B. and Esp, D. (Eds) *The Supply and Recruitment of School Teachers*, Harlow: Longman.

Green, H. (1992) 'Strategies for management development: towards coherence?' in Bennett, N., Crawford, M. and Riches, C. (Eds) *Managing Change in Education*, London: Paul Chapman Publishing.

Griffiths, F. and McLachlan, N. (1993) 'Licensed to learn' in Fidler, B., Fugl, B. and Esp, D. (Eds) *The Supply and Recruitment of School Teachers*, Harlow: Longman.

Guest, D. (1987) 'Human resource management and industrial relations'. *Journal of Management Studies*, **24**, 5, pp.503–521.

Handy, C. (1985) *Understanding Organizations*, third edn, Harmondsworth: Penguin.

Handy, C. (1990) *The Age of Unreason*, London: Arrow Books.

Handy, C. and Aitken, R. (1986) *Understanding Schools as Organizations*, Harmondsworth: Penguin.

HMI (Her Majesty's Inspectorate) (1992) *The Induction and Probation of New Teachers*, London: DES.

Knight, B. (1983) *Managing School Finance*, London: Heinemann Educational.

LACSAB (Local Authorities Conditions of Service Advisory Board) (1990) *Local Management of Schools and Colleges: Personnel Management Implications*, London: LACSAB Advisory Service.

Morgan, C., Hall, V. and MacKay, H. (1983) *The Selection of Secondary School Headteachers*, Milton Keynes: Open University Press.

Mortimore, P., Mortimer, J., Thomas, H., Cairns, R. and Taggart, B. (1992) *The Innovative Uses of Non-teaching Staff in Primary and Secondary Schools Project*, final report, London: Institute of Education, University of London.

Murgatroyd, S. and Morgan, C. (1993) *Total Quality Management and the School*, Milton Keynes: Open University Press.

NCE (National Commission for Education) (1993) *Learning to Succeed*, London: Heinemann.

Ofsted (Office for Standards in Education) (1993) *The Management and Provision of Inservice Education Funded by the Grant for Education Support and Training (GEST)*, London: Ofsted.

Pryke, R. (1992) 'Local management in action'. *Education Today*, **42**, 2, pp.2–6.

Ranson, S. (1992) *The Role of Local Government in Education: Assuring Quality and Accountability*, Harlow: Longman.

Riches, C. and Morgan, C. (1989) *Human Resource Management in Education*, Milton Keynes: Open University Press.

Schuster, R. and Kindall, A. (1974) 'Management by objectives — where we stand today'. *Human Resource Management*, **13**, 1, pp.8–11.

Straker, N. (1991) 'Teacher supply in the 1990s: an analysis of current developments' in Grace, G. and Lawn, M. (Eds) *Teacher Supply and Teacher Quality, Issues for the 1990s*, Clevedon: Multilingual Matters.

Thomas, H. (1985) 'Teacher supply: problems, practice and possibilities' in Hughes, M. (Ed) *Managing Education*, Eastbourne: Holt, Rinehart and Winston.

Trethowan, D. (1987) *Appraisal and Target Setting*, London: Harper and Row.

West, M. (1991) 'Providing an advisory service to schools in the 1990s' in McLoughlin, C. and Rouse, M. (Eds) *Supporting Schools*, London: David Fulton.

West-Burnham, J. (1990) 'Human resource management in schools' in Davies, B., Ellison, L., Osborne, A. and West-Burnham, J. *Education Management for the 1990s*, Harlow: Longman.

11 Motivation

Colin Riches

Work motivation and its relevance to management

❏ The understanding of motivation and managing motivation

A study of work motivation has two basic strands; first, why people behave in the way they do in the workplace and secondly how they can be helped to engage in work behaviours which are beneficial to the organization — and themselves. If the experience of work has a negative effect on individuals they cannot give of their best in that sphere of their lives. If we are to make some relevant application of theoretical knowledge about motivation in educational management we need to understand something about the relationship between theories of motivation and theories of managing motivation. This will be an important consideration in this chapter.

Motivating people to get results through them is central to the purposes of management.

> Apart from developing the skill to work well ... we need to look for ways of developing the will to work well (Evenden and Anderson, 1992).

Motivation and its management is a core element of human resource management (HRM) just as the whole of the latter is the backbone of all effective management.

> Of all the resources at the disposal of a person or organization it is only people who can grow and develop and be motivated to achieve certain desired ends. The attaining of targets for the organization is in their hands and it is the way people are managed ... which is at the heart of HRM ... and optimum management. (Riches and Morgan 1989, p. 1).

An expanding interest in motivation has arisen because of an increasing emphasis on HRM. Katz and Khan (1978) have argued that organizations need people who are:

(a) attracted to staying in an organization as well as initially joining it
(b) perform their tasks in a dependable manner
(c) go beyond this to engage in some type of creative, spontaneous and innovative behaviour. In a nutshell, effective organizations have to get to grips with how people are stimulated to participate and be productive at work

Two factors in particular have contributed to an interest in motivation and its management:

1. A new environment of competition in western societies (and schools and colleges are no exception), in which organizational 'slack' is less tolerated and performance is paramount, forces attention on obtaining full benefit in particular from the human resources which are available. Thus attention is drawn to how management can best motivate employees to achieve the goals of the organization;

2. The increasing sophistication of technology in industry, and to a lesser extent in education, has heightened awareness that machines may be necessary for increasing efficiency and effectiveness in organizations but people and their motivation are seen more than ever as irreplacable in key areas of operation. Thus personnel development programmes have come to the fore to help to provide a continuing reservoir of well-trained and highly motivated people. We can see this demonstrated increasingly in education as elsewhere, although the education service, with its concepts of 'professionalism' and teacher 'autonomy', has hitherto paid limited attention to motivation and personal development.

❏ Defining motivation

One of the difficulties surrounding the study of motivation is that there is no overarching or single theoretical model which explains motivation. Smith et. al. (1990) have described the concept of motivation as:

> probably the most confused, confusing and poorly developed concept in organizational psychology.

The etymological root of the term 'motivation' is the Latin word movere, meaning 'to move'. However such a definition is inadequate here. A preliminary definition of motivation is that it refers to individual differences with regard to the priorities, attitudes and aspects of life style that people seek to fulfil in work, i.e. those things which drive them on and make them feel good about doing so.

Different definitions emphasize to varying degrees a number of facets which constitute motivation. They are:

- The goals which people have which direct their behaviour towards something, e.g. power, status, friends, money
- The mental processes or energetic forces by which individuals (a) pursue/are driven towards particular goals, including decisions about what to aim for and how to go about it and (b) maintain or sustain such behaviour
- The social processes through which some individuals, e.g. managers, seek to retain or change the behaviour of others

A comprehensive definition which incorporates all these aspects has been given by Johannson and Page (1990, p. 196):

> Processes or factors that cause people to act or behave in certain ways. To motivate is to induce someone to take action. The process of motivation consists of:
> - identification or appreciation of an unsatisfied need
> - the establishment of a goal which will satisfy the need
> - determination of the action required to satisfy the need

Clearly the concept is multi-faceted in that it incorporates what gets people activated (arousal) and the force exerted by an individual to engage in desired behaviour (direction or choice of behaviour).

A basic general model of motivation has the following building blocks:

(a) needs or expectations
(b) behaviour
(c) goals
(d) some form of feedback

For example, an expectation that more effort in doing a job will lead to promotion or the need to be socially acceptable in the organization will usually result in a state of disequilibrium within individuals which they will try to reduce (behaviour) by working towards a goal, and information will be fed back to the individual concerning the impact of such behaviour (Dunnette and Kirchner, 1965, quoted in Steers and Porter, 1991). However what actually happens is never so simple or straightforward. First, motives behind actions can never be seen; they are always inferred, when in fact motives may be multiple, disguised, and expressed in different ways according to the person and the culture in which the action takes place. Secondly, motives change and may be in conflict with one another. Thirdly, selection of motives and their intensity will vary between individuals. Finally, when certain prime motives for action are reduced, e.g. through thirst being satisfied, then other motives may become primary ones (see Herzberg, Mausner and Synderman, 1959; and below).

❏ Some concepts related to motivation

Stress

Up to this point we have written of motivation in somewhat neutral terms and as if it was sanitised from negative manifestations. What happens to our basic model if a person's drive is blocked before reaching its desired goal? There are two possible sets of outcomes: constructive behaviour or frustration. Potential frustration may be reduced by managers addressing the problem in a positive way and employing various strategies according to the issue to reduce that frustration, e.g. effective recruitment, selection and training, careful job design and work organization, equitable handling of people, effective communications and a participative style of management. If the problem is not forseen then actual frustration may well take place, and stress, in the negative sense of distress (for some stress may well be a beneficial driving force) is most likely to occur.

Job satisfaction

The relationship between motivation to work and job satisfaction is not at all clear. One view is that the motivation required for a person to achieve a high level of performance is satisfaction with the job but, although the level of job satisfaction may well affect the strength of motivation this is not always so. Locke and Latham (1990) claim that the motivation to work (exert effort) and satisfaction are relatively independent outcomes. Job satisfaction is not the same as motivation in that it is more an attitudinal state being associated with a personal feeling of achievement, either quantitative or qualitative. All that can be said with certainty is that motivation is a process which may lead to job satisfaction. Neither does job satisfaction necessarily lead to improved work performance. Vroom, (1964) after examining twenty studies found a low correlation (0.14) between job satisfaction and job performance. Luthans, (1989) has concluded that,

> Although most people assume a positive relationship, the proponderance of research evidence indicates that there is no strong linkage between satisfaction and productivity.

Morale

'Morale' usually relates to the way people think about their work, and, while the term is sometimes applied to individuals (see for example, D. Evans, 1992), it usually refers to group feelings, thoughts, actions etc., whereas motivation is applied to individuals. Thus Kempner (1971, p.260) defines morale as:

> The extent to which the members of a group identify with the aims and activities of the group.

In examining the state of morale in schools, Lawley (1985) suggests that there are three basic ways of identifying low morale:

- The psychological and physiological state of teachers
- The existence of injustice
- The undermining of status, or threats to personal equilibrium or personal insults

Theories of motivation

❑ Some factors affecting motivation

As we have seen, the variables affecting motivation are very numerous. Text books which deal with the subject have innumerable categorizations of those influences, and diagrams to indicate the way they impact on motivation. The most comprehensive scheme is provided by Betts (1993, p. 145) and is set out in Figure 11.1.

The categories are largely self-explanatory. Betts (p.146) claims that 'override' factors:

> upset the effect of all the previous factors, often regardless of their combined strength to motivate. Override comes into play on the spot: it has an immediate, powerful and dominating effect on motivation by altering behaviour because of some mental incapability, physical incapability or sudden change in the situation surrounding the individual.

The categories, listed are not discreet; they interact with one another in complex ways. However, the mapping is helpful in raising awareness of the multiplicity of factors which go to make up motivation.

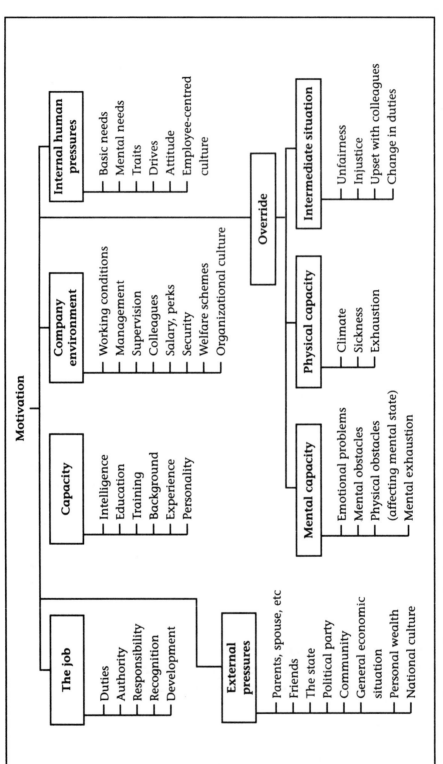

Figure 11.1 The main factors affecting motivation (Betts 1993, p.145)

Needs

Betts includes 'needs' as one aspect of 'internal human pressures'. Needs may be classified as physiological (for food, drink, protection, work) or psychological (for security, belongingness, esteem), and the potency of each will vary between individuals. Drives are sometimes divided into basic or primary drives which are not learned and are derived from physiological needs such as thirst, sex, sleep; general drives that are not learned but are more psychological in character, like competence, curiosity, seeking affection and being active; and finally secondary drives which are learned and tend to take over from primary and general drives if the opportunity occurs. Examples of secondary drives are:

- *aggressiveness:* the drive to be powerful which expresses itself in hostility, awkwardness and being quarrelsome, which extremely is expressed in violence and can be very close to the desire to escape
- *acquisitiveness:* the desire for protection and possession
- *self-assertion:* the drive to be important often arising out of the need to be given credit for achievement
- *constructiveness:* the desire to be creative
- *gregariousness:* the urge to belong to a group and be accepted by it

Needs and drives can, of course, come up against obstacles, which can be within one's own personality or external to it such as other people, the demands of society and culture and many other restrictions. Identifying obstacles to achieving goals and recognizing the way these are dealt with by individuals are highly significant for managers if they are to adopt strategies for dealing with them. However, as various theorists of motivation have pointed out, the processes and content of motivation make a linear understanding (need–drive–obstacle–solution–goal–achievement) less than satisfactory because so many variables intervene to complicate the picture.

Theories of motivation

Theories of motivation can be divided into content theories and process theories. The former concentrate on the specific things which motivate individuals at work. The latter attempts to identify and examine the dynamic relationships among the different variables which make up motivation. As the name suggests they are primarily concerned with the actual process of motivation; with how behaviour is initiated, directed and sustained.

❑ Content theories of motivation

Maslow's hierarchy of needs

This is one of the most widely known theories of motivation and concentrates on a supposed needs hierarchy. Maslow (1943) suggests that human needs are arranged hierarchically and that needs which are low in the hierarchy must be largely satisfied before those which are higher in the hierarchy will motivate behaviour. These needs may be defined as:

- *Physiological:* for sunlight, sex, food, water and similar inputs which are basic to human survival

- *Safety-Security:* for freedom from environmental threat, animals and people, for shelter, security, order, predictability and for a generally organized world

- *Belonging or Social:* the need to associate with one's own kind, for relationships, affection, giving and receiving love, for feelings of belonging

- *Esteem and Status or Ego:* for strength, achievement, adequacy, confidence, independence and for reputation, prestige and recognition

- *Self-actualisation:* the need to reach one's ultimate goals in life, to fulfil ones own destiny

---

Self-Actualisation

Esteem and Status
or Ego

Belonging or Social

Safety or Security

Physiological

Figure 11:2 Maslow's needs hierarchy
(Based on Gray and Starke 1988, p. 109)

This hierarchy (caricatured as from 'belly to brains'!) rests on two assumptions: that (a) unsatisfied needs motivate behaviour and (b) as a particular need becomes satisfied it becomes less of a motivator and the next in line takes on more importance. For most people the higher order needs will be less satisfied than the lower ones and differences in satisfaction will depend on cultures and individuals. This theory has not been confirmed by empirical work (see the review by Wahba and Bridwell, 1976). While it may be useful to see the theory as operating over time at a general societal level, at the individual level it has serious drawbacks which include:

- There is a methodological issue: the theory was intended to predict changes in individuals' needs but most of the research has been cross-sectional comparing the needs of different people at one point in time
- It is not easy for psychologists to define constructs such as self-actualisation, let alone to test them
- It is difficult to see how the theory can predict behaviour by assessing the amount of satisfaction that one has to achieve at one level before passing on to the next
- People do not satisfy their needs, especially the higher order ones, through the work situation alone; they are satisfied through other areas of their lives as well
- The hierarchy 'may simply have reflected American middle-class values and the pursuit of the good life, and may not have hit on fundamental universal truths about human psychology' (Buchanan and Huczynski 1985, p. 54)
- Individuals attach different values to the same need
- Some outcomes at work satisfy more than one need
- Even for people with the same hierarchical level the motivating factors may well be different
- The theory seems to ignore the notion of altruistic behaviour
- The theory does not acknowledge gender variables (see chapter 9).

McGregor's 'X' AND 'Y' theory

McGregor (1970), drawing on Maslow's hierarchy of needs model, states that there are two basic suppositions about human nature which will help determine the mode of management which is adopted to motivate people. Theory 'X' incorporates the following assumptions about human nature:

- people are usually lazy and work shy
- most must be coerced, controlled and threatened with punishment to achieve objectives
- the average person avoids responsibility and seeks direction, is unambitious and prefers security to anything else

- motivation (in Maslow's terms) occurs at the physiological and security levels only

Theory 'Y' on the other hand, is based on the assumptions that:

- for most work is natural
- people will be self-directed and controlled if they are committed to definite objectives
- commitment to objectives is because of rewards attached to achievement
- people usually want to accept responsibility
- motivation happens at the affiliation, esteem, and self-actualisation levels

These contrasting theories of motivation are, of course, extremes and an over-simplification, but for McGregor theory 'Y' is the preferred way to motivate people because it is more likely to achieve the desired results.

Herzberg's two–factor theory

This theory, first proposed by Herzberg and his colleagues in 1959, was a major departure in thinking about work motivation. A study of 200 engineers and accountants concluded that satisfaction and dissatisfaction were conceptionally distinct factors caused by different phenomena in the work environment. The research found that feeling good was associated with a preponderance of factors dealing with the work itself and feeling bad with the work environment. Thus, one group of factors was found to cause job satisfaction and another job dissatisfaction. He called the former 'motivators' and the latter 'hygiene' factors, which when present caused dissatisfaction. Motivators generally relate to job content (the nature of the work itself) and hygienes to work context (the environment in which the work is performed). So Hertzberg believes that job satisfaction and job dissatisfaction are different because the sources of each are different.

The theory has generated a good deal of criticism because the empirical evidence suggests that he has oversimplified reality. There are four major criticisms:

- The methodology causes the results: unless Herzbergs's methodology is used it is difficult to support his theory
- The two factors are not distinct: empirical studies suggest that specific job content factors are sometimes listed by individuals as hygienes and job context factors, e.g pay, as motivators. Female workers often list inter-personal relations as motivators while males see them as not

- Human nature explains the findings: people tend to take credit for their own achievement (motivators) and blame others, e.g. the work organization, for their failures (hygienes)
- Hygienes have been ignored under Hertzberg's influence: his ideas may have led to an over emphasis on higher level needs (particularly outside the sphere of professional workers) at the expense of basic needs

The general conclusion is that empirical evidence does not support the two-factor theory although it does not clearly refute it. Maybe the construct of satisfaction/dissatisfaction is correct but hygienes and motivators will vary between individuals. Therefore, if managers knew which content or context factors operated as motivators or hygienes, in a given task for a given individual, this information could be used to effect individual performance.

Nias (1981) has applied Herzberg's theory to an educational context. Using a sample of 135 primary school teachers, she found that job satisfaction arose out of factors which were intrinsic to the job, but also identified 'negative satisfiers', which if removed would result in more job satisfaction, whereas the contextual dissatisfiers would not do so.

> The removal of the 'dissatisfier' does not provide a 'satisfier'. Thus teachers' views on leadership of their heads tend, by definition, to be expressed in negative terms. When they are satisfied with the management of their schools they do not mention it because good management is not, under normal circumstances, a 'satisfier' in its own right. Bad management is, by contrast, a 'dissatisfier' (Nias 1980, p. 258).

Where there was purposeful leadership, and a close fit between the ideologies of teachers and the ideologies of the schools, then satisfaction was high. The most important single dissatisfier was the absence of a sense of purpose in the ethos of the school.

In more recent small-scale studies of primary school teachers Evans (1992, p.8) concluded that:

> school-specific issues are generally more influential on teachers'... satisfaction levels than are centrally initiated policies and conditions of service ... of the 18 teachers who participated in the research ... six reported a strong desire (sometimes even a determination) to change schools due to (*sic*) dissatisfaction .

The evidence on job satisfaction for *heads* seems to suggest that achievement on task or in reaching specific standards of competence are significant (Vroom, 1964; Locke, 1965; Herzberg, 1966). Conversely, the loss of autonomy, e.g. trying to deal with problems over which they have no control, and the powerlessness, e.g. the moving goalposts of government legislation, lead to job dissatisfaction. Steps which may be taken to reduce 'innovation shock' includes the development of teams to share the burdens, and careful preparation for headship.

❑ Process theories of motivation

So far we have considered content theories only, which are concerned with identifying specific things which motivate the individual to work and the relative strengths of those needs, i.e. what motivates. Now we turn to process theories which look at the dynamic relationships between motivational variables concerning the initiation, direction and sustaining of behaviour, i.e. the actual process of motivation. These approaches are represented by expectancy, equity and goal theories.

Expectancy theories

The basis of expectancy theory is that people are influenced by what they expect to be the impact of their actions. Expectancy theory is based on:

1. An individual's perceptions that she/he has about the results of alternative behaviours

2. As the theory is based on individual perceptions it helps to explain individual differences in motivation and behaviour, unlike Maslow's universal content theory

3. It attempts to measure the strength of the individual's motivation

4. Expectancy theory is based on the assumption that human behaviour is to some extent rational and individuals are conscious of their goals and motives and therefore it is possible to predict behaviour

The managerial implications of this complex but popular theory are that, because of its rational basis, it can be used to diagnose and resolve organizational problems. Neider (1980) has argued that managers need to realize that people work well only when they expect their efforts to produce good performance. Ideally, managers should:

- seek to give appropriate rewards for individual performance

- attempt to establish clear relationships between effort-performance and rewards as seen by the individual
- establish clear procedures for evaluating levels of performance (appraisal)
- give attention to intervening variables like abilities, traits, organizational procedures and support facilities, which might affect performance albeit, indirectly (Mullins, 1993)

Equity theory

According to equity theory (Adams 1965), the motivation of individuals in organizations is influenced by the extent to which they feel they are being treated in a fair and equitable manner in comparison with the treatment received by others. Equity theory is based on staff inputs, what they believe will contribute to their job or organization, and their outcomes, what they perceive the organization provides in return. Because of the idea of trading inputs for outcomes, equity theory is often called exchange theory, which is closely related to micro-political behaviour (see chapter 2). When both are in balance according to the perception of a given individual then there is equity, and in the case of inbalance, inequity. The theory assumes that on feeling inequity the individual is motivated to reduce it and this may result in a number of different behaviours:

- Altering inputs, e.g. choose to put more or less effort into the job
- Altering outcomes, e.g. pay or working conditions, without changing inputs
- Distorting inputs or outcomes rather than actually changing them so that a person may change her/his perceptions of what she/he is putting into the organization
- Leaving the situation — asking for a transfer or quitting
- Taking actions to change the inputs or outcomes (either actual or perceived) of others, e.g. saying to a colleague, 'You shouldn't work so hard, it's not worth it.'
- Changing the person one is comparing with to someone else, e.g. I may be worse off compared with X but I am getting a fair deal compared with Y.'

Equity theory argues that perceived inequity creates feelings of discomfort and tension in a person and hence that a person experiencing such inequity will be motivated to restore equity via one of the previous methods (Feldman and Arnold 1983, p.118).

The theory seems to have usefulness in predicting staff behaviour and motivational levels. Its value in the sphere of education might increase as attempts are made to relate pay to performance (however defined), but paradoxically, in times of retrenchment, it has relevance as educational managers seek to assess the relationship between inputs and outcomes of staff when financial rewards are limited and satisfactions need to be engendered in different ways.

Goal theory

Locke (1968) argues that there are three cognitive processes which intervene between events which occur in the environment around a person, e.g. conditions of work, and that person's subsequent performance. They are the perception of that event by the person, his/her evaluation of it and the setting of goals and formulating of intentions. At this point a conscious decision is made about what to do. All types of incentive — direct and powerful, e.g. setting time limits on work to be done, and indirect and less influential, e.g. money, verbal praise, reproof and participation in decision-making — have an influence on behaviour via their effect on staff goals. However, what goals are set is important and there are a number of critical attributes or characterisitcs of goals to be considered. First goal difficulty: the more difficult the goal set, the higher the level of performance brought about, provided it is not unrealistically high. Second, the more specific the goal set the greater is its impact on subsequent performance. Third, for a goal to have a positive impact on a person's performance it must be accepted by that person, and thus participation in goal setting is very important. There is considerable potential in goal theory for influencing motivation and performance of members of organizations provided managers are trained to develop the necessary skills in handling the goal-setting process sensitively and tactfully.

The high-performance cycle

A recent model of work motivation (Locke and Latham, 1990) provides both incorporation of many of the theories discussed above and a trenchant critique of what has gone before to give a guide through a maze of often conflicting theories. Their 'high performance cycle' has as its well attested basis the view that motivation to work (exert effort) and satisfaction, are relatively independent outcomes. They have pieced together several theories into a coherent whole which 'explains' both the motivation to work and job satisfaction. (see Figure 11.3).

The model takes the view that job satisfaction comes as the result of rewards measured against one's own appraisal of the job matched to one's value standards. The consequences of satisfaction or dissatisfaction appear to be many, depending on the individual choices which people make. Responses to dissatisfaction might be avoidance (most frequent), complaint, formal protest,

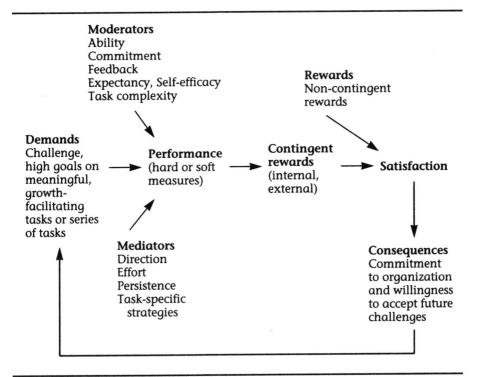

Figure 11.3 The high performance cycle
(Locke and Latham, 1990.p.4)

illegal acts, passive-aggressive response, or even substance abuse (Henne and Locke, 1985). Satisfaction is reinforced through commitment to the goals and values of the organization and a desire to stay in the organization (Mowday et al. 1982). This brings us back again to the beginning of the 'circle' in the diagram. The 'high performance cycle' provides a coherent, advanced and enhanced explanation of the way individuals are motivated, perform and receive satisfaction in an organization.

❏ Summary of approaches to motivation

Motivation is what drives individuals to work in the way they do to fulfil goals, needs or expectations. These are numerous, varied and changing. Both content theories, which emphasise what motivates, and the relative strengths of these motivators, and process theories, which stress the dynamic variables operating as motivation proceeds, have all evolved to try to explain the complex phenomenon of motivation. It has become apparent that there is not an all-embracing theory of work motivation and job satisfaction, but the model of Locke and Latham, (1990) has been put forward as a useful integrating theory which has considerable explanatory power.

When motivation fails

In defining stress early in the chapter we indicated that when people fail to be motivated in a positive direction they behave in two possible ways; they either act constructively to overcome the problem, or they can be frustrated in various ways — and this leads to stress. Kyriacou and Sutcliffe (1978, p.159) have defined stress among teachers as:

> a response syndrome of negative effects (such as anger or depression) resulting from the teacher's job and mediated by the perception that demands made on the teacher constitute a threat .

The signs and symptoms of stress will be personal, but may be divided into symptoms which are *internal*, e.g. feeling sick, moodiness, or *external*, e.g. throwing things, not talking. High levels of arousal associated with stress reactions (stressors) will be experienced as tension. *Eustress*, or 'good' stress, is when the stressors produce a response of rising to the challenge (positive motivation). However demotivation/distress/'bad' stress is when a person is asked to do too much over a long period, so that what might have once been a challenging motivator becomes a strong demotivator leading to distress.

Dunham (1992) has made reference to three theoretical perspectives for understanding teacher stress:

- the stages of   (a) alarm reaction,
  - (b) the resistance stage and
  - (c) the stage of exhaustion

- the relationship between demands and performance — if the demands are too few this will lead to *boredom* (Fisher, 1993) and if too many may well lead eventually to *burnout*. The most effective performance will occur when these two are balanced

- as a person passes through different thresholds he/she may experience more failure, anxiety may build up and a new coping behaviour threshold is reached; if the new coping strategy fails to solve the problem, the frustration threshold is reached and severe stress may lead to psychosomatic conditions as all other strategies fail

Coping strategies are many and varied. Hughes (1990) has placed them into four categories:

- direct action, e.g. modifying the demands of the job
- indirect action, e.g. through peer support or counselling
- compensatory, e.g. taking up leisure interests outside the sphere of work
- palliative, e.g. drinking a great deal of coffee, over-eating

An individual may employ a combination of these strategies. Hughes suggests that these four categories are useful for diagnosing the sources of stress and identifying ways in which they may be turned into stimulants (motivators) for improved work.

The implications of theories of motivation for educational management

In this section we give a broad summary of some of the most significant implications that our theoretical knowledge has for the motivation of people by managers. We start with the significance of the 'summarising' cycle of Locke and Latham for management.

The broad implications of the 'high performance cycle' for management are as follows:

- Effective organizations should expect much from the people who work for them. Low expectations are certainly demotivating in the long run and will not help the school or college overall

- Managers must ensure that a sense of satisfaction is gained in return for effort

- Satisfaction will derive in part from personally meaningful work which members ore capable of and in part from managers taking pains to reward performance. Managers need to ensure that they understand what influences each individual to be satisfied, or otherwise, in her/his employment

- Managers should encourage staff to set specific, challenging but realistic goals for high performance by them. Consultation and training are needed to ensure commitment to these goals

- Feedback on work performance helps staff to effective task strategies and to be motivated towards self-efficacy and to reveal discrepancies between the goal set and present performance.

When thinking about managing motivation we always come back to the individual nature of the enterprise. The different needs of individuals usually demand different strategies to satisfy them. Kakabadse (1988) has suggested some potential strategies related to meeting the needs of staff in organizations including:

- results-focused appraisal: in which performance is measured against pre-determined goals, the achievement of which can lead to reward
- job enrichment or 'vertical job loading', where individuals can gain more responsibility, autonomy and control over the tasks they perform
- quality circles, where there is an emphasis on participative problem-solving and decision-making
- management training which can provide opportunities for evaluating skills, attitudes and on-the-job behaviour
- situational leadership where the appropriate style is fitted to the situation
- autonomous work groups where groups are given whole tasks and significant autonomy to decide how they should be completed
- staff benefits or rewards which are not tied to individual performance
- job design by accountablilities, in which jobs are clarified according to the different accountabilities of those who hold them

One significant issue arising from motivation theory is the importance of valuing staff. Torrington and Weightman (1989) have linked this aspect to Maslow's esteem needs. They identified four types in the secondary schools they studied:

- *consideration:* that an interest should be taken in staff by their managers, e.g. the basic etiquettes of smiling, saying 'thank you', offering words of encouragement and praise, having a good working environment in the staffroom and elsewhere

- *feedback:* the need for tangible indications of success from colleagues, involving informal as well as formal assessment like evaluation and appraisal

- *delegation:* 'members of staff are valued when responsibility is delegated to them' (p. 49), and they are not just given a job to do

- *consultation and participation:* lack of consultation and participation in decision-making and in developing the culture of the school was a dissatisfier whereas the opposite engendered feelings of their opinions being valued because they counted for something

The authors conclude that:

> valuing of colleagues is something for *all* the adults in the organization to
> offer each other: it is not just for the mighty to confer on the lowly (p.52).

Conclusion

Certain management policies emerge from the evidence. As Guest (1984,
p.23) observes:

> ... on the one hand it may be possible to obtain high and productive
> motivation through judicious job selection and by using reactance
> principles (i.e. not seeing individuals as passive receivers and responders) to
> obtain high commitment to organizational goals, by using goal setting
> techniques, by careful job design to provide personal or group control over
> effort-performance-control links and by adopting facilitative leadership. On
> the other hand management may attempt to impose tight control using
> conventional control systems such as technology, authority structures and
> careful allocation of punishment and reward. The result will be a passive,
> compliant but possible resentful workforce; the day-to-day work will be done
> but there will be little enthusiasm, initiative or commitment.

Further reading

A straightforward introduction to motivation is contained in Everard, K.B. and
Morris, G. (1992) *Effective School Management*. Riches, C. and Morgan, C.
(1989) *Human Resource Management in Education*, provides a useful chapter on
motivation by Furukawa, as well as one on teacher stress and burnout by
Kyriacou. For more specific reading on motivation in education one needs to
turn to journal references e.g. Mercer (1993) or Nias (1981). Dunham (1992a),
Stress in Teaching, is the best overall volume on the subject as applied to
education.

References

Adams, J.S. (1965) 'Inequality is social exchange' in Berkowitz, L. (Ed) *Advances in
Experimental Social Psychology*, **2**, New York: Academic Press.

Betts, P.W. (1993) *Supervisory Management*, sixth. edn. London: Pitman.

Buchanan, and Huczynski, (1985), *Organizational Behaviour. An Introductory Text*, New York: Prentice Hall.

Dunham, J. (1992) *Stress in Teaching*, second. edn. London: Routledge.

Evans, D. (1992) *Supervisory Management: Principles and Practice*, third. edn. London: Cassell.

Evans, L. (1992) 'Teachers' morale and satisfaction: the importance of school specific factors'. *Paper presented at the 1992 Annual Conference of the British Educational Research Association.*

Evenden, R. and Anderson, G. (1992) *Management Skills, Making the Most of People*, Wokingham: Addison-Wesley.

Feldman, D.C. and Arnold, H.J. (1983) *Managing Individual and Group Behaviour in Organizations*, Auckland: McGraw-Hill.

Fisher, C.D. (1993) 'Boredom at work: a neglected concept'. *Human Relations*, **46**, 3, pp.395–417.

Gray, J.L. and Starke, F.A. (1988) *Organizational Behaviour, Concepts and Application*, fourth, edn. Colombus: Merrill.

Guest, D. (1984) 'What's new in motivation?', *Personnel Motivation*, May, pp.21–23.

Henne, and Locke, E.A. (1985), 'Job dissatisfaction: what are the consequences?,' *International Journal of Applied Psychology*, **20** ,pp.221–240.

Herzberg, F. (1966) *Motivation to Work*, New York: John Wiley.

Herzberg, F., Mausner, B. and Synderman, B.B. (1959) *The Motivation to Work*, New York: John Wiley.

Hughes, J. (1990) 'Stress, scourge or stimulant?' *Nursing Standards*, 5, 4, pp.30–33.

Johannson, H. and Page, G.T. (1990) *International Dictionary of Management*, fourth. edn. London: Kogan Page.

Katz, D. and Kahn, R. (1978) *The Social Psychology of Organizations*, New York: John Wiley.

Kempner, T. (Ed) (1971) *A Handbook of Management*, London: Penguin.

Kyriacou, C. and Sutcliffe, J. (1978) 'Teacher stress, prevalence, sources and symptoms'. *Educational Psychology*, **48**, pp.159–167.

Lawley, (1985), 'Tackling morale', *Education Administration and Management*, **13**, 3, pp.199 –206.

Locke, E.A. (1965) 'The relationship of task success to task liking and satisfaction'. *Journal of Applied Psychology*, **49**, pp.379–385.

Locke, E.A.(1968) 'Towards a theory of task motivation and incentives'. *Organizational Behaviour and Human Performance*, **3**, pp.157–189.

Locke, E.A. and Latham, G.P. (1990) 'Work motivation: the high performance cycle' in Kleinbeck, U., Quast, H-H. and Hacker, H. (Eds.) *Work Motivation*, Lawrence Erlbaum Associates.

Luthans, F. (1989) *Organizational Behaviour*, fifth. edn. New York: McGraw-Hill.

Maslow, A. (1943) 'A theory of work motivation'. *Psychological Review*, **50**, 4, pp.370–396.

McGregor, (1970) *The Human Side of Enterprise*, Maidenhead: McGraw-Hill.

Mowday, R.T., Porter, L.W. and Steers, R.M. (1982) *Employee Organization Linkages*, Academic Press.

Mullins, L.J. (1993) *Management and Organizational Behaviour*, third. edn. London: Pitman.

Neider, L. (1980) 'An experimental field investigation utilizing an expectancy theory view of participation'. *Organizational Behaviour and Human Performance*, **26**, 3, pp.425–442.

Nias, J. (1980) 'Leadership styles and job satisfaction in primary schools' in Bush, T, Glatter, R., Goodey, J. and Riches, C. *Approaches to School Management,* London: Harper and Row.

Nias, J. (1981) 'Teacher satisfaction and dissatisfaction: Hertzberg's 'two-factor' hypothesis revisited'. *British Journal of Sociology of Education*, **2**, 3, pp. 235–246.

Riches, C and Morgan, C (1989) *Human Resource Management in Education*, Milton Keynes: Open University Press.

Smith, M., Cooper, C., Cox, C., Ottaway, D. and Talbot, R. (1990) *In Introducing Organizational Behaviour*, London: Macmillan.

Steers, R.M. and Porter, L.W. (1991) *Motivation and Work Behaviour*, New York: McGraw-Hill.

Torrington D. and Weightman, J. (1989) *The Reality of School Management*, Oxford: Blackwell.

Vroom, V.H. (1964) *Work and Motivation*, New York: Wiley.

Whaba, M.A. and Bridwell, L.G. (1976) 'Maslow reconsidered: a review of research on the need hierarchy theory'. *Organizational Behaviour and Human Performance*, **15**, pp.212–240.

12 Communication

Colin Riches

Communication and theory

Communication is an everyday experience which we all claim to know something about but, in fact, is a quite complex activity. Without communication all that we think of as human experience would cease to exist for it is a vital component of all spheres of life. Management could not take place without communication, and organizations could not exist without it. It is a common complaint within organizations that communications are unsatisfactory and need improving. Mistakes are often made because communication is not seen as a two-way exchange, but as a directive from above, without any consideration of those for whom the communication is intended, or of *their* views. Negotiation in communication is often vital if the message is to be fully received, accepted by the parties concerned and acted upon. Successful organizations, and schools and colleges are no exception, need good communications. Because so many changes are taking place in educational institutions, effective communication is more than ever critical for their effectiveness.

Among the significant changes are:

- an increased *complexity*, both in structure and technology, even in the smallest primary school

- the *market forces* which are operating within education highlight the need for effective communication between the organization and clients (potential and actual) and within the organization itself

- Government education and general *legislation*, e.g with regard to employment law, has brought about so many changes which require careful communication if misunderstandings are to be avoided and if colleagues are to take 'ownership' (if they can!) of such developments

- increased complexity in the organization of schools and colleges highlighting the importance of both *vertical* and *horizontal* (e.g. within departments) two-way communication

- an increasing concentration on *efficiency* and *effectiveness*, arising partly out of LMS and competition within the education service, points up the need for communicating this with clarity and sensitivity to all staff within organizations

Of course all this begs the question, 'What is communication?'

❑ What is communication?

A straightforward definition of 'communication' is that it is an activity which takes place when a message is transferred satisfactorily from one party to another so that it can be understood and acted upon if necessary. It has been defined (by Rasberry and Lemoine 1986, p. 23) as 'sorting, selecting, forming and transmitting symbols between people to create meaning'.

For communication to take place there has to be a *source, transmission* through *channels* and a *receiver*. Communication involves the meeting of minds through the ebb and flow of actions, reactions, questions and answers. Windahl et al. (1992, p.221) have defined it in a rather more comprehensive way as, 'The exchange and sharing of information, attitudes, ideas and emotions'. This emphasizes that communication is not confined to written or oral exchange of simple messages only but embraces the collective activity of sharing an experience at a variety of verbal and non-verbal levels. Modern thinking about the subject has moved away somewhat from thinking about a linear model of communication as a movement from a *source–sender–message–channel–receiver* model to the notion of communication as shared experience. While much of the discussion which follows is within the linear model of communication it is a very useful corrective to think of communication as very much a two-way experience involving whole *personalities* to varying degrees.

We have been considering the outline nature of communication in general up to this point but it is useful to think too of a classification of the activity into different spheres of communication. These are the:

- *basic mechanical aspects of communication:* the use of mechanical/electronic devices to transmit (encode) and receive (decode) messages. Systems theory has also been used to make sense of how communication inputs are transformed through management functions like planning, organizing and leading into outputs

- *interpersonal communication:* this concerns the behaviour of people when transferring information etc. from one to another and involves verbal, non-verbal and listening behaviour. Teaching has its roots in such communication

- *organizational communication:* this recognises the fact that within an organization all the members are sending and receiving signals simultaneously in dynamic interaction with one another. In other words there is a *network* of communication experiences and all within that network (and outside it) influence the process. Analysis of these processes is important in schools and colleges

Communication takes place for a variety of *reasons* and through a variety of *methods*. Reasons for communicating might be to inform, explain, persuade, reprimand, encourage, thank, appraise, propose, consult, apologise or praise (and one can think of many others). Methods might be *written* in the form of letters, memos, reports, minutes, telex, telemessages, oral through conversations, face-to-face casual encounters, interviews, meetings, conferences, telephone, teleconferences, or *visual* in the shape of diagrams, graphs, illustrations, slides, VDU, video, television, body language (Smithson and Whitehead, 1990).

Communication models

❑ The simple communication model

This is made up of three elements: the source (or sender), message, and receiver. The source may be an object, e.g. a book or a person: the message may take many forms such as a question, an appeal, or even a smile. The receiver is the person to whom the message is directed. The characteristic of the receiver will influence the way she/he perceives the message and interprets it. In communication the three elements can take many forms. The message may have wider implications than we intend because we communicate more than the spoken word. This simple model makes a fundamental conceptualisation, even if it is not sophisticated enough to understand the intricacies of most communication in organizations (see Figure12.1).

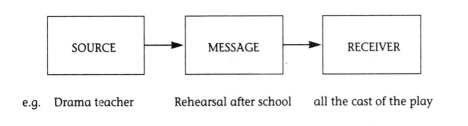

e.g.   Drama teacher   Rehearsal after school   all the cast of the play

Figure 12.1 A simple communication model

❏ The general communication model

A more complex model is encapsulated in Laswell's statement that communication is really about the five W's: 'Who says What, to Whom, in Which channel, with What effect' (Laswell, 1948). The variables here are as follows: starting with the information source (the sender), the message, filtered by the sender, is encoded into words, gestures or postures as the case may be. These are transmitted along various channels, which can be blocked by noise (i.e. distractors). The receiver picks up these audio-visual stimuli, which are then decoded into understandable meanings or ideas. The communication destination is reached when there is a shared understanding between the sender and the receiver. By means of feedback the sender will know that the receiver has interpreted the message correctly (Lopez, 1965) (See Figure12.2):

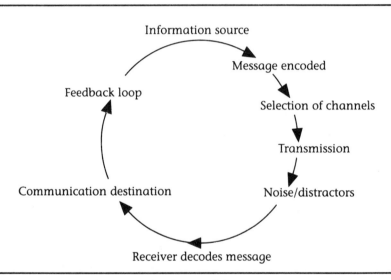

Figure 12.2 A general communication model

If, in this case, for example, the information source is the drama teacher, the message is filtered by the sender and encoded in her perceptions that the school play is the most important event at the moment, and indeed this is demonstrated in the enthusiastic tone of her memo and by every gesture when she meets those involved. A general atmosphere exists in the school so that many channels are being used to convey the message that 'the play's the thing'. However, some staff literally make a noise while others put blocks on the activities surrounding the production, thinking, for example, that many members of the cast should be concentrating on study as public examinations draw near. Others have never liked the idea of a school play anyhow, believing it allows a few to shine instead of concentrating on developing interpersonal communication through drama! The receiver picks up the message having filtered it (decoded) through her/his own perceptions and maybe conveyed to those concerned with a special twist of elation or irony. The communication reaches its destination and there is some joint understanding of it by the sender and receiver which is fed back from the latter to the former at a convenient moment. Processes like this example happen many times daily in a school or college situation.

Using slightly different wording Rasberry and Lemoine (1986) have produced a diagram (Figure 12.3) which introduces other variables influencing the communication process — and adding to its complexity. The significant new variables referred to here emphasise the influences on *meaning* which affect the way messages are encoded and decoded, the fact that there are competing messages (they cause 'noise'), the process takes place over *time* and *space* in a situation of existing *relationships*. In short, communication takes place within an *organizational environment*. One could apply this model to teacher appraisal, for example.

Research on *source* credibility indicates that high-credibility sources have a greater potential for influencing behaviour than low-credibility ones. The content of a message is often interpreted according to the source. Other research has shown, more interestingly, that source credibility has no effect upon the *attention* of the receiver (Secord and Backman, 1964). A source can gain credibility by using a high prestige medium to carry the message.

The *channels* of communication (which in the literature generally refer to both the methods and paths of communication) can be enormously varied. They can be both formal and informal. The choice of channel to be used will depend on personal preference based on the sender's knowledge of the receiver, experience and the environment.

> The channels form patterns or networks which, diagrammatically, are interconnecting lines between people who may be grouped in various ways with one- or two-way communication facilities (Betts, 1993).

Formal channels are related to a hierarchical chain of command and are usually connected with official activities like meetings, formal memos, reports and so on. Informal channels operate unofficially through 'the grapevine', which can often be a speedy way of helping the official channels convey a message or correct the misinformation of a previous message through a formal channel. However, the grapevine can be a vehicle for unwarranted gossip, scandal or rumour — and a sign that managers have been indiscreet

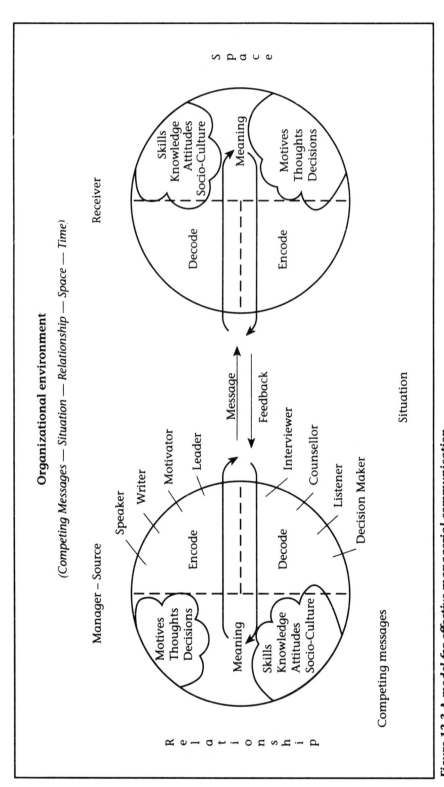

Figure 12.3 A model for effective managerial communication
(Rasberry and Lemoine, 1986)

in the way they communicate or have failed to inform people when they should have been informed.

In *decoding* it is helpful if there is an 'understanding' between the sender and receiver, say because they are of similar status or background, i.e. 'they speak the same language'. The major point to be made about the receiver is that she/he will perceive a communication in the manner that is consistent with previous experiences, and communications that are not so will tend to be rejected.

Feedback completes the cycle of communication and shows that the model is not restricted to one direction. It takes the linearity away from the model and suggests the reciprocal and sharing aspect of communication referred to earlier in this chapter. Feedback can be verbal, non-verbal or in written form The sender of a message might observe one of four possible reactions to the message: agreement, partial acceptance but a wish to negotiate its meaning, disagreement or apathy. Speed of feedback will have an influential effect.

The term *noise* can be taken literally but in communication theory is usually used to mean conceptual noise, that is those differences in individuals which confound and complicate the ability of individuals to understand one another. Noise, or distortion, can operate at each stage of the communication process, but the sender or receiver are specially vulnerable to it.

Barriers to communication

There are various barriers to communication which may be broken down into a number of sources of distortion:

Language or semantic problems words and symbols may mean different things to different people and jargon can be confusing. We each interpret messages in terms of our own backgrounds, needs and purposes and in relationship to the particular context or situation. Also disorganized ideas and the use of the wrong word or phrase may lead to poorly expressed messages which confuse rather than enlighten.

Attitudinal problems participants in communication can easily have different values, which may reflect deep emotions, beliefs and prejudices, and refuse to recognise and understand other people's viewpoints. This affects the way in which messages are represented and interpreted and can be a fundamental barrier to communication, particular in the sphere of interpersonal relations.

Different perceptions of the problem

Undue emphasis on status we speak of people 'standing on their dignity' and remaining so aloof and superior that easy exchange becomes difficult.

Excessive selective perception hearing what we expect to hear, related to our experience and background and/or what we know or believe. For example, if a person is favoured the 'halo' effect operates in which everything is seen in a favourable light and if the opposite is the case the 'cloven hoof' perception takes over, and all is seen unfavourably.

Selective retention/rejection a failure to hear (and see) what is being heard (or shown) and forgetting what has been told. This can happen because of lack of interest (the passive receiver) and concentration. Perhaps there are physical barriers contributing to this as well, such as fatigue, discomfort, excessive comfort, and a stuffy environment; or the barriers of indifference or prejudice.

The witholding of information because knowledge is power.

Premature evaluation of what is being said one's mind is made up without hearing the full message.

An artificial wall of silence which has developed between the sender and the receiver which clearly prevents a full communication exchange.

Poor choice of communication channels the failure to select the right medium to convey the message.

Natural reserve, fear or lack of confidence which tend to silence people.

Effective communication is learned through training and experience. We learn to communicate more effectively by having the appropriate techniques or skills, having the opportunity to practise them and having our performance reviewed by experienced commentators in a non-threatening environment. We have to realise that it takes two *willing* communicators to make full communication possible. A clear flow of communication within an organization can greatly aid its effectiveness.

Communication flow

❏ Downward communication

Communication flows within three main directions in the typical organization: downward, upward and horizontally. *Downward communication* is crucial to the function of an organization; it concerns messages and information sent from senior management to other staff. On organizational charts the flow normally follows the formal lines of authority downward from position to position. This is usually the strongest flow of the three major ones. Management has the power to put messages in motion and start them on their downward journey — either to be received or not, or to arrive distorted, or late.

The common reasons for poor downward communication are as follows:

- *growth of an organization causes isolation:* face-to-face contact is less frequent, formal lines of communication are established and individuals tend to isolate themselves so that close contact between the various levels is lost

- *clearly defined objectives are missing:* management is sometimes confused about the information it thinks its subordinates need and want to know. This confusion is seldom sorted out

- *when management does not audit its communication techniques:* established habits are rarely examined and ineffective communication practices continue unquestioned

- *confusion arises as to who is responsible for what communication activities*

- *segregation between senior and other levels in the organization:* a non-participatory management style can isolate managers from the wants and needs of staff and devalue the downwards communication

Downward flow can be improved by establishing objectives about what the manager wishes to communicate and the content of the messages to be communicated.

❏ Upward communication

Upward communication flows from subordinates to superordinates and depends on the trust and confidence felt by the former towards the latter. Effective upward flow is premised on the assumption that participation of staff is accepted within the organization. Reasons for poor upward communication include:

- *size and complexity of an organization:* the larger the organization the more common the barriers to upward flow

- *unrealistic assumptions* that others are listening and understanding the messages in the correct way

- *filtering and distortion:* each step upwards allows for a filtering and consequential distortion of messages

- *the manager–staff relationship:* this can affect the free flow of messages as staff feel inhibited by those with status in the organization

- *others in the hierarchy can create bottlenecks:* e.g. a gatekeeper such as a deputy or a secretary, a status seeker within the organization who uses the information for his/her own benefit, the promotion rival who keeps information that could help others to obtain promotion

❏ Horizontal communication

Lateral or horizontal flow of communication is beneficial because it acts as a coordinating device across departments and units at the same level, for people who are working for the same objective but are performing differentiated tasks. Horizontal flow of communication is the most frequent because individuals at the same level usually talk to each other about work-related events, management and personal matters. It is a flow which is strongly associated with group and team activities. Poor horizontal communication can divide a team, whether it be a managerial team or any other type. Departmental rivalries and personality clashes and conflicts are often felt in the lateral flow of messages. Improvement depends on developing inter-departmental contacts and developing communication skills like conflict management.

Communication networks

A more sophisticated perspective on communication flows is the study of the relative effectiveness of various communication *networks*. There are specific flows (or networks) which exist within the broad categories discussed above.

Beginning in the 1950s, many research studies have been conducted to test the importance of various networks on the effectiveness of communication (e.g. Guetzkow and Simon, 1960). The most frequent networks examined have been the circle, all-channel, wheel and chain, although there is also the pattern both upwards and downwards (see Figure12.4). The circle corresponds to a group working in a physical arrangement so that they can communicate with their immediate neighbour but not with others. The all-channel network is analogous to communication patterns in a task force or functional team. The wheel arrangement corresponds to a manager at the hub with the subordinates on the periphery obtaining information from that one source, while the chain describes the one-way downward communication process of a heavily hierarchical organization.

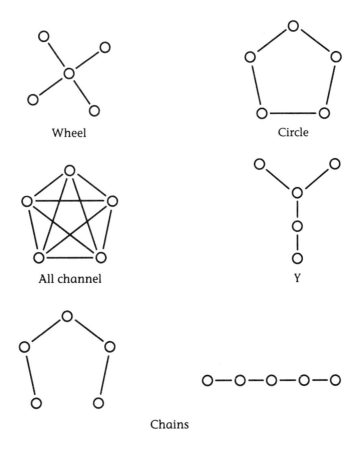

Figure 12.4 Patterns of networking (Mullins 1993, p.203)

There are conflicting views about the evidence obtained but the general consensus is that for performance on simple tasks the wheel and all-channel networks have the best scores and the circle the worst. When complex tasks are performed the all-channel network tends to score highly. The chain network is useful only on simple tasks and morale is low at the end of the chain! Lewis (1975) has elaborated on these findings in diagrammatic form (see Figure12.5).

Characteristic	Circle	Chain	Wheel	All-Channel
Speed	Slow	Fast	Very fast	Slow/fast
Accuracy	Poor	Good	Good	Poor/excellent
Morale	High	Low	Very low	Very high
Leadership stability	None	Marked	Very pronounced	None
Organization	Unstable	Emerging stability	Very stable	Unstable
Flexibility	High	Low	Low	High

Figure 12.5 Communication and organizational structure
(Lewis, 1975, p. 86, quoted in Rasberry and Lemoine, 1986, p.108)

One should approach these findings with some caution because there is evidence that other factors influence the communication process, such as the powerful influence of the task structure within the group on performance. Once the structure has been set up the task is more readily achieved irrespective of the basic network set up. But undoubtedly there is enough evidence to say that communication networks influence the communication process in a significant way. There is also sufficient evidence to challenge how a school for example, does its networking as an organization and to analyse the sub-networks which exist, say within departments. One can also ask the question about how effective the respective networks are as vehicles of communication. Does the network exclude those who should be included?

Communication content

The purpose of examining communication from a content perspective is to look at what research has taught us about the potential for various types of content for changing attitudes. The value of one-sided communication, i.e., communicating the favourable side of an argument only as against a two-sided communication which gives a rounded picture of the issue, appears to depend largely on the level of knowledge possessed by the receiver prior to the communication. Given a relatively low level of knowledge, both types produce about the same kind of attitudinal change in the receiver. However, if the initial knowledge is high the one-sided communication is less successful. Thus in managerial terms, putting both sides of an issue is likely to decrease resistance to attitudinal change in most circumstances.

Two points of view exist with regard to the ordering of communication content, one arguing for primacy (the message received first is the most persuasive) and the other for recency (the message received last having the greater influence). Two factors seem to favour recency over primacy in that it leaves no time for unfavourable messages to be put across and it will be easier to recall.

A final issue with regard to content is the comparative appeal to emotion and reason. The divisions are not in practice as clear cut as this in that the same message may be seen in different ways by people. For example, a manager may announce that staff are to be made redundant in the college and the emotional reaction might be, 'I wonder if it will be my turn next'. In handling change both elements need to be addressed. Emotional resistance to change has to be met at an emotional level as well as at a rational one.

The issues of content cannot be entirely separated from that of communication flow. For example a 'leaked' communication may be more effective than a formally presented one. Perhaps the deciding factor in the content/flow issue is the importance and relevance of a communication to the receiver. Information that does not have such a direct effect on the receiver could be sent through formal channels, but if it does have a direct effect then a multi-channel approach may be preferable.

Communication skills

Examining the communication process from a skills perspective has problems. First, it is difficult to generalize about the effectiveness of a given skill because skills are individual in nature and can be practised in many different ways. Secondly, the list of communication skills is so vast that we can never be sure that we have covered them all. For these two reasons little is known scientifically about communication skills. Also the teaching of a skill may be limited because of the personality involved particularly if it is a skill requiring some modification of personality.

Of the vast field of communication/inter-personal skills we have chosen to select three exemplars for limited analysis: effective listening, non-verbal communication and negotiation. Collectively they have a contribution to make to developing skills in the more specific area of interviewing (selection, appraisal, counselling and so on) where communication skills are so important.

❑ Effective listening

Carl Rogers and Fritz Roethlisberger (1952) argued that ineffective listening is the greatest barrier to effective communication. Too often we say in communication with a person, 'Go ahead, I'm listening' when, although we hear a voice, the words are not listened to and the *mind* is not engaged. Listening is a most difficult skill to learn. Perhaps this is because, throughout our lives, we develop improper listening habits and become expert in the art of not listening when appearing to listen; having an interested expression when all the time we may be thinking about something entirely different!

Real listening is *active* in the sense that what is said is taken in, thoughtfully considered and, if relevant, shapes future exchanges. A good listener listens with understanding, looks for what is actually meant through inflexions and words that could be clues to hidden and double meanings. Active listening requires getting inside the sender's point of view. However, we have to recognise from the outset that effective listening is never total; when we listen we engage in *selective perception*. Because we are all different and have different purposes in our listening we will listen to different stimuli and, although we have 'heard' the same message we are likely to assign a different significance to it.

Listening involves the *filtering* of a variety of stimuli. For a two-person model of communication exchange, Hunt (1980 pp.67–68) has identified seven basic factors which influence a receiver's power to listen:

1. *Auditory and visual:* the ability to see and hear with acuity.
2. *Concentration:* the ability to focus exclusively on the communication exchange.
3. *Situational constraints:* such as external factors and the physical environment.
4. *The history of the relationship:* between the sender and receiver.

5. *The perceived purpose of the communication exchange.*
6. *The perceived degree of difficulty of the message:* without understanding attention will slacken.
7. *The perceived usefulness of the message.*

As the receiver, in particular, we need to engage in in-depth listening. We must go beyond words to discern their real meaning.

❏ Non-verbal communication

One dimension of listening which has not been emphasized, as yet, is the non-verbal behaviour associated with it. We will certainly be aided in our listening, and in the whole process of communication, if we can understand to the full the non-verbal communication signals that are sent out by senders and receivers, either deliberately or involuntarily.

> Probably more feelings and intentions are communicated non-verbally than through all the verbal methods combined (Tortoriello, Blatt and DeWine 1978, p.23).

However, there are problems of interpretation in seeking to understand specific pieces of non-verbal communication (NVC). In the first place NVC is culturally conditioned. Secondly, we can never be absolutely sure that we attach the same meaning to other people's bodily cues as we do. Thirdly, not all NVC is intentional; there is a fair amount of our NVC which 'leaks' through to the other person in spite of oneself. A final difficulty is that although for purposes of discussion and analysis we draw a distinction between verbal communication (VC) and NVC, they are all of a unity. The whole of this behaviour may be subsumed under the term 'body language'.

The functions of NVC may be broken down into the following categories:

repeating what a person has said in a NV gesture

contradicting words through NV behaviour

substituting a clear NV message for a word

complementing when VC reinforces NVC

relating and regulating: i.e. giving a signal

and *accenting* or putting a NV emphasis on a word that is spoken

Each of these functions can help or hinder communication flow between people. There is a good deal of evidence that when verbal cues and non-verbal cues are contradictory the non-verbal ones win (McMahan, 1976).

❑ Communication and negotiation

One arena where the spoken word and NVC are closely married is in negotiation, particularly if conflict has been part of the process! In such a situation a wide variety of communication skills will be called into play. Negotiation has been defined as

> a way of reconciling interests and reducing conflict in situations where people have to interact with one another but where no side is powerful enough to impose its will. All human relationships have an element of cooperation and competition and negotiation is lubrication between these two tendencies (Lowe and Pollard 1989, p. 120).

By argument and compromise, in a close and concentrated communication exchange, a *mutually acceptable* outcome is hopefully arrived at.

We must not suppose that negotiators start from equal positions of strength; indeed it is common to hear it said that so-and-so starts from a strong or weak negotiating position. The factor of differential power cannot be ignored: *position* power where a person(s) controls resources, *personal* power through the force of personality, and *negative* power, possessed by everyone, can fuel the conflict. Both groups and individuals, consciously and unconsciously, spend time and energy developing these sources of power. Lowe and Pollard suggest that the effectiveness of negotiators is dependent upon the *frame of mind* adopted by the negotiator, the procedures used and the process of interpersonal communication. Pennington and Gooderham (1987) provide a useful map of the process (see Figure 12.6). So interpersonal communication becomes vital in a negotiation scenario.

Negotiation calls for the exercise of general skills, but there is also a specialized language of negotiation which has its own specific central speech-acts, or words and phrases. Mulholland (1991, p.186) has classified these as:

(a) call for agreement
(b) give reasons why there should be agreement
(c) compare and contrast options
(d) judge or evaluate ideas and options
(e) clarify and test the views expressed
(f) assess the strength of feelings
(g) establish and reiterate goals

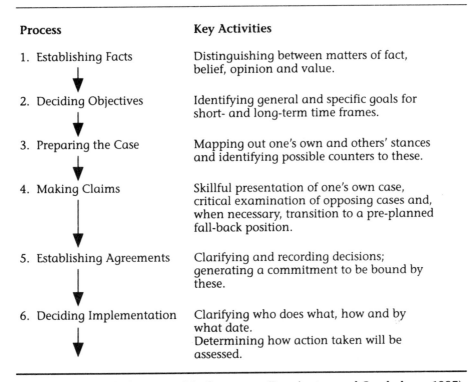

Process	Key Activities
1. Establishing Facts	Distinguishing between matters of fact, belief, opinion and value.
2. Deciding Objectives	Identifying general and specific goals for short- and long-term time frames.
3. Preparing the Case	Mapping out one's own and others' stances and identifying possible counters to these.
4. Making Claims	Skillful presentation of one's own case, critical examination of opposing cases and, when necessary, transition to a pre-planned fall-back position.
5. Establishing Agreements	Clarifying and recording decisions; generating a commitment to be bound by these.
6. Deciding Implementation	Clarifying who does what, how and by what date. Determining how action taken will be assessed.

Figure 12.6 Negotiation: a model of a process (Pennington and Gooderham, 1987)

Non-linguistic behaviours play an important part in this process, but talk has a major function and any speech acts which bring about conflict, obstruction and obstinacy are inappropriate.

Conclusion: some managerial implications

This chapter has covered a wide range of concepts, theoretical positions, and strategies involved in the communication process, but it has been by no means comprehensive. The reader will have observed many points which are relevant to educational management. Effective management has to start from a full understanding of the details of how the communication process impacts on every management activity and be as precise as possible on the way that communication theory can be translated into effective practice.

All schools and colleges would find value in examining the stages, content and processes of communication discussed above in relation to their own internal and external patterns of communication. For effective communications, whether written, oral or non-verbal, managers in schools and colleges would benefit from an audit of formal and informal procedures, and any barriers they engender. They should establish a positive communication policy, based on sound theory, making sure that this policy is *communicated!*

One major improvement in communications might be to achieve more *empathy*, i.e. understand more closely the receiver's needs, attempt to predict the impact of a message on the receiver's feelings and attitudes and adjust it to attune with his or her vocabulary, interests and values. For example, bluntness which is acceptable to one teacher (or student) may well be anathema to another. School and college managers need to know their staff and customers. A second area of improvement might be through feedback to ensure that a communication has been accurately transmitted. Other strategies might include using simpler and more direct language, making sure that the message is really the one intended, attempting to break down the levels of communication in a hierarchical organization (a difficult task without changing those structures) and using a number of channels to ensure that the message is conveyed fully. The methods should be matched to the needs and circumstances of the school or college. Effective communication in school and college management is never a luxury but always an absolute necessity.

Further reading

Books which discuss communication in an educational context do not seem to exist, and even references to the subject in educational management texts are quite sparse. Thus these suggestions are largely for the general literature on communication and management. A useful and detailed but readable text on communication is Rasberry and Lemoine (1986) *Effective Managerial Communication*, while Betts P.W. (1993) *Supervisory Management*, fifth edn. has a good chapter on the theme. For some points on interpersonal communication in general and communication in the interview, in particular, see Riches, C.R. (1992) 'Developing communication skills in the interview' in Bennett N., Crawford M. and Riches C. *Managing Change in Education: Individual and Organizational Perpectives*, Paul Chapman.

References

Betts, P.W. (1993) *Supervisory Management*, fifth edn. London: Pitman.

Guetzkow, H. and Simon, H.A.(1960) 'The impact of certain communication nets upon organization and performance in task-oriented groups' in Rubenstein, A.H. and Haberstroh, C.J. (Eds) *Some Theories of Organizations*, Homewood, Ill: Dorsey Press.

Hunt, J.W.(1980) Managing People at Work: a Manager's Guide to Behaviour in Organizations, London: McGraw-Hill.

Laswell, H.D.(1948) 'The structure and function of communication in society' in Bryson, L. (Ed) *The Communication of Ideas*, New York: Harper and Bros.

Lewis, P. (1975) *Organizational Communications*, second edn. Colombus, Ohio: Grid.

Lopez, F.M. (1965) *Personnel Interviewing, Theory and Practice*, New York: McGraw-Hill.

Lowe, T.J. and Pollard, I.W. (1989) 'Negotiation skills' in Riches, C. and Morgan, C., (Eds), *Human Resource Management*, Milton Keynes: Open University Press.

McMahan, E.M. (1976) 'Non-verbal communication as a function of attribution in impression formation'. Paper presented at the Speech Communication Convention, San Francisco, December.

Mulholland, J. (1991), *The Language of Negotiation, A Handbook of Practical Strategies for Improving Communication*, London: Cassell.

Mullins, L.J. (1993), *Management and Organization Behaviour*, third edn. London: Pitman.

Pennington, R.C. and Gooderham, D.G. (1987) *Negotiation in Schools*, Middlesborough: Department of Management Studies, Flatts Lane Centre.

Rasberry, R.W. and Lemoine, L.F. (1986) *Effective Managerial Communication*, Boston, Mass: Kent Publishing.

Rogers, C.R., and Roethlisberger, F.J. (1952) 'Barriers and gateways to communication'. *Harvard Business Review*, **30** (July-August), pp.44–49.

Secord, P.F. and Backman, C.W. (1964) *Social Psychology*, New York: McGraw-Hill.

Smithson, S. and Whithead, J. (1990) *Interpersonal Skills, A Handbook for Management Trainees*, Kingston upon Thames: Croner Publications.

Tortoriello, T.R., Blatt, S.J. and DeWine, S. (1978) *Communications in the Orgnization: An Applied Approach*, New York: McGraw-Hill.

Windahl, S., Signitzer, B. and Olson, J.T. (1992) *Using Communication Theory*, London: Sage.

13 Managing with teams

Marianne Coleman and Tony Bush

Introduction

All schools and colleges operate partly on the basis of teams. These often have a place in the formal structure of the organization. Examples include senior management teams and departmental teams in secondary schools, course or faculty teams in further education and whole staff teams in primary schools. Teachers and lecturers who belong to these groups are expected to act collaboratively with colleagues in pursuance of institutional or team objectives.

Teams may also exist outside the formal structure. Working parties may be established to deal with specific issues, disbanding when the task has been completed. Informal groups may also be influential through powerful inter-personal links rather than any acknowledged role within the school or college hierarchy.

Trethowan (1985, pp.3–4) offers the following classification of teams:

- *Senior management teams* — aims and policy
- *Middle management teams* — heads of department, heads of year
- *Staff teams* — within departments or pastoral units
- *Project teams* — ad hoc groups established to achieve short term goals
- *Interdisciplinary teams* — comprise members from various departments to deal with long term issues.

Inter-disciplinary teams may include teaching and non-teaching staff, (Mortimore et al. 1993). Collaborative teams of teachers and members of the support services have particular strengths:

A well co-ordinated team can, in many cases, lead to better use of individual skills and more effective implementation of resources especially when there is a danger of duplication or of children 'slipping through the net' (Lacey and Lomas 1993, p. 141).

The trend towards collegial approaches in schools and colleges is noted in Chapter 2. They are attractive models because they encourage the participation of teachers in decision making, leading to a sense of ownership and an enhanced prospect of successful innovation. One of the main features of collegiality is its emphasis on team work. It is regarded as an effective approach because it harnesses the talents of all team members. Development planning is one important process which is more likely to work well if it is handled by collegial teams.

❑ Self-management

The shift towards autonomous schools and colleges in England and Wales since the 1988 Education Reform Act has been parallelled by similar trends towards self-management in several other countries, including Australia, Canada and the United States.

Self-management is advocated on the basis that decisions are likely to be more appropriate for schools and colleges if they are taken by those inside the institution rather than those in central and local government who are necessarily at arms' length from the organization concerned and the community it serves. Caldwell and Spinks (1992, p.18) have written extensively on self-managing schools. They argue that devolving power to institutions should be matched by the empowerment of people *inside* schools.

> Certain groups of people in the school community now have the opportunity to influence the course of events in the life of the school to a greater extent than in the past.

The implication is that improvement is dependent on dispersed management *within* the school as well as devolution of power to the institutional level.

This international trend towards self-management means that schools and colleges are responsible for major strategic decisions which were previously the preserve of national and local government. In Chapter 4, West-Burnham suggests that strategic management requires a different approach with a reduced role for groups in the formal hierarchy and more involvement of teams drawn from all parts of the school, including support staff and governors. Successful schools and colleges utilise teams to liberate the talents of all their members.

What is team-work?

Teams should not be regarded as synonymous with 'groups'. A group is a looser notion than that of a team which is a body established to fulfil certain specified tasks or activities. Everard and Morris (1990, p.172) provide a suitable definition:

> A team is a group of people that can effectively tackle any task which it has been set up to do ... The contribution drawn from each member is of the highest possible quality, and is one which could not have been called into play other than in the context of a supportive team.

West-Burnham (1992a, p.119) stresses that teams need to be nurtured and developed if they are to be an effective vehicle for organizing work:

> There is a substantial gap between labelling a group a team and creating an effective work team which is able to function in a total quality environment. Too often teams are established and expected to operate simply by virtue of having delegated tasks — little consideration is given to the way in which the team functions.

Bell (1992) points out that there is rarely a shared perception in schools and colleges of what the term 'staff team' means. Building effective teams is a major responsibility of the headteacher or principal and other senior staff. Bell (1992, p.45) describes team-work as 'playing from the same sheet of music'. Figure 13.1 outlines the nature of team-work:

A group of people working together on the basis of:

- Shared perceptions
- A common purpose
- Agreed procedures
- Commitment
- Co-operation
- Resolving disagreements openly by discussion.

Figure 13.1 What is team-work? (adapted from Bell 1992, p. 45)

Team-work, then, is much more than meetings of groups. It has to involve agreed aims, active commitment and co-operation, adopt a problem-solving approach and devote time to team-building if it is to achieve its potential as a vehicle for school or college improvement.

Team membership

For permanent teams, such as senior management teams in schools and colleges, membership is largely determined by functional role designations. However, selection for a particular role, such as deputy head, does not guarantee that the person selected will automatically work effectively with the other members of the team.

In the case of teams that are set up for specific purposes, for example to introduce a new course, or to plan a centenary event, team membership is likely to be determined by the interests of the individuals. Alternatively, personal or institutional factors, such as career development, or perceived departmental responsibility, may play a part. Whatever the type of team: 'rarely will the capabilities of the person as a team member be a factor.' (West-Burnham, 1992a, p.125)

❏ Team roles

The ways in which team members interact, and the resulting links with team performance, have been analysed and categorized by Belbin (1981, 1993). Belbin's theories regarding the optimum combination of team roles were developed in the context of training in a business setting, but the theories have been widely applied in education. In both contexts there are implications for the selection and training of teams.

In observing the way in which groups succeeded in a management game, Belbin and his colleagues found that those teams containing high-achievers, the 'A' teams, did not automatically succeed as might have been expected, nor did they always 'gel' together as a team (Belbin, 1993). Observation over a long period of time showed which combinations of roles tended to produce the most successful outcomes:

> The types of behaviour in which people engage are infinite. But the range of useful behaviours, which make an effective contribution to team performance, is finite (p.21).

The teams that were most successful in the management games were those that included members who were complementary in their range of team roles.

There is a practical distinction between the role that a person occupies in their work, such as head of a faculty or year head and the team role that they occupy, which 'refers to a tendency to behave, contribute and interrelate with others at work in certain distinctive ways.' (p.25).

Type	Characteristics	Positive Qualities	Allowable weaknesses
Company Worker now called **Implementor**	Translates ideas into practice. Gets on with the job. Works with care and thoroughness.	Organising ability. Common sense. Integrity. Hard working. Self disciplined. Loyal.	Lack of flexibility and adaptability.
Chair now called **Co-ordinator**	Controls and co-ordinates. Driven by objectives. Utilises team resources.	Enthusiastic. Assertive. Flexible. Strong sense of duty.	Not really creative or inspirational.
Shaper	Pushes to get the job done. Inspires. Makes things happen.	Drive. Enthusiasm. Challenges roles. Commands respect. Intolerant of vagueness.	Needs to be in charge. Impulsive. Impatient. Unduly sensitive to criticism.
Innovator	Advances new ideas. Synthesises knowledge.	Intelligence. Imagination. Creativity. Unorthodox.	Prefers ideas to people. Ignores practical issues.
Resource Investigator	Identifies ideas and resources from outside the team. Questions and explores.	Very good at networking. Positive. Cheerful. Sustains the team.	Lacks self discipline. Impulsive. Quick to lose interest.
Monitor Evaluator	Critical thinker. Analyses ideas. Constantly reviews the team.	Interprets complex data. Judgement, hard-headed, objective.	Over critical. Negative. Intellectually competitive, sceptical and cynical.
Team Worker	Socially orientated. Loyal to the team. Promotes harmony. Perceptive of feelings, needs and concerns.	Stable, extrovert, good listener. Promotes strengths. Underpins weaknesses.	Indecisive, can forget a task.
Completer Finisher	Drives for task completion – on time and according to specification.	Obsessed with detail. Strong sense of purpose. Driven by targets.	Anxious, compulsive, can lower morale.
Specialist (this role added to original eight)	Having pre-existing specialist skills and knowledge.	Contributes specialist skills and expertise.	Narrow and specific vision.

Figure 13.2 Belbin's team roles (West-Burnham 1992, p.128)

Belbin and his team have developed a series of psychometric tests on personality, mental ability and values and motivations which together act as predictors of the team role that individuals are likely to play. However, team behaviour may still be modified by life experience, by particular constraints, such as the presence of someone the team member wishes to impress, and by the process of training in team work.

Taking the Belbin categorisation of team roles, it is possible to identify why it is that some teams will act more effectively than others. A team that contains several shapers and/or chairs will experience internal leadership problems that may lead to the team being unable to operate at all. Similarly, a team that has a large number of team workers and company workers may lack sufficient drive and direction to accomplish very much.

An alternative approach which has also focused on the dynamics of team roles, has been the development of the 'Team Management Index' (TMI) (Chaudhry-Lawton et al., 1992), which measures the profile of an individual team member on the basis of four issues:

1. Relationships with others
2. Ways in which information is obtained and used
3. Ways in which decisions are taken
4. The preferred method of organization of people

A questionnaire based on the four issues allows the development of a profile for an individual which identifies the potential team member's major preference in contributing to the team. The broad categories identified are known as Explorers, Organizers, Controllers and Advisers (p.115). The system seeks to identify 'how individual work preferences match up with the necessary ingredients of a well-balanced, high-performing team' (p.114). The resulting benefits relate both to selection and to team development. It is possible to select balanced teams and to ensure that members understand both what they and the other team members can contribute to the team so that all contributions are valued.

Selection for teams on the basis of this analysis should maximise the possibility of:

An appropriate mix of technical competence

Compatible personalities

Appropriate work styles (p.133).

Key questions relevant to selection of team members include the nature of the tasks to be achieved, the size, structure and permanence of the team and the necessity for technical knowledge. In both the Belbin and the TMI models it is presumed that there is an optimum size of team.

> Experience suggests that teams of over ten and under three perform less well. In smaller teams it is more difficult to bring together the range of skills and approaches that lead to the significant enhancement of problem solving, creativity and enthusiasm found in teams of five to seven people (Chaudhry-Lawton et al. 1992, p.137).

For many primary schools the number of staff employed falls within this 'ideal' range and management through team-work is particularly relevant.

Contributions to teams

> Team-work is a group of individuals working together towards some common purpose and, in so doing, achieving more than they could alone (Bell 1992, p.47).

Selection of team members who can work together in a complementary fashion contributes to the success of the team. However, it is also important that there is a common understanding of objectives and a systematic approach if all members of a team are to participate effectively. In addition, team efficiency will be enhanced by giving due attention and consideration to the individual contributions of members to team discussion.

Everard and Morris (1990, pp. 182–3) identify the major types of contributions to meetings as including:

- Seeking suggestions, allowing the broadening of discussion
- Suggesting
- Agreeing, offering supportive behaviour
- Disagreeing, including presenting difficulties that might arise if a suggestion were adopted
- Seeking clarification
- Clarifying, including re-capping and summarizing
- Interrupting.

The role of observer is implicit in identifying the roles and the contributions of team members. Such an observer may act as a consultant or 'coach' in analysing the ways in which teams are operating. In so doing the observer could:

> bring a useful amount of objectivity and detachment into the proceedings, and get the team to confront issues that, left to itself, it would probably suppress (p.183).

Such observation can therefore be useful in identifying areas where teams, or team members, may benefit from training and development. Use of the Belbin analysis may indicate the absence of a role such as completer finisher in the team, raising the issue of staff development for a team member.

Team building

We noted earlier that team building is an important determinant of effectiveness in the operation of teams. According to Bell (1992, p.53), there are four central factors in the development of successful teams:

- the *objectives* of the team should be clearly understood by all team members
- *procedures* for decision-making and planning should involve all team members
- all members should be clear about team *processes* — what has to be done, by whom, by when, with what resources
- the team should *review* its work regularly as part of a development process.

Trethowan (1985, p. 11) offers some guide-lines for team building:

- team building takes time. It may be years rather than months before a sound and effective team is created
- team leaders must listen to and support the problems and solutions being proposed by the team
- team changes need to be built into the routines or structures of the team. The team should not be allowed to slip back into its old ways once improvements have been agreed
- team decision making increases commitment so allow the team to decide
- team building needs constant maintenance and servicing to enable members to develop and grow.

Earley and Fletcher-Campbell's (1987, 1992) research on heads of department indicates the need for middle managers to develop the skills necessary for team building within their departmental team. They report that effective practitioners link team building to the active promotion of staff development. They also refer to three factors which facilitate collective working and are features of effective departments:

- free flow of information
- well-organized meetings
- sharing of responsibilities

Free flow of information occurred when department heads willingly shared their own professional experience (lesson ideas, resources, etc.), professional expertise from without the school (professional associations, courses) and information regarding broader curricular and professional matters affecting the whole school community. The effective practitioners were trying to widen the decision-making base (Earley and Fletcher-Campbell 1992, p.189).

The Earley and Fletcher-Campbell research illustrates the maxim that effective teams do not happen by chance, they have to be deliberately created and systematically managed. Tuckman (1985) suggests that teams go through a series of stages in the move to effectiveness (see Figure 13.3).

Tuckman suggests that the initial 'forming' stage is accompanied by anxiety as team members seek to establish the purpose of the team and their own roles within it. The subsequent 'storming' stage is characterized by conflict as differences of view are articulated.

West-Burnham (1992a, p.125) argues that effective team building is facilitated by minimising the time spent on forming and storming and devoting more attention to the creative stages of 'norming' and 'performing'. During norming, working procedures are established and the team builds its own sense of identity. In the performing stage, high levels of trust are evident and the team becomes effective in solving problems and in decision-making.

Team leadership

Theories and styles of leadership are considered in Chapter 3. Adair (1988) has identified three inter-linking aspects of team leadership:

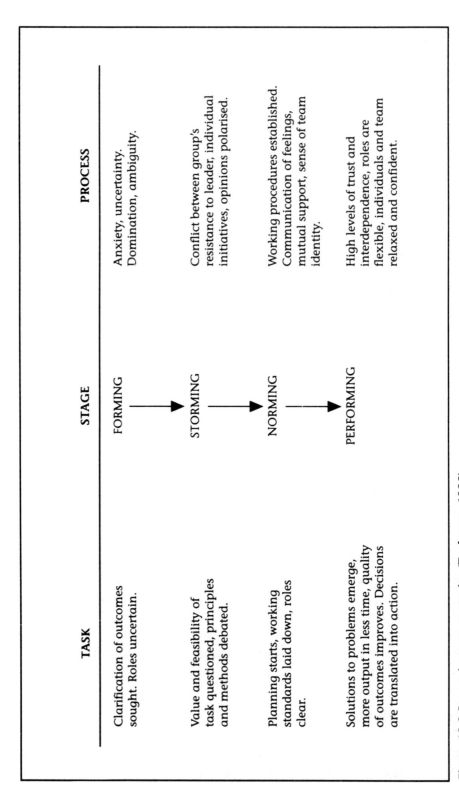

The table contains the following information:

TASK	STAGE	PROCESS
Clarification of outcomes sought. Roles uncertain.	FORMING	Anxiety, uncertainty. Domination, ambiguity.
Value and feasibility of task questioned, principles and methods debated.	STORMING	Conflict between group's resistance to leader, individual initiatives, opinions polarised.
Planning starts, working standards laid down, roles clear.	NORMING	Working procedures established. Communication of feelings, mutual support, sense of team identity.
Solutions to problems emerge, more output in less time, quality of outcomes improves. Decisions are translated into action.	PERFORMING	High levels of trust and interdependence, roles are flexible, individuals and team relaxed and confident.

Figure 13.3 Stages in team maturity (Tuckman, 1985)

achievement of the task

development and maintenance of the team

development of the individual

The three areas are not only linked but interdependent, (see Figure 13.4). For example, if the team, or its individual members, are not functioning well it is likely that task achievement will be impaired. Whilst all team members carry some responsibility for the three areas, the leader is seen as holding a particular position; 'half-in and half-out' of the circles, (Adair, 1988, p.44) and is considered to be accountable both to a higher authority and to the group.

Figure 13.4 What a leader has to do (Adair 1988, p.44)

It may be that a particular function of the leader is to link with the wider organization, both in terms of the harmonization of goals and in dealing with any external interference with the group's activities.

In such circumstances, the decision to appoint a team leader involves consideration of:

The culture of the wider organization, the familiarity of the team member with teamworking, [and] the complexity of the team's goal (Chaudhry-Lawton et al. 1992, p.144).

However, school effectiveness is linked with a style of leadership that empowers other participants and fosters an understanding of the aims and values of the school or college (Caldwell and Spinks, 1992). In this context, team leaders may be most effective where they enable the members of their teams to 'assume control according to the needs of the situation' (West Burnham 1992a, p.122). For the empowering leader 'the dominant component of this approach is allowing the team members to proceed on their own.' (Chaudhry-Lawton et al. 1992, p.121).

For schools that have adopted a collegial style of management it may be true to say that:

> team leadership is the only form of leadership acceptable in a society where power is shared and so many people are near equals (Belbin 1993, p.107).

In teams operating within a collegial environment, expertise rather than status can determine the leadership of a team. For a project or inter-disciplinary team it could be that:

> Team leaders will tend to be those people with direct and relevant expertise. (Bell 1992, p.47).

For example, the head of a department may count a member of the senior management of the school as a member of his or her team; or a team investigating a key area of development in a school or college may be led by an individual who is not part of the traditional senior management team:

> Under functional management a degree of ambiguity is introduced. A person may be a simple team member in one function but be exercising a large measure of direct responsibility in another or be the holder of a high position in the hierarchy. The key to success is to see the tasks clearly and to guide our actions by what needs to be done, not by the extraneous and often irrelevant considerations of status (Headteacher, quoted in Jenkins 1991, p. 59–60).

The ambiguity of status may make it even more important that the team leader recognises the importance of sensitivity with regard to the 'psychological processes' at work within the team and the need to adopt strategies to deal with potential problems. Bell (1992, p. 48) identifies three 'interactions' between an individual and the team. The implication is that the leader must not only recognize them, but be able to build on or counteract them where necessary. These interactions are identified as:

1. *Compliance* on the part of the individual, which would be rewarded by the acceptance of the team

2. *Identification* of the desired course of action of the individual with the course of action of the team

3. *Internalization* of the aims of the team, which would provide the strongest form or 'contract'

Observation of the operation of the team then allows the leader to check the extent to which responsibility is shared within the team and whether they are working effectively together. The continuing sensitivity and support of the team leader is also essential where the tasks or membership of a team may change over time:

> Team members may need encouraging, reassuring and appreciating in order to establish and retain their membership in an active sense (Bell 1992, p.52).

The leader of a team has a particular responsibility to ensure understanding of the values and aims of the school or college. The understanding of the team is dependent partly on the role of the team leader, but also on the clear development of aims within the larger organization:

> This means that the team leader has to understand and communicate to colleagues the rationale which underpins the work of the staff team. ... the existence within the school of a clear and agreed approach to education, as formulated in the school's statement of aims and approached through the school development plan is a crucial element in the effectiveness of the staff team (Bell 1992, p.48).

The team leader has a particular role in monitoring the link with the development plan, including the staff development needs of the team, and in ensuring that the work of the team is reviewed and evaluated.

The special role of the leader of a team is summarized by Trethowan (1985, p.6) as the following:

- To set the aims of the team
- To clarify personal expectations within the team
- To use the skills and qualities of individuals in the team effectively
- To set an example through personal performance

- To talk through all problems as they appear
- To monitor both individual and group performance regularly and give feedback regularly
- To represent and speak for the team in the school and outside it
- To ensure there is a healthy relationship between the team and other teams within the school
- To ensure the task is achieved

Teams in primary schools

It may be that the operation of teams in primary schools warrants particular consideration. Much of what is written about teams in educational institutions presupposes that they exist within a larger organization such as a secondary school or a college. For most primary schools, the number of staff is conducive to effective teamwork. (see page 271).

> Primary schools are usually groups of six to twelve people, often working in close physical proximity, interacting frequently, exhibiting a common set of professional skills, needing to be interdependent in developing an agreement about the continuity of the education children will receive as they move from year to year (Yeomans 1987, p.130).

Unlike secondary schools, primary schools often use a staff meeting as an opportunity for detailed discussion of policy matters. (Bolam et al. 1993, p.48)

Collegial models of management are closely identified with primary schools. The 'image' is of 'an atmosphere, ethos or climate distinctive to collegiality' (Campbell 1989, p.43). The process is associated with collaborative effort and the devolution of responsibility. The increasing demands of curriculum management in primary schools requires the development of subject expertise by individual teachers. It seems likely that school appointments are being made:

> based on clear statements about areas of expertise and curriculum leadership rather than on classroom experience alone (Bell 1989, p.126).

If such expertise is to benefit the school, it must be made available through appropriate management structures and strategies. Since expertise will tend to be spread through the whole staff:

> it is crucial that all members of the staff in primary schools understand the processes involved in managing and leading teams (Bell 1989, p.132).

There is evidence that the teacher with responsibility for a curriculum area takes charge at the appropriate meetings and leads on policy statements in that area. (Bolam et al. 1993, p.49) The head's overall responsibility for school management is balanced with the requirement to act as a member of smaller teams.

> Since a primary staff is numerically a small group of adults, leaders and members cannot easily escape each other, and leadership and membership should not be treated as watertight compartments (Yeomans 1987, p.139).

Developing effective teams

Teams are an important element in school and college management. They have the potential to enhance the quality of decision-making, and of relationships, providing that they operate effectively. Nine components of team effectiveness have been identified by West-Burnham (1992a, 1992b).

1. *Explicit and shared values*
West-Burnham (1992a, p.121) stresses that no team can operate effectively unless it is working in a context where the values are clear and agreed and translated into a mission.

2. *Situational leadership*
The team is sufficiently mature to base leadership on function and need rather than power and status. Skills are more important than hierarchical factors. This requires a willingness by the designated leader to stand back and allow other team members to assume control according to the needs of the situation.

3. *Pride in the team*
This implies commitment and involvement and is manifested in high morale and loyalty. Team members have self-belief, and confidence in others and the team as a whole.

4. *Clear task*
The outcome that the team is created to achieve is clear, realistic and understood. Teams are motivated by tangible goals, clear outcomes and a firm time-scale.

5. *Review*
Effective teams learn and develop by a process of continuous feedback and review. Team review is a permanent feature of every activity and leads to more effective working.

6. Openness

Teams achieve a high level of candour in review and exchange. There are no 'hidden agendas' and there is praise and criticism. The latter is frank and direct but constructive rather than negative.

7. Lateral communication

Team members are able to communicate with each other without reference to the team leader. Networks are formed and nourished by the team.

8. Collaboration

Decisions are shared and have full commitment. Quality decisions emerge from the full utilisation of the knowledge and skills of team members.

9. Action

Team decisions are expressed in terms of action. Each team member knows what has to be done, by whom and when. Effective teams issue agreed actions after their meetings.

(Adapted from West-Burnham 1992a, pp.121-124)

The benefits and weaknesses of team-work

Effective teams should produce certain clear-cut benefits for the school or college, the team and its members. The realisation of those benefits serves to reinforce commitment to the team while the lack of beneficial outcomes may lead to demotivation. Bell (1992, p.46) argues that there are significant benefits from effective team-work. These are summarized in Figure 13.5. These are ambitious claims and are not likely to be achieved without excellent leadership and a high level of commitment from all team members.

These benefits may not be achieved in practice because teams are often 'immature' or problematic, operating well below their potential. This may be because of one or more of the weaknesses identified by West-Burnham (1992a, p.120) (see Figure 13.6).

These weaknesses may be alleviated by the process of review and team development discussed earlier. However, there is a danger that loyalty to teams may impede progress towards institutional goals. Ball (1987) refers to the 'baronial politics' of inter-departmental feuding, and Levacic (1993, p.105) to the importance of integration, particularly in light of financial delegation, which has:

Figure 13.5 The benefits of team-work (Bell 1992, p.46)

- agreeing aims

- clarifying roles

- sharing expertise and skills

- maximising use of resources

- motivating, supporting and encouraging members of the team

- improving relationships within the staff group

- encouraging decision-making

- increasing participation

- realising individual potential

- improving communication

- increasing knowledge and understanding

- reducing stress and anxiety

Table 13.6 Limitations of teams in schools (adapted from West-Burnham 1992a, p.120)

- School 'teams' place great emphasis on tasks or agendas and little emphasis on processes

- 'Teams' in schools spend too little time solving problems and formulating solutions and too much time debating issues over which they may have little control. They lack 'a bias for action'

- Poorly managed 'teams' in schools are reactive — responding to events rather than anticipating them

- 'Teams' spend insufficient time recognizing, reinforcing and celebrating each other nor will they seek to develop their skills as a team.

reinforced a further differentiation — that between the class and subject teachers, and those in the 'senior management team', all or some of whom are primarily involved in budget management.

Critchley and Casey (1986, p.413) provide a more fundamental critique of team-work. They argue that the 'harsh reality is at odds with this cosy view of teams, team-work and teambuilding'.

Critchley and Casey (p.414) claim that most decisions in organizations are operational and do not require team-work:

> In these conditions, high levels of trust and openness may be nice, but are not necessary; consensus is strictly not an issue and in any case would take up far too much time. There is therefore no need for high levels of interpersonal skills.

They conclude that there is a very large proportion of most managers' work where team-work is not needed and may be dysfunctional. Only that small part devoted to strategic management requires team-work.

Critchley and Casey's analysis is not based on the educational context but many teachers would echo their cautions about excessive reliance on team-work. They worry about the need to attend meetings at the end of the teaching day when they are tired and may wish to devote time to preparation and marking rather than team-work, especially where the focus of the meeting is not central to their interests (Bush 1993).

Despite these concerns, team-work remains a vital component of school and college management, not least because of the professional nature of decision-making in education. Decisions made by teams with appropriate membership and skills, are more likely to be the right decisions and should lead to ownership by those who have to implement them. Teams remain an essential part of the fabric of educational management but should be used sparingly if they are not to demand too much of team members.

Summary

Teams of people form part of the management structure of all educational institutions.

Teams are a particularly appropriate vehicle for the devolution of power to smaller groups, a trend that echoes the devolution of responsibility to individual institutions. The trend towards empowerment of groups and individuals places particular emphasis on the role of the leaders of teams, where it is argued that leading a team and membership of the team may overlap.

If teams are to play an important role in the management of schools and colleges and operate effectively, the ways in which members are selected, and the opportunities for team building and development, are particularly significant.

Whilst effective team-work brings certain benefits to educational institutions, the operation of teams may also be characterised by problems and limitations.

Further reading

Bell, L. (1992) *Managing Teams in Secondary Schools*, London: Routledge.

Everard, K.B. and Morris, G. (1990) *Effective School Management*, London: Paul Chapman.

West-Burnham, J. (1992) *Managing Quality in Schools*, Harlow: Longman.

References

Adair, J. (1988) *Effective Leadership*, London: Pan Books

Ball, S.J. (1987) *The Micro-Politics of the School: Towards a Theory of School Organization*, London: Routledge.

Belbin, M. (1981) *Management Teams: Why They Succeed or Fail*, London: Heinemann.

Belbin, M. (1993) *Team Roles at Work*, London: Butterworth Heinemann.

Bell, L. (1989) *Management Skills in Primary Schools*, London: Routledge.

Bell, L. (1992) *Managing Teams in Secondary Schools*, London: Routledge.

Bolam, R. et al. (1993) *Effective Management in Schools*, London: HMSO.

Bush, T. (1993), 'Exploring collegiality: theory and practice' in *E326 Managing Educational Change*, Milton Keynes: The Open University.

Caldwell, B. and Spinks, J. (1988) *The Self-Managing School*, London: Falmer Press.

Caldwell, B. and Spinks, J. (1992) *Leading the Self-Managing School*, London: Falmer Press.

Campbell, J. (1989) 'Towards the collegial primary school' in Bush, T. *Managing Education: Theory and Practice*, Milton Keynes: Open University Press.

Chaudhry-Lawton, R., Lawton, R., Murphy, K. and Terry, A. (1992) *Quality: Change Through Teamwork*, London: Century Business.

Critchley, B. and Casey, D. (1986) Team building in Mumford, A. (Ed) *Handbook of Management Development*, Aldershot: Gower.

Earley, P. and Fletcher-Campbell, F. (1987) *The Time to Manage: Department and Faculty Heads at Work*, Windsor: NFER-Nelson.

Earley, P. and Fletcher-Campbell, F. (1992) 'How are decisions made in departments and schools' in Bennett, N., Crawford, M. and Riches, C. *Managing Change in Education*, London: Paul Chapman.

Everard, K.B. and Morris, G. (1990), *Effective School Management*, London: Paul Chapman.

Jenkins, H.O. (1991) *Getting It Right: A Handbook for Successful School Leadership*, Oxford: Blackwell.

Lacey, P. and Lomas, J. (1993) *Support Services and the Curriculum: A Practical Guide to Collaboration*, London: David Fulton.

Levacic, R. (1993) 'Coupling financial and curriculum decision-making in schools' in Preedy, M. (Ed) *Managing the Effective School*, London: Paul Chapman.

Mortimore, P., Mortimore, J. (1993) *The Innovative Uses of Non-Teaching Staff in Primary and Secondary Schools: Final Report*, London: Institute of Education.

Trethowan, D. (1985) *Teamwork*, The Industrial Society.

Tuckman,B.W. (1985) 'Developmental sequence in small groups' *Psychological Bulletin*, **63**.

West-Burnham, J. (1992a) *Managing Quality in Schools*, Harlow: Longman.

West-Burnham, J. (1992b) 'Total quality management in education' in Bennett, N., Crawford, M. and Riches, C., *Managing Change in Education*, London: Paul Chapman.

Yeomans, R. (1987) 'Leading the team, belonging to the group?' in Southworth, G. (Ed) *Readings in Primary School Management*, London: Falmer Press.

14 Managing professional development

John O'Neill

This chapter is concerned with the nature of professional learning and development. It has three main themes:

- the relationship between personal and organizational improvement
- the management of adult learning
- models of professional development

Together these constitute a theoretical perspective on major aspects of the management of professional development. The themes are explored within a framework which is determined by key management issues generated from that theoretical perspective:

- organizational context
- needs analysis
- learning theory and style
- support
- approach

The final section of the chapter examines the difficulties associated with translating theory into institutional practice.

Definitions of professional development

At its most generalized level the in-service education and training of teachers (INSET) has been defined as 'professional development activities engaged in by teachers to enhance their knowledge, skills and attitudes in order to educate children more effectively' (Brown and Earley 1990, p.4).

Professional development in education embraces two related concepts (Hoyle, 1982). In the first, professional development is seen as a process, spanning an individual's career, 'whereby the teacher continues to develop the knowledge and skills required for effective professional practice as circumstances change and as new responsibilities are accepted' (p.164). In the second is the notion that knowledge acquisition and skills development 'should to a greater degree than in the past be more directly related to the substantive problems faced by teachers' (ibid.). This perception of professional development emphasizes the changing nature of development needs at different stages of career and suggests that development activities be given a meaningful context in terms of actual teacher experience.

Three types of development are identified by Main (1985, p.8). They have an organizational focus inasmuch as the chosen categories reflect the interactive, group-based nature of many aspects of professional work in educational organizations.

Instructional development   (e.g. evaluation, methods and technologies and curriculum development)

Organizational development   (e.g. team-building, decision-making and management development)

Personal development   (e.g. interpersonal skills training and career development)

Eraut (1972, p.1) refers to the problematic distinction between 'in-service *training* in which a teacher–*employee* is told what to do and how to do it', and 'in-service *education* in which a teacher–*professional* is supported in his (*sic*) task of trying to answer the questions for himself'.

The distinction may be clarified by examining the way needs analysis is conducted according to each definition.

A training perspective is intended to provide externally identified solutions to problems associated with curriculum *delivery* by teachers as employees. Needs analysis is *extrinsic*, normally not carried out or informed by practitioners themselves. The need is defined more readily in terms of providing a response to a specific training need.

An education perspective encourages the analysis of problems and potential solutions by professional teachers themselves. Needs analysis is of necessity *intrinsic*, conducted in the context of self-generated priorities. Needs analysis is an essential part of a process designed to generate a range of possible professional responses to a problem.

286

Jones et al. (1989, p.5) suggest that staff development 'provides the means for teachers to experience continuing education as part of a team of professionals'. *Staff development* in this definition is seen as related to the needs of staff within a given institution. *Professional development* is the broader career and personal development of the individual (ibid. p.12).

The salient features of each perspective are incorporated in Figure 14.1.

Term	Target	Needs analysis	Purpose	Focus
training	groups or individuals with like needs	extrinsic	specific solution to fill gap in provision	short-term
staff development	whole staff	intrinsic	priorities of institution or functional groups	medium-term
professional development	individuals or groups with like needs	intrinsic or extrinsic	career-orientated personal needs	longer-term

Figure 14.1 Definitions of professional development[1]

The generic term adopted in the remainder of this chapter is professional development which here encompasses the concepts of:

> meeting the needs of professional role responsibilities at various career stages ; and

> improving professional performance and capability

Purposes of professional development

Definitions of professional development vary according to perceptions about what such development activity is intended to achieve. These perceptions will determine how professional development is managed within the school or college. The stated objective of any programme or activity will dictate, to a large extent, its structure, its location and the type and level of support it may expect to receive within the institution. Equally, financial and organizational constraints will help delimit the range of development opportunities made available in any given institution.

Within the context of this chapter professional development is treated in isolation. In reality, however, the structure and process of professional development will be informed and constrained by other areas of management activity. Thus the media through which professional development takes place will reflect, for example, the institution's culture (see chapter 5) its associated management structures (see chapter 5) and the levels of authority and autonomy devolved to curriculum area teams (see chapter 13). In short, the school or college's definition of professional development will inevitably reflect interpretations of how and where it can most effectively be carried out, and by whom it should be controlled and managed, as well as directly influencing the content and style of the learning activities themselves.

Professional development and the curriculum

The notion that the principal objective of professional development is to enhance the quality of student learning experience (Brown and Earley op. cit.) has implications for the management both of single activities and of planned programmes of professional development. In the context of enhancing the quality of learning experience, professional development may be defined not so much as an outcome in its own right but rather as a means of facilitating the attainment of other educational objectives.

> The ultimate aim of staff development is to improve the quality of teaching and learning. The immediate aim is to improve the performance of those with teaching and management responsibilities (Bolam 1987, p.9).

Bolam's perspective is helpful because it focuses on the assertion that professional development should contribute, directly and indirectly, to an improvement in the quality of student learning experience. Thus professional development is seen as curriculum-focused in the broadest sense of the term.

Professional development may thus be interpreted from a variety of perspectives along a continuum of provision. (Figure 14.2) At one end of that continuum its purpose is to serve as a medium for enhancing the capability of teachers and managers to improve the quality of the management of learning, i.e. of students and of their own. Professional development is therefore driven by a professionally determined agenda, without necessarily

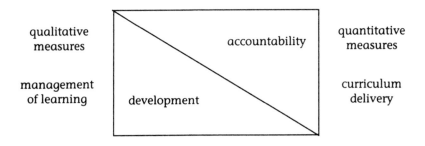

Figure 14.2 The purposes of professional development

having any preferred measurable outcomes for an individual activity. It is a *development* perspective in which the predominant focus is the professional *capability* of the individual practitioner. The appropriate performance indicators for such a perspective would be qualitative in nature because development is seen as *process* oriented.

At the other end of the continuum professional development may be seen as a means of ensuring effective and efficient curriculum *delivery*. Such a perspective suggests that the purpose of professional development is to ensure faithful curriculum implementation. It is an *accountability* perspective. Here the predominant focus is the *performance* of the sum of professionals working within the institution. The appropriate performance indicators according to this perspective would be quantitative in nature reflecting a view of development which is seen as *product* oriented.

In the reality of a school or college situation however it is likely that a number of perspectives will be adopted and will vary according to:

- The objectives of those sponsoring the development activity
- the type of curriculum area involved in the development activity
- the personnel involved
- the timescale
- the level of change involved

Nevertheless, the two perspectives outlined in Figure 14.2 remain in some senses mutually incompatible (e.g. Kelly,1989) and thus reflect the professional tensions and management difficulties associated with professional development in educational organizations.

Control of professional development

Day (1986), building on the work of Rogers and Shoemaker, offers a view of a *superordinate* and a *subordinate* group of decision-makers who dominate the management of professional development programmes. The relative control of one group over the other determines the level at which decisions in practice are made about professional development activity at system (i.e. local or national government) level and within the institution itself. In essence, the locus and direction of control may be said to be bottom-up or top-down (Figure 14.3).

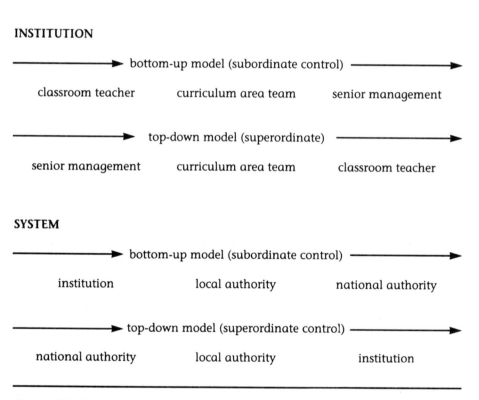

INSTITUTION

⟶ bottom-up model (subordinate control) ⟶

classroom teacher   curriculum area team   senior management

⟶ top-down model (superordinate) ⟶

senior management   curriculum area team   classroom teacher

SYSTEM

⟶ bottom-up model (subordinate control) ⟶

institution   local authority   national authority

⟶ top-down model (superordinate control) ⟶

national authority   local authority   institution

Figure 14.3 Control of professional development

A critical management task arising from the potential conflict over control is the need for organizations to agree a working definition of professional development and its purposes and objectives in the context of the individual institution. The inherent tensions identified above may then be accommodated within the working priorities of the establishment.

A framework for management analysis

It is possible to identify key issues which influence the nature of the management response to professional development within the institution. These issues are analysed below. In terms of application of theory they are intended to provide a management agenda for promoting an effective organizational interpretation of professional development provision.

Organizational context

Effective professional development occurs in a school or college environment which encourages individuals and groups of staff to engage in and then have successful experience of problem-solving within the institution (Schmuck, 1980; Holly and Southworth, 1989). The importance of an appropriate organizational culture for professional development may be understood in terms of the necessary environment in which individual, functioning group (e.g. the staff of a subject department, key stage, or senior management team), and organizational development takes place. Everard and Morris's matrix of training and organization development (1990, p.173) suggests that organizational improvement depends on the increased effectiveness over time of the individuals and teams which comprise the staff of the institution. Individual growth demands acceptance of individual responsibility for personal development. Organizational growth relies on acceptance of collective responsibility for the development of functioning groups and individuals.

Within a macro-context for educational management, evidence from other sectors would suggest that organizations in general are having to be more flexible in response to what Handy (1990) terms discontinuous, rather than planned or incremental, change. To cope with discontinuous change professional development activities at all levels need to encourage the development of 'meta-qualities' (Burgoyne, 1978) which transcend the requirements of particular activities but improve individual capability to respond to a variety of ever changing demands on professional and managerial expertise. Thus several writers advocate the desirability of establishing a positive learning culture (e.g. Holly and Southworth, 1989) or learning organization (e.g. Jenkins, 1991). Such organizations are characterized, in a highly normative way, by a synergy of curriculum, team and organization development which provides an environment for individual development.

The organizational context for professional development incorporates three management imperatives, each of which suggests that professional development needs to be grounded in the framework of the school or college development plan.

1. *Professional activity* takes place at three levels:
    - individual
    - functioning group
    - whole institution

2. Effective management of *professional development* needs to rationalize and integrate perceived priorities from each of these levels to best promote individual and organizational development.

3. Development activities need to be directly linked to the *organizational context* or environment in which they are to be implemented if they are to have any prospect of success.

Needs analysis

This section examines needs analysis from various perspectives. It is suggested that the analysis of professional development need should focus on different levels within the school or college and on disparate career stage needs. In the following section needs analysis is considered in relation to adult learning theory and linked to the design considerations for effective development activities.

❑ Levels of needs analysis

Professional development needs may be identified at three levels within the organization.

The needs of individual teachers
The needs of functioning groups within the school
The needs of the school as a whole (ACSTT 1980, p.426)

In a fully integrated approach, professional development is seen as a 'development partnership' (Main 1985, p.4) between individual and organization. Implicit in the relationship is the notion that individual and organizational needs are considered simultaneously given their interdependence at the various levels within the organization.

The alleviation of organizational needs and the facilitation of organizational growth as a whole is now considered by many educators and senior personnel as being a legitimate purpose of any staff development program (Main 1985, p.7).

However, the fact that disparate needs may exist demands that the structuring of development provision displays awareness of different types of development need. Schmuck (1980) distinguishes between in-service education for teachers and training in organizational development for faculties, suggesting that professional development activity be grounded in its organizational context. Thus needs analysis and associated development programmes should be constructed and managed with organizational constraints and opportunities in mind:

Many educational reforms have collapsed or been absorbed without effect mainly because of the limited attention given to the organizational context in which the reforms have been attempted (ibid. p.406).

❑ Stages of career

The analysis of professional development needs is complex inasmuch as it relates both to the priorities of the organization and to the particular needs of those individuals who work there. Hence the James report (1972) argues for provision to meet career development needs of professional staff at various stages of their careers. This is refined in the Bolam (1987, p.10) model to demonstrate that there are distinct development needs not only in relation to whole career but also in terms of stages within a particular post:

the preparation stage (when they wish to apply for a new job)
the appointment stage (when they are selected or rejected)
the induction stage (e.g first two years in-post)
the in-service stage (e.g. 3-5, 6-10, 11+ years in post)
the transitional stage (i.e.promotion, redeployment, retirement)

The management of these issues is further complicated by macro-economic developments (Handy, 1990) which reflect a change in *employment patterns*. Autonomous educational establishments are not immune from these and institutions are increasingly evidenced by a smaller core of full-time, permanent contract staff supplemented by a periphery of part-time, temporary, fixed-term and supply contract professionals all of whose development needs will vary considerably.

The School Management Task Force (DES, 1990) and the National Development Centre for Educational Management and Policy (McMahon and

Bolam, 1990) address the local and national systems implications for the effective management of professional development provision. In both models there is the recognition that individual establishments are unable to achieve the necessary perspectives or the economies of scale necessary to provide for effective manpower, career or succession planning for the education service as a whole. There remains a need, therefore, to plan for recruitment and retention strategies at national and local levels via nationally identified priorities, continuing LEA initiatives and professional development ventures between groups of schools or colleges who choose to collaborate in order to provide that breadth of perspective and economy of scale.

Learning theory and style

A focus on the development needs of individuals implicitly acknowledges that individual professional staff will have preferences (Honey and Mumford, 1982) for particular ways of updating their professional knowledge and enhancing their ability to do the job. These preferences will range from independent study to delivered sessions, from action-learning to reflective self-analysis, from group learning to solitary study. They will be affected also by the individual's level of motivation to take part in the activity and to implement changes in professional practice as a result (Fullan, 1988).

Thus, whilst professional staff may have shared group training or development needs all will have individual learning needs (Jones et al. 1989). Both these sets of needs will be reflected in:

(a) a preferred *learning style* as perceived and experienced by the individual; and

(b) a proposed *activity format* which reflects the objectives of the activity designer

There is a very basic development polemic facing managers in schools and colleges whose brief it is to design or commission professional development activities. That is, how best to match the requirements of the learning process with the preferences of the individual learner (Ballinger, 1986), how to provide an effective match between identification of professional development need and the provision of an appropriate programme of development activities.

❏ Activity design

Figure 14.4 illustrates the design considerations which need to be built into professional development activities and programmes. The terms on the right

MODE

cognitive ———————————————————— affective

FORMAT

passive ———————————————————— active

ENVIRONMENT

simulated ———————————————————— real

Figure 14.4 Design issues affecting the management of adult learning

hand side of the figure represent those predominantly affective characteristics of the management of effective adult learning. These are generally considered the more difficult to effect (Coulson, 1985) and evaluate in terms of lasting changes in performance or attitude (Fullan, 1989), and are those which are most demanding of participants in the course of the development activities themselves.

Everard (1986) suggests that within the teaching profession preferences are usually for cognitive modes of learning which allow participants to remain outside the learning process by focusing on information transfer rather than analysis of individual experience, personal behaviour and interpersonal relationships. This distinction between cognitive and affective modes of learning lies at the heart of decisions related to the management of professional development. Passive formats of adult learning fail to address the need for individuals to engage in learning which encourages self-awareness and self-analysis (Coulson, 1985). Nor do they promote the benefits in terms of 'the shared insights of groupwork' (Turner et al. 1988, p.196) to be gained from collaborative forms of professional development. This would suggest the need for a more creatively managed approach to professional development which provides opportunities for professional colleagues to collaborate and support each other in the process of learning and 'exploring mutual professional problems' (Easen 1985, p. 16).

A learning mode which intends simply to raise participant awareness operates at a cognitive level, is non-threatening to the learner, merely *promotes* changes in performance but *demands* comparatively little from the learner in terms of modified behaviour. A performance oriented activity, such as the improvement of classroom or behaviour management skills, however, falls into the affective mode and in Everard's and Fullan's terms is correspondingly more difficult to manage because the development activity is intended to change practice *and* attitudes.

❑ Changing performance

The move in education towards institution-based and organization-focused models of professional development is chronicled by SMTF (DES, 1990) and Williams (1991). Such moves have been prompted both by increasing financial constraints within the education service as a whole and a perception that the learning environment should be closer to the 'context of practice' (Wallace 1986, p.68). Wallace identifies a 'missing link' between training and performance which indicates that off-the-job training courses suffer from difficulties of transfer of learning to the work situation. Wallace suggests that designers of training and development activities have a responsibility to ensure that the learning activity incorporates strategies for implementing desired changes in school or college practice.

The change in focus exemplified in the SMTF model incorporates attempts to overcome such difficulties of transfer. Learning therefore becomes much more closely linked to workplace requirements and evaluation to changes in performance. Everard's (1986) suggestion that workplace development is more effective *per se* underpins the notion that the purpose of development is to improve specific aspects of performance. Evaluation of professional development should therefore aim to establish an explicit relationship between development activity and enhanced performance in post.

Of greater management significance, however, is the contention that the *location* of training is of secondary importance to the *environment* which is necessary for effective learning and that consideration of the most appropriate environment will determine the structure of the learning activity.

The Kolb (1983) learning cycle indicates a sequence of essential elements in the adult learning process:

- reflective observation
- abstract conceptualisation
- active experimentation
- concrete experience

The Kolb cycle is adapted by Coates (1989) who suggests that appropriate simulated learning environments provide learners with opportunities to reflect upon and theorize about their practice, and to devise and experiment with potential solutions to problems. Real learning environments, e.g. the school or college workplace itself, provide opportunities to implement, monitor, evaluate and modify strategies in practice (Turner et al. 1988, p.196). The value of the simulated learning environment is perceived to be that it allows learners to engage in professional development in a safe, non-threatening environment. The learning cycle may only be completed, however, by including the 'concrete experience' phase which leads to actual changes in performance.

Joyce and Showers (1980) postulate a model which allows specific *components* of a training activity to be assessed in terms of their potential *impact* on performance. Central to their model is the premise that learners should be given feedback, coaching and support during the learning process if changes in practice are to take place. Within the Joyce and Showers model the 'missing link' identified by Wallace is addressed via coaching and support in the workplace and, as such, constitutes an integral part of the learning process.

The essential features of the Kolb, the Coates and the Joyce and Showers models provide a comprehensive guide to the analysis of training or development activities in terms of:

- choice of appropriate *learning style*
- necessary *components* of the learning activity
- the appropriate *environment* for that activity
- the anticipated *outcomes* for the learner
- the levels of *support* needed to manage the learning process

The provision of an effective learning environment for professional development assumes awareness both of the varied ways in which adults learn and of the learning conditions most conducive to ensuring application of learning in terms of enhanced performance. In particular, school and college managers have a responsibility to ensure that development activities are designed so that they:

- provide a *safe environment* for learning
- provide appropriate strategies to support *transfer of learning*
- allow *appropriate evaluation* of learning and learning transfer

Support

The complexities of effective professional development provision suggest that for professional development activities to benefit both learner and organization a comprehensive framework of support for those activities is needed to ensure appropriate transfer of learning and lasting changes in performance. The need for a framework of support indicates that effective professional development is not a peripheral, bolt-on, area of school or college activity but is, rather, an integral feature of day-to-day work. As such professional development becomes an important but routine aspect of managerial and professional activity within the organization, with consequent implications for the way that managers support the work of professional colleagues.

The essential purposes of a framework of support may be defined as:

- to ensure appropriate *needs analysis*
- to ensure appropriate *match* between need and learning activity
- to *resource* agreed activities
- to facilitate *performance enhancement* as a result of learning
- to *monitor* the effectiveness of the learning experience
- to *evaluate* the effectiveness of the development activity

It is essential to assess the outcome of learning back in the school setting, in terms of a change in behaviour, in order to be satisfied that school management training is worthwhile. Although the same problem undoubtedly exists in industry, there is less of a tendency to value the acquisition of knowledge for its own sake than in an educational institution, and correspondingly more pressure to get a return on investment in learning (Everard 1986, p. 202).

Effective professional development does not take place in a vacuum and as such needs to become fully integrated with other aspects of educational management within the organization. It is possible to identify three models of institutionally managed support, illustrated in Figure 14.5, which are intended to aid the application of learning in the workplace.

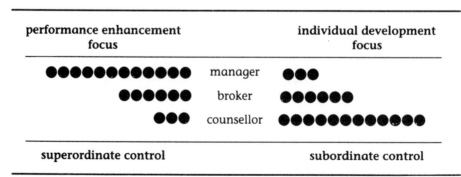

Figure 14.5 Models of institutional support for professional development

1. The manager

The *manager* is an important feature of a support framework amongst proponents of workplace based, task oriented forms of development (Everard, 1986; DES, 1990) based on the assertion that the most effective and appropriate forms of development take place within the routine working environment. Such a perception is reflected in the move away from course driven models of professional development:

> The main shift has been from a view that training is the sole source of knowledge and skills acquisition towards a recognition that experience, advice, support and encouragement must be made regularly available in everyday working conditions and relationships.(DES 1990, p.7).

This perspective views development in the context of performance enhancement and emphasizes the importance of the line manager, or team leader, in terms of supporting personal development within an institutional context:

> The key agent in the organization for helping people to do a better job is their immediate manager (Everard 1986, p.146).

A focus on the line manager implicitly argues that professional development needs to have a team (Everard and Morris, 1990) or functioning group (ACSTT, 1980) emphasis. Such a view is endorsed by those advocates of a move toward self-managing teams (Jenkins, 1991; West-Burnham, 1992) as a feature of emerging management structures in educational organizations. Such a move argues that professional development should address the needs of functioning groups and, as such, would best be addressed via group rather than solitary learning.

2. The broker

The role of the *broker* is articulated in the James report (1972) in terms of provision of advice and support both for longer-term career development and more immediate in-post responsibilities. The model of support is important inasmuch as it is seen as a means of harmonizing the, at times, disparate needs of individual and institution. It may be labelled a brokering function in that expressed needs are matched with appropriate activities within the resources available, with advice being given in respect of the most appropriate choice from amongst several options:

> This may involve deciding on priorities, balancing the various sets of needs and choosing or providing the most effective form of training or new experience (Gane 1986, p.9).

Thus it is possible to envisage the role of the INSET co-ordinator or professional tutor as a support both for individuals and line managers, and which serves two principal functions:

- acting as a clearing house of appropriate activities to support the development at individual, functioning group and organizational levels
- arbitrating between the various demands made upon the system by those three levels of activity

3. The counsellor

An alternative model of support, focusing on 'colleague-to-colleague counselling', is advocated by Main (1985, p.115). Responsibility for professional development in this model resides with the individual professional. The professional has access to an academic counsellor or mentor whose role is to:

(a) act as a catalyst for the analysis and development of teaching; and
(b) indicate possible strategies for improvement (ibid.).

The *counsellor* support model then incorporates elements of the broker role but, significantly, sees professional development driven by the individual, with the organization providing logistic support for the counsellor-professional relationship.

Approach

The manager, broker and counsellor models of institutionally managed support may thus be distinguished according to focus and control. Equally, the way that professional development is approached will vary from institution to institution. The chosen approach(es) will not only reflect the school's or college's interpretation of the importance of professional development but, significantly, will also indicate how well professional development is integrated with other areas of management activity within the institution. Such an overview is essential in management terms because schools and colleges need to establish an appropriate and integrated balance of development at individual, team and organizational levels if they are to improve the quality of learning experience of pupils and students. Analysis of preferred current approaches therefore allows and encourages an organization to promote a 'balance of interests' (Holly and Southworth 1989, p.14) in terms of professional development activity.

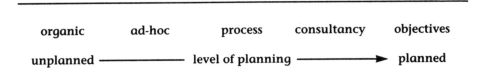

Figure 14.6 Approaches to professional development

Figure 14.6 illustrates a range of approaches to provision at organizational level, distinguished by the level of planning in each type. The five approaches are discussed below:

❑ Organic approaches

Organic approaches to professional development are rooted in the concept of change as 'evolutionary' (Stake 1987, p.57). In these approaches development occurs naturally as a normal consequence of experience and social interaction. Dissemination is via informal networks of colleagues on a shared basis (Havelock, in Turner et al. 1988). The only purpose of planning within these approaches is to 'design studies that provide descriptions of practice which can serve as vicarious experiences for practitioners, which in turn will stimulate reflection, insights, natural generalizations and personal change in practice' (Fullan 1987, p.218). Such approaches assume that learners are motivated to engage independently in affective modes of learning.

❑ Ad-hoc approaches

Ad hoc or *laissez-faire* approaches are characterized (e.g. Southworth 1984;) as lacking in planning or integration. Bradley (1991) implies that many in-service programmes at national and local levels have reflected this narrow stimulus–response approach to development. Professional development in these approaches is reactive and opportunistic and lacks any systematic attempt to integrate organizational and individual needs within a managed programme (Burgoyne, 1988).

❑ Process-based approaches

Process-based approaches include those models of professional development which emphasise reflection (Schon, 1983), analysis and self-generated review. Typically these approaches are considered developmental processes in their own right (Hopkins, 1987). They aim to enhance practice through a cycle of learning leading to the testing of potential solutions to problems in practice. Essential to the principle of this approach is the generation of development priorities by the learners themselves (Main, 1985). Developing an appropriate organizational environment for this process suggests a 'need for openness, co-operation, shared ownership and responsibility as underlying values for staff development' (ibid. p.115). Typically process approaches employ actual organizational practice as a context for learning.

❑ Consultancy approaches

Consultancy approaches involve the use of an outside agent in the analysis of individual, group or whole organization work. Murgatroyd and Reynolds (1984) identify three forms of consultancy in education:

Consultative assistance as in technical assistance in relation to a specific problem.

Content consultation is non-directive in nature and aims to assist sub-groups within the organization to improve practice in a given area.

Process consultation is the most extensive form of consultancy which is directed at the structures and relationships within the organization as a whole.

The authors suggest that a significant strength of consultancy as a form of development is that it provides alternative perspectives on organizational and functioning group practice within a structure of review and support. The approach is helpful because it offers the prospect of overcoming obstacles to changes in professional practices discussed above in relation to adult learning, for, according to Murgatroyd and Reynolds (p.333):

> consultancy encourages changes in behaviour, hoping that attitude and relationship changes may follow; conventional teacher education encourages attitudinal change that may never have behavioural effects.

❑ Objectives approaches

Objectives approaches, in one sense, are typical manifestations of superordinate models of control described by Day (op. cit.). These give preeminence to the needs of the organization at the expense of individual career or professional development needs (Southworth, 1984). In such approaches needs analysis is conducted in many instances from a competence perspective. Staff development needs are analyzed in terms of what is needed to deliver organizational objectives (e.g. Everard ,1986; Squire ,1987) Development in these approaches is regarded as training in specific deficit areas rather than broader personal development. Its purpose is to 'promote effective curricular change and improvements in teaching quality throughout the school' (ACSET 1988, p.337). At a more sophisticated level an objectives approach to professional development would advocate integrated strategies for recruitment and retention, career and succession-planning, in order to plan for and meet the needs of the organization over a period of time (Burgoyne, 1988).

Application

Theory suggests that effective professional development programmes should:

(a) acknowledge the professional as an adult learner
(b) begin from an analysis of the professional's own practice
(c) explicitly link learning and workplace environments
(d) promote shared reflection
(e) focus on thoughts and feelings in addition to actions
(f) integrate whole school and individual development
(g) establish learning objectives for the purposes of evaluation

There are, however, certain polemics associated with the management of professional development which militate against the ready translation of such principles into action. Several of these difficulties arise from the discussion, at the beginning of the chapter, about the various, and at times conflicting, interpretations of what professional development should be about. Those difficulties are compounded by the fact that, in the 1990s, priorities and associated funding levels for professional development are still largely decided at national and local levels. Thus autonomous schools and colleges may be faced with the problem of conflicting demands which, despite greater levels of institutional choice than ever before, constrain their freedom to interpret and manage professional development according to internally determined priorities (Kelly 1989, p.169). The management of professional development, therefore, should be seen in terms of not only the effective internal management of longer term institutional priorities, but also as the ability to respond to external demands for short-term improvements in curriculum performance.

The move towards institutionally based and focused programmes of professional development has implications for the school or college in respect of potential insularity of outlook. A purely introspective focus for professional development restricts opportunities for professionals to engage in reflection and experimentation with colleagues from other institutions and different experiences.

This difficulty is compounded by the combined effects of an international movement towards delegation of financial responsibility to site level and of curriculum accountability to central government level. Within the framework suggested by Figure 14.2 it is possible to anticipate pressures against development activities at the more broadly focused management of learning end of the continuum in favour of those towards the curriculum delivery end. The 1988 Education Reform Act and subsequent, related, legislation have led to significantly increased levels of individual and organizational accountability in the area of curriculum delivery. Increased accountability demands the identification of specific training priorities with quantifiable and measurable outcomes in terms of enhanced performance.

Accountability and financial probity constraints need to be set against the theoretical perspectives outlined above. This suggests that effective professional development, in the broadest sense, may be possible only in organizations which can develop an appropriate learning or problem-solving culture for individuals and groups of professional staff. The nature of change in educational organizations argues for the development of a flexible, highly-skilled, committed team of professional staff. External pressures for quality curriculum delivery urge professional development programmes to concentrate on the training of a narrower range of curriculum related competences. The essential challenge for those involved with the management of professional development in practice is to effectively balance the demands of short-term external accountability with those of longer-term individual and institutional improvement.

Summary

This chapter has analysed major management concerns in the area of professional learning. Control and accountability issues are seen to exercise considerable delimiting effects in terms of programme purpose and design at the level of the individual institution. Nevertheless, institutional culture represents a powerful vehicle for the promotion of effective individual and organizational growth. Theories of adult learning suggest that the structure of activities should provide a safe learning environment which encourages reflection and analysis together with the identification of appropriate strategies for application of learning in the workplace. Effective application in turn depends on the provision of appropriate institutionally managed networks of support for both the learner and the intended innovation, together with appropriate mechanisms for needs analysis and evaluation of learning.

Note

1. The complexities of educational management suggest that the figures in this chapter are treated as illustrative of a range of possible features rather than prescriptive and rigid categories. Within any educational organization or particular institution it is probable that provision will be characterized by more than one type of approach to the management and delivery of professional development activity. The range will vary typically according to the size, structure and culture of the organization, and idiosyncratically according to the perceptions and preferences of individual professional staff.

Further reading

Main, A (1985) *Educational Staff Development*, London: Croom Helm.

Wideen, M. and Andrews, I. (Eds) (1987) *Staff Development for School Improvement: A Focus on the Teacher*, Lewes: Falmer Press.

References

ACSET (Advisory Committee for the Supply and Education of Teachers) (1988) 'Making INSET work' in Glatter, R., Preedy, M., Riches, C. and Masterton, M. (Eds) *Understanding School Management*, Milton Keynes: Open University Press.

ACSTT (Advisory Committee for the Supply and Training of Teachers) (1980) 'Making INSET work' in Bush, T., Glatter, R., Goodey, J. and Riches, C. (Eds) *Approaches to School Management*, London: Harper and Row.

Ballinger, E.A. (1986) 'The training and development needs of managers: an overview' in Day, C. and Moore, R. (Eds) *Staff Development in the Secondary School: Management Perspectives*, London: Croom Helm.

Bolam, R. (1987) *What is Effective INSET?*, Paper addressed to the Annual Members Conference of the National Foundation for Educational Research.

Bradley, H.(1991) *Staff Development*, Lewes: Falmer Press.

Brown, S. and Earley, P. (1990) *Enabling Teachers to Undertake In-service Education and Training. A Report for the DES*, Windsor: National Foundation for Educational Research.

Burgoyne, J. (1978) 'Managerial skills' in Burgoyne, J. and Stuart, R. (Eds) *Management Development: Context and Strategies,* Aldershot: Gower Press.

Burgoyne, J. (1988) 'Management Development for the individual *and* the organization' *Personnel Management,* **20,** 6, pp.40–45.

Coates, J. (1989) 'How people learn on management courses! a learning styles model of management courses' *Industrial and Commercial Training,* **21,** 2, pp.3–10.

Coulson, A. (1985) 'Recruitment and management development for primary headship' *School Organization,* **5,** 2, pp.111–123.

Day, C. (1986) 'Staff development: some problems in promoting professional learning and change' in Day, C. and Moore, R.(Eds) *Staff Development in the Secondary School: Management Perspectives,* London: Croom Helm.

DES (Department of Education and Science) (1990) *Developing School Management: The Way Forward. A Report by the School Management Task Force,* London: HMSO.

Easen, P. (1985) *Making School-centred INSET work,* London: Routledge.

Eraut, M. (1972) *In-Service Education for Innovation,* Occasional paper 4, National Council for Educational Technology (NCET), NCET publications.

Everard, K.B. (1986) *Developing Management in Schools,* Oxford: Blackwell.

Everard, K.B. and Morris, G. (1990) *Effective School Management,* second edn. London: Paul Chapman Publishing.

Fullan, M. (1987) 'Implementing the implementation plan' in Wideen, M. and Andrews, I. (Eds) *Staff Development for School Improvement: A Focus on the Teacher,* Lewes: Falmer Press.

Fullan, M. (1988) 'Research into educational innovation' in Glatter, R., Preedy, M., Riches, C. and Masterton, M. (Eds) *Understanding School Management,* Milton Keynes: Open University Press.

Fullan, M. (1989) 'Managing curriculum change' in Preedy, M. (Ed) *Approaches to Curriculum Management,* Milton Keynes: Open University Press.

Gane, V. (1986) *Appraisal for Staff Development: Implications for Teacher Education,* report on the Annual Conference of the Standing Conference on the Education and Training of Teachers, Leicester, 21–23 Nov.

Handy, C. (1990) *The Age of Unreason,* London: Century Hutchinson.

Holly, P. and Southworth, G. (1989) *The Developing School*, Lewes: Falmer Press.

Honey, P. and Mumford, A. (1982) *Manual of Learning Styles*, Honey Publications.

Hopkins, D. (1987) 'Teacher research as a basis for staff development' in Wideen, M. and Andrews, I. (Eds) *Staff Development for School Improvement: A Focus on the Teacher*, Lewes: Falmer Press.

Hoyle, E. (1982) 'The professionalization of teachers: a paradox'. *British Journal of Educational Studies*, **30**, 2, pp.161–171.

James Report (1972) *Teacher Education*, Report of Committee of Inquiry under the chairmanship of Lord James of Rusholme, London: HMSO.

Jenkins, H. (1991) *Getting It Right: A Handbook for Successful School Leadership*, Oxford: Blackwell.

Jones, K., Clark, J., Figg, G., Howarth, S. and Reid, K. (1989) *Staff Development in Primary Schools*, Oxford: Blackwell Education.

Joyce, B. and Showers, B. (1980) 'Improving in-service training: the messages of research', *Educational Leadership*, **37**, 5, pp.379–386.

Kelly, A.V. (1989) *The Curriculum, Theory and Practice*, third edn. London: Paul Chapman Publishing.

Kolb, D. (1983) *Experiential Learning Experience As The Source of Learning and Development*, New York: Prentice Hall.

Main, A. (1985) *Educational Staff Development*, London: Croom Helm.

McMahon, A. and Bolam, R. (1990) *Management Development and Educational Reform: A Handbook for LEAs*, second edn. London: Paul Chapman Publishing.

Murgatroyd, S. and Reynolds, D. (1984) 'The creative consultant: the potential use of consultancy as a method of teacher education, *School Organization*, **4**, 4, pp.321–335.

Schmuck, R. (1980) 'Interventions for strengthening the school's creativity' in Bush, T., Glatter, R., Goodey, J. and Riches, C. (Eds) *Approaches to School Management*, London: Harper and Row.

Schon, D. (1983) *The Reflective Practitioner*, London: Temple Smith.

Southworth, G. (1984) 'Development of staff in primary schools (some ideas and implications)'. *British Journal of In-Service Education*, **10**, 3, pp.6–15.

Squire, W. (1987) *Education Management in the UK: A Defective Mode and Its Remedies*, Aldershot: Gower.

Stake, R. (1987) 'An evolutionary view of programming staff development', in Wideen, M. and Andrews, I. (Eds) *Staff Development for School Improvement: A Focus on the Teacher*, Lewes: Falmer Press.

Turner, E., Long, A., Foley, R. and Kidd, J. (1988) 'Towards a strategy for implementing change'. *British Journal of In-Service Education*, **14**, 3, pp.191–201.

Wallace, M. (1986) 'Training and performance—a missing link?', *British Journal of In-Service Education*, **12**, 2, pp.68–72.

West-Burnham, J. (1992) *Managing Quality in Schools*, Harlow: Longman.

Williams, M. (1991) *In-service Education and Training: Policy and Practice*, London: Cassell.

15 Accountability in education

Tony Bush

Introduction

In this chapter, we explore the concept of accountability and apply it to education. We consider several definitions of accountability and contrast the term with similar notions of responsiveness and responsibility. Kogan's (1986) four-part model of accountability is discussed and the different conceptions of accountability within educational management theory are also addressed. Finally, we consider how patterns of accountability have changed in the United Kingdom in the two decades since the 'Great Debate' initiated by former prime minister James Callaghan in 1976.

The context of accountability

Accountability is an important concept in the management of education. It has gained credence in the United Kingdom since Callaghan's seminal Ruskin speech in 1976. Expressed in terms which now appear to be modest, he asserted that teachers had a responsibility to explain and justify their decisions to a wider audience, including parents, employers, and the LEAs and central government which fund their activities.

The notion of accountability has been given a new emphasis in England and Wales by the shift to autonomous or quasi-autonomous institutions following the 1988 Education Reform Act. The advent of independent colleges, grant maintained (GM) schools and local management of schools (LMS) has loosened or removed the previous accountability framework, substituting other, less well articulated, modes of accountability.

Definitions of accountability

Accountability is a multi-faceted concept which may have several different interpretations:

The trouble is that people understand many different things by accountability ... [it] can be of many kinds: personal, professional, political, financial, managerial, legal, contractual (Burgess 1992, p.5).

At minimum, accountability means being required to give an account of events or behaviour in a school or college to those who may have a legitimate right to know. One of the central aspects of accountability relates to establishing which individuals and groups have that legitimacy.

Sockett (1980) argues that accountability has both a simple and a complex meaning. At its most basic, it is 'to hold someone to account' (p.10). He goes on to suggest that accountability means being *obliged* to deliver an account as well as being able to do so. He says that the principle usually means being accountable for outcomes and results but, in certain professions, it has come to mean responsibility for adherence to codes of practice rather than outcomes. In these cases, including law and medicine, answerability is for due process rather than the results of professional activity.

Kogan (1986, p.25) acknowledges the wide range of terms in use but adopts a rigorous definition of the concept. Accountability is:

a condition in which individual role holders are liable to review and the application of sanctions if their actions fail to satisfy those with whom they are in an accountability relationship .

He distinguishes between those who have 'hard' sanctions, such as pay, promotion or continued employment, and those who may have 'softer' sanctions such as disapproval.

Forms of accountability

Sockett (1980) asks three central questions in delineating forms of accountability:

- is the school or teacher accountable?
- to whom should the school or teacher be accountable?
- for what is the school or teacher accountable?

❑ School or teacher

Sockett advocates that teachers should be regarded as the unit of account. This is partly because only individual teachers can be held to account for their behaviour and partly because accountability should have both an internal and external dimension. The internal dimension is valid only if individuals are separately accountable, to one another as well as to the external community.

❏ To whom is a teacher accountable?

Sockett distinguishes between teachers' perceptions of their accountabilities and the views of others about this issue. He argues that teachers ought to be accountable to the following groups whether or not teachers recognise and accept all these levels of responsibility:

(a) individual pupils and parents
(b) pupils and their parents as part of the community
(c) the teacher's employers, e.g. the LEA
(d) the providers of the resources, both LEA and Government
(e) professional peers inside and outside the school
(f) other relevant educational institutions, e.g. universities, secondary schools
(g) the 'public'
(h) industry, including the Trade Unions

Elliott (1979, p.69) focuses on the school rather than the individual teacher and stresses the complexity of this important question:

> In an ideal situation one might argue that a school is accountable to all those groups and agencies who have either a legal or moral right to know about and influence its work. But within any given political context the answers are not so simple.

He goes on to argue that there may be conflicting requirements arising from different accountabilities. One example is the tension between meeting the needs of children and being accountable to parents. There may also be conflict between accountability to parents and to those who have political responsibility for schools and colleges, although this is less of an issue in an era of autonomous institutions.

❏ For what is a teacher accountable?

Sockett (1980) argues that teachers should be accountable for outcomes and for the process leading to those outcomes. He notes that the various constituencies may expect different results from the educational process but stresses that teachers can be held to account only for what is in their control.

Elliott (1979) says that this is an ambiguous question because schools and their various 'audiences' may not agree about the nature and aims of education. This may become a conflict over values and schools may be reluctant to accept that certain demands for accountability are legitimate. However, in an increasingly pluralist educational system, acceptance of alternative values may be an essential element in the process of accountability.

Accountability, responsibility and responsiveness

❑ Responsiveness

Responsibility and responsiveness may be regarded as alternatives to accountability in conceptualising the relationship between educational institutions and their external environments. Scott (1989, p.17) rejects the suggestion that *responsiveness* is simply a synonym for accountability and distinguishes between them as follows:

> Responsiveness describes the willingness of an institution — or, indeed, an individual — to respond on its own or their own initiative, i.e. the capacity to be open to outside impulses and new ideas. Accountability, in contrast, describes the submission of the institution or individual to a form of external audit, its capacity to account for its or their performance ... Responsiveness is freely arrived at; accountability is imposed from outside ... the first concept subsumes the second — it is a much broader idea.

This distinction is sharpened by Scott's use of a narrow definition of accountability but the notion of responsiveness permeates the accountability literature and a clarification of both terms is an important element in understanding the significance of accountability for schools and colleges in the 1990s.

Elliott (1979, p.69) claims that responsiveness is acceptable only if it results in change:

> A school's audiences are most likely to accept the responsive approach when the school positively demonstrates its ability to modify its practices in the light of public discussion. If a school can demonstrate its openness to rational influence exerted through discussion then its public audiences will feel less need to adopt coercive methods for influencing its practices.

Scott (1989) elaborates his distinction between accountability and responsiveness and seeks to integrate them into a four-part model:

Political accountability

Scott (1989) argues are that there are two senses in which schools and colleges must be accountable to government:

- because the system is largely supported by public funds, it must be accountable in a managerial sense for the best possible use of those funds

- government has a right and even a duty to determine the broad character of the schools and colleges which it supports so that they contribute fully to economic development, social progress, cultural conservation, individual fulfilment and other goals which enjoy widespread support

Market accountability

Here the role of the customer, whether student or employer, is emphasized. If the customer can be placed in a direct relationship with the supplier of the services they seek, then a self-regulatory market can be allowed to operate. Both choice and efficiency will be maximized without the need for political interventions. However, Scott identifies three important limitations of the market model of accountability and responsiveness:

- the difficulty of definition — who is the customer? The pupil or student, or their parents? Or is the government the real customer so long as education is largely tax-supported? The complexity and ambiguity of these questions undermine the idea of a market in education

- it is a managed not a free market. The education system's position as a near-monopoly supplier is maintained by a range of regulations, including compulsory attendance at school, the qualification and registration of teachers and, in England and Wales, the imposition of a National Curriculum. A free market would require all these controls to be lifted

- there are external benefits that accrue to society from education which cannot be attributed to particular individuals

Scott argues that, as a result of this complexity, education is resistant to a market version of accountability. However, the changes introduced in England and Wales by the Education Reform Act, including LMS, open enrolment and GM schools, serve to enhance the market aspects of education, encouraging schools to compete for pupils and the resultant income. Schools have to be responsive to parental needs if they are to recruit successfully.

Professional responsibility

Scott suggests that the accountability of teachers and educational institutions may be captured best within a web of professional obligations. These norms embody codes of practice and sets of values that are all the more influential because they are self-imposed. He claims that professionals know that it is the student who is at the centre of the accountability process:

> In discussing ways to improve the responsiveness of institutions and individuals in education it would be wrong to ignore the professional model. It does allow accountability to be exercised outside the immediate context of politics and the market (p.20).

Cultural responsibility

Scott defines this as the allegiance to rationality, trust and knowledge (p.20). Real change in education comes from new insights, knowledge and understanding:

> This may be the ultimate form of responsiveness ... An institution that fails to foster such things or an individual who has little regard for them can hardly be regarded as responsive ... without this primary responsibility education would be truly a dead world. Its external utility is rooted in its internal validity, its private integrity.

❏ Responsibility

Kogan (1986, p.26) contrasts moral and legal obligations in distinguishing between accountability and *responsibility:*

> Accountability assumes institutional authority to call an individual or a group to account for their actions. It is to be contrasted with responsibility which is the moral sense of duty to perform appropriately. Responsibility need not evoke the duty to answer in any legal or contractual setting, that is to act accountably

Kogan acknowledges that his definition of accountability is narrower than that of some other writers. Others subsume responsibility within a broader statement of accountability. Elliott et al. (1979, p.8) reject the notion of public accountability which they call 'a model of social control'. They substitute the concept of responsibility which they regard as more appropriate for 'autonomous' professionals:

> The ideas of 'autonomy' and 'responsibility' [are] conceptually linked with that of 'a profession'. An association of people would not be entitled to the

status of a profession if it was not in a position to accept 'responsibility' for its activities. People can be held responsible for their activities only if they are free to decide between alternatives. In other words, 'responsibility' can only be ascribed to those who are free to act 'autonomously'.

Edwards (1991, p.30) points to the difficulty of reconciling the 'closely entwined' concepts of autonomy and accountability and says that a balance is required between these twin demands:

> The issue lies in the degree to which accountability and autonomy are applied in relation to each other in order to ensure that people work simultaneously within guidelines and with a degree of independence.

Edwards adds that accountability leads to control while autonomy fosters the release of human potential.

There is a contradiction for teachers who have to operate as professionals within an organizational framework. A measure of autonomy is required for practitioners to be effective while the school remains accountable for their performance. Hughes' (1976) model explains how schools are able to accommodate the conflicting demands of professionalism and bureaucracy. His conceptualization describes headteachers as both leading professionals and chief executives by virtue of their background as experienced teachers and their formal position as official leaders of the school. Within this model, the 'chief executive' is accountable to external stakeholders while the 'leading professional' facilitates a measure of teacher autonomy.

While the distinctions between accountability, responsibility and responsiveness are valid, it may be more useful to regard all these categories as simply different modes of accountability. As we shall see in the next section, most models of accountability incorporate responsiveness and responsibility rather than treating them as separate concepts.

Models of accountability

Kogan (1986) proposes a normative model of accountability. It is normative in the sense that 'descriptions of potential relationships and their consequences are given whether or not they exist in the empirically observable world' (Kogan 1986, p.33). In other words, these are conceptual distinctions rather than models arising from research evidence. He identifies three models but one of these has two variants so I shall treat them as four different categories:

- public or state control and managerialism
- professional accountability
- consumerist control: partnership
- consumerist control: free market

The Kogan models will be used to structure the discussion but insights from other writers will be included as appropriate.

❏ Public or state control

Kogan argues that the dominant mode of accountability in the UK is that of public control. Its main formal characteristic is that of a managerial hierarchy. For example, the teacher is legally an 'assistant' who is required by contract to perform tasks set by the head and is subject to review by him or her. Teachers are held accountable by the head for their work. The teacher's career prospects, whether in terms of internal promotion or in the judgements made in references, are strongly affected by evaluations made by the head. The head cannot directly secure dismissal of a teacher for poor performance, but can institute a process to be implemented by others. In turn, the head is accountable for the work of the school and has authority to discharge that accountability.

Kogan (1986, p.40) argues that the managerially accountable school within a local authority is legitimated by the electoral process, a similar point to that made by Scott (1989):

> That may mean, however, that it is tied into the political–administrative system of the local authority and less capable of being influenced by its immediate clientele.

This judgement is less valid in the 1990s in England and Wales where local political and administrative control is weakened for all schools and absent for grant-maintained schools and newly-autonomous colleges. Accountability to governing bodies is the dominant mode of public accountability in self-governing establishments and is increasingly important in all schools. In this climate, accountability to clients is enhanced and that to the local political system is much reduced.

❏ Professional accountability

This mode of accountability relates to professional self-control. Teachers are judged by peers on the basis of their adherence to professional norms and values. Kogan says that groups of professionals should establish detailed codes of conduct in relation to each aspect of their work. Teachers are expected to be responsive to clients and this may take the form of a 'contract' with interested parties.

Kogan argues that advocates of this model are seeking to meet two objectives:

- to protect schools from demands for product-orientated outcomes. Self-evaluation by teachers forms the basis for lay judgements of school effectiveness
- responsiveness to clients. The stronger the professional autonomy of teachers and schools the more responsive to their clients they will be

Elliott et al. (1979) advocate a professional model linked to the notion of autonomy and to the concept of responsiveness discussed earlier. They argue that a school is professionally accountable if it is under an obligation to demonstrate to the teaching profession that its policies protect and foster educational values.

Sockett (1980, p.19) also advocates a professional accountability model, based on principles rather than results, but gives more attention than Elliott et al. to the need to be responsive to other 'constituencies'. His professional model has the following characteristics:

(a) accountability would be for adherence to *principles of practice* rather than for results embodied in pupil performances

(b) accountability would be rendered to *diverse constituencies* rather than to the public alone

(c) the teacher would have to be regarded as an *autonomous professional*, not as a social technician, within the bureaucratic framework of a school

(d) evaluation through measurement of pupil performances would be replaced by a *conception of evaluation* as providing information for constituents allied to a system of proper redress through a professional body.

Burgess (1992, p.7) argues that professional accountability is effective in securing 'proper performance':

> Professionals are judged by other professionals: they are accountable to their peers ... Legal and contractual accountabilities exist and can be used

317

in extremes, but they are not what secures proper performance. Commitment to pupils and their parents, to the outcomes of training, to best practice and to ethical standards are more effective here .

In the climate of the 1990s the concept of professional accountability may be criticised by some for its inward, producer-dominated focus in contrast to the consumer stance espoused by governments in the United Kingdom and elsewhere. Alternatively, it may be regarded as legitimate if considered alongside that of public accountability and Kogan's two consumerist models.

❑ Consumerist control : partnership

Kogan (1986) draws much of the material for this model from the work of Sallis (1979). The essence of this approach is that parents as clients should participate in a partnership and not in a dependency relationship with teachers. According to Sallis, links between professionals and clients should contain three elements:

- consensus about objectives
- an exchange of information about methods
- dialogue about the success of what has been done

Sallis argues that a partnership between parents and teachers is required if there is to be an accountable relationship. Schools and parents must be accountable to each other for their contributions to a shared task. She claims that 'true accountability can only exist in an acceptance of shared responsibility for success at the level of the child, the school and the service' (Sallis 1988, p.10).

The partnership model is idealistic and normative, based on the Sallis' notion of good practice. It may be the least relevant of the accountability models for schools and colleges in the 1990s. Kogan's (1986, p.33) caution about the models not being evident in the 'empirically observable world' applies to the partnership model in particular.

❑ Consumerist control : free market

This model provides for accountability through market mechanisms rather than through publicly maintained systems of control. Kogan (1986, p.52) says that these are largely 'social' market rather than free market models:

> They assume that consumer preference will be elucidated and met through schemes which enable public authorities to pursue public goals whilst giving maximum play to private wishes.

Kogan illustrates this model by reference to voucher schemes in operation in parts of the United States. The approach is underpinned by the view that the goals of education should not be determined by teachers alone:

> Teachers will indeed become accountable but not to publicly appointed bodies or other professionals in public authorities. The head and staff will have their behaviour conditioned by the degree of success that they achieve in attracting pupils (p.53).

Kogan's work was completed before the ERA of 1988 which enshrined many of these free market principles in English and Welsh education. The introduction of local management of schools, which ties schools' income to their ability to recruit pupils, and open enrolment, which removes artificial limits on pupil recruitment, are powerful elements of a free market strategy. The provision for grant-maintained (GM) schools extends this principle by giving governing bodies and parents the right to opt out of LEA control. GM schools receive their income from the Department for Education, largely on the basis of pupil numbers. Research on the first 100 GM schools concludes that:

> The main accountability of the GM schools is to the market-place and their effectiveness is increasingly assessed by their ability to recruit pupils and to perform well in public examinations (Bush et al. 1993, p.178).

The market place has sharpened notions of client accountability. In 1980 Barton et al. referred to 'answerability' to clients as 'moral accountability', a weak mode compared with the strict accountability which schools were said to owe to LEAs. In the 1990s market accountability has assumed much greater significance. The requirement to publish examination and test results, and the production of the 'parents' charter', further enhance the importance of this mode of accountability in England and Wales.

Kogan (1986) criticizes the market mechanism as likely to be damaging to teachers' professionalism. The ERA places the emphasis on accountability to consumers through the market mechanism and through parental participation in school government. The explicit objective of much of government policy is to reduce the producer 'domination' of the education system and, by implication, to reduce the significance of professional accountability.

Accountability and educational management theory

In Chapter 2 of this volume, I review the main theories of educational management. Five models are presented which portray different ways of conceptualizing the management of schools and colleges. In this section, I will link the notion of accountability to these five theories of educational management.

❏ Bureaucratic theories

These approaches assume a hierarchical structure in schools and colleges with staff accountable to their immediate superordinate in the pyramid:

> The hierarchy is the general structure in all developed cultures for achieving work objectives that are beyond the control of the single individual. Through a series of manager-subordinate relationships it explicitly locates accountability for work. The manager in the hierarchy is accountable not only for his, or her, performance, but also for the work of subordinates (Packwood 1977, p.1).

This internal accountability is matched by an external dimension. Heads and principals are accountable to governing bodies and funding agencies for the activities of their institution. The treatment of accountability in this theory fits Kogan's (1986) public accountability model.

❏ Collegial theories

These approaches stress the professional nature of schools and colleges and advocate decision-making by staff. Teachers' authority of expertise is emphasised in contrast to the positional authority associated with the bureaucratic theory. Their expertise reinforces their right as professionals to a measure of autonomy in the classroom, and to participate in institutional decision-making. Accountability is to fellow professionals who have the expertise to judge other teachers. This approach is consistent with the professional accountability model discussed by Kogan (1986), Sockett (1980) and Elliott et al. (1979).

The focus of accountability in collegial theories is firmly on the internal dimension. There is a problem in relation to the external aspect of accountability. Leaders are expected to explain decisions to governing and sponsoring bodies. However, these decisions are the product of a participative process and it is possible that the leader may not agree with the outcome. Heads are then in the invidious position of justifying decisions which do not enjoy their personal support.

This issue arose in research at Churchfields school in the English West Midlands. The head is committed to a collegial approach and was prepared to defend decisions at meetings of the governing body even where he disagreed with them:

The headteacher works on the principle that if he thinks a decision is 'wrong' but there is a consensus in favour of it, it is more likely to be made to work successfully than the decision he would have favoured. It is a matter of commitment to a decision by those who will have to make it work. Thus accountability is for successful implementation of policies, rather than for the policies themselves (Bush 1993, p.38).

While this stance gives primacy to professional accountability, it may be difficult to sustain if there is disagreement over major issues or if the school fails to recruit well.

❏ Political theories

These theories stress the importance of sub-units such as faculties and departments rather than the whole school or college. Accountability is to other members of the department rather than to the head, other teachers or external groups. The main exception to this generalisation is the accountability of specialist staff to the norms established by external subject groups. Associations of English teachers or science staff, for example, may exert influence on departments and impact on internal decision-making.

In political theories it is assumed that conflict is resolved by the exercise of power. The most powerful groups or coalitions strongly influence the outcomes of policy debates. When heads explain decisions to governing bodies and other external groups, they may be reporting the outcomes of power struggles rather than the results of a collegial or bureaucratic process. However, leaders are participants in the decision process and also have substantial resources of power. In many, but not all, cases, heads will be able to determine outcomes and thus experience little difficulty in explaining them to external bodies.

❏ Subjective theories

These approaches focus on individuals within organizations rather than the whole institution or its sub-units. Each person is thought to have a selective and subjective perception of the school or college. Individuals may have different interpretations of the same event or situation. These meanings may be influenced by external influences, both professional and personal.

In this model, the emphasis is on the answerability of individual teachers rather than that of the school or college, consistent with Sockett's (1980) view referred to earlier. Elliott et al. (1979) suggest that accountability may be primarily to the individual's own beliefs and values. They report the results of interviews with teachers participating in their research on accountability in secondary schools. Their findings show that answerability to 'myself' is rated as the most important of the different sets of accountabilities.

Elliott et al.'s research lends support to the subjective model but it is difficult to conceptualise how personal accountability can be compared with other models which involve rendering an account to other individuals or groups. However, if people evaluate their performance against high professional standards it may be the vehicle for individual and school improvement and lead to a better service for clients.

❑ Ambiguity theories

These theories stress uncertainty and complexity in organizations. The emphasis is on the instability and unpredictability of institutional life. In this approach, schools and colleges are characterized by problematic goals, unclear technology and fluid participation in decision-making.

These theories portray the external environment as turbulent and the source of much of the ambiguity which pervades schools and colleges, an assessment which has considerable validity in the Britain of the 1990s. The uncertainty inside and outside the institution makes the process of accountability unpredictable and its outcomes unclear. Any or all of the models of accountability discussed in this chapter may apply but the procedures may be blurred and participation may vary from one accountability setting to another.

Conclusion — accountability in a changing world

The 1988 ERA has changed the context of accountability in England and Wales. When Callaghan opened the debate in 1976, schools operated within a clearly defined structure with a powerful role for LEAs. Teachers also exerted substantial influence on the curriculum, albeit within the limitations imposed by public examinations in secondary schools and colleges. The decline in the authority of the LEAs has been paralleled by increased powers for central government, notably in respect of the curriculum and the creation of GM schools, and for the governing bodies of both schools and colleges.

These developments mean that the nature of *public accountability* has changed and its importance may have diminished. Schools and teachers are responsible more to their governing bodies and less to the LEAs. As we noted earlier, Kogan (1986) stresses the significance of sanctions to stiffen the accountability relationship. LEAs in the 1990s have few sanctions for LMS schools and none at all for colleges, and schools in the expanding GM sector. Governing bodies have the power to 'hire and fire' staff and to deploy budgets. The Department for Education, through the new inspection arrangements and the Secretary of State's powers to rationalize school places, also has important sanctions over schools and, indirectly, teachers. The location of these sanctions inevitably influences the locus of public accountability.

Parents have increased representation on governing bodies and the opportunity to press the case for the wider parent body, insofar as they can be truly representative of such a heterogeneous group. The governing body has representation from teachers and the local community as well as parents and may become the forum for the partnership activity advocated by Sallis (1988). However, research in GM schools suggests that there is little evidence of increased involvement by parents, other than parent governors, in school decision-making (Bush et al. 1993). The *partnership model* remains an ideal rather than a reality for most schools.

The ERA has also enhanced and institutionalized the market approach, giving parents increased choice of school and the collective power to determine the income and, perhaps, the future of schools. The notion of *market accountability* has been re-inforced by the legislation and this model is probably the most relevant for schools and colleges in the 1990s. Satisfying consumers and potential consumers is now the most important indicator of success although the 'satisfaction' may take different forms. According to West-Burnham (1992), 'the customer is at the heart of quality organizations' and market accountability may be regarded as consistent with this aspect of total quality management. However, quality depends on many factors and there is no firm evidence to link a market orientation to higher standards.

The position of teachers has not been enhanced by the legislation of the 1980s and 1990s. Although they *are* represented on governing bodies, their influence has been reduced by the growing importance of the market ethic and the government's increased control of the school curriculum. These developments form part of a wider, ideologically-motivated drive to reduce 'producer' influence in the management of public services. The concept of *professional accountability* is marginalised by these developments. Schools are increasingly answerable to their external audiences and this has reduced the significance of the professional model.

Summary

The radical changes to the British educational system in the 1980s and 1990s have been accompanied by shifts in the pattern of accountability for schools and colleges. Accountability is a complex concept but Kogan's (1986) four models provide a useful framework for the analysis of the seismic changes experienced by educational establishments since 1988. Accountability differs from related terms such as responsibility and responsiveness in that sanctions may be imposed in an accountability relationship.

The move to a market economy in education, with school and college income tied firmly to recruitment, increases the salience of the market model and reduces the significance of professional accountability. The locus of public accountability has changed, with an increased role for governing bodies and central government at the expense of LEAs. In its modified form, public accountability remains important but it is less significant than before the ERA because the ultimate sanctions of reduced income and possible closure depend more on market appeal than on the judgements of the political and administrative system.

Further reading

Kogan, M. (1986) *Education Accountability*, London: Hutchinson.
This book provides a detailed discussion of Kogan's four models of accountability.

Scott, P. (1989) 'Accountability, responsiveness and responsibility' in Glatter, R. (Ed), *Educational Institutions and their Environments : Managing the Boundaries*, Milton Keynes: Open University Press.
This chapter provides a succinct discussion of accountability and the related terms of responsibility and responsiveness.

References

Barton, J., Becher, T., Canning, T., Eraut, E. and Knight, J. (1980) 'Accountability and education' in Bush, T., Glatter, R., Goodey, J. and Riches, C. (Eds), *Approaches to School Management*, London: Harper & Row.

Burgess, T. (1992) 'Accountability with confidence' in Burgess, T. (Ed), *Accountability in Schools*, Harlow: Longman.

Bush, T. (1993) 'Exploring collegiality : theory, process and structure' in *E326 Managing Schools : Challenge and Response*, Milton Keynes: The Open University.

Bush, T., Coleman, M. and Glover, D. (1993) *Managing Autonomous Schools: The Grant Maintained Experience*, London: Paul Chapman.

Edwards, W. (1991) 'Accountability and autonomy : dual strands for the administrator' in Walker, W., Farquhar, R. and Hughes, M. *Advancing Education: School Leadership in Action*, London: The Falmer Press.

Elliott, J. (1979) 'Self-accounting schools: are they possible?'. *Educational Analysis*, **1**, 1, pp.67–71.

Elliott, J., Bridges, D., Ebbutt, D., Gibson, R. and Nias, J. (1979) 'School accountability: social control or dialogue', *Cambridge Accountability Project*, Interim Report to the Social Science Research Council.

Hughes, M. (1976) 'The professional-as-administrator: the case of the secondary school head' in Peters, R. (Ed), *The Role of the Head*, London: Routledge and Kegan Paul.

Kogan, M. (1986) *Education Accountability*, London: Hutchinson.

Packwood, T. (1977), 'The school as a hierarchy', *Educational Administration*, **5**, 2, pp.1–6.

Sallis, J. (1979), 'Beyond the market place: a parent's view', in Lello, J. (Ed), *Accountability in Education*, London: Ward Lock.

Sallis, J. (1988) *Schools, Parents and Governors: A New Approach to Accountability*, London: Routledge.

Scott, P. (1989) 'Accountability, responsiveness and responsibility' in Glatter, R. (Ed), *Educational Institutions and their Environments: Managing the Boundaries*, Milton Keynes: Open University Press.

Sockett, H. (1980), 'Accountability: the contemporary issues' in Sockett, H. (Ed), *Accountability in the English Educational System*, London: Hodder and Stoughton.

West-Burnham, J. (1992) 'Total quality management in education', in Bennett, N., Crawford, M. and Riches, C. (Eds) *Managing Change in Education*, London: Paul Chapman.

16 Managing resources

Brent Davies

In order to manage resources effectively in educational institutions it is necessary to have a clear understanding of the budgetary process and of the detailed costing assumptions that underlie it. This chapter aims to take these two areas, budgeting and costing, in turn and explore the nature and dimensions of each to establish the basic theoretical concepts that underpin them.

When examining financial matters, such as budgeting and costing, there can be a certain resistance on behalf of the reader who is not experienced in financial matters. This chapter aims to overcome that resistance by proving that finance is not only fun(!) but, more importantly, that if scarce resources are to be efficiently and effectively managed, then a good level of financial understanding is vital.

Budgeting in educational organizations

The first misconception to dispel is that budgets are merely about money. Wildavsky (1974, p.xxiii) provides a useful perspective on this:

> One is likely to think of budgeting as an arid subject, the province of stodgy clerks and dull statisticians. Nothing could be more mistaken. Human nature is never more evident than when people are struggling to gain a larger share of funds or to apportion what they have among myriad claimants.

This suggests that the budgeting process is a dynamic one with competing forces vying for funds to meet differing expenditure needs. Indeed, this quotation draws parallels with the standard definition of economics which is often considered to deal with the problem of 'unlimited wants and limited resources'.

This section of the chapter seeks to develop the theme that budgets are not just about spending money but they are about a large number of management processes and functions that help relate:

Educational Needs ⟶ To ⟶ Resources

The most important strategic understanding to develop is that educational institutions should be education-driven not resource-driven. They should plan to spend 105 per cent, thereby releasing the creative energy of the organization and drawing up a prioritized list of expenditure options. Obviously, in the real world of financial constraints, choices have to be made to bring that expenditure within the 100 per cent budget limit, but ideas will have been generated and educational choices made. The alternative strategy is to be ultra-cautious, plan to spend 95 per cent and, by doing so, suppress the creative ideas because the members of the organization are generating only a limited number of alternative expenditure options. Budgeting should be seen as an activity that facilitates the educational process.

It is useful to look at the position of budgeting in the cycle of educational management activity as demonstrated in Figure 16.1:

Figure 16.1 The educational management cycle

Figure 16.1 demonstrates that budgeting is part of the overall educational management process and not a separate or bolt-on activity.

The functions of the budgetary process

Many writers (see for example Schick, 1972 or Irvine, 1975) see budgeting as a means of relating expenditure to the achievement of objectives. However, in breaking the budgetary process down, it can be seen that it also enables the organization to plan, co-ordinate, control and evaluate its activities. How budgeting is managed in terms of the decision-making process, and the participation of individuals, will have an effect on the people involved and, therefore, on their commitment to outcomes. For example, budgeting can be seen to have not only planning and co-ordinating components but also communicating and motivating aspects. Irvine (1975, p.74) provides a useful comment as to why it is important to consider that how the budgetary process is managed may be as important as what is managed in terms of the final success of the process:

> A budget, as a formal set of figures written on a piece of paper, is in itself merely a quantified plan for future activities. However, when budgets are used for control, planning and motivation, they become instruments which cause functional and dysfunctional consequences both manifest and latent which determine how successful the tool will be.

Therefore, it is important to consider not only the components of the budgetary process but how they are managed. This can be demonstrated in Figure 16.2 which considers the budgetary what and how.

Budgetary:

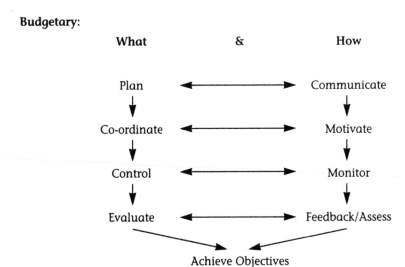

Figure 16.2 The budgetary 'what and how'

The budgetary process can be seen to have four key components. The *first* is planning: budgets are financial expressions in a quantified form of an organization's activities. They will lay down that 'x' amount of money is to be spent on an activity in a specific time period. A budget can demonstrate that the organization plans to spend a certain amount on staffing or spend another amount on an extension to its buildings. It is therefore a quantified plan for action. The *second* component of budgeting is that of co-ordination: budgets bring together a series of activities so that the amounts to be spent are organized in such a way that they contribute to meeting the organization's objectives. Organizations will fail unless the diverse set of expenditure activities on staffing, materials, equipment etc. are brought into focus by operationalising the plan so that it is managed to achieve its objectives. A *third* component of the budgetary process is that of control. By approving expenditure on one particular activity, and not on another, an organization regulates and governs the activities of its employees to the achievement of specific objectives. The *fourth* component of budgeting, that of evaluation, is the process of checking whether the expenditure has been undertaken as planned, whether the outcomes have been achieved and whether the best alternatives were utilized.

Even if the organization undertakes each of these activities in an organized and careful way, whether or not it fully achieves its objectives may depend on other factors. Management has often been defined as 'getting things done through people'. This highlights the 'how' dimension of budgeting. How the people in the organization are involved in the process is a crucial factor in the success of that process. Thus, focusing on how the budget is operationalised, by effective communication and motivation strategies, together with the monitoring of the activity and the provision of feedback, contributes as much as the component areas to the organization's achieving its objectives. Therefore it is important to consider both the component areas and the human aspects of budgeting, the 'what' and the 'how' in order to formulate a successful strategy.

The budgetary cycle

If budgets are the means of relating expenditure to needs it is necessary to consider how that process operates. The budgetary element in Figure 16.1 can itself be seen as a cycle of activity comprising four stages. Davies and Ellison (1990, p.43) see these stages as budgetary review, budgetary forecasting, budgetary implementation and budgetary evaluation:

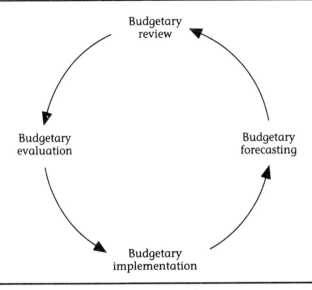

Figure 16.3 The budgetary cycle

❏ 1. Budgetary review

This first stage of the budgetary cycle involves an assessment of the current financial position of the institution and the underlying causal factors. This review has two elements to it. One is a check of current levels of income and expenditure in key categories such as:

Income	*Expenditure*
• Funds from funding formula linked to student numbers	• Staffing
• Funds from student charges	• Premises-related expenses
• Funds from specific bidding projects/categories	• Curriculum-related expenses
• Community-based financial support	• Organization-related expenses
• Income from investments	
• Income from lettings	

Once current levels of income and expenditure have been checked, the managers in the institution should move on to the second element of the audit and ask some fundamental management questions:

- Is the institution balancing its income and expenditure?

- Are there significant levels of over- or underspending in particular areas?

- Can financial resources be reallocated (vired) from one area to another to another to increase educational outputs or organizational efficiency?

❏ 2. Budgetary forecasting

Having assessed the current position, it is important that the impact of likely future financial trends is assessed to set any budgetary decisions in context. This is a significant activity which is new to many educational managers, as budgeting within the education sector has traditionally taken place on an annual basis. It is now necessary to examine the impact of financial decisions and the general resource environment over a longer period to establish a multi-year-time-horizon (MYTH) to provide this context.

In a resource-constrained environment, educational organizations struggle to achieve their objectives while keeping their educational income and expenditure in balance. It is a mistake to view budgetary decisions within a one-year time-frame. There are several examples that illustrate this. One would be the adoption of learning schemes that use a workbook approach and thus have considerable future material costs. Another would be planned replacement of computers over time. In the staffing field, an example is provided by choosing between two members of staff where the initial difference in salary (owing to the point on the salary spine) of £7,000 can, over a five-year period, cost in the region of £35,000 depending on progress up the salary spine.

Another key management factor in the budgetary forecasting context is whether the institution has an increasing or decreasing resource base and the relationship of that to the budget balance. If the student population is increasing then, on formula-based funding, a positive financial framework will be created. This can overcome any marginal over-spending in the current budget. This longer-term perspective is necessary before the manager takes action to adjust the current budget otherwise unnecessary cutbacks may be made. Conversely, if the institution is facing declining numbers, owing to either increased competition or demographic factors or both, then remedial action on the budget needs to be taken promptly or the deficit will get out of hand. Table 16.1 provides a useful checklist of factors that should be included in a financial forecasting exercise:

Table 16.1 Factors in budgetary forecasting

- Pupil/student roll
- Changes in the make up of the overall roll — more older/younger students with their different formula weightings would affect the budget
- Changes in the formula-funding mechanism either by the LEA or the central government funding agency
- Projections of extra support funds i.e. gifts, donations (PTAs etc), income from lettings
- Projections of success in bidding for specific Central Government or Private Sector grants
- Costs of extent of staffing changes, retirements, movement up the pay spine and their subsequent financial implementations
- Costs of new curicula or predictable replacement costs for learning schemes
- Costs of essential maintenance cycle
- Planned expansion/contraction costs re capital and revenue
- New sources of income identified or additional areas of necessary expenditure

When this context has been set then the next stage, budgetary implementation, can be undertaken.

☐ 3. Budgetary implementation

When drawing up the annual budget, reference back to the previous two stages needs to take place in order to set current decisions in the context of both the audit and future projections. A useful staged implementation process could be:

- Set out headings and sub-headings of the budget
- Allocate fixed costs to headings
- Allocate recurrent costs
- Bring forward items from the audit and forecast stages to establish a priority list for available expenditure
- Decide between alternative projects and courses of action
- Put budget forward for approval by the institution's governors
- Set check points during the year for possible virement opportunities

It has to be appreciated that, even at this stage, as with all financial statements, this is a snapshot at a particular moment in time and that adjustments will have to take place as events unfold. Finally, the cycle moves on to the evaluation stage.

❏ 4. Budgetary evaluation

It is important that institutions do not ignore this vital stage of the budgetary process which can be split into two parts, one concerned with outcomes and one with process. The evaluation of *outcomes* must involve a consideration of how well the resource allocation decisions have enabled the institution to meet its objectives in an effective but also efficient way. The questions to be asked might be: did we achieve what we wanted? Was the money well spent? Would alternatives have given us a better use of resources?

As well as evaluating the output of the budgetary process it is necessary to evaluate the process itself and the role of the people involved. Davies and Ellison (1992) provide a useful list (see Table 16.2):

Table 16.2 Evaluating the budgetary process

- Who is involved in the budgetary process?
- What are the roles and responsibilities of governors, staff and parents? To what extent are they consulted about, or take part in, the decision-making process?
- How is the review to be structured?
- Is the resourcing of certain areas to be examined in more depth on an occasional basis?
- Who is to summarize the review information, indicating priorities?
- When is the summary to be presented to the Governing Body?
- Who is involved with making forecasts?
- Who provides the data?
- Who makes final decisions about choices and allocations?
- Are these decisions based on the priorities identified in the school development plan?

Having considered the nature of budgeting and the budgetary cycle, the next section examines some key management points which are essential when setting up a budgetary system in an educational institution.

Points to consider when establishing a budgetary system

First and foremost, the budgetary process should link into the overall management planning cycle and not be seen as a bolt-on activity which is the sole responsibility of the financial manager or bursar. It is only the integration of the budgetary process into the general management cycle that will enable priorities to be taken into account in an educational context and, subsequently, facilitate the achievement of organizational objectives.

Secondly, budgetary activity should not be seen solely as an annual activity but should facilitate long-term planning by the development of a multi-year-time-horizon. Thus, short-term policies should always be considered with their longer-term implications if effective and efficient decision-making is to take place.

Thirdly, the 'how' of budgetary decision-making needs careful consideration and management in terms of the people involved. It is necessary, at the initial stage of the budgetary process, to determine the level of participation and consultation to be employed. This is an issue that will be explored in Chapter 17.

This links into a fourth point, a consideration of whether the institution employs centralized or decentralized decision-making structures. Just as decentralization in decision-making has profound consequences when applied to allocations to organizations it also has these consequences when applied to allocations within organizations. Institutions that operate in a decentralized environment must therefore examine their internal management philosophies to consider whether the decentralization concept should also apply to resource allocations within the school or college.

Finally, the budgetary process itself should have positive characteristics. It should be a flexible process that encourages innovation and not have an enterprise-choking system of internal controls. The process should be easily understood and should not incur substantial costs in operation.

All these five factors will contribute to the process being widely accepted within the organization and thus reinforce its organizational effectiveness.

Costing in educational organizations

Whereas budgeting is concerned with drawing up an overall financial plan as part of the institutional management process, costing is concerned with determining the specific costs of an educational activity, often with the focus of providing data about the viability of competing activities. Although it would at first appear that costing is a precise, value-free activity dealing with facts, this is not necessarily the case. We shall see in this part of the chapter that both the way that an activity is costed and the particular aspects which are costed have a large element of subjectivity originating from the value system of the person who is making the decisions.

This part of the chapter will consider key factors in the costing process, aids to decision-making and, finally, a recommended sequence of activity for those engaged in the costing process.

Key factors in the costing process

1. Scale of operation
2. Time frame
3. Fixed costs
4. Variable costs
5. Total costs and economies of scale
6. Average costs
7. Marginal costs and thresholds
8. Cash flow

❏ 1. Scale of operation

The first questions to ask in the costing process are 'How many students will use a piece of equipment?' 'How many textbooks will be needed?' or 'How many classrooms will be used?' Basically, what is the volume being costed? This is not as easy as it seems. For example, it is difficult to be precise about how many students would use a piece of science equipment over a ten-year period in order to make calculations about the cost per student. To a certain extent, this can be considered to have a degree of subjectivity based on the assumptions relied upon by the individual making the decision. However, it is important to proceed on the best estimates drawn from professional assessments but to realise that these may have to be adjusted as circumstances change.

❏ 2. Time-frame

The second factor seems deceptively easy to answer but is in fact inherently more complex. If, for example, we say that a computer (which costs £2,000) lasts five years and over that period 1000 students use it (i.e. 200 per year), then the cost can be expressed as £2,000 divided by the number of students (1000) as:

$$\frac{£2000}{1000} = £2 \text{ per student.}$$

However, experience has shown that, despite more technologically advanced machines being available, institutions have used their equipment for considerably longer than originally planned. Thus, if the machines last ten years, instead of five, the costing equation changes to £2,000 divided by 2000 students (200 per year x ten years), so

$$\frac{£2,000}{2,000} = £1 \text{ per student.}$$

When preparing bids for funding, the decision on the time-frame can have a significant impact on the cost profile. This is especially true when both the scale of operation and the time-frame are considered. If another fifty students could use the equipment and it could last another two years, a significantly lower cost profile will emerge. Therefore, it can be seen that the initial assumptions of the decision-maker about both scale and time have a considerable impact on the costing outcomes.

This example has been used to demonstrate that costs need to be considered over a period of time. However, in the real world two factors impinge on the example to make it less straightforward. First, assets depreciate and either incur maintenance costs or replacement costs, making estimates of capital expenditure difficult. Indeed, in the example computers may become obsolete — throwing out all calculations. Secondly, when comparing different expenditure alternatives over a period of time, especially where replacement or other future costs are involved, then rates of inflation need to be considered.

❑ 3. Fixed costs

When assessing the nature of costs, it is important to distinguish between those costs which the decision-maker can adjust quickly and those that take a longer time to impact upon. Fixed costs are often considered as those where no short-term adjustments are possible and which do not vary with levels of output. A common example would be permanent buildings and the loan costs associated with them. Thus if more or fewer students use the building the fixed costs will not change. This is in contrast to variable costs.

❑ 4. Variable costs

These are costs which can be adjusted quickly and which can be seen to vary directly with the level of activity. For example, extra students in a classroom generate requirements for more books and paper. Such variable costs would move up or down depending on the number of students in the class. The ease of adjustment and the short time period are the factors that determine the degree of responsiveness and flexibility of variable costs.

However, some categories of cost are not that easy to define. Teacher costs, for example, are theoretically possible to reduce in terms of the three-months resignation period. However, practice would suggest that this is unrealistic and that reducing teacher costs takes longer.

It is not always straight forward to decide which are fixed costs and which are variable. Figure 16.4 provides a useful guide:

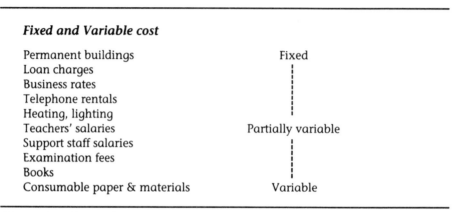

Figure 16.4 The graduation of costs

❑ 5. Total costs and economies of scale

As the name suggests, total costs are the sum of all expenditures undertaken in a given time period. Total Costs (TC) are a combination of Fixed Costs (FC) and Variable Costs (VC), i.e. TC = FC + VC. While it is true that total costs increase as more students are taught, they increase less than proportionately. This is because fixed costs stay the same and the only additional costs are the variable ones. The fixed costs are therefore spread over a larger student base and become a smaller part of the cost associated with each individual student. Thus economies of scale occur until capacity cannot be increased any further and a new series of fixed costs have to be incurred.

❑ 6. Average costs

Average costs are often called unit costs and are the cost of providing for each student, e.g. if the total cost of an educational programme is £10,000 and 500 students are involved in the programme, then

$$AC = \frac{£10,000}{500} = £20 \text{ per student.}$$

However if 800 pupils are involved with no extra costs, the average will fall, i.e.

$$\frac{£10,000}{800} = £12.50 \text{ per student.}$$

In most cases the cost structure is more complex than this. Average costs are made up of both fixed and variable costs so even where more variable costs are being incurred, average costs will continue to fall until it is necessary to pay more fixed costs. For example, to teach science £500 of fixed costs have to be incurred in terms of equipment, plus £2 per student for the variable cost. The first student costs £502, the second student gives an average cost of £252 (£500 + £2 per student = £504/2), the third student brings the average cost to £168.67. This falling average cost will continue until the optimum point is reached and then, if a second set of equipment is needed, additional fixed costs will be incurred and average costs will increase.

Educational institutions with declining rolls have fewer students over whom to spread the costs (notably the fixed cost element) and have a higher average or unit cost. Conversely, those that have an increasing roll can spread their costs over more students and the cost per student (the average cost) will fall.

❑ 7. Marginal costs and thresholds

Marginal costs are a significant costing factor and relate closely to the concept of threshold levels of expenditure. The marginal cost is the cost of taking one extra student or reducing a group by one student; it is the student at the margin! Take, for example a classroom that will hold 30 pupils taught by one teacher. If the class currently has 25 pupils, the one extra (marginal) student brings the total up to 26 with only minor increases in terms of books and materials costs, the premises and teaching costs already having been met. This is true until the class size increases to 30. The 31st student may cause the class to be split in two with an extra teacher employed and possibly incurring the building costs of an extra classroom. The marginal cost of this student is considerable as the cost schedule has gone through a significant *threshold* triggering a whole new series of costs.

Marginal costs are especially important when related to marginal revenue (the money received for one extra student). Under a funding formula where an institution receives £2,000 per student, filling up spaces, for example in an existing class, will mean that marginal revenue will exceed marginal costs, but once a threshold is triggered, marginal costs in terms of extra buildings and staff will far exceed marginal revenue. Extra students, therefore, are not necessarily a good thing; it depends how they relate to the school's cost profile.

❏ 8. Cash flow

Although not strictly a costing factor, cash flow is included here because of its importance. Cash flow is important because it is a measure of *when* money is spent. Thus, if an organization has £1,500 of income one year and £2,500 the next, the fact that the organization has to meet costs of £2,000 in each of the years means that, although it would have enough to cover the total expenditure, the project may not start as the cash flow in year one is inadequate. More sophisticated financial planning in educational organizations will allow cash flow to be matched with peak financial demands such as replacement costs which tend to bunch rather than being spread evenly.

Making decisions based on costing data

Decision-making can utilize a number of costing approaches. The first would be to cost two alternative educational schemes using the techniques described in points 1–8 above. This can be shown in the following example where two alternative educational schemes are costed to aid the decision making process. The costing exercise seeks to determine:

(i)   Fixed Costs
(ii) Variable Costs
(iii) Total Costs
(iv) Average Costs
(v)   Cash Flow

❏ Educational schemes to be costed:

Scheme A is a learning scheme that has high initial costs but has subsequently low running costs and has the following cost profile:

Fixed Cost	=	£500 (initial materials last 5 years)
Variable Cost	=	£1 in consumable material per user per year
Scale	=	100 individuals use it per year — 500 over the life of the scheme

Scheme B is a learning scheme that has low initial costs but has subsequently high running costs and has the following cost profile:

Fixed Cost	=	£200 (initial materials last 5 years)
Variable Cost	=	£2 per user per year
Scale	=	100 individuals use it per year — 500 over the life of the scheme

While the decision to choose Scheme A or B is primarily an educational one, the costing analysis (see Figure 16.5) may inform the debate:

Scheme A

Year	F.C.	V.C.	T.C. to date	No of students to date	A.C.	Cash flow
1	£500	£100	£600	100	£6	£600
2	–	100	700	200	3.50	100
3	–	100	800	300	2.67	100
4	–	100	900	400	2.25	100
5	–	100	1000	500	2.00	100

Scheme B

Year	F.C.	V.C.	T.C. to date	No of students to date	A.C.	Cash flow
1	£200	£200	£400	100	£4	£400
2	–	200	600	200	3	200
3	–	200	800	300	2.67	200
4	–	200	1000	400	2.50	200
5	–	200	1200	500	2.40	200

Figure 16.5 A costing schedule

A consideration as to which is the best scheme from an educational perspective may provide an overwhelming conclusion but, if it is a marginal decision or one of afford ability then a costing perspective is useful. The information in Figure 16.5 tells us several things:

(i) Scheme A is the most cost-effective in the long run — average costs are lower in year four onwards;

(ii) Scheme B, however, has lower initial fixed costs and if there is a shortage of funds at the start of the scheme this lower drain on cash flow may be considered desirable even if it is more expensive in the long run;

    (iii) in both schemes predictions of total cost, cash flow and average costs provide invaluable information. This is particularly so when bidding for resources internally or externally. For the purpose of this exercise inflation has been ignored.

A second costing approach would be to build on the perspectives already established but to utilise a Cost-Benefit Analysis approach. Cost–benefit puts a financial value on all inputs (costs) and all outputs (benefits).

The rationale for a cost-benefit analysis would be that individuals or organizations should go ahead with projects in which the benefits exceed the costs, or exceed them by some predetermined amount. Putting an exact price on some costs and benefits is reasonably straightforward but other costs and benefits depend on the value system of the individual making the choice. So, while cost benefit is useful in listing all inputs and outputs and putting a value on them it should be used with care. When proposing the closure of a small village primary school, a wide range of factors could be seen as costs. These would include the use of the school facilities by the community, the school as a centre of village life and the stress on young children caused by travelling to an alternative school. While these are definite costs they cannot be easily calculated. This then poses the dilemma of a cost-benefit analysis: what to include in the calculations and how to value them.

Thirdly, it is always important to consider Opportunity Costs when making decisions. This is the term used to describe the choice between two alternatives. If a school has a fixed budget it can only spend up to the total amount. It may have a number of plans or programmes which it wishes to fund. However, as in most organizations, there are more activities than there is finance to pay for them. Where the choice is between new computer equipment or library books, if the school chooses computer equipment, the opportunity cost is the library books forgone. The concept of opportunity costs thus involves valuing one alternative in terms of the other alternative given up. This illustrates a key factor in delegated budgeting — that of choice between alternatives.

Stages in implementing an educational costing activity

Managers in educational institutions should consider the following four-stage process when undertaking a costing activity. First, there must be a clear identification of the project being costed and of the items to be costed. This is not as straightforward as it seems. New innovations, such as microcomputers in schools in the late 1970s and early 1980s, were easy to cost because they did not previously exist and all expenditure was new. It is not the same with a new language scheme where use of some material from previous schemes and the teachers'/lecturers' previous experience are utilised. It is then very difficult to isolate precise new costs. Identifying these and putting a value on items such as teachers' goodwill (concerning extra preparation and training) are complex calculations. Thus, it is very important to identify the cost components at the outset of the project.

Secondly, deciding on the approach and the measurements used is critical. Is it a total costing activity or a unit (average) costing that is required? Are marginal costs to be calculated? Similarly, judgements about the time-frame and scale of the operation to be costed are critical in affecting the success of the approach.

Thirdly, the collection and analysis of costing data has to take place. It is important that this stage is planned carefully and is sequenced after the first two stages have been fully considered and completed otherwise a lack of focus will lead to time and effort being wasted collecting irrelevant data.

Finally, careful consideration needs to be given to the presentation of results. Who is the audience to whom the costing results will be presented? The nature of the audience, professional or lay, economic specialists or general members of the public, will determine the complexity and detail of the final report.

Conclusion

A clear understanding of the budgetary process and of the costing dimensions that underlie it provide the manager in an educational organization with the ability to use financial information as a facilitating device. There is no more 'hidden curriculum' than finance. It is hoped that this chapter has broken down some of those walls surrounding the financial curriculum!

Further reading

Davies, B. and Ellison L. (1990) *Managing the Primary School Budget*, Northcote House.

Knight, B. (1993) *Financial Management for Schools*, London: Heinemann.

Levacic, R. (Ed), (1989) *Financial Management in Education*, Milton Keynes: Open University Press.

Thomas, H. (1990) *Education Costs and Performance*, London: Cassell.

References

Davis, B. and Ellison, L. (1990) *Managing the Primary School*, Northcote House: Budget.

Davis, B. and Ellison, L. (1992) *School Development Planning*, Harlow: Longman.

Irvine, V.B. (1975) 'Budgeting:functional analysis and behavioural implications' in Rappaport, A. (Ed) *Information for Decision-making, Quantitative and Behavioural Dimensions*, second edn. Englewood Cliffs, New Jersey: Prentice Hall.

Schick, A. (1972) 'The road to PPB: the stages of budget reform' in Lyden, F.J. and Miller, E.G. (Eds) *Planning Programming Budgets — A Systems Approach to Management*, Markham Publishing.

Wildavsky, A. (1974) *The Politics of the Budgetary Process*, second edn. Little, Brown & Co.

17 Models of decision–making in resource allocation

Brent Davies

This chapter follows on from Chapter 16, which established some of the general characteristics of the resource management and costing processes, by examining the decision-making process that underlies the effective management of resources. The chapter considers two major themes: 1. rational and political frameworks as a means of understanding the decision-making process and 2. models of effective decision-making in decentralized financial systems.

Frameworks for resource decision-making

Organizational culture defines the framework in which resource decisions are made. The culture is reflected in the way that resource decision-making frameworks operate. Two broad decision-making frameworks or approaches, into which differing budgetary processes can be located will be examined in this section. These are the rational and political approaches.

❑ The rational framework

Rational approaches are based on the hypothesis that organizations directly relate resource expenditure to the achievement of organizational objectives. They assume that organizations have clear objectives and that resource allocation is organized in a systematic way to facilitate the achievement of those objectives. This means that, after assessing the alternative expenditure options, the finance spent and the resources acquired should maximize those outputs which contribute to fulfilling organizational objectives. It is possible to isolate three key elements which underpin a rational budgetary approach:

(i)   Output budgeting
(ii) Zero-based resource decisions
(iii) Multi-year-time-horizon

Output budgeting

In a rational framework, budgets should focus on outputs rather than on inputs. Expenditure patterns should relate to outputs rather than being characterized by a list of resource inputs. In that way they relate directly to fulfilling the objectives of the organization. The use of an output budgeting approach, it is claimed, facilitates more effective management processes. Firstly, by definition it necessitates the formulation of clear outputs and objectives. Secondly, organizations must engage in systematic planning because resources must be clearly related in advance to objectives. Thirdly, priorities are established because assessing, and opting between, alternatives is necessary. Finally, performance indicators can be defined in terms of how far objectives have been met utilising the current mix of resources.

There has been a significant shift in educational funding throughout the 1980s and 1990s. The trend has been to put considerable emphasis on the outcomes to be achieved from differing resource inputs. In England and Wales, the government has sought to engender a debate about outcomes and the resources that are expended to achieve them. One example of this can be seen in the number of 'specific grants' that central government has tied to detailed output and performance criteria. It has also been achieved by giving schools budgetary discretion through LMS and GMS while, at the same time, setting in place arrangements for national testing.

Zero-based budgeting

A fundamental part of a rational approach to budgeting is the adoption of a zero-based perspective to resource allocation. This involves taking a fresh look at expenditure by starting with a 'clean slate' rather than by basing decisions on previous practice. This is not just taking a fresh look at additional expenditure but also about examining existing core expenditure patterns or allocations. There is a need to justify all expenditure, as Wildavsky (1978 p.501) states:

> ... the past, as reflected in the budgetary base ... is explicitly rejected. There is no yesterday. Nothing is taken for granted, everything at every period is subjected to searching scrutiny.

The incorporation of the former polytechnic and further education institutions, together with the introduction of LMS and GMS in schools, is an attempt to cash-limit budgets and force these institutions to take a zero-based view of their expenditure patterns. The ability of these institutions to take a fresh look initially or to vire funds already committed is an example of this influence of zero-based thinking. Perhaps one of the most famous examples was Margaret Thatcher who, as Secretary of State for Education in the 1970–73 Heath government, earned the title 'Margaret Thatcher — milk snatcher!' What she decided to do was not to increase or decrease the central government subsidy on school milk in an incremental way but to take a zero-based view of that expenditure item and abolish the subsidy altogether. Site-based management in LM and GM schools has replaced the previous LEA allocation system where fixed amounts of resources (in terms of teachers, support and administrative staff, materials and equipment, building maintenance and other costs) were predetermined for the school. Now these schools are encouraged to take a fresh look by deciding for themselves the appropriate mix of resources.

Multi-year-time-horizon

This third element in a rational approach concerns the abandonment of simplistic one-year financial planning in favour of multi-year financial planning. Most lecturers and teachers have previously been faced with the dilemma of having to spend money by the end of the financial year instead of doing what, in many cases, would yield better outcomes i.e. spreading the expenditure over a longer time-period.

Traditional budgets have been on a one-year time scale. The weakness of this approach is that it fails to view education as an ongoing process with long-term resource needs that cannot be easily packaged into 12 month spending bouts. Pupils are in schools for five years or more and students are in higher education for three years. What is needed is longer-term financial planning that makes some attempt to match the nature of education with resource expenditure which must, of necessity, be of the same time duration.

Some move to this type of thinking has been operationalized by schools under LMS and GMS legislation as they are allowed to carry balances forward, giving them the flexibility to save for larger scale expenditure. However, this flexibility is limited to saving money and carrying it forward as they are not allowed to plan deficits and borrow money as commercial firms can through business loans. The incorporation of further education colleges and former polytechnics together with the establishment of GMS schools and City Technology Colleges has meant that these institutions are now responsible for capital as well as revenue expenditure. This responsibility is particularly significant with premises related costs which require longer term financial planning. Thus, consideration of a multi-year-time-horizon budget is necessary if longer term financial planning and budgeting is to take place.

❑ The political framework

However logical the key elements in the rational framework discussed above appear it is nevertheless true that political budgetary approaches show a remarkable capacity to persist. There are three key factors that influence the persistence of traditional budgeting processes. These can be seen as:

(i) Incrementalism
(ii) Micro-political forces
(iii) The organizational process approach.

Incrementalism

The incremental process bases its decisions on the previous year's budget and level of expenditure. Wildavsky (1974 p.13) makes the point that 'the largest determining factor of the size and content of this year's budget is last year's budget'. Attention is given to minor adjustments in the spending pattern or the justification of additional spending. There is no significant attempt to reassess existing spending patterns; the existing budget is not challenged — there is general acceptance that it is valid. This approach provides a predictable and stable organizational climate. It also needs very little in terms of information and time requirements compared with zero-based approaches. Discussions focus around the 5 per cent increase or decrease in the budget, not about its fundamental composition. Marginal shifts in the budget occur so that a fluctuating or disjointed pattern of change occurs around an unchanging central core. This has become known as 'disjointed incrementalism or the science of muddling through'. In the past, local authority budgets and institutional budgets have been incremental but in the early 1990s, through the pressure of resource restraints, they show evidence of zero-based influences while retaining (through formula-based funding) strong elements of incrementalism. For example, central government's funding of the university sector has shown significant attempts to break incremental tendencies by making fundamental shifts in funding for particular groups of students.

Micro-political forces

Resource decisions may not depend so much on what is clearly correct for the organization but on a number of other 'people-dependent' factors. For example, it is important to consider who is making the decisions because his/her value system may be a critical factor. Similarly, individuals may coalesce into groups having significant power that rivals the power ascribed to the formal organizational structure. Everyone is familiar with the saying 'It's not *what* you know but *who* you know that is important'. Thus, who is making the decision, influenced by what group in what organizational setting, may be more critical factors in determining the decision taken rather than the apparently rational alternative considerations. These sorts of influences and factors underlie the micro-political dimension of budgeting. A micro-political analysis therefore, is based on the view that budgetary decisions are not necessarily made on rational-economic grounds but that the deciding factors may be other influences such as the power base of individuals or groups and their value systems. Wildavsky (1968, p.193) states:

> If politics is regarded as conflict over whose preferences are to prevail in the determination of policy, then the budget records the outcomes of this struggle.

Therefore, gaining resources may not depend on the logic of the case but on a number of other factors. Greenwood et al. (1980, p.29) express this as:

> A department's share of scarce resources depends upon the skill of its advocates in the use of essentially political tactics such as knowing how much to bid for, how far to pad estimates, how far to over/underspend, how to 'read' the political climate, how to generate and utilize public support.

It is clear that the way in which the budgetary process is managed by the people involved may be as important as what is being managed as far as outcomes are concerned. If resource patterns are to be understood, asking questions about the political forces at work may be as important as asking rational questions. In assessing the political dimension Simkins and Lancaster (1983, p.30) suggest the following questions:

1. Which are the key groups that compete for resources in the budgetary process?

2. What differences in values and interests exist among them and how are these expressed in budgetary terms?

3. What sources of power can groups and key individuals bring to bear on the budgetary process?

4. Who controls the budgetary process itself and what means do they use to do so?

5. What political strategies and tactics are used to influence budget allocations?

6. What kinds of coalitions are formed and bargains struck?

7. Who gains and who loses from the budgetary process?

These dimensions should be considered when assessing resource allocation patterns from a political perspective.

The organizational process approach

The organizational process approach as a concept puts forward the idea that there is a number of factors which organizations pursue as well as the corporate objectives. Organizations try to balance these factors with the achievement of set objectives in order to ensure harmony. For example, in the business sector it is often assumed that profit maximization is the main goal. However, managers may prefer to safeguard their position by reducing competition through takeovers instead of maximizing profits by competition. They may also aim to produce satisfactory levels of profit to keep shareholders happy and may grant over-generous wage rises to avoid labour conflicts. The aim is to provide a series of acceptable solutions which meet the needs of the various constituencies that make up the organization.

In budgetary terms it may be preferable to produce a budget that keeps the main interest groups and constituencies of the organization happy rather than being involved in radical solutions which dissatisfy key stakeholders. Allocating time and money for a school's Christmas production may have little educational value and cause a great deal of disruption to the teaching programme but it is done because 'the parents expect it' and it is important to please this key group of stakeholders. Thus, the organizational process approach would suggest that an acceptable solution which satisfies the different goals and objectives in an organization may be preferred to the most efficient one on rational grounds.

❑ Analysing budgetary practice

Earlier in this chapter the three key elements of a rational approach to resource decision-making were identified as: output budgeting, zero-based resource decisions and a multi-year-time-horizon. The three key elements of a political approach to resource decision-making were identified as: incrementalism, micro-political forces and the organizational process approach. Readers can make their own assessment about the dominance of rational or political frameworks in their own organization and the impact they have on the effectiveness and efficiency of the resource management process. Since the mid-1980s the national government in the United Kingdom has pursued a policy of moving away from incrementalism within the public sector and has set performance targets with decentralized financial decision-making. This has been in an attempt to encourage more rational approaches to meeting client needs. While it could be argued that some progress has been made in adopting more rational approaches in improving resource allocation *to* institutions, there is little evidence that the culture has changed *within* organizations. While it is possible to describe decision making-structures in existing organizations (which have an incremental element) it would seem that it may prove more profitable to consider the key factors in successful resource management in the future as educational organizations grapple with the challenge of managing in this new environment.

Effective resource decision-making in financially decentralized education organizations

The latter part of the 1980s and the early 1990s have seen a radical shift from centralized to decentralized systems of educational finance in the United Kingdom. This has happened in all sectors: local education authority controlled polytechnics have become self-managing incorporated bodies and then joined the university sector; further education colleges have become self-managing incorporated bodies independent of LEAs, but funded through a national funding council; schools have achieved self-management through the three formats of local management of schools, grant maintained status and city technology colleges.

The belief in the benefits of decentralized institutions has been a major theme in many countries as well as the United Kingdom. Developments in Australia, Canada, New Zealand and the United States provide significant examples. The rhetoric that supports this change is well articulated by Osbourne and Gaebler (1993) in their seminal book *Reinventing Government*. They state (p.252–253):

> Decentralized institutions have a number of advantages: First, they are far more flexible than centralized institutions; they can respond quickly to changing circumstances and customers' needs. ... Second, decentralized institutions are more effective than centralized institutions. ... Third, decentralized institutions are far more innovative than centralized institutions. ... Fourth, decentralized institutions generate higher morale, more commitment, and greater productivity.

As can been seen, the claims are extensive. They highlight increased flexibility, effectiveness and innovation leading to a whole set of benefits for the people involved in the organization in terms of morale, commitment and greater productivity. Why should this be so? Earlier work by Thomas (1987, p.226) gives an interesting perspective by providing a rationale as to why these benefits might arise. He makes the point that decentralized unit managers are better able to make choices to maximise efficiency because:

> The unit managers are (i) closer to the clients and (ii) better able than more remotely sited managers to identify the needs of the clients. In addition unit managers (iii) will give primacy to satisfying these needs; and (iv) will also know the best, i.e. most efficient, way of combining available resources to meet as many of these needs as possible. Finally, in making decisions on resource combinations the unit managers will vary the proportion of different resources as (v) production requirements and (vi) relative prices change.

It can be seen that there are powerful arguments both for the benefits of decentralization and for the mechanism by which it operates. As a result, the rhetoric of decentralized management has achieved considerable acceptance.

Moving beyond the rhetoric, the question should be asked 'how should the resource management process at the institutional level be organized to achieve the benefits that the proponents of decentralized management claim for it?' Brown (1990, p.262) argues that decentralization involves five factors which he organizes in what he describes as a decentralization diamond as in Figure 17.1.

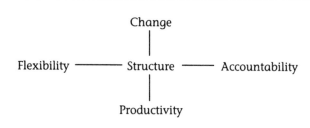

Figure 17.1 Brown D. J.: The decentralization diamond

Brown states that the benefits of decentralization are improved flexibility, accountability and productivity. While change is the attendant issue, the fundamental idea for the success of decentralization lies in the structure of organizations. It would seem that Brown sees similar benefits to Osbourne and Gaebler but to achieve them fundamental change to the structure of decentralized organizations is necessary. This restructuring theme will be developed in the rest of this section.

While the external changes (from national government) have been radical and zero-based, it is debatable whether the operationalization of decentralized budgets at the site level has shown a similar zero-based approach. Have incremental approaches persisted which reflect past resource management patterns but not the needs of managing within this new decentralized environment?

❏ Reconceptualizing resource decision-making structures

This section now looks at concepts that may assist in building the effective decision-making structures that are necessary in the radically different organizations that have been formed by the decentralization of financial decision-making in the education system of the United Kingdom.

In considering the design of effective resource decision-making structures, the temptation is to seek to adjust or improve present practice. This improvement approach is typified by the quality movement which seeks better ways of doing existing things. However, it is debatable whether we should try to improve the present resource management practice by using approaches such as total quality management because there are doubts about the incremental improvement approach being sufficient or desirable. What may be needed is a more fundamental reappraisal of what an organization does, rather than trying to get better at the way we operate by using total quality approaches.

Using this perspective we should not look to improve present resource practices but should fundamentally reassess what we are doing. Hammer and Champy (1993) argue in their book *Re-engineering the Corporation* that what is needed is a re-engineering approach. This they define as follows:

> Business re-engineering means starting all over, starting from scratch (p.2).
> ... At the heart of business re-engineering lies the notion of discontinuous thinking — identifying and abandoning the outdated rules and fundamental assumptions that underlie current business operations (p.3).

They consider that three forces are driving organizations in new ways. They are the three C's of Customers, Competition, and Change. They see *customers* taking charge with demands for products and services that meet their particular needs. They seek a change from dealing with customers en mass and a change in emphasis to servicing *this* customer now. This is very evident in education: institutions are highly dependent on students for funding so pleasing the customer or client safeguards the cash flow to the budget. Responding quickly to client needs and organizing flexible budgets that can react to those needs is paramount in this environment.

Hammer and Champy see *competition* as intensifying with the rapid growth of niche competitors. This certainly has a parallel in the education sector with the government encouraging schools to specialize and diversify to provide more choice for parents and pupils. Schools, colleges and universities all face competition from institutions in their own sectors. However, responding quickly to competition is difficult if resource spending patterns have to be adjusted rapidly as most of the resource management culture is rooted in the old incremental LEA cartel days.

Hammer and Champy state that *change* has become both 'pervasive and persistent … it is normality' (p.23). Despite the very rapid change engineered by the 1988 Education Act, and what has followed, there is a belief that we have now reached a new plateau and that more stable planning frameworks are possible. This is likely to be an illusion as change gathers pace in the 1990s.

Caldwell and Spinks (1990, 1992) propose a means of managing resources effectively in a decentralized environment. The key elements of the Caldwell and Spinks model are shown in Figure 17.2.

This model proposes a charter agreed between the external accountability body(s) and a policy group (in solid black lines) interacting with a series of programme teams. While it has a lot to commend it, the model replicates a number of traditional features. They include belief in the effectiveness of long term planning, an approach that seems rather 'top down' and a series of very structured planning cycles. How can the organization build a structure that is less rigid to deal with the basic re-engineering that is necessary to operate within the dynamic environment described by Hammer and Champy?

In taking a fresh look at creating an effective resource decision-making framework, some useful perspectives can be drawn upon. Central to these perspectives is the achievement of real decentralization within the organization as a means of empowering groups to utilize fully the decentralized financial framework. Lawler (1992, pp.257–267) considers that effective management must deliver information, knowledge, power and rewards to employees in order to gain commitment and high involvement from those employees. He writes:

> Information Managers must regularly and honestly share with employees valid data about the organization's and the work unit's past performance and future plans. Without some sense of where the organization is going, it is hard for employees to identify with and contribute to its success …

CENTRAL FRAMEWORK

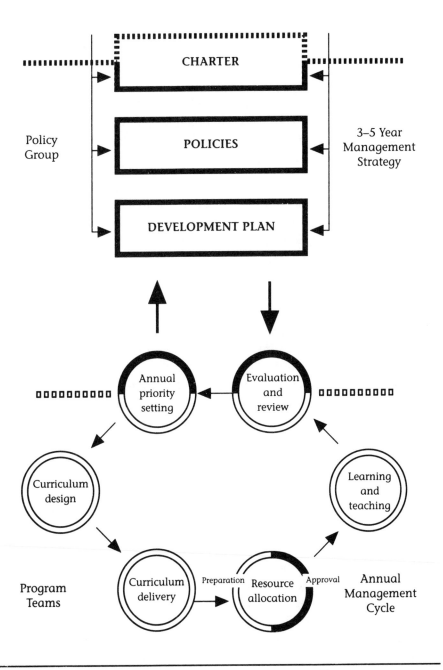

Figure 17.2 Caldwell and Spinks — The refined model of self-management

Knowledge Managers usually are in a position to add to the knowledge and expertise of the employees in their work area. Employees in a high-involvement organization must have knowledge of how the organization operates and how a particular work area operates. It is almost as critical that they understand and act on the kind of financial and other information that is provided by the organization's information system. In the absence of this knowledge, it is difficult for employees to be meaningful participants in any decision-making processes.

Power The key to moving power downward in an organization is a manager who is willing to allow employees to influence a number of the decisions that affect their day-to-day work life... sharing power must be preceded by or done in concert with, sharing knowledge and information, for power without knowledge and information is dangerous.

Rewards When work units are successful, managers should be sure that everyone involved is acknowledged and that celebrations and other forms of recognition occur... The important point is that performance in the work area be recognized as the product of everyone and that the rewards and recognition that come from good performance be shared broadly in the work unit.

It is clear that, in financially decentralized systems information, knowledge, power and rewards have passed to the organizations but there is little clear evidence that in educational organizations these key factors have been decentralized *within* them. To make decentralization effective within organizations, and therefore to provide the framework that will enable organizations to react to the very rapidly changing environment, in which they find themselves, the decentralization of fiscal structures to smaller sub-groups seems to be essential.

An interesting structure is suggested by West-Burnham (1992) who proposes that resource and other decisions should be made close to the client by teams of staff given authority by a central strategic management team. This can be seen in Figure 17.3.

This model means giving effective resource power, once the strategic dimensions have been set, to much smaller groups in organizations. However, giving power is not in itself enough. The sub-units need to be given the same information and knowledge as managers at the senior or strategic levels in the organization so as to be able to make effective decisions. Control over information is linked to power and therefore disseminating information and knowledge is very challenging to those in traditionally structured hierarchical

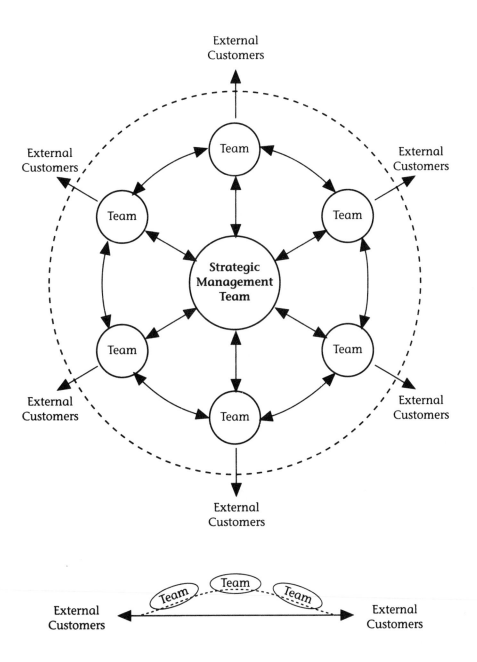

Figure 17.3 (Adapted from West-Burnham, 1992) Decision-making in financially decentralized organizations

organizations because it threatens their power base. Rewards need to be structured so that they can relate directly to the performance of the group. The group also needs to perceive a direct relationship between performance and reward.

What would effective groups look like? Groups could be of ten in a faculty or department in a secondary school and similar sizes in further and higher education. Traditionally, only power over capitation for books and materials has been delegated to this level but would they take responsibility for staffing as well? We need to consider what is the most effective resource decision-making unit in education and devolve desision-making power to it.

If Hammer and Champy's (1993) view that re-engineering is necessary because customer expectations, competition and change are operating in a fundamentally different way, then the West-Burnham model may be the only way of achieving responsive organizations that can operate in this new environment. The key may be locating information, knowledge, power and rewards with a group that is flexible enough to adjust its resource mix to directly meet the needs of the clients. It is at this team/client interface that resource decisions have to be made in the dynamic environment of the 1990s. The challenge therefore is to rethink both the organizational and financial structures of schools and colleges to empower those teams working directly with clients.

Further reading

Davies, B. and Anderson, L. (1992) *Opting for Self-Management: the Early Experiences of Grant-Maintained Schools*, London: Routledge.

Caldwell, B. J. and Spinks, J.M. (1992) *Leading The Self-Managing School*, Lewes: Falmer Press.

Hammer, M. and Champy, J. (1993) *Re-engineering the Corporation*, New York: Harper Collins.

Lawler, E.E. (1993) *The Ultimate Advantage: Creating the High Involvement Organization*, San Francisco: Jossey-Bass.

Simkins, T. and Lancaster, D. (1983) *Budgeting and Resources Allocation in Educational Institutions*, Sheffield City Polytechnic (now Sheffield Hallam University) papers in Education Management No.35.

References

Brown, D.J. (1990) *Decentralization and School-Based Management*, Lewes: Falmer Press.

Caldwell, B .J. and Spinks J.M. (1990), *The Self-Managing School*, Lewes: Falmer Press.

Caldwell, B .J. and Spinks J.M. (1992), *Leading the Self-Managing School*, Lewes: Falmer Press.

Daily Telegraph (1993) 'IBM reveals $8bn charge and job cuts'. p.21, 27 July.

Greenwood, et al. (1980), 'Incremental budgeting and the assumption of growth: the experience of local government' in Wright, M. (Ed), *Public Spending Decisions: Growth and Restraints in the 1970's*, London: Allen and Unwin.

Hammer, M. and Champy, J. (1993), *Re-engineering the Corporation*, New York: Harper Collins.

Lawler, E.E. (1992) *The Ultimate Advantage: Creating the High Involvement Organization*, San Francisco: Jossey-Bass.

Osbourne, D. and Gaebler, T. (1993) *Reinventing Government: How the Entrepreneurial Spirit is Transforming the Public Sector*, New York: Penguin Books.

Simkins, T. and Lancaster, D. (1983) 'Budgeting and resources allocation in educational institutions'. Sheffield City Polytechnic papers in *Education Management*, 35.

Thomas, H. (1987) 'Efficiency and opportunity in school finance' in Thomas, H. and Simkins, T. *Economics and the Management of Education: Emerging Themes*. London: Falmer Press. pp.224–234.

West-Burnham, J. (1992) *Managing Quality in Schools*, Harlow: Longman.

Wildavsky, A. (1968) 'Budgeting as a political process' in Sills, D.L. (Ed) *International Encyclopedia of the Social Sciences*, 2, London: Crowell, Collier and Macmillan.

Wildavsky, A. (1978) 'A budget for all seasons: why the traditional budget lasts'. *Public Administration Review*, 38, 6, pp.501–509.

18 Marketing and external relations

Marianne Coleman

Marketing, and the part it plays in the strategic management of schools, provides the context for examination of the relationships of schools and colleges with their customers, including parents, the wider community and business and industry. The changing relationship with the local education authority (LEA) and the Department for Education (DFE) will also be discussed.

There are difficulties in identifying who is inside and who outside the 'boundaries' of a school or college. The decision:

> may reflect a value position, a personal view about the desirable relationship of that particular group of stakeholders with the institution. ... For the community educator, the boundaries would be inclusive and permeable. for the 'marketeer' they would be exclusive and fairly firm (Glatter 1989, p.3).

Governing bodies, school boards and other non–professional policy-making bodies, are particularly difficult to place. However, changes in the role and power of governors in England and Wales following the legislation of the 1980s would seem to make it more appropriate to consider them as internal to the organization of the school.

Schools and colleges have external relations with other phases of education; in particular, the interface between primary and secondary schools and relations between secondary schools and higher and further education. Schools and colleges also relate to support services, particularly with regard to provision for special educational needs. It is not proposed to cover these areas of external relations, and references will be given to relevant further reading in the final section of the chapter.

A market environment

The Education Reform Act (1988) in England and Wales incorporated a series of reforms that decreased the powers held by local education authorities over schools and theoretically gave parents the right to choose any school for their child. The Act also gave greater responsibilities to the schools for financial management, whether through local management of schools (LMS) or through allowing schools to opt for grant-maintained status (GMS) and completely sever the links with the LEA.

> the combined effect of GM schools, open enrolment and local management of schools seeks to open up what is at present a predominantly publicly-funded service to the priorities and values of an enterprise culture (Flude and Hammer 1990, p.51).

Educational policy-making has stressed the autonomy of schools and the benefits to be gained by schools diversifying and competing with each other for 'customers':

> The underlying dynamic is that schooling is shifting from a public service driven by professionals towards a market-driven service, fuelled by purchasers and customers (Murgatroyd and Morgan 1993, p.1).

The incorporation of colleges and the increased autonomy of schools, appear to indicate that the accountability of educational institutions is moving towards the consumerist control of the free market described by Kogan (1988) and away from local public accountability (see chapter 15).

Marketing

Demographic change in Great Britain has dramatically affected the numbers of pupils and students in the population. It is estimated that 'the total population of young people in Britain has declined by up to one-third since the 1970s' (Gray 1991, p.6). In the climate engendered by the demographic turn-down and the educational reforms of the 1980s, many schools and colleges have considered the issue of marketing. This consideration reflects practice in many non-profit making organizations:

> Their administrators are struggling to keep them alive in the face of rapidly changing societal needs, increasing public and private competition, changing client attitudes, and diminishing financial resources (Kotler et al. 1987, p.4).

Marketing is often identified simply with promotion. However, in the context of non-profit making organizations, marketing is better defined as 'market-orientated institutional planning' (Kotler et al. 1987, p.4) and a promotion such as the exuberant gesture of releasing balloons filled with scholarship offers to North Kentucky State University does not rank as marketing since it does not show 'any real improvement in competitive positioning, teaching quality, or student services' (Kotler et al. 1987, p.5).

Marketing is defined as 'a management process, responsible for anticipating, identifying and then satisfying consumer wants and needs with a view to making profit' (Institute of Marketing, quoted by Gray 1991, p.2). This is a very much broader approach than that indicated by a promotional gimmick or a re-vamped prospectus. The marketing process can involve a 'dialogue' with customers enabling the identification of needs through market research, followed by planning, the use of the marketing mix (see below) and the application and evaluation of the resulting strategy.

Marketing in education

The tools of marketing were first developed in the context of production in the private sector. The application to education of such techniques might be questioned:

> Given the service-collaborative culture that has characterized the best of schooling anywhere, what role has marketing to play in the life of the school today and tomorrow? (Styan ,1991).

However, in a more competitive environment and in the context of general use of strategic development planning in schools and colleges, marketing concepts have been adopted, and Styan goes on to say:

> Schools are encouraged to consider marketing as an integral part of their development plan, to see all who work there as having an important part to play in marketing the school.

Marketing can be built into development planning. The cycle of marketing audit, marketing planning, and the execution and evaluation of the process can be part of the wider cycle. In this context, marketing will build on the aims and values of the school and thus:

> should disarm critics of marketing who accuse it of polluting education with alien commercial ideas and strategies (Gray 1992, p.26).

❏ The impact of educational marketing

The 'collaborative culture' referred to by Styan reflects a value system where marketing can be seen as inimical. Caldwell and Spinks (1992, p.77) have developed a view of marketing compatible with an educational setting which is based on the needs of the customer, but sees competition occurring only:

> where such competition will not produce demonstrable harms, all in a manner that preserves or enhances the student's or society's well-being.

By concentrating on the needs of the student, and operating within the normal planning cycle, it seems that the 'label' of marketing is almost unnecessary. What is important is that: 'educational integrity in the day-to-day activities associated with the marketing effort' is ensured.

Such a view of marketing in education is unlikely to raise moral concern. Kotler (1987, p.13) suggests, it is 'the fallacy of viewing marketing as primarily promotional' that is at the root of the fear of marketing.

However, competition and market forces do not safeguard the interests of all institutions and individuals at all times, and Kotler's (p.13) view of the outcome of marketing seems somewhat sanguine:

> marketing competition at its best, creates a pattern of varied institutions, each clear as to its mission, market coverage, needs specialization and service portfolio.

Murgatroyd and Morgan (1993) have analysed the ways in which schools and colleges might develop a strategy of marketing taking into account the following:

- access, including the ability and right of the institution to select its students
- resources, including the people, technology and links with industry available
- curriculum — allowing for the fact that much of this is set, schools and colleges still have some freedom to prioritize certain areas such as personal and social development
- management and organization needed to handle the chosen strategy

Having analysed these four variables, the school or college might develop one of four generic strategies. Whilst resources and management are central in delivering the strategy, access and the curriculum mix are the two variables that are most important in making the analysis.

The four generic marketing strategies are:

1. Broad open — here the school or college seeks to provide an all-round education to all who apply.

2. Enhanced open — the school or college has open access and offers a broad education enhanced by extra-curricular or other 'value-added' activities.

3. Basic niche — the school or college adopting this strategy offers a broad all round education but seeks to develop a niche in the market, either by developing a speciality in one area of the curriculum, or by appealing to a particular group, or market segment, for instance one defined by its religion

4. Enhanced niche — the school or college in this instance will tend to be 'at the leading edge' in a particular field. They will develop special expertise in a curricular area and select pupils.

The marketing process

❑ The marketing audit

Marketing decisions should only be based on a full range of information about the school and its actual and potential customers. The analysis of information can take place on the basis of a 'systematic review of the school's internal organization and external environment' (Barnes 1993, p.19). Sometimes referred to as a 'SWOT' analysis, this involves the listing of the institution's:

Strengths
Weaknesses
Opportunities
Threats

❑ Market research and analysis of the market

The potential market can be 'segmented' so that it is possible to target a portion of the market in the most effective way. The actual and potential customers can be identified by such differentials as social class, employment, ethnicity, religion or 'geography'. The aim may be to increase the school or college's share of the market, known as 'market penetration' or to establish a niche in the market, as in two of the market strategies identified by Murgatroyd and Morgan above.

The tools of market research are those applicable to any form of social research, and the main areas of research have been identified as:

- researching the markets and their segments
- examining aspects of institutional responsiveness such as customer satisfaction
- resolving specific marketing problems (Gray 1991, p.55).

❏ The marketing plan

The planning of marketing is on the basis of the marketing mix of the four 'ps'.

Product — for instance, developing a particular 'product mix', possibly specializing in curricular or extra-curricular mix for a 'niche market'.

Place — giving particular consideration to the location of the school or college and the facilities on offer.

Price — although education is a merit good in economic terms, and state education is provided 'free' by the government, there are still pricing considerations for customers. The main consideration is opportunity cost, the giving up of the next best alternative.

Since price may indicate *quality* to the consumer, such items as travel cost, expensive uniform and the expected level of both parent and pupil commitment to the school, may carry distinct marketing messages.

Promotion comes last of the four 'ps' since it concerns the communication of the outcome of all the processes associated with audit and planning. Schools and colleges can consider alternative strategies on the basis of suitability and cost.

To these four, originally applied to manufacturing, Gray has added a fifth 'p':

People — in any service industry, but particularly in education, the people who work in the institution are involved in its marketing. Both students and teachers give messages about the school or college. There is therefore a need for internal marketing to staff, implying the desirability of a level of commitment to the values of the institution by both teaching and non-teaching staff. The anticipation might then be that staff will:

enthuse about their work and the institution in which they deliver it externally, both formally through promotional events and informally through social and casual contacts (Gray 1991, p.144).

The role of students in a school or college is not just that of consumer or customer. Groups of students work together for long periods of time and, particularly with the increasing use of active teaching methods are instrumental in the provision of their own learning. Students also act as ambassadors for their institution. It is therefore important that there is internal marketing to students:

> Students at every age need to be made to feel an important part of the educational community, and this needs to be structured so as to shape as quickly as possible their models of a quality service. (Gray, 1991 p.143).

Analysis of product, place, price, promotion and people enables the organization to establish its marketing strategies.

The management implications of marketing

Marketing as strategic management
If marketing is embraced as a key element of strategic management, it will be closely linked with the statement of aims and visions for the school or college. Marketing will be 'part of a series of activities dedicated to the continuous improvement of the organization'. (Gray 1991, p.43).

Marketing and staff management
Internal marketing ensures that staff are committed to the values of the institution and therefore agreed as to the messages that they give intentionally and unintentionally to external groups. This carries implications for staff development for both the teaching and non-teaching staff.

The idea of rewarding staff for effective marketing sits uneasily with the concept of the teacher as a professional, and with the public service ethic of education. However performance-related pay could be used:

> for institutions to invest in imaginative forms of public and private recognition for those marketing activities which contribute to organizational survival and prosperity (Gray 1991, p.35)

In addition, the logic of the market would be that customer evaluation would play a part in the appraisal process.

Marketing as a specialist function

Both economic factors, and the concept of marketing as part of the school's strategic planning, emanating from its aims and values, make it inappropriate to employ an external marketing specialist. The existence of an internal specialist in marketing is more common in further and higher education. For secondary schools, responsibilities may be split, giving a lack of integrity to the marketing strategy. It is common for links with business to be the responsibility of the careers staff, whilst liaison with primary schools is the responsibility of the head of the lower school. In both secondary and primary schools the headteacher and other senior managers are likely to interface with external bodies and bear overall responsibility for the level of admissions.

Marketing and resource management

Marketing carries implications for resource management, both in the sense that time will be devoted to research and implementation, and also that overt promotional techniques are expensive.

In a survey of 600 independent schools and 100 maintained schools, the latter in the Metropolitan Borough of Solihull, it was found that lack of resources was the most commonly mentioned obstacle to marketing success, for the maintained schools, and was also important to the independent schools. (Barnes 1993, pp. 169–70)

One of the main aims of marketing, particularly for further and higher education institutions, may also be to obtain resources. They may therefore incorporate a department to administer alumni relations. Schools also raise funds through deeds of covenant and through specific fund-raising events. In addition colleges and schools may look to industrial sponsorship. Internal support for such initiatives will depend on how successfully the marketing plan reflects the aims of the school and on the quality of the internal marketing.

Marketing and curriculum management

If the aims and values of the school or college are integral to the marketing of the institution, the curriculum must be regarded as central to any marketing considerations. The school or college may identify through research that there is a need for a particular course either amongst its existing or potential customers. However, the National Curriculum imposes limitations on the freedom of schools to introduce variety. Emphasis may then be on the nature of the delivery of the course, as in the 'enhanced' models of Murgatroyd and Morgan (1993) considered above.

The customer

The central importance of the customer or client is emphasised in marketing. In education there can be considerable difficulty in identifying who is the customer. Gray describes the customer as 'students and those acting on their behalf', and adds 'those employers who select vocational education and training courses for their workers' (p.3). Pardey (1991) differentiates between 'primary clients', the pupils and 'secondary clients' the parents, employers and the community, whilst also indicating the client status of the funding bodies which pay for the service. It appears then, that the customer may be regarded as defined by a situational relationship:

> Thus the child is the customer in the classroom, the parent is the customer
> for reporting procedures, the LEA, DES and HMI are equally customers in
> context (West-Burnham 1992, p.57).

In a completely free market situation, schools and colleges would be responsive to and accountable only to the paying customer. The market for education is not free, but distorted by statutory controls and criteria for admission to schools and colleges which are other than financial.

> market accountability can only be made to work by drastically simplifying
> the process and indeed the essence of education (Scott 1989, p.19).

In addition, professional educators would experience difficulties in being entirely accountable to the customer in the market:

> No one seriously argues that teachers, doctors or engineers, ... should be
> unaccountable to those they ultimately serve. But it may be that this
> essential accountability is best captured within a web of professional
> obligations. (Scott 1989, p.19).

Parents and students as customers

Whilst students play a large part in choosing a place at college, parents now hold the major responsibility for decisions about admission to schools:

> The Education Reform Act 1988, through its open enrolment provisions,
> secured more choice for parents, requiring schools to admit pupils up to the
> limits of their physical capacity (DFE 1992, para. 1.17).

369

Maintained schools have moved from being 'domesticated', where a 'steady flow of clients is assured' (Carlson, 1964, p.266) to being 'wild' organizations which:

> struggle for survival. Their existence is not guaranteed, and they do cease to exist. Support for them is closely tied to quality of performance, and a steady flow of clients is not assured (p.267).

In this changing relationship of the school with its environment, the question of why parents and students choose a school becomes more prominent. However: 'The literature on this offers rather few general findings.' Geographical considerations plus 'traditional academic qualities and good discipline ... are generally held as more important for secondary schools' (Westoby 1989, p.69).

One set of research findings based on a community school showed that parents and representatives of the community gave considerable weight to these 'traditional' qualities:

> It is clear that the 'trappings' are not highly rated and the importance attaching to outcomes demonstrates that results are seen to be amongst the most important criteria for evaluation (Glover 1992, p.41).

Parents of children recently admitted were concerned with 'work emphasis, subject help and discipline' (Glover 1992, p.41) whilst 20 per cent of these parents considered the school brochure as unimportant.

The creation of city technology colleges (CTCs) and the possibility that a school may opt to become grant-maintained are indications of a growing diversity of schools and might be expected to have a considerable effect on parental choice. However, evidence from a small scale study at Kingshurst CTC (Walford,1991) showed that children played as large a part as their parents in choosing the school. One conclusion of the research was that 'It is likely that children will make their choice of school using criteria very different from those which a disinterested adult would use' (Walford 1991, p.73).

An investigation of parental choice involving GM schools, showed that:

> The most that one can say is that GM status consolidated already existing patterns of first choice preference, particularly where it coincided with selective schooling, rather than altering relative positions between either sectors or individual schools (Fitz et al. 1993, p.16).

It would appear possible that marketing techniques may make only a marginal difference to the choices made by students and parents. In interpreting the findings of his study, Glover (1992, p.41) points out that his survey population have a 'varied knowledge of contemporary educational debate', and that the community may judge the school by 'the values by which they were judged whilst at school.'

However, in a competitive environment, schools and colleges may adopt a marketing culture not just for the short-term recruitment of additional students but in the sense that:

> the primary marketing effort should be focused in very powerful ways on ensuring that each student and, through the student, the parent, receives the very best of educational services (Caldwell and Spinks 1992, p.82).

❏ Parental involvement in schools

The effect of government legislation in the 1980s has been not only to increase the role of parents as consumers in choosing the school, but also to 'strengthen their position in schools as organizations' (Westoby 1989, p,70).

The Government anticipates that parents will play an increasing part in the life of the school. Since the 1986 and 1988 Acts parents have increased participation as parent governors and there is the mechanism of the governors' annual report to parents. Most of all, it has been expected that grant-maintained status will give parents the opportunity to influence the development of the education:

> The better the service, the greater the commitment of parents and pupils and the greater the willingness of parents to be involved with the life and performance of the school. The stronger the commitment, the stronger the school. GM status is already showing just how effective this process can be and pointing the way to the future (DFE 1992, para. 1.6).

❏ 'Exit' and 'voice'

The Government claims that increased parental influence on schools would bring about higher standards of education:

> There is the claim that educational standards and the quality of education for the mass of the population will not improve until state controls, particularly those of the local state, are drawn back to a level compatible with maximizing parental choice (Flude and Hammer 1990, p.56).

The question of how this mechanism might work has been approached by Westoby using Hirschman's concepts of 'exit' and 'voice'. There are two classic responses to dissatisfaction with an organization, to 'exit' or to 'voice' your complaint. 'Voice' is considered to be a more 'information-rich' guide to the improvement of the school, as compared to simple 'exit'. Where parents can choose to exit, they do not complain and therefore the impetus to improvement is lost:

> Making exit easier may well atrophy voice; voice may be loudest, and perhaps of greatest effect, when monopoly conditions prevail and customers are securely 'locked-in' (Westoby 1989, p.71).

Certainly research evidence does not indicate that parental 'voice' has been increased as a result of opting out. Despite the necessity for parental support in the opting out process: 'the majority of (GM) schools report little change. Where there is impact on the level of parental involvement, it tends to be mildly favourable' (Bush et al. 1993, p.175).

It is however possible that 'voice' could be effective when coupled with the possible sanction of threatened 'exit', and that therefore parents could stay within a school and exercise such influence.

As truly 'wild' organizations, those schools from whom parents 'exit' might respond vigorously through effective marketing to re-capture parents and pupils.

❏ The partnership model

> Involving parents successfully as partners in the process is the key to so many of the other problems. We have the beginnings of mutual accountability, or at the least the climate for it, in that parents have naturally accepted that something is expected of them. (Sallis 1988, p.178)

It may be useful to distinguish between involvement and partnership, the former 'usually occurs as a matter of course, participation implies a stronger role' (Caldwell and Spinks 1992, p.130). A high level of involvement and support is referred to as the 'social capital' of the school, and appears to be positively related to school effectiveness. Caldwell and Spinks advocate parent development programmes to increase parents' knowledge about education and to enable them to encourage and support their children for example through having high expectations. Joint developmental training for parents and teachers is also advocated.

The Parent's Charter (DES, 1991) promises parents annual written reports on their children, a school prospectus and an annual report from the governors. It adds the promise of regular inspections of schools and the publication of information to enable comparison of schools.

Parents are told that 'Teachers need your support in their efforts to help your child do the best he or she can' (DES, 1991). This rather limited contract can be contrasted with other proposals such as the twelve point minimum programme outlined for a parent teacher partnership by Macbeth (1993). This suggests for example that parents should have the right to see official records on their child, and that parental wishes should be consulted in the case of all educational decisions, and where there might be disagreement 'every effort might be made to accommodate parental wishes' (Macbeth 1993, p.195).

❏ The management implications of parental involvement

Strategic management
The ethos and style of management of the school will have an impact on parental involvement:

> The extent to which a head is autocratic or democratic, defends existing structures or encourages innovation, is prepared to reassess goals and is sensitive to staff and client needs, to research evidence and to changes in society — all these can have impact on a school's home-school ethos (Macbeth 1993, p.202).

The statutory duty to produce a development plan requires the involvement of the governors. It was suggested at the beginning of this chapter that the governors could now best be considered as 'internal' to school management. Parents are represented on the governing body, but it can be argued that they, as a group, should be involved to a greater extent in the school's development plan:

> if a tripartite agreement is secured between school, governors and parents then mutual understanding and confidence will grow and will surely enhance the school's development and the management of change (Holly and Southworth 1989, p.35).

The management of the curriculum
Parental involvement is one of the twelve factors linked with effective junior schools. (Mortimore et al. 1993) The help of parents in the classroom, active discussion with staff on their children's learning and help given to the

children with schoolwork at home 'was beneficial both to the children and the school' (Holly and Southworth 1989, p.80). However the involvement of parents in children's learning has implications for marketing, resource and staff management.

Marketing implications

If it is seen as desirable to increase the level of parental participation, marketing techniques might be used to encourage attitude change, since:

> parents have been on the periphery of schooling for so long ... It is therefore not just a matter of permitting parental involvement; the idea requires a 'hard sell' by determined teachers, supported by well-informed publicity' (Macbeth 1993, p.196).

Resource implications

Marketing may carry cost implications in terms of increased communication with parents. There are also resource implications in an increased work-load for staff in focusing on relations with parents.

Staff development

There are implications for staff development. If the leadership and ethos of the school are favourable to parental participation, staff development planning will ensure that there is a programme of appropriate staff training.

The partnership of parents with teachers can be seen in the wider context of the partnership of schools with the community in which they are placed.

Schools and colleges in the community

The relationship of school and community has not always been one of partnership. The traditional ethos of pre-comprehensive education was more concerned with the isolation of the scholar. Sayer (1989, p.4) describing the pre-1944 Act grammar schools claims that:

> Far from being part and parcel of the local community, secondary schools were about protecting able young people from local limitation; there was something of the monastic ideal, matched by the habits of uniformed segregation.

Mitchell (1989) points to a range of factors that have led to there being a partnership between school or college and community. The educational factors include:

- recognition of the benefits of home-school links;
- the introduction of a 'broader' concept of education, including personal, social and moral development
- a blurring of the distinction between education and training and a recognition of the need for life-long learning

In addition, Mitchell isolates economic factors such as the desire to obtain better value from the high capital cost of school and college buildings.

There is general acceptance of the idea that there should be a relationship between the school or college and its community. The nature of the relationship varies from the most informal, to one where the school or college is open to provide community education to adults alongside children.

❑ Community education

The terms community and community education are difficult to define, although:

> Community educators are likely to offer five criteria to be met by community education in any form, ... They are access, involvement, shared governance, use of the community as a learning resource, and a relationship with lifelong learning (Sayer 1989, p.12).

Of the criteria listed above, shared governance may differentiate community schools and colleges from those which are only providing for the community in the more informal sense.

❑ Management implications of community education

Implications for financial management
Where schools and colleges are providing education to the whole community and have shared governance with user councils, potential problems have emerged since the advent of local financial management:

> This (the Education Reform Act) effectively returns the control of community activity in the school to the headteacher and governors (Watts 1992, p.154).

Implications for staff development
Teachers, trained to work with children, may need new skills to communicate successfully with adults in the community:

There are other skills essential to teachers as potential support systems for community education — and they involve the development and experience of social skills as well as intellectual ones: a commitment to practise stamina in the face of difficulties, and an ability to think around contentious issues (Mitchell 1989, p.102).

Implications for marketing

If the school is to be the provider of community education it becomes particularly important to establish the needs of the community by undertaking appropriate market research.

Relationships with business and industry

The development of personal and social education, and the recognition of the importance of lifelong learning, have put a particular emphasis on links between schools and colleges and the business life of the community.

The School Curriculum Industry Partnership (SCIP), identifies the curricular benefits from links with business as:

1. Education for business — providing and improving careers education and guidance

2. Education about business — contributing to economic and industrial understanding

3. Education through business — providing a context or environment through which young people learn, for example an enterprise activity

Various practical initiatives have helped to nurture the development of the local relationship:

1. Technical and Vocational Education Initiative, which initially linked vocational school courses with local industrial needs, a recognition of the employer as a 'customer'

2. Development of work experience, so that now the vast majority of pupils aged 15 and over have placements in local firms

3. Economic and industrial understanding as a cross-curricular theme, incorporating the opportunities for pupils to 'talk and work with adults from industry and the community' (NCC 1990, p.6)

4. Existence of compacts, which attempt to place school leavers in jobs in return for their achievement of agreed targets within school

5. Representation of local industry on boards of governors

6. Development of teacher placements in industry and of industrial placements in schools and colleges

7. Institution of Education-Business Partnerships as a joint initiative of the TECs and the LEAs. The EBP contains:
    > a formal agreement committing the partners to work together to improve education and employment opportunities in their local area. (Employment Department, 1990).

Ninety per cent. of secondary schools and over half the primary schools have links with local industry (NCC 1990, p.2).

> The vision for the partnership between education and business is that the two cultures, for too long kept apart, can work together to improve each other's performance and, thereby, raise everyone's standard and quality of life (Marsden, 1990).

❏ Management implications of implementing links

Staff development
As with the introduction of any initiative there is an implication for staff training and development.

The involvement of adults other than teachers in the classroom may have implications for styles of teaching and learning. The more active and experiential methods appropriate for joint education-industry ventures may lead to a re-evaluation of classroom management.

Strategic management and responsibilities
If the development of any initiative or link with external groups is to be successful it carries implications both for developmental priorities and for the work-load of staff:

> any initiative must gain the support of the senior management team of a school and that of the governing body if it is to stand a chance of succeeding (Fullick 1992, p.133).

❑ The common interests of education and business

Britain's relative economic and industrial decline has been linked with the need to examine the nature and provision of education.

> With increasing economic competitiveness, both in the European Community and world-wide, the nation's prosperity depends more than ever on the knowledge, understanding and skills of young people (NCC 1990, p.1).

There has been government recognition that education and training for young people must be extended. Targets adopted as the National Education and Training Targets epitomise the need for education and business to work together in common interest. The Foundation Learning Targets include the aim that by 1997 at least 85 per cent of all young people should have attained a Level 2 National Vocational Qualification (NVQ) or academic equivalent.

The establishment of Training and Enterprise Councils (TECs) in 1989 marked a development in the relationship of education and business. The 82 TECs in England and Wales are largely funded through the Department of Employment and represent the interests of the local business community. The TECs, using their funds for work-related further education, fund college courses and, increasingly act as 'bankers' for training credits with which school-leavers 'purchase' courses from FE colleges.

A market for courses operates between local businesses and TECs:

> The theory is that employers will use the TECs, 'their' institutions for monitoring and equipping the local labour market, to contract with free-standing, commercially alive colleges to provide ... national programmes of education and training (Walker, 1993).

Colleges, although largely funded by the Further Education Funding Council, receive most of their remaining funding from TECs for the provision of the contracted courses. This has implications for the accountability of the colleges, who are providing education that is responsive to the needs of the local employment market, but via the intermediary of the local TEC.

Management implications of training initiatives

A change in the way that Government initiatives concerned with training and vocational education are funded has implications not only for financial management but also for the way in which planning priorities in education may be established. For example, the then Manpower Services Commission

(MSC), when establishing TVEI offered seven million pounds to ten LEAs whose submissions best met the suggested criteria. TECs also operate this system, which has been called 'honeypot management' (Knight 1987, p.204).

This system of funding is typified by the intention to achieve change as quickly as possible and by the invitation for submissions, to be measured by the 'donor's' criteria. The process is competitive and as such, this type of management has benefits of stimulating initiative, but it imposes priorities:

> It is haunted with the problem of opportunity costs. It is very well for the donor to lay down priorities, but what opportunities are lost which the bidder perceives as more important? (Knight 1987, p.210).

The provision of public funds via the 'honeypot' involves following market principles within what is ultimately public accountability.

The autonomous school — support and accountability

Before the Education Reform Act (1988) maintained schools were supported and regulated by the local education authority. Local Management of Schools (LMS) has given schools control of the bulk of their finances and put them in a position of contracting LEA services where they wish to do so. The school or college is now responsible for the selection and employment of staff and for its own industrial relations.

Although it might seem that the result of the changes imposed by the Education Reform Act is that LEAs: 'are squeezed between institutional autonomy and central controls' (Mann 1989, p.118), there are claims that there is a continuing need for the support of the LEA:

> It is the genuine, positive professional need for the right kind of help and information that should form the basis for better partnership in the future between provider, client and support service (Cobb 1992, p.48).

However, some commentators expect the market will prevail in the area of support services:

> we believe that fear of a lack of support services under the market model will be alleviated as skilful consultants currently employed by school systems at the central, regional or district levels gain confidence and experience success as they move into private practice (Caldwell and Spinks 1992, p.195).

❏ Grant-maintained schools

The creation of GM schools, under a provision of the Education Reform Act (1988), was aimed: 'to break the local authorities' monopoly of 'maintained' schooling' (MacLure, 1988). Further, schools were able to take the option of applying for grant-maintained status if threatened with LEA closure or re-organization, thus frustrating LEA planning capacities.

Research on the first 100 schools to opt out of LEA control showed that independence from the LEA was the reason most often given for seeking GM status. Of the respondents, 70 per cent mentioned independence, 43 per cent giving it as their main reason. A further 36 per cent gave their main reasons for opting out as being to avoid closure, or some form of LEA re-organization (Bush et al. 1993).

❏ GM schools and their relations with LEAs

Although the LEA loses all influence and control over a GM school, it is still required to provide services to pupils of opted out schools, including support for statemented pupils, education welfare services and home to school transport.

Most of the first 100 schools to opt out were continuing to use some LEA services, the most popular being pay-roll services and INSET, which at that time were purchased by nearly a half of the schools. A later survey of 229 GM schools carried out by the Public Services Privatisation Research Unit suggests that the purchase of LEA services might by then have slightly declined. (Nash, 1993)

Expected changes in the powers of LEAs

Despite the overall reduction in the role of the LEA, some of the powers of LEAs are somewhat enhanced by the Education Act 1993, since an LEA will have the right to require a school — whether GM or LEA maintained (including voluntary schools), to take a child who would otherwise be without a place if not admitted or permanently excluded from all accessible schools. Similarly, an LEA has the right to direct any maintained school, including those that are GM, to accept a pupil named in a School Attendance Order (DFE 1992, para. 5.11).

As the role of LEAs diminishes, the role of the Funding Agency for Schools (FAS) will expand. The primary duty of the Agency will be responsibility for the payment of grants to, and financial monitoring of, GM schools. However, in addition, the new FAS will share responsibilities with the LEAs for the overall provision of school places in an area, where at least 10 per cent of the pupils are in grant-maintained schools.

The FAS will be a quango, its members appointed by the Secretary of State, as such it will not itself be directly accountable to Parliament or to local democracy.

Nevertheless, it will be necessary for schools to include the FAS in their frame of reference when planning a policy of external relations.

Schools and the DFE

At the same time that schools have become more autonomous, they have become more subject to central government control, notably through the imposition of the National Curriculum. Whilst most schools have little direct contact with the DFE, this is not true for GM schools. The Secretary of State has a direct influence over GM schools, deciding in the first place whether to give them GM status, and reserving the right to appoint new first governors in the case of serious problems of governance in the school. GM schools apply to the DFE direct for capital grants.

Until the establishment of the FAS, the DFE serviced the GM schools directly with regard to the payment and monitoring of recurrent grants. Evidence from the first 100 schools to opt out shows that the DFE has had excellent relationships with the schools, being helpful and non-interfering. However:

> This degree of helpfulness may have something to do with the relatively generous staffing allowed for DFE handling of GM schools (Bush et al. 1993, p.170).

It remains to be seen how GM schools and schools in areas where LEAs cease to exist build their relationship with the FAS and with private consultants offering training and advice on the open market.

Summary

Schools and colleges are experiencing greater degrees of autonomy within an environment increasingly more subject to market forces. They are responding to the pressures of a more competitive environment by using marketing techniques, borrowed and adapted from the commercial world, but used effectively in education as part of strategic management.

Despite political claims and the increased importance of the consumer, there does not seem to be a radical increase in parental involvement as customers in education.

Schools and colleges work within communities and bear differing degrees of responsibility for education for all. The partnership between education and business is recognized as being mutually beneficial, both at a local level and for its wider effects on the future workforce and thus the economy.

The diminished role of the LEA has implications both for accountability of the education service and for support for schools and colleges. The external relations of some schools will expand to include the FAS.

Further reading

References for external relations with other educational institutions:

Part 2 of Foskett, N. (Ed) (1992) *Managing External Relations in Schools: A Practical Guide*, London: Routledge, covers links with the educational environment including:

Messer, J. 'Links across the primary/secondary interface — a primary perspective'.

Campbell, G. 'Links with educational support services'.

Snell, M. 'Links with further education'.

Foskett, N. 'Links with higher education'.

Part 2 of Glatter, R. (Ed) *Educational Institutions and their Environments: Managing the Boundaries*, Milton Keynes: Open University Press, including:

Mann, J. (1989) 'Institutions and their local education authority'.

Parkes, D. and Thomson, C. (1989) 'Towards the responsive college'.

General

Foskett, N. (Ed) *Managing External Relations in Schools: A Practical Guide*, London: Routledge.

Glatter, R. (Ed) *Educational Institutions and Their Environments: Managing the Boundaries*.

Sayer, J. and Williams, V. (Eds) *Schools and External Relations: Managing the New Partnership*, London: Cassell.

Education business links

Gibbs, B., Hedge, R. and Clough E. (1991) *The Reality of Partnership: Developing Education Business Relationships*, Harlow: Longman.

Marketing

Barnes, C. (1993) *Practical Marketing for Schools*, Oxford: Blackwell.

Davies, B. and Ellison, L. (1991) *Marketing for Secondary Schools*, Harlow: Longman.

Devlin, T. and Knight, B. (1990) *Public Relations and Marketing for Schools*, Harlow: Longman.

Gray, L. (1991) *Marketing Education*, Milton Keynes: Open University Press.

Pardey, D. (1991) *Marketing for Schools*, London: Kogan Page.

Sullivan, M. (1991) *Marketing Your Primary School: A Handbook*, Harlow: Longman.

References

Barnes, C. (1993) *Practical Marketing for Schools*, Oxford: Blackwell.

Bush, T., Coleman, M. and Glover, D. *Managing Autonomous Schools: The Grant-Maintained Experience*, London: Paul Chapman.

Caldwell, B. and Spinks, J. (1992) *Leading the Self-Managing School*, London: Falmer Press.

Carlson, R.O. (1964) 'Environmental constraints and organizational consequences: the public school and its clients' in Griffiths, D.E. (Ed) *Behavioral Science and Educational Administration: The Sixty-third Yearbook of the National Society for the Study of Education*, The University of Chicago Press.

Cobb, T. (1992) 'From paternalism to partnership: links with the LEAs' in Foskett, N. (Ed) *Managing External Relations in Schools: A Practical Guide*, London: Routledge.

Department of Education and Science (1991) *The Parent's Charter: You and Your Child's Education*, DES.

Department for Education (1992) *Choice and Diversity: A New Framework for Schools*, (Cmnd 2021), London: HMSO.

Employment Department (1990) *The Partnership Primer*, London: HMSO.

Fitz, J., Power, S. and Halpin, D. (1993) 'Opting for grant-maintained status: a study of policymaking in education', *Policy Studies*, **14**, 1, pp.4–20

Flude, M. and Hammer, M. (1990) *Opting for an Uncertain Future: Grant-Maintained Schools*, London: Falmer Press.

Fullick, P. (1992) 'Links with industry and employers' in Foskett, N. (Ed) *Managing External Relations in Schools: A Practical Guide*, London: Routledge.

Glatter, R. (1989) *Educational Institutions and Their Environments: Managing the Boundaries*, Milton Keynes: Open University Press.

Glover, D. (1992) 'An investigation of criteria used by parents and community in judgement of school quality'. *Educational Research*, **34**, 1, Spring.

Gray, L. (1991) *Marketing Education*, Milton Keynes: Open University Press.

Holly, P. and Southworth, G. (1989) *The Developing School*, London: Falmer Press.

Knight, B. (1987) 'Managing the honeypots' in Thomas, H. and Simkins, T. (Eds) *Economics and the Management of Education: Emerging Themes*, London: Falmer Press.

Kogan, M. (1988) 'Normative models of accountability' in Glatter, R., Preedy, M., Riches, C. and Masterton, M. (Eds) *Understanding School Management*, Milton Keynes: Open University Press.

Kotler, P., Ferrell, O.C. and Lamb, C. (1987) *Strategic Marketing for Nonprofit Organizations: Cases and Readings*, Englewood Cliffs, NJ: Prentice-Hall, Inc.

Macbeth, A. (1993) 'Parent-teacher partnership: a minimum programme and a signed understanding', in Preedy, M. (Ed) *Managing the Effective School*, London: Paul Chapman.

Maclure, S. (1989) 'Parents and schools: opting in and opting out', in Lawton, D. (Ed) *The Education Reform Act: Choice and Control*, London: Hodder and Stoughton.

Mann, J. (1989) in Glatter, R. *Educational Institutions and Their Environments: Managing the Boundaries*, Milton Keynes: Open University Press.

Marsden, C. (1990) *Education and Business: A Vision for the Partnership*, Alton: BP Educational Service.

Mitchell, G. (1989) 'Community education and school: a commentary' in Glatter, R. (Ed) *Educational Institutions and Their Environments: Managing the Boundaries*, Milton Keynes: Open University Press.

Mortimore, P., Sammons, P., Stoll, L. and Lewis, D. (1993) 'Key factors for effective junior schooling'. in Preedy, M. (Ed) *Managing the Effective School*, London: Paul Chapman.

Murgatroyd, S. and Morgan, C. (1993) *Total Quality Management and the School*, Milton Keynes: Open University Press.

Nash, I. (1993) 'Authorities fail to win GM contracts'. *Times Educational Supplement*, 15 January.

National Curriculum Council (1990) *Education for Economic and Industrial Understanding*, York: NCC.

Pardey, D. (1991) *Marketing for Schools*, London: Kogan Page.

Sallis J. (1988) *Schools, Parents and Governors: A New Approach to Accountability*, London: Routledge.

Sayer, J. (1989) 'The public context of change' in Sayer, J. and Williams, V. (Eds) *Schools and External Relations: Managing the New Partnership*, London: Cassell.

Scott, P. (1989) 'Accountability, responsiveness and responsibility' in Glatter, R. (Ed) *Educational Institutions and their Environments: Managing the Boundaries*, Milton Keynes: Open University Press.

Styan, D. (1991) in Stott, K. and Parr, H. *Marketing Your School*, London: Hodder and Stoughton.

Walford, G. (1991) 'Choice of school at the first city technology college'. *Educational Studies*, **17**, 1, pp. 65–75.

Walker, D. (1993) 'Funders in search of a new role'. *Times Educational Supplement*, 2 July.

Watts, J. (1992) 'The school within the community' in Foskett, N. (Ed) *Managing External Relations in Schools: A Practical Guide*, London: Routledge.

West-Burnham, J. (1992) 'Total quality management in education' in Bennet, N., Crawford, M, and Riches, C. *Managing Change in Education: Individual and Organizational Perspectives*, London: Paul Chapman.

Westoby, A. (1989) 'Parental choice and voice under the 1988 Education Reform Act' in Glatter, R. (Ed) *Educational Institutions and Their Environments: Managing the Boundaries*, Milton Keynes: Open University Press.

University of Leicester MBA in educational management by distance learning

The MBA in educational management by distance learning is a unique qualification which combines an academically rigorous programme with personal development in the context of institutional improvement. The degree is a *partnership* between the teacher, their school or college and the University.

The course balances knowledge with reflection leading to application; this is achieved through:

- *High quality, relevant and up-to-date course materials*
- *Resources designed to help understanding and personal reflection*
- *Assessment linked to practical management outcomes*

The degree is academically and professionally demanding but will form the basis for enhanced management effectiveness, career development and personal growth.

The degree can be made up of a combination of distance learning materials, school- or college-based activity and, in appropriate circumstances, the accreditation of prior learning.

The MBA is a genuinely distance learning qualification. This means that you decide:

- *when you start to study*
- *the pace at which you study*
- *the specialist focus of your degree*
- *the topics for assessment*
- *where and when you study*

There are no compulsory residentials or formal tutorials. Advice and support are available through:

— *Telephone and fax advice lines*
— *A regional network of tutors*
— *High quality course materials*
— *Study groups*
— *Linking with school/college based activities*
— *Networking with other course members*

Further information is available in the course handbook. This information is subject to confirmation by the University of Leicester Senate.

Course structure

The degree programme is made up of a planning unit and five modules:

1. Leadership and strategic management

2. Managing the curriculum

3. The management of professional and support staff

4. Managing finance and external relations

5. Research methods

The planning unit is designed to help you plan your programme of study and the most effective ways of integrating the degree into your work, professional and career development.

Each module is made up of a core unit which is compulsory, an elective unit chosen from a range of options and a 5,000 word assignment. Module 5 is a compulsory course in research methods followed by a 20,000 word project on a management subject.

	Planning Unit		
Module			
1	Core	Elective	→ Assignment
2	Core	Elective	→ Assignment
3	Core	Elective	→ Assignment
4	Core	Elective	→ Assignment
5	Core		→ Management Project

❏ Examples of elective units

Total Quality Management; Relationships with the Governing Body; The Curriculum and Learning in the Secondary School; Women in Educational Management; Management of Teams in the Special School; Managing Staff Development in the Primary School and Quality Assurance in Further Education.

Course materials

When you have been accepted on to the course you will receive a copy of *The Principles of Educational Management*. This is the core text which will serve as an introduction to the advanced study of education management and be a major reference work throughout the course.

When you register for a particular unit you will receive a learning pack which will include:

— an authoritative discussion of the topic

— activities, exercises and readings

— application to real cases in schools and colleges

— coverage of current issues

— suggestions for further study and reading

Awards

1 Module	=	Advanced Certificate in Educational Management
4 Modules	=	Postgraduate Diploma in Educational Management
5 Modules	=	MBA in Educational Management

For further information please contact: Carolyn Vincent, Course Manager, University Centre, Queens Building, Barrack Road, Northampton, NN2 6AF. Tel: 0604 30180

University of Leicester
Educational Management Development Unit

The Educational Management Development Unit (EMDU) is a specialist unit within the University of Leicester School of Education. It was established in January 1992 with the specific brief to offer high quality training and development programmes to meet the management needs of professionals working in schools and colleges.

The EMDU offers:

- Accredited courses leading to Higher level qualifications
- School-based development activities
- Consultancy
- Distance learning packages

EMDU aims to build on the recommendations of the School Development Task Force and offers management training to meet the needs of senior managers and those aspiring to such positions. It offers qualifications geared to the management needs of schools and colleges in the 1990s.

EMDU aims to meet the needs of individuals and institutions. The MBA in Educational Management is offered in part-time and distance learning modes.

It covers all aspects of educational management and is designed for people holding or aspiring to senior management positions in schools and colleges.

The Advanced Certificate (school-based) in Educational Management is an exciting new opportunity for schools to negotiate a tailor-made programme, designed to meet the school's needs, at a much lower cost than conventional University taught modules.

EMDU offers consultancy and associated training/development activities to schools and colleges on an individual basis. EMDU staff provide advice and expertise in all aspects of educational management.

EMDU is engaged in a range of research activities — current topics include:

— Quality management in education

— Self-governing schools

— Middle management

— Theories of educational management

— Women in educational management

— Mentoring and school management

— Managing the curriculum

EMDU works with individuals, individual schools and colleges, and also with groups of teachers or institutions. EMDU aims to help education professionals determine training and development needs and then sets out to provide high quality training packages designed to meet those needs. EMDU aims to provide development packages which can be combined to lead to a variety of qualifications in Educational Management.

The Centre for Total Quality in Education and the Community is based in EMDU. This is the first centre to be specifically dedicated to research and development into Total Quality in schools and colleges.

For further information about the work of EMDU please contact: Professor Tony Bush, EMDU, School of Education, Queens Building, Barrack Road, Northampton, NN2 6AF

Author index

Index